O9-BUB-886

SIXTH EDITION

Rules for Writers

Diana Hacker

Contributing Authors

Nancy Sommers
Tom Jehn
Jane Rosenzweig
Harvard University

Contributing ESL Specialist

Marcy Carbajal Van Horn
Santa Fe Community College

Bedford/St. Martin's
Boston ◆ New York

For Bedford/St. Martin's

Executive Editor: Michelle M. Clark
Development Editor: Mara Weible
Senior Production Editor: Anne Noonan
Production Supervisor: Jennifer Peterson
Senior Marketing Manager: John Swanson
Editorial Assistant: Alicia Young
Assistant Production Editor: Katherine Caruana
Copyeditor: Barbara G. Flanagan
Text Design: Claire Seng-Niemoeller
Cover Design: Donna Lee Dennison
Composition: Monotype Composition Company, Inc.
Printing and Binding: Quebecor World Eusey Press

President: Joan E. Feinberg
Editorial Director: Denise B. Wydra
Editor in Chief: Karen S. Henry
Director of Marketing: Karen Melton Soeltz
Director of Editing, Design, and Production: Marcia Cohen
Managing Editor: Elizabeth M. Schaaf

Library of Congress Control Number: 2009924669 (student edition)
2009924672 (tabbed student edition)

Manufactured in the United States of America.

3   2   1   0   9
e   d   c   b   a

For information, write: Bedford/St. Martin's, 75 Arlington Street, Boston, MA 02116
(617-399-4000)

ISBN-10: 0-312-59339-2   ISBN-13: 978-0-312-59339-1 (student edition)
ISBN-10: 0-312-59340-6   ISBN-13: 978-0-312-59340-7 (tabbed student edition)

Acknowledgments

Scott Adams, "Dilbert and the Way of the Weasel." Copyright © 2000 by United Features Syndicate. Reprinted with permission of United Media.
American Heritage Dictionary, definition for "regard" from *The American Heritage Dictionary of the English Language, Fourth Edition.* Copyright © 2006 by Houghton Mifflin Company. Reproduced with permission.
R. I. Berkowitz, T. A. Wadden, A. M. Tershakovec, and J. L. Cronquist, "Behavior Therapy and Sibutramine for the Treatment of Adolescent Obesity" from *Journal of the American Medical Association* 289 (2003): 1807–1809. Copyright © 2003 by the American Medical Association. Reprinted with permission.
Eugene Boe, excerpt from "Pioneers to Eternity" from *The Immigrant Experience,* edited by Thomas C. Wheeler. Copyright © 1971 by Thomas C. Wheeler. Reprinted with the permission of Doubleday, a division of Random House, Inc.

Acknowledgments and copyrights are continued at the back of the book on page 592, which constitutes an extension of the copyright page. It is a violation of the law to reproduce these selections by any means whatsoever without the written permission of the copyright holder.

Preface for Instructors

Publisher's Note

> This book is grounded in my many years of teaching first- and second-year composition to a wide range of students: young and mature, mainstream and multiethnic, talented and underprepared. As I've drafted and revised *Rules for Writers,* my goal has never been to sell students on my own views about language and politics — or to endorse popular trends in the teaching of English. Instead, I've tried to look squarely at the problems students face and come up with practical solutions.
>
> —Diana Hacker, from the preface to
> *Rules for Writers,* Fifth Edition

First and foremost a teacher, Diana Hacker (1942–2004) was clear about why her handbooks have been so successful: They give students practical solutions to real writing problems. Her many innovations — both large and small — were always at the service of giving students the advice they need in a way they can understand. She was able to take everything she knew from her thirty-five years of teaching and put it to work on every page of her books. As a result, she was one of the most successful college textbook authors of all time, with her handbooks assigned at more than half of the two- and four-year colleges in the United States.

Of all of her handbooks, *Rules for Writers* was Diana Hacker's favorite; it was the one she assigned and taught from at Prince George's Community College. Her innovative quick-reference features were time-savers for her students, and her simplified, value-priced handbook option was a money-saver. In *Rules for Writers,* Diana and Bedford/St. Martin's had produced the best value in college publishing — a handbook that helped students answer all of their writing questions quickly and that was priced to fit any student's budget.

With a new team of coauthors, *Rules for Writers* still offers class-tested advice in a language students can understand and at a low price. In the Hacker tradition, the new contributing authors—Nancy Sommers, Tom Jehn, Jane Rosenzweig, and Marcy Carbajal Van Horn—have crafted solutions for the writing problems of today's college students. Together they give us a new edition that provides more help with academic writing and research and that works better for a wider range of multilingual students. And at Bedford/St. Martin's, we have worked hard to maintain the same high standards that have informed every Hacker handbook.

Joan Feinberg
President, Bedford/St. Martin's

Features of the Sixth Edition

What's new

NEW CHAPTER ON WRITING ABOUT TEXTS. Reading and responding to texts is a core skill for academic writing in any discipline. The new edition includes helpful guidelines for analyzing texts along with two new annotated samples—a summary and an analysis. New guidance for writing about visual texts helps students apply critical thinking skills when writing about advertisements, photographs, cartoons, and other visual media.

MORE HELP WITH WRITING ARGUMENTS. Revised coverage of counterargument teaches students how to strengthen their writing by anticipating and responding to objections. A new annotated sample paper demonstrates the effective use of counterargument.

NEW VISUALS TEACH CITATION AT A GLANCE. New full-color, annotated facsimiles of original sources show students where to look for publication information in a book, a periodical, a Web site, and a source accessed in a database. These visuals help students find the information they need to cite print and online materials accurately and responsibly.

ADVICE THAT HELPS STUDENTS MAINTAIN THEIR VOICE WHILE WRITING FROM SOURCES. Thoroughly revised coverage of integrating sources teaches students how to go beyond patchwork research writing. Section 56 shows students how to lead into — and get out of — sources while keeping the source material in context and maintaining their own line of argument.

MORE HELP FOR WORKING WITH SOURCES. New advice helps students determine what role each of their sources will play in their paper, a skill useful in composition and beyond. Students are encouraged to question whether a source will function as background material, expert testimony, counterargument, and so forth. Clear examples do the teaching.

NEW QUICK-ACCESS CHARTS. The sixth edition features new charts to help writers navigate common writing challenges: understanding a writing assignment, reading actively, analyzing visuals, determining scholarly sources, and avoiding Internet plagiarism.

MORE ESL HELP FOR GENERATION 1.5 STUDENTS. Thoroughly revised ESL coverage considers the experiences of college students who may be proficient English speakers but who continue to struggle with writing in English. The sixth edition offers stronger support — with handy charts and advice — for using verbs, articles, and prepositions correctly.

NOW WITH ADVICE ON ACADEMIC CONVENTIONS — FOR NATIVE AS WELL AS NONNATIVE SPEAKERS. New boxed tips teach *academic English* — or how to go about writing well at an American college. Throughout the book, these nuggets of advice — on topics such as plagiarism, writing arguments, and understanding writing assignments — help students meet college expectations.

NEW SAMPLE PAPERS. Two new research papers use current print and electronic sources and are annotated to show both good writing and proper formatting. The new MLA-style research essay examines Internet monitoring in the workplace, and the new APA-style paper is a review of the literature on treatments for childhood obesity. A new essay in section 46, "Writing about Texts," demonstrates effective analysis of an article.

NEW EXERCISE ITEMS. Revisions of two hundred exercise items reflect a diversity of experience and offer practice through high-interest topics. These new items, along with the existing ones, provide students abundant opportunities for practice on every topic in the handbook.

What's the same

We have kept the features that have made *Rules for Writers* work so well for so many students and instructors. These features, detailed here, will be familiar to users of the previous edition.

A BRIEF MENU AND A USER-FRIENDLY INDEX.   Designed for student use, a brief menu inside the front cover displays the book's ten parts and lists only the numbered sections. The traditional, more detailed handbook menu, which is useful for instructors but too daunting for many students, appears inside the back cover.

The handbook's index (which Diana Hacker wrote herself and which was carefully updated for this edition) helps students find what they are looking for even if they don't know grammar terminology. When facing a choice between *I* and *me,* for example, students may not know to look up "Case" or even "Pronoun, case of." They are more likely to look up "*I* " or "*me,*" so the index includes entries for "*I* vs. *me*" and "*me* vs. *I.*" Similar user-friendly entries appear throughout the index.

QUICK-REFERENCE CHARTS.   Many of the handbook's charts help students review for common problems in their own writing, such as fragments and subject-verb agreement. Other charts summarize important material: a checklist for global revision, strategies for avoiding sexist language, guidelines for evaluating Web sites, and so on.

EXTENSIVE EXERCISES, SOME WITH ANSWERS.   At least one exercise set accompanies nearly every grammar section of the book. Most sets begin with five lettered sentences with answers in the back of the book so students can test their understanding independently. The sets then continue with numbered sentences whose answers appear only in the Instructor's Edition. Students who need more practice can go to the book's companion Web site (see pp. xvii–xviii for details).

DISCIPLINE-SPECIFIC RHETORICAL ADVICE FOR MLA AND APA STYLES. Advice on drafting a thesis, avoiding plagiarism, and integrating sources is illustrated for both documentation styles — MLA and APA — in color-coded sections. Examples are tied to topics appropriate to the disciplines that typically use each style: English and other humanities for MLA and social sciences and health professions for APA.

What's on the companion Web site
<http://dianahacker.com/rules>

RESOURCES FOR WRITERS AND TUTORS. New writing center resources on the companion Web site offer help for both tutors and writers: checklists for responding to a wide array of assignments, tips for preparing for a visit to the writing center, hints for making the best use of advice from tutors, and helpsheets for common writing problems — the same kinds of handouts students see in the writing center — all available in printable format.

GRAMMAR EXERCISES. For online practice, students can access more than one thousand exercise items — on every grammar topic in the handbook — with feedback written by Diana Hacker. Most of the exercises are scorable. Exercises that call for editing are labeled "edit and compare"; students are asked to edit sentences and compare their versions with possible revisions.

RESEARCH AND WRITING EXERCISES. Scorable electronic exercises on matters such as avoiding plagiarism, integrating sources, using MLA and APA documentation, and identifying citation elements give students ample practice with these critical topics. Scorable exercises on thesis statements, peer review, point of view, transitions, and other writing topics support students throughout the composing process.

EXTRA HELP FOR ESL WRITERS. For native and nonnative speakers alike, this area of the site offers advice and strategies for understanding college expectations and for writing well on college assignments. It includes many helpful charts, exercises and activities, advice for working with sources, and an annotated student essay.

LANGUAGE DEBATES. These twenty-two brief essays encourage students to explore controversial issues of grammar and usage (such as split infinitives and *who* versus *whom*), think about the rationales for a rule, and then make their own rhetorical decisions.

MODEL PAPERS. Model papers for MLA, APA, *Chicago,* and CSE styles illustrate both the design and the content of researched writing. Annotations highlight key points about each paper's style, content, and documentation.

RESEARCH AND DOCUMENTATION ONLINE. This online resource helps students conduct research and document their sources. Reference librarian Barbara Fister has updated her advice on finding sources and has provided new links to resources in a variety of disciplines. Guidelines for documenting print and online sources in MLA, APA, *Chicago,* and CSE styles are also up-to-date.

ACCESS TO PREMIUM CONTENT. With the purchase of a print version of the handbook, students can access premium content including an e-book version of *Rules for Writers* as well as a series of tutorials.

Ancillaries for students

Both print and electronic ancillaries are available for students.

PRINT RESOURCES

Developmental Exercises to Accompany RULES FOR WRITERS

Answers to Exercises in RULES FOR WRITERS

Working with Sources: Exercises to Accompany RULES FOR WRITERS

Research and Documentation in the Electronic Age, Fourth Edition

Language Debates, Second Edition

Extra Help for ESL Writers

Writing about Literature

Writing in the Disciplines: Advice and Models

Designing Documents and Understanding Visuals

ONLINE RESOURCES

Rules for Writers companion Web site (see pp. xvii–xviii)

Comment with *Rules for Writers*

Ancillaries for instructors

Classroom and professional resources for instructors are available in print form. Other resources appear on the instructor portion of the book's companion Web site.

PROFESSIONAL RESOURCES FOR INSTRUCTORS

Teaching Composition: Background Readings

The Bedford Guide for Writing Tutors, Fourth Edition

The Bedford Bibliography for Teachers of Writing, Sixth Edition

WEB RESOURCES FOR INSTRUCTORS

Rules for Writers instructor site < http://dianahacker.com/ rules/instructor >

- Exercise Masters, print-format versions of all the exercises in the book
- Quiz Masters, print-format quizzes on key topics in the book
- Electronic Diagnostic Tests, a test bank for instructors' use
- Transparency Masters, useful charts, examples, and visuals from the book
- *Preparing for the CLAST*
- *Preparing for the THEA*

In addition, all of the resources within *Re:Writing* < http:// bedfordstmartins.com/rewriting > are available to users of *Rules for Writers.* Resources include tutorials, exercises, diagnostics, technology help, and model documents — all written by our most widely adopted authors.

Acknowledgments

We called on a number of individuals to help us develop the sixth edition with Diana Hacker's goals as a foundation.

Contributors

The following contributing authors brought expertise, enthusiasm, and classroom experience to the revision. They wrote new content and rethought existing content to make certain that *Rules for Writers* reaches a broader range of students and meets their various needs. Nancy Sommers, Tom Jehn, and Jane Rosenzweig helped revise the coverage of the writing process, writing about texts, and research. Marcy Carbajal Van Horn revised the ESL coverage.

Nancy Sommers, Sosland Director of Expository Writing at Harvard University, has also taught composition at Rutgers

University and at Monmouth College and has directed the writing program at the University of Oklahoma. Diana was a longtime admirer of Nancy Sommers's work because it focused on student writing. A two-time Braddock Award winner, Nancy is well known for her research and publications on student writing. Her articles "Revision Strategies of Student and Experienced Writers" and "Responding to Student Writing" are two of the most widely read in the field. Her recent work involves a longitudinal study of undergraduate writing.

Tom Jehn teaches composition and directs the writing across the disciplines program at Harvard University. A recipient of numerous teaching awards both at Harvard and at the University of Virginia, he also leads professional development seminars on writing instruction for public high school teachers through the Calderwood Writing Fellows Project.

Jane Rosenzweig, a published author of fiction and nonfiction, teaches composition and directs the writing center at Harvard University. She has also taught writing at Yale University and the University of Iowa.

Marcy Carbajal Van Horn, assistant professor of English and ESL at Santa Fe Community College (FL), teaches composition to native and nonnative speakers of English and teaches the advanced ESL writing course. She has also taught university-level academic writing and critical thinking at Instituto Technológico y de Estudios Superiores in Mexico. Marcy creates practical and accessible content for a broad range of students — starting with her own — as Diana always did.

Reviewers

For their many helpful suggestions, we would like to thank a perceptive group of reviewers.

Eileen Abel, Bluegrass Community and Technical College

James Beasley, DePaul University

Lisa Beckelhimer, University of Cincinnati

Allegra Blake, Central Michigan University

Christina Bowman, California State University, Long Beach
Addison Bross, Lehigh University
Elaine Brousseau, Providence College
Cynthia L. Butos, Trinity College
Anita L. Cook, Bridgewater College
Susan Jean Cooper, College of the Canyons
Diana Federman, Holyoke Community College
Deborah Fleming, Ashland University
Douglas B. Hoehn, Community College of Philadelphia
Noha Kabaji, Golden West College
Elana Kent-Stacy, College of the Canyons
Mary T. Lane, Anne Arundel Community College
Benjamin Lareau, Casper College
Maurice L'Heureux, Northern Virginia Community College
Deborah B. Luyster, University of North Florida
David Marlow, University of South Carolina Upstate
Mark R. Matthews, Anne Arundel Community College
D. Erik Nielson, Northern Virginia Community College
Denee Pescarmona, College of the Canyons
Anne M. Rector, Emory University
Angela D. Schlein, University of Florida
Leta McGaffey Sharp, University of Arizona
Ann L. Smith, Modesto Junior College
Catherine Sutton, Ithaca College
Carol Ann Theuer, Wake Technical Community College
Amy Ulmer, Pasadena City College
Donald Wildman, Wake Technical Community College
Cynthia Schoolar Williams, Tufts University

Student contributors

We are indebted to the students whose essays appear in this edition—Jamal Hammond, Luisa Mirano, Anna Orlov, Emilia Sanchez, and Matt Watson—not only for permission to use their work but also for allowing us to adapt it for pedagogical purposes.

Our thanks also go to the students who granted permission to use their paragraphs: Celeste Barrus, Rosa Broderick, Diana Crawford, Jim Drew, Connie Hailey, Craig Lee Hetherington, William G. Hill, Linda Lavelle, Kathleen Lewis, Laurie McDonough, Chris Mileski, Leon Nage, Julie Reardon, Kevin Smith, Margaret Smith, Margaret Stack, John Clyde Thatcher, and David Warren.

Bedford/St. Martin's

Rules for Writers had always been a team effort between Diana Hacker and her editors at Bedford/St. Martin's. The Hacker team is still in place. Joan Feinberg, president, was the editor on the first editions of every Hacker handbook, including *Rules for Writers*, and has been a part of every book since. Special thanks go to Chuck Christensen for understanding what makes a great handbook author and for knowing he had found one in Diana Hacker. At the heart of the Hacker team is Diana's longtime editor, executive editor Michelle Clark, the most skilled, creative editor we could wish for. Development editor Mara Weible expanded the new media offerings, making them as easy to use as the book itself. Claire Seng-Niemoeller has designed every Hacker handbook since the first and has again retained the clean, uncluttered look of the book while making more use of color. Having copyedited every Hacker handbook, Barbara Flanagan has helped to develop the clarity and consistency that is a Hacker hallmark. Senior production editor Anne Noonan kept the team on track with her persistence, sharp eye, and concern for every detail. Assistant production editor Katie Caruana provided detailed assistance throughout the page proof review. Editor in chief Karen Henry and managing editor Elizabeth Schaaf have worked on these books from the beginning and remain committed to maintaining the high level of quality of Hacker handbooks. Editorial assistant Alicia Young managed various projects and made sure that we heard from many users. The team remains committed to maintaining the high level of quality of Hacker handbooks.

How to Use This Book and Its Web Site

Though it is small enough to hold in your hand, *Rules for Writers* will answer most of the questions you are likely to ask as you plan, draft, and revise a piece of writing: How do I choose and narrow a topic? What can I do if I get stuck? How do I know when to begin a new paragraph? Should I write *each was* or *each were*? When does a comma belong before *and*? What is the difference between *accept* and *except*? How do I cite a source from the Web?

The book's companion Web site extends the book beyond its covers. See pages xvii–xviii for details.

How to find information with an instructor's help

When you are revising an essay that has been marked by your instructor, tracking down information is simple. If your instructor marks problems with a number such as *16* or a number and letter such as *12e,* you can turn directly to the appropriate section of the handbook. Just flip through the orange tabs at the top of the pages until you find the number in question. The number *16,* for example, leads you to the rule "Tighten wordy sentences," and *12e* takes you to the subrule "Repair dangling modifiers." If your instructor uses an abbreviation such as *w* or *dm* instead of a number, consult the list of abbreviations and revision symbols on the next to the last page of the book. There you will find the name of the problem (*wordy; dangling modifier*) and the number of the section to consult.

How to find information on your own

With a little practice, you will be able to find information in this book without an instructor's help — usually by consulting the brief menu inside the front cover. At times, you may consult the detailed menu inside the back cover, the index, the Glossary of Usage, the list of revision symbols, or one of the directories to documentation models. The tutorials on pages xix–xxii give you opportunities to practice finding information in different ways.

THE BRIEF MENU.   The brief menu inside the front cover displays the book's contents as briefly and simply as possible.

Let's say that you are having problems writing parallel sentences. Your first step is to scan the menu for the appropriate numbered topic — in this case "9 Parallelism." Then you can use the orange tabs at the top of the pages to find section 9. The information in the tabs — the section number and the symbol for parallelism — will tell you that you are in the section you need.

THE DETAILED MENU.   The detailed menu appears inside the back cover. When the numbered section you're looking for is broken up into quite a few lettered subsections, try consulting this menu. For instance, if you have a question about the proper use of commas after introductory elements, this menu will lead you quickly to section 32b.

THE INDEX.   If you aren't sure which topic to choose from one of the menus, consult the index at the back of the book. For example, you may not realize that the issue of whether to use *have* or *has* is a matter of subject-verb agreement (section 21). In that case, simply look up "*has* vs. *have*" in the index and you will be directed to specific pages in two sections covering the topic of subject-verb agreement.

THE GLOSSARY OF USAGE.   When in doubt about the correct use of a particular word (such as *affect* and *effect, among* and *between,* or *hopefully*), consult the Glossary of Usage at the back of the book. This glossary explains the difference between commonly confused words; it also lists words that are inappropriate in formal written English.

DIRECTORIES TO DOCUMENTATION MODELS.   When you are documenting a research paper with MLA or APA style, you can find documentation models by consulting the appropriate directories. For MLA in-text citation and works cited directories, see the pages marked with a vertical band of orange; for APA in-text citation and reference list directories, see the pages marked with a vertical band of gray.

How to use this book and its Web site for self-study

In a composition class, most of your time will be spent writing. So it is unlikely that you will study all of the chapters in this book in detail. Instead you should focus on the problems that tend to crop up in your own writing. Your instructor (or a tutor in your college's writing center) can help you design a program of self-study.

Rules for Writers has been designed so that you can learn from it on your own. By providing answers to some exercise sentences, it allows you to test your understanding of the material. Most exercise sets begin with five sentences lettered a–e and conclude with five numbered sentences. Answers to the lettered sentences appear in an appendix at the end of the book.

The following list describes the features on the book's companion Web site < dianahacker.com/rules >. Each feature — whether an electronic exercise or a Language Debate or a writing center helpsheet — has been developed for you to use on your own whenever you need it.

ON THE WEB dianahacker.com/rules

> **Writing exercises**
Interactive exercises on topics such as choosing a thesis statement and conducting a peer review

> **Grammar exercises**
Interactive exercises on grammar, style, and punctuation

> **Research exercises**
Interactive exercises on topics such as integrating quotations and documenting sources in MLA and APA styles

> **Model papers**
Annotated sample papers in MLA, APA, *Chicago*, and CSE styles

ON THE WEB (continued)

> **ESL help**

Resources and strategies to help nonnative speakers improve their college writing skills

> **Language Debates**

Mini-essays exploring controversial issues of grammar and usage, such as split infinitives

> **Research and Documentation Online**

Advice on finding sources in a variety of disciplines and up-to-date guidelines for documenting print and online sources in MLA, APA, *Chicago*, and CSE styles

> **Tutorials**

Interactive resources that teach essential skills such as integrating sources in MLA style and writing paraphrases and summaries

> **Resources for writers and tutors**

Revision checklists and helpsheets for common writing problems

> **Additional resources**

Print-format versions of the exercises in the book and links to additional online resources for every part of the book

Tutorials

The following tutorials will give you practice using the book's menus, index, Glossary of Usage, and MLA directory. Answers to the tutorials begin on page 578.

TUTORIAL 1
Using the directories

Each of the following "rules" violates the principle it expresses. Using the brief menu inside the front cover or the detailed menu inside the back cover, find the section in *Rules for Writers* that explains the principle. Then fix the problem. Examples:

> *Tutors in*
> ~~In~~ the writing center/ ~~they~~ say that vague pronoun reference is
> ^
> unacceptable. *23*
>
> *come*
> Be alert for irregular verbs that have ~~came~~ to you in the
>   ^
> wrong form. *27a*

1. A verb have to agree with its subject.
2. Each pronoun should agree with their antecedent.
3. About sentence fragments. You should avoid them.
4. Its important to use apostrophe's correctly.
5. Check for *-ed* verb endings that have been drop.
6. Discriminate careful between adjectives and adverbs.
7. If your sentence begins with a long introductory word group use a comma to separate the word group from the rest of the sentence.
8. Don't write a run-on sentence, you must connect independent clauses with a comma and a coordinating conjunction or with a semicolon.
9. A writer must be careful not to shift your point of view.
10. When dangling, watch your modifiers.

TUTORIAL 2
Using the index

Assume that you have written the following sentences and want to know the answers to the questions in brackets. Use the index at the back of the book to locate the information you need, and edit the sentences if necessary.

1. Each of the candidates have decided to participate in tonight's debate. [Should the verb be *has* or *have* to agree with *Each*?]
2. We had intended to go surfing but spent most of our vacation lying on the beach. [Should I use *lying* or *laying*?]
3. We only looked at two houses before buying the house of our dreams. [Is *only* in the right place?]
4. In Saudi Arabia it is considered ill mannered for you to accept a gift. [Is it okay to use *you* to mean "anyone in general"?]
5. In Canada, Joanne picked up several bottles of maple syrup for her sister and me. [Should I write *for her sister and I*?]

TUTORIAL 3
Using the menus or the index

Imagine that you are in the following situations. Using either the menus or the index, find the information you need.

1. You are Ray Farley, a community college student who has been out of high school for ten years. You recall learning to put a comma between all items in a series except the last two. But you have noticed that most writers use a comma between all items. You're curious about the current rule. Which section of *Rules for Writers* will you consult?
2. You are Maria Sanchez, a peer tutor in your university's writing center. Mike Lee, a nonnative speaker of English, has come to you for help. He is working on a rough draft that contains a number of problems with articles (*a, an,* and *the*). You know how to use articles, but you aren't able to explain the complicated rules on their correct use. Which section of *Rules for Writers* will you and Mike Lee consult?
3. You are John Pell, engaged to marry Jane Dalton. In a note to Jane's parents, you have written, "Thank you for giving Jane and myself such a generous contribution toward our honeymoon." You wonder if you should write "Jane and I" or "Jane and me." What does *Rules for Writers* say?
4. You are Selena Young, an intern supervisor at a housing agency. Two of your interns, Jake Gilliam and Susan Green, have writing problems involving *-s* endings on verbs. Jake tends to drop *-s* endings; Susan tends to add them where they don't belong. You suspect that both problems stem from nonstandard dialects spoken at home.

Susan and Jake are in danger of losing their jobs because your boss thinks that anyone who writes "the tenant refuse" or "the landlords agrees" is beyond hope. You disagree. Susan and Jake have asked for your help. Where in *Rules for Writers* can they find the rules they need?

5. You are Joe Thompson, a first-year college student. Your friend Samantha, who has completed two years of college, seems to enjoy correcting your English. Just yesterday she corrected your sentence "I felt badly about her death" to "I felt bad about her death." You're sure you've heard many educated people, including professors, say "I felt badly." Upon consulting *Rules for Writers,* what do you discover?

TUTORIAL 4
Using the Glossary of Usage

Consult the Glossary of Usage to see if the italicized words are used correctly. Then edit any sentences containing incorrect usage. If a sentence is correct, write "correct" after it. Example:

> *an*
> The pediatrician gave my daughter a̶ injection for her allergy.

1. Changing attitudes *toward* alcohol have *effected* the beer industry.
2. It is *mankind's* nature to think wisely and act foolishly.
3. This afternoon I plan to *lie* out in the sun and work on my tan.
4. Our goal this year is to *grow* our profits by 9 percent.
5. Most sleds are pulled by no *less* than two dogs and no more than ten.

TUTORIAL 5
Using the directory to MLA works cited models

Assume that you have written a short research essay on the origins of hip-hop music. You have cited the following sources in your essay, using MLA documentation, and you are ready to type your list of works cited. Turn to page 437 and use the MLA directory to locate the appropriate models. Then write a correct entry for each source and arrange the entries in a properly formatted list of works cited.

A book by Jeff Chang titled *Can't Stop, Won't Stop: A History of the Hip-Hop Generation.* The book was published in New York by St. Martin's Press in 2005.

An online article by Kay Randall called "Studying a Hip-Hop Nation." The article appeared on the University of Texas at Austin Web site, which you accessed on October 13, 2008. The last update was October 9, 2008.

A journal article by H. Samy Alim titled "360 Degreez of Black Art Comin at You: Sista Sonia Sanchez and the Dimensions of a Black Arts Continuum." The article appears in the journal *BMa: The Sonia Sanchez Literary Review*. The article appears on pages 15–33. The volume number is 6, the issue number is 1, and the year is 2000.

A sound recording entitled "Rapper's Delight" performed by the Sugarhill Gang on the CD *The Sugarhill Gang*. The CD was released in 2008 by DBK Works.

A magazine article accessed through the database *Expanded Academic ASAP*. The article, "The Roots Redefine Hip-Hop's Past," was written by Kimberly Davis and published in *Ebony* magazine in June 2003. The article appears on pages 162–64. You found this article on October 13, 2008.

Contents

The Writing Process   1

Document Design 59

Clarity 79

Grammar

ESL Challenges   223

The Writing Process

Writing is not a matter of recording already developed thoughts but a process of figuring out what you think. Since it's not possible to think about everything all at once, most experienced writers handle a piece of writing in stages. You will generally move from planning to drafting to revising, but be prepared to return to earlier stages as your ideas develop.

1

Generate ideas and sketch a plan.

Before attempting a first draft, spend some time generating ideas. Mull over your subject while listening to music or driving to work, jot down inspirations, and explore your insights with anyone willing to listen. Ask yourself questions: What do you find puzzling, striking, or interesting about your subject? What would you like to know more about? At this stage, you should be collecting information and experimenting with ways of focusing and organizing it to reach your readers.

1a Assess the writing situation.

Begin by taking a look at the writing situation in which you find yourself. The key elements of the writing situation include your subject, the sources of information available to you, your purpose, your audience, and constraints such as length, document design, review sessions, and deadlines.

It is likely that you will make final decisions about all of these matters later in the writing process — after a first draft, for example. Nevertheless, you can save yourself time by thinking about as many of them as possible in advance. For a quick checklist, see the chart on page 3.

ACADEMIC ENGLISH What counts as good writing varies from culture to culture and even among groups within cultures. In some situations, you will need to become familiar with the writing styles — such as direct or indirect, personal or impersonal, plain or embellished — that are valued by the culture or discourse community for which you are writing.

Checklist for assessing the writing situation

Subject

- Has the subject (or a range of possible subjects) been given to you, or are you free to choose your own?
- What interests you about your subject? What questions would you like to explore?
- Why is your subject worth writing about? How might readers benefit from reading about it?
- How broadly can you cover the subject? Do you need to narrow it to a more specific topic (because of length restrictions, for instance)?

Sources of information

- Where will your information come from: Reading? Personal experience? Observation? Interviews? Questionnaires?
- What sort of documentation is required?

Purpose and audience

- Why are you writing: To inform readers? To persuade them? To entertain them? To call them to action? Some combination of these?
- Who are your readers? How well informed are they about the subject? What do you want them to learn?
- How interested and attentive are they likely to be? Will they resist any of your ideas?
- What is your relationship to them: Student to instructor? Employee to supervisor? Citizen to citizen? Expert to novice? Scholar to scholar?

Length and document design

- Do you have any length specifications? If not, what length seems appropriate, given your subject, purpose, and audience?
- Must you use a particular format for your document? If so, do you have guidelines to follow or examples to consult?

Reviewers and deadlines

- Who will be reviewing your draft in progress: Your instructor? A writing center tutor? Your classmates? A friend? Someone in your family?
- What are your deadlines? How much time will you need to allow for the various stages of writing, including proofreading and printing the final draft?

Subject

Frequently your subject will be given to you. In a psychology class, for example, you might be asked to explain Bruno Bettel-heim's Freudian analysis of fairy tales. Or in a course on the history of filmmaking, you might be assigned an essay on the impact of D. W. Griffith's silent film *The Birth of a Nation.* In a composition course, assignments often ask you to respond to readings. In the business world, your assignment might be to draft a quarterly sales report.

At other times, you will be free to choose your own subject. Then you will be wise to select a subject that you are curious to learn more about. Make sure that you can reasonably investigate your subject in the length you have been assigned.

Whether or not you choose your own subject, it's important to be aware of the expectations of each writing situation. The chart on page 7 suggests ways to interpret assignments.

ON THE WEB > dianahacker.com/rules
Additional resources > Subjects for writing

Sources of information

Where will your facts, details, and examples come from? Can you develop your topic from personal experience, or will you need to search for relevant information through observation, interviews, questionnaires, or reading?

PERSONAL EXPERIENCE   If your interest in a subject stems from your personal experience, you will want to ask what it is about your experience that would interest your audience and why. For example, if you volunteered at a homeless shelter, you might have spent some time talking to homeless children and learned about their fears. Perhaps you can use your experience to broaden your readers' understanding of the issues involved, to persuade an organization to fund an after-school program for homeless children, or to propose changes in legislation.

READING   Reading is an important way to deepen your under-standing of a topic and enlarge your perspective. Reading will be your primary source of information for many college assign-ments, which will generally be of two kinds: (1) analytical es-says that call for a close reading of one book, essay, or literary

Ways to narrow a subject to a topic

Subdividing your subject

One way to subdivide a subject is to ask questions sparked by reading or talking to your classmates. If you are writing about teen pregnancy, for example, you might wonder why some cities have different rates of teen pregnancy. This question would give you a manageable topic for a short paper.

Restricting your purpose

Often you can restrict your purpose. For example, if your subject is preventing teen pregnancy, you might at first hope to call readers to action. Upon further reflection, you might realize that this goal is more than you could hope to accomplish, given your word limit. By adopting a more limited purpose — to show that an experimental health class targeted at sixth graders results in lower rates of teen pregnancy — you would have a manageable topic and a better chance of success.

Restricting your audience

Consider writing for a particular audience. For example, instead of writing for a general audience on a broad subject such as teenage pregnancy, you might address a group with a special interest in the subject: young people, parents, educators, or politicians.

Considering the information available to you

Look at the information you have collected. If you have gathered a great deal of information on one aspect of your subject (for example, counseling programs for pregnant teenagers) and less information on other aspects (such as birth control education), you may have found your topic.

work and (2) research assignments that ask you to find and consult a variety of sources on a topic. (See the chart "Guidelines for active reading" on p. 347.)

For an analytical essay, you will select details from the work not to inform readers but to support an interpretation. You can often assume that your readers are familiar with the work and have a copy of it on hand, but provide enough context so that someone who doesn't know the work well can still follow your interpretation. When you quote from the work, page references are usually sufficient. When in doubt about the need for documentation, consult your instructor.

For a research paper, you cannot assume that your readers are familiar with your sources. Therefore, you must formally document all quoted, summarized, or paraphrased material (see 51c).

OBSERVATION   Observation is an excellent means of collecting information about a wide range of subjects, such as male-female relationships on a popular television program, the clichéd language of sports announcers, or the appeal of a local art museum. For such subjects, do not rely on your memory alone; your information will be fresher and more detailed if you actively collect it, with a notebook or tape recorder in hand.

INTERVIEWS AND QUESTIONNAIRES   Interviews and questionnaires can supply you with detailed and interesting information on many subjects. A nursing student interested in the care of terminally ill patients might interview hospice nurses; a political science major might speak with a local judge about alternative sentencing for first offenders; a future teacher might conduct a survey on the use of computers in local elementary schools.

It is a good idea to tape-record interviews to preserve any lively quotations that you might want to weave into your essay. Circulating questionnaires by e-mail will facilitate responses. Keep questions simple and specify a deadline to ensure that you get a reasonable number of replies. (See also 49g.)

Purpose

Your purpose will often be dictated by your specific writing situation. Perhaps you have been asked to draft a proposal requesting funding for a student organization, to report the results of a biology experiment, or to write about the stem cell research controversy for the school newspaper. Even though your overall purpose is fairly obvious in such situations, a closer look at the assignment can help you make a variety of necessary decisions. How detailed should the proposal be? How technical does your biology professor want your report to be? Do you want to inform students about the stem cell research controversy or change their attitudes toward it?

In many writing situations, part of your challenge will be discovering a purpose. Asking yourself why readers should

Understanding an assignment

For many college papers, you will be given a written assignment that outlines your instructor's expectations. When you receive an assignment, read through it carefully. Don't assume that all assignments are alike — spend some time making sure you understand what is required of you. When in doubt, ask your instructor.

Determining the purpose of the assignment

Instructors assign writing projects for a variety of reasons. You might be expected to summarize information from textbooks, lectures, or research (see 46c); to analyze ideas and concepts (see 46d); to take a position on a topic and defend it with evidence (see 47); or to create an original argument by combining ideas from different sources (see 47). The wording of an assignment will often suggest which of these purposes your instructor has in mind.

Understanding how to answer an assignment's question

Many assignments will ask you to answer a *how* or *why* question. Such a question cannot be answered using only facts; you will need to take a position. For example, the question "*What* are the survival rates for leukemia patients?" can be answered by reporting facts. The question "*Why* are the survival rates for leukemia patients in one state lower than in a neighboring state?" must be answered with both facts and interpretation.

If a list of prompts appears in the assignment, be careful — instructors rarely expect you to answer all of the questions in order. Look instead for topics, themes, or ideas that will help you ask your own questions.

Recognizing implied questions

When you are asked to *discuss, analyze, agree or disagree,* or *consider* a topic, your instructor will often expect you to answer a *how* or *why* question. For example, "*Discuss* the effects of the No Child Left Behind Act on special education programs" is really another way of saying "*How* has the No Child Left Behind Act affected special education programs?" Similarly, the assignment "*Consider* the recent rise of attention deficit hyperactivity disorder diagnoses" is asking you to answer the question "*Why* are diagnoses of attention deficit hyperactivity disorder rising?"

care about what you are saying can help you decide what your purpose might be. Perhaps your subject is magnet schools — schools that draw students from different neighborhoods because of features such as advanced science classes or a concentration on the arts. If you have discussed magnet schools in class, a description of how these schools work probably will not interest you or your readers. But maybe you have discovered that your county's magnet schools are not promoting diversity as had been planned and you want to call your readers to action. Or maybe you are interested in comparing student performance at magnet schools and traditional schools.

Although no precise guidelines will lead you to a purpose, you can begin by asking yourself which one or more of the following aims you hope to accomplish.

PURPOSES FOR WRITING

to inform	to evaluate
to persuade	to recommend
to entertain	to request
to call readers to action	to propose
to change attitudes	to provoke thought
to analyze	to express feelings
to argue	to summarize

Writers often misjudge their own purposes, summarizing when they should be analyzing or expressing feelings about problems instead of proposing solutions. Before beginning any writing task, pause to ask, "Why am I communicating with my readers?" This question will lead you to another important question: "Just who are my readers?"

Audience

Audience analysis can often lead you to an effective strategy for reaching your readers. A writer whose purpose was to persuade teenagers not to smoke began by making some observations about her audience (see the top of p. 9).

This analysis led the writer to focus more on the social aspects of smoking than on the health risks. Her audience analysis also warned her against adopting a preachy tone that her readers might find offensive. Instead of lecturing, she decided to draw examples from her own experience as a smoker: burning holes in her best sweater, driving in zero-degree weather

AUDIENCE ANALYSIS

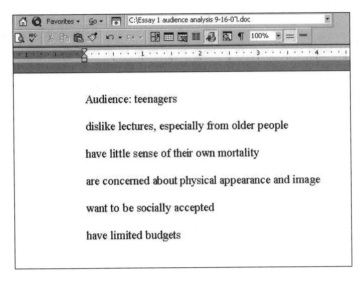

late at night to buy cigarettes, and so on. The result was an essay that reached its readers instead of alienating them.

Of course, in some writing situations the audience will not be neatly defined for you. Nevertheless, many of the choices you make as you write will tell readers who you think they are (novices or experts, for example), so it is best to be consistent.

For help with audience analysis, see the chart on page 3.

ACADEMIC AUDIENCES   In the academic world, considerations of audience can be more complex than they seem at first. Your instructor will read your essay, of course, but most instructors play multiple roles while reading. Their first and most obvious roles are as coach and judge; less obvious is their role as an intelligent and objective reader, the kind of person who might reasonably be informed, convinced, entertained, or called to action by what you have to say.

Some instructors specify an audience, such as a hypothetical supervisor, readers of a local newspaper, or fellow academics in a particular field. Other instructors expect you to imagine an audience appropriate to your purpose and your subject. Still others prefer that you write for a general audience of educated readers—nonspecialists who can be expected to read with an intelligent, critical eye.

BUSINESS AUDIENCES Writers in the business world often find themselves writing for multiple audiences. A letter to a client, for instance, might be distributed to sales representatives as well. Readers of a report might include persons with and without technical expertise or readers who want details and those who prefer a quick overview.

To satisfy the demands of multiple audiences, business writers have developed a variety of strategies: attaching cover letters to detailed reports, adding boldface headings, placing summaries in the margin, and so on.

Length and document design

Writers seldom have complete control over length. Journalists usually write within strict word limits set by their editors, businesspeople routinely aim for conciseness, and most college assignments specify an approximate length.

Certain document designs may be required by your writing situation. Specific formats are used in business for letters, memos, and reports. In the academic world, you may need to learn precise conventions for lab reports, critiques, research papers, and so on. For most undergraduate essays, a standard format is acceptable (see 6a).

In some writing situations, you will be free to create your own design, complete with headings, displayed lists, and perhaps visuals such as charts and graphs. For a discussion of the principles of document design, see 5.

Reviewers and deadlines

Professional and business writers rarely work alone. They work with reviewers, often called editors, who offer advice throughout the writing process. In college classes, too, the use of reviewers is common. Some instructors play the role of reviewer for you; others may ask you to visit your college's writing center. Still others schedule peer review sessions in class or online. Such sessions give you a chance to hear what other students think about your draft in progress—and to play the role of reviewer yourself.

Deadlines are a key element of any writing situation. They help you plan your time and map out what you can accomplish in that time. For complex writing projects, such as research papers, you'll need to plan your time carefully. By working backward from the final deadline, you can create a schedule of target dates for completing parts of the process. (See p. 382 for an example.)

ON THE WEB > dianahacker.com/rules
Writing exercises > E-ex 1–1

1b Experiment with ways to explore your subject.

Instead of just plunging into a first draft, experiment with one or more techniques for exploring your subject, perhaps one of these:

> talking and listening
>
> annotating texts and taking notes
>
> listing
>
> clustering
>
> freewriting
>
> asking the journalist's questions
>
> keeping a journal

Whatever technique you turn to, the goal is the same: to generate a wealth of ideas that will lead you to a question, a problem, or an issue that you want to explore further. At this early stage of the writing process, don't censor yourself. Sometimes an idea that initially seems trivial or far-fetched will actually turn out to be worthwhile.

Talking and listening

Since writing is a process of figuring out what you think about a subject, it can be useful to try out your ideas on other people. Conversation can deepen and refine your ideas before you even begin to set them down on paper. By talking and listening to others, you can also discover what they find interesting, what they are curious about, and where they disagree with you. If you are planning to advance an argument, you can try it out on listeners with other points of view.

Many writers begin a writing project by brainstorming ideas in a group, debating a point with friends, or chatting with an instructor. Others turn to themselves for company — by talking into a tape recorder. Some writers exchange ideas by sending e-mail or instant messages, by joining an Internet chat group, or by following a mailing list discussion. If you are part of a networked classroom, you may be encouraged to exchange ideas with your classmates and instructor in an electronic workshop. One advantage of engaging in such discussions is that while you are "talking" you are actually writing.

Annotating texts and taking notes

When you write about reading, one of the best ways to explore ideas is to mark up the work — on the pages themselves if you own a copy, on photocopies if you don't. Annotating a text encourages you to look at it more carefully — to underline key concepts, to note contradictions in an argument, to raise questions for investigation. (See also 46a.) Here, for example, is a paragraph from an essay on medical ethics as one student annotated it.

What break-throughs?
Do all break-throughs have the same consequences?

Breakthroughs in genetics present us with a promise and a predicament. The promise is that we may soon be able to treat and prevent a host of debilitating diseases. The predicament is that our newfound genetic knowledge may also enable us to manipulate our own nature — to enhance our muscles, memories, and moods; to choose the sex, height, and other genetic traits of our children; to make ourselves "better than well." When science moves faster than moral understanding, as it does today, men and women struggle to articulate their unease. In liberal societies they reach first for the language of autonomy, fairness, and individual rights. But this part of our moral vocabulary is ill equipped to address the hardest questions posed by genetic engineering. The genomic revolution has induced a kind of moral vertigo.

Stem cell research?

What does he mean by "moral understanding"?

Is everyone really uneasy?
Is something a breakthrough if it creates a predicament?

Which questions? He doesn't seem to be taking sides.

— Michael Sandel,
"The Case against Perfection"

After reading and annotating the entire article, the student read through his annotations and looked for patterns. He noticed that several of his annotations pointed to the larger question of whether a scientific breakthrough should be viewed in terms of its moral consequences. He decided to reread the article, taking detailed notes on his reading, with this question in mind. (See also 52c.)

Listing

Listing ideas — a technique sometimes known as *brainstorming* — is a good way to figure out what you know and what questions you have. Here is a list one student writer jotted down for an essay about funding for college athletics:

Football receives the most funding of any sport.

Funding comes from ticket sales, fundraisers, alumni contributions.

Biggest women's sport is soccer.

Women's soccer team is only ten years old; football team is fifty years old.

Football graduates have had time to earn more money than soccer graduates.

Soccer games don't draw as many fans.

Should funding be equal for all teams?

Do alumni have the right to fund whatever they want?

The ideas and questions appear here in the order in which they first occurred to the writer. Later she felt free to rearrange them, to group them under general categories, to delete some, and to add others. These initial thoughts led the writer to questions that helped her narrow her topic. In other words, she treated her early list as a source of ideas and a springboard to new ideas, not as an outline.

Clustering

Unlike listing, clustering highlights relationships among ideas. To cluster ideas, write your topic in the center of a sheet of paper, draw a circle around it, and surround the circle with related ideas connected to it with lines. If some of the satellite ideas lead to more specific clusters, write them down as well. The writer of the following diagram was exploring ideas for an essay on obesity in children.

CLUSTER DIAGRAM

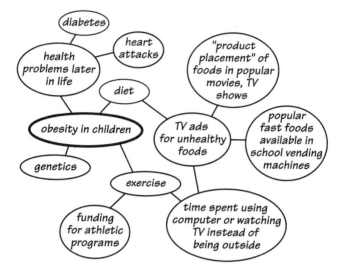

Freewriting

In its purest form, freewriting is simply nonstop writing. You set aside ten minutes or so and write whatever comes to mind, without pausing to think about word choice, spelling, or even meaning. If you get stuck, you can write about being stuck, but you should keep your fingers moving. The point is to loosen up and see what happens. Even if nothing much happens, you have lost only ten minutes. It's more likely, though, that something interesting will emerge — perhaps an eloquent sentence, an honest expression of feeling, or an idea worth further investigation. Freewriting also lets you ask questions without feeling that you have to answer them. Sometimes a question that emerges at this stage will point you in an unexpected direction.

To explore ideas on a particular topic, consider using a technique known as *focused freewriting*. Again, you write quickly and freely — without regard for punctuation, word choice, spelling, or paragraphing — but this time you focus on a subject and pay some attention to the connections among your ideas.

TIP: If you get stuck while freewriting, try imagining that you are writing an e-mail to a friend about your subject.

Asking the journalist's questions

By asking relevant questions, you can generate many ideas — and you can make sure that you have adequately explored your subject. When gathering material for a story, journalists routinely ask themselves Who? What? When? Where? Why? and How? In addition to helping journalists get started, these questions ensure that they will not overlook an important fact: the date of a prospective summit meeting, for example, or the exact location of a neighborhood burglary.

Whenever you are writing about events, whether current or historical, asking the journalist's questions is one way to get started. One student, whose topic was the negative reaction in 1915 to D. W. Griffith's silent film *The Birth of a Nation*, began exploring her topic with this set of questions:

> *Who* objected to the film?
>
> *What* were the objections?
>
> *When* were protests first voiced?
>
> *Where* were protests most strongly expressed?
>
> *Why* did protesters object to the film?
>
> *How* did protesters make their views known?

As often happens, the answers to these questions led to another question the writer wanted to explore. After she discovered that protesters objected to the film's racist portrayal of African Americans, she wondered whether their protests had changed attitudes. This question prompted an interesting topic for a paper: Did the film's stereotypes lead to positive, if unintended, consequences?

Keeping a journal

A journal is a collection of personal, exploratory writing. An entry in a journal can be any length — from a single sentence to several pages — and it is likely to be informal and experimental.

In a journal, often meant for your eyes only, you can take risks. In one entry, for example, you might freewrite. In another, you might pose questions, whether or not you have the answers. You might comment on an interesting idea from one of your classes or keep a list of questions that occur to you while reading. A journal is also an excellent place to play around with language for the sheer fun of it: experimenting with prose style, for instance, or parodying a favorite songwriter.

Keeping a journal can be an enriching experience in its own right, since it allows you to explore issues of concern to you without worrying about what someone else thinks. A journal can also serve as a sourcebook of ideas to draw on in future essays.

1c Formulate a tentative thesis.

As you explore your topic and begin to identify questions you would like to investigate, you will begin to see possible ways to focus your material. At this point, try to settle on a tentative central idea. The more complex your topic, the more your initial central idea will change as your drafts evolve.

For many types of writing, you will be able to assert your central idea in a sentence or two. Such a statement, which will ordinarily appear in the opening paragraph of your finished essay, is called a *thesis*. A thesis is often the answer to a question you have posed, the resolution of a problem you have identified, or a statement that takes a position on a debatable topic. A successful thesis — like the following, which are all taken from articles in *Smithsonian* — points both the writer and the reader in a definite direction.

> Much maligned and the subject of unwarranted fears, most bats are harmless and highly beneficial.

> The American Revolution was the central event in Washington's life, the crucible for his development as a mature man, a prominent statesman, and a national hero.

> Raging in mines from Pennsylvania to China, coal fires threaten towns, poison air and water, and add to global warming.

The thesis sentence usually contains a key word or controlling idea that limits its focus. The preceding sentences, for example, prepare for essays that focus on the *beneficial* aspects of bats and the role of the American Revolution in the *development* of George Washington. The third example uses a controlling idea: the *effects* of coal fires.

It's a good idea to formulate a tentative thesis early in the writing process. This tentative thesis will help you organize your draft. It will probably be less graceful than the thesis you include in the final version of your essay. Don't worry too soon about the exact wording of your thesis because your main point

Testing a tentative thesis

Once you have come up with a tentative thesis, you can use the following questions to refine it.

- Does the thesis require an essay's worth of development? Will you be able to include all of your support? Or will you run out of points too quickly?
- Is the thesis too obvious? If you cannot come up with interpretations that oppose your own, consider revising your thesis.
- Can you support your thesis with the evidence available?
- Can you explain why readers will want to read an essay with this thesis?

may change as you refine your ideas. Here, for example, is one student's early effort:

> In *Rebel without a Cause*, the protagonist, Jim Stark, is often seen literally on the edge of physical danger — walking too close to the swimming pool, leaning over an observation deck, and driving his car toward a cliff.

The thesis that appeared in the student's final draft not only was more polished but also reflected the evolution of the student's ideas.

> The scenes in which Jim Stark is seen on the edge of physical danger — walking too close to the swimming pool, leaning over an observation deck, driving his car toward a cliff — provide viewers with a visual metaphor for his mental state; as Jim teeters on the edge of physical danger, he also becomes more and more agitated by the constraints of family and society.

For a more detailed discussion of the thesis, see 2a.

1d Sketch a plan.

Once you have generated some ideas and formulated a tentative thesis, you might want to sketch an informal outline to see how you will support your thesis and to figure out a tentative structure for your ideas. Informal outlines can take many forms. Perhaps the most common is simply the thesis followed by a list of major ideas.

Thesis: Television advertising should be regulated to help prevent childhood obesity.

- Children watch more television than ever.
- Snacks marketed to children are often unhealthy and fattening.
- Childhood obesity can cause diabetes and other health problems.
- Solving these health problems costs taxpayers billions of dollars.
- Therefore, these ads are actually costing the public money.
- But if advertising is free speech, do we have the right to regulate it?
- We regulate liquor and cigarette ads on television, so why not advertisements for soda and junk food?

If you began by jotting down a list of ideas (see p. 13), you may be able to turn the list into a rough outline by crossing out some ideas, adding others, and putting the ideas in a logical order.

When to use a formal outline

Early in the writing process, rough outlines have certain advantages over their more formal counterparts: They can be produced more quickly, they are more obviously tentative, and they can be revised more easily should the need arise. However, a formal outline may be useful later in the writing process, after you have written a rough draft, especially if your topic is complex.

A formal outline helps you see whether the parts of your essay work together and whether your essay's structure is logical. A formal outline does not set your paper in stone. In fact, it will often make clear which parts of your draft should be rearranged and which parts don't fit at all.

The following formal outline brought order to the research paper that appears in 56b, on Internet surveillance in the workplace. Notice that the student's thesis is an important part of the outline. Everything else in the outline supports it, either directly or indirectly.

Thesis: Although companies often have legitimate concerns that lead them to monitor employees' Internet usage — from expensive security breaches to reduced productivity — the benefits of electronic surveillance are outweighed by its costs to employees' privacy and autonomy.

I. Although employers have always monitored employees, electronic surveillance is more efficient.
   A. Employers can gather data in large quantities.
   B. Electronic surveillance can be continuous.
   C. Electronic surveillance can be conducted secretly, with keystroke logging programs.

II. Some experts argue that employers have legitimate reasons to monitor employees' Internet usage.
   A. Unmonitored employees could accidentally breach security.
   B. Companies are legally accountable for online actions of employees.

III. Despite valid concerns, employers should value employee morale and autonomy and avoid creating an atmosphere of distrust.
   A. Setting the boundaries for employee autonomy is difficult in the wired workplace.
      1. Using the Internet is the most popular way of wasting time at work.
      2. Employers can't tell easily if employees are working or surfing the Web.
   B. Surveillance can create resentment among employees.
      1. Web surfing can relieve stress, and restricting it can generate tension between managers and workers.
      2. Enforcing Internet usage can seem arbitrary.

IV. Surveillance may not increase employee productivity, and trust may benefit it.
   A. It shouldn't matter to the company how many hours salaried employees work as long as they get the job done.
   B. Casual Internet use can actually benefit companies.
      1. The Internet may spark business ideas.
      2. The Internet may suggest ideas about how to operate more efficiently.

V. Employees' rights to privacy are not well defined by the law.
   A. Few federal guidelines exist on electronic surveillance.
   B. Employers and employees are negotiating the boundaries without legal guidance.
   C. As technological capabilities increase, there will be an increased need to define boundaries.

Guidelines for constructing an outline

1. Put the thesis at the top.
2. Make items at the same level of generality as parallel as possible (see 9).
3. Use sentences unless phrases are clear.
4. Use the conventional system of numbers and letters for the levels of generality.

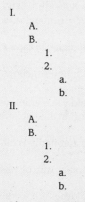

```
I.
    A.
    B.
        1.
        2.
            a.
            b.
II.
    A.
    B.
        1.
        2.
            a.
            b.
```

5. Always use at least two subdivisions for a category, since nothing can be divided into fewer than two parts.
6. Limit the number of major sections in the outline; if the list of roman numerals (at the first level) gets too long, find some way of clustering the items into a few major categories with more subcategories.
7. Be flexible; be prepared to change your outline as your drafts evolve.

2

Rough out an initial draft.

As you rough out an initial draft, focus your attention on ideas and organization. You can deal with sentence structure and word choice later.

Before you begin to write, gather your prewriting materials — lists, diagrams, outlines, freewriting, and so on. In addition to helping you get started, such notes and blueprints will encourage you to keep moving. With your earlier thoughts close by, you won't need to stare at a blank page or screen in search of ideas. Writing tends to flow better when it is drafted relatively quickly, without many stops and starts.

If writer's block becomes a problem for you, consider whether you're being too hard on yourself. Do you demand that your sentences all be stylish and perfectly grammatical right from the start? Do you get stuck trying to perfect your introduction — the hardest part — before you can move forward?

Professional writers look at drafting as a process of discovery, so they expect their first attempts to be messy. Most writers discover ideas as they write. As Joan Didion puts it, "I write entirely to find out what I'm thinking, what I'm looking at, what I see, and what it means."

ON THE WEB > dianahacker.com/rules
Additional resources > Links Library > The writing process

2a For most types of writing, draft an introduction that includes a thesis.

The introduction announces the main point; the body develops it, usually in several paragraphs; the conclusion drives it home. You can begin drafting, however, at any point. If you find it difficult to introduce a paper that you have not yet written, try drafting the body first and saving the introduction for later.

Your introduction will usually be a paragraph of 50 to 150 words (in a longer paper, it may be more than one paragraph). Perhaps the most common strategy is to open with a few sentences that engage the reader and establish your purpose for writing, your main point. The sentence stating the main point is called a *thesis*. (See also 1c.) In the following examples, the thesis has been italicized.

> Credit card companies love to extend credit to college students, especially those just out of high school. Ads for credit cards line campus bulletin boards, flash across commercial Web sites for students, and get stuffed into shopping bags at college bookstores. Why do the companies market their product so vigorously to a population that lacks a substantial credit history and often has no steady sources of income? The answer is that significant

profits can be earned through high interest rates and assorted penalties and fees. *By granting college students liberal lending arrangements, credit card companies often hook them on a cycle of spending that can ultimately lead to financial ruin.*

— Matt Watson, student

As the United States industrialized in the nineteenth century, using desperate immigrant labor, social concerns took a backseat to the task of building a prosperous nation. The government did not regulate industries and did not provide an effective safety net for the poor or for those who became sick or injured on the job. Luckily, immigrants and the poor did have a few advocates. Settlement houses such as Hull-House in Chicago provided information, services, and a place for reform-minded individuals to gather and work to improve the conditions of the urban poor. Alice Hamilton was one of these reformers. Her work at Hull-House spanned twenty-two years and later expanded throughout the nation. *Hamilton's efforts helped to improve the lives of immigrants and drew attention and respect to the problems and people that until then had been virtually ignored.*

— Laurie McDonough, student

Ideally, the sentences leading to the thesis should hook the reader, perhaps with one of the following:

a startling statistic or an unusual fact

a vivid example

a description

a paradoxical statement

a quotation or a bit of dialogue

a question

an analogy

an anecdote

Whether you are writing for a scholarly audience, a professional audience, or a general audience, you cannot assume your readers' interest in the topic. The hook should spark curiosity and offer readers a reason to continue reading.

Although the thesis frequently appears at the end of the introduction, it can just as easily appear at the beginning. Much work-related writing, in which a straightforward approach is most effective, commonly begins with the thesis.

Flextime scheduling, which has proved its effectiveness at the Library of Congress, should be introduced on a trial basis at the

main branch of the Montgomery County Public Library. By offering flexible work hours, the library can boost employee morale, cut down on absenteeism, and expand its hours of operation.

— David Warren, student

For some types of writing, it may be difficult or impossible to express the central idea in a thesis sentence; or it may be unwise or unnecessary to put a thesis sentence in the essay itself. A personal narrative, for example, may have a focus too subtle to be distilled in a single sentence, and such a sentence might ruin the story. Strictly informative writing, like that found in many business memos, may be difficult to summarize in a thesis. In such instances, do not try to force the central idea into a thesis sentence. Instead, think in terms of an overriding purpose, which may or may not be stated directly.

ACADEMIC ENGLISH If you come from a culture that prefers an indirect approach in writing, you may feel that asserting a thesis early in an essay sounds unrefined and even rude. In the United States, however, readers appreciate a direct approach; when you state your point as directly as possible, you show that you value your readers' time.

Characteristics of an effective thesis

An effective thesis sentence is a central idea that requires supporting evidence; it is of adequate scope for an essay of the assigned length; and it is sharply focused. (See also 1c.)

When constructing a thesis sentence, you should ask yourself whether you can successfully develop it with the sources available to you and for the purpose you've identified. Also ask yourself if you can explain why readers should be interested in reading an essay that explores this thesis. If your thesis addresses a question or problem that intrigues you, then it will probably interest your readers as well. If your thesis would be obvious to everyone, then your readers will be less compelled to read on.

A thesis must require proof or further development through facts and details; it cannot itself be a fact or a description.

TOO FACTUAL   The first polygraph was developed by Dr. John A. Larson in 1921.

REVISED Because the polygraph has not been proved reliable, even under the most controlled conditions, its use by private employers should be banned.

A thesis should be of sufficient scope for your assignment, not too broad and not too narrow. Unless you are writing a book or a very long research paper, the following thesis is too broad.

TOO BROAD Mapping the human genome has many implications for health and science.

REVISED Although scientists can now detect genetic predisposition to specific diseases, not everyone should be tested for these diseases.

A thesis should be sharply focused, not too vague. Avoid fuzzy, hard-to-define words such as *interesting, good,* or *disgusting.*

TOO VAGUE The way the TV show *ER* portrays doctors and nurses is interesting.

The word *interesting* is needlessly vague. To sharpen the focus of this thesis, the writer should be more specific.

REVISED In dramatizing the experiences of doctors and nurses as they treat patients, navigate medical bureaucracy, and negotiate bioethical dilemmas, the TV show *ER* portrays health care professionals as unfailingly caring and noble.

In the process of making a too-vague thesis more precise, you may find yourself outlining the major sections of your paper, as in the preceding example. This technique, known as *blueprinting,* helps readers know exactly what to expect as they read on. It also helps you, the writer, control the shape of your essay.

EXERCISE 2-1 In each of the following pairs, which sentence might work well as a thesis for a short paper? What is the problem with the other one? Is it too factual? Too broad? Too vague?

1a. By networking with friends, a single parent can manage to strike a balance among work, school, a social life, and family.

  b. Single parents face many challenges as they try to juggle all of their responsibilities.

2a. At the Special Olympics, disabled athletes are taught that with hard work and support from others they can accomplish anything: that they can indeed be winners.

 b. Working with the Special Olympics program is rewarding.

3a. History 201, taught by Professor Brown, is offered at 10:00 a.m. on Tuesdays and Thursdays.

 b. Whoever said that history is nothing but polishing tombstones must have missed History 201, because in Professor Brown's class history is very much alive.

4a. So far, research suggests that zero-emissions vehicles are not a sensible solution to the problem of steadily increasing air pollution.

 b. Because air pollution is of serious concern to many people today, several US government agencies have implemented plans to begin solving the problem.

5a. Anorexia nervosa is a dangerous and sometimes deadly eating disorder occurring mainly in young, upper-middle-class teenagers.

 b. The eating disorder anorexia nervosa is rarely cured by one treatment alone; only by combining drug therapy with psychotherapy and family therapy can the patient begin the long, torturous journey to wellness.

ON THE WEB > **dianahacker.com/rules**
Writing exercises > E-ex 2–1 and 2–2

2b   Draft the body.

The body of the essay develops support for your thesis, so it's important to have at least a tentative thesis before you start writing. What does your thesis promise readers? Try to keep your response to that question in mind as you draft the body.

You may already have written an introduction that includes your thesis. If not, as long as you have a thesis you can begin developing the body and return later to the introduction. If your thesis suggests a plan (see 2a) or if you have sketched a preliminary outline, try to block out your paragraphs accordingly. Draft the body of your essay by writing a paragraph about each supporting point you listed in the planning stage. If you do not have a plan, you would be wise to pause for a moment and sketch one (see 1d).

Keep in mind that often you might not know what you want to say until you have written a draft. It is possible to begin without a plan — assuming you are prepared to treat your first attempt as a "discovery draft" that will most likely be tossed (or radically rewritten) once you discover what you really want to say. Whether or not you have a plan when you begin drafting, you can often figure out a workable order for your ideas by stopping each time you start a new paragraph to think about what your readers will need to know to follow your train of thought.

For more detailed advice about paragraphs in the body of an essay, see 4.

2c Attempt a conclusion.

A conclusion should remind readers of the essay's main idea without dully repeating it. Often the concluding paragraph can be relatively short. By the end of the essay, readers should already understand your main point; your conclusion simply drives it home and, perhaps, leaves readers with something larger to consider.

In addition to echoing your main idea, a conclusion might briefly summarize the essay's key points, propose a course of action, discuss the topic's wider significance, offer advice, or pose a question for future study. To conclude an essay analyzing the shifting roles of women in the military, one student discusses her topic's implications for society as a whole:

> As the military continues to train women in jobs formerly reserved for men, our understanding of women's roles in society will no doubt continue to change. When news reports of women training for and taking part in combat operations become commonplace, reports of women becoming CEOs, police chiefs, and even president of the United States will cease to surprise us. Or perhaps we have already reached this point.
> — Rosa Broderick, student

To make the conclusion memorable, you might include a detail, an example, or an image from the introduction to bring readers full circle; a quotation or a bit of dialogue; an anecdote; or a witty or ironic comment. To end a narrative describing a cash register holdup, one student uses an anecdote that includes some dialogue:

It took me a long time to get over that incident. Countless times I found myself gasping as someone "pointed" a dollar bill at me. On one such occasion, a jovial little man buying a toy gun for his son came up to me and said in a Humphrey Bogart impression, "Give me all your money, Sweetheart." I didn't laugh. Instead, my heart skipped a beat, for I had heard those words before.

— Diana Crawford, student

Whatever concluding strategy you choose, keep in mind that an effective conclusion is decisive and unapologetic. Avoid introducing wholly new ideas at the end of an essay. Finally, because the conclusion is so closely tied to the rest of the essay in both content and tone, be prepared to rework it (or even replace it) when you revise.

3

Make global revisions; then revise sentences.

For most experienced writers, revising is rarely a one-step process. Global matters — focus, purpose, organization, content, and overall strategy — generally receive attention first. Improvements in sentence structure, word choice, grammar, punctuation, and mechanics come later.

3a Make global revisions: Think big.

By the time you've written a draft, your ideas will probably have gone in directions you couldn't have predicted ahead of time. As a result, global revisions can be quite dramatic. It's possible, for example, that your thesis will evolve as you figure out how your ideas fit together. You might drop whole paragraphs of text and add others or condense material once stretched over several paragraphs. You might rearrange entire sections. You will save time if you handle global revisions before turning to sentence-level issues: There is little sense in revising sentences that may not appear in your final draft.

Many of us resist global revisions because we find it difficult to view our work from our audience's perspective. To distance yourself from a draft, put it aside for a while, preferably overnight or even longer. When you return to it, try to play the role of your audience as you read. Ask questions such as "What is the main point of this paragraph?" "Why have I put these paragraphs in this order?" "How will readers respond to this point?" If possible, enlist the help of reviewers to play the role of audience for you, or perhaps visit your school's writing center to go over your draft with a writing tutor. Ask your reviewers to focus on the larger issues of writing, not on the fine points. The following checklist may help you and your reviewers focus on global concerns.

Checklist for global revision

Purpose and audience

- Does the draft accomplish its purpose—to inform readers, persuade them, entertain them, call them to action?
- Is the draft appropriate for its audience? Does it account for the audience's knowledge of the subject, level of interest in the subject, and possible attitudes toward the subject?

Focus

- Is the thesis clear? Is it prominently placed?
- If there is no thesis, is there a good reason for omitting one?
- Are any ideas obviously off the point?

Organization and paragraphing

- Are there enough organizational cues for readers (such as topic sentences and headings)?
- Are ideas presented in a logical order?
- Are any paragraphs too long or too short for easy reading?

Content

- Is the supporting material relevant and persuasive?
- Which ideas need further development?
- Are the parts proportioned sensibly? Do major ideas receive enough attention?
- Where might material be deleted?

Point of view

- Is the draft free of distracting shifts in point of view (from *I* to *you*, for example, or from *it* to *they*)?
- Is the dominant point of view—*I, we, you, he, she, it, one,* or *they*— appropriate for your purpose and audience?

ON THE WEB > dianahacker.com/rules
Resources for writers and tutors > Preparing to visit the writing center

ON THE WEB > dianahacker.com/rules
Writing exercises > E-ex 3–1 and 3–2

3b Revise and edit sentences; proofread the final draft.

When you revise sentences, you focus on effectiveness; when you edit, you check for correctness. Proofreading is a slow and careful reading in search of typos and other obvious mistakes.

Revising and editing sentences

Much of the rest of this book offers advice on revising sentences for clarity and on editing them for grammar, punctuation, and mechanics.

Some writers handle sentence-level revisions directly at the computer, experimenting on-screen with a variety of possible improvements. Other writers prefer to print out a hard copy of the draft, mark it up, and then return to the computer to enter their revisions. Here, for example, is a rough-draft paragraph as one student edited it for a variety of sentence-level problems:

Although some cities have found creative ways to improve access to public transportation for physically handicapped passengers, ~~and to fund other programs, there have been problems in~~ our city has struggled with ~~due to the need to address~~ budget constraints and competing ~~needs~~ priorities. ~~This~~ The budget crunch has led citizens to question how funds are distributed.~~?~~ For example, last year ~~when~~ city officials voted to use available funds to support ~~had to choose between allocating funds for accessible transportation or allocating funds to~~ after-school programs rather than transportation upgrades. ~~, they voted for the after-school programs.~~ It is not clear to some citizens why ~~these~~ after-school programs are more important.

The original paragraph was flawed by wordiness, a problem that can be addressed through any number of revisions. The following revision would also be acceptable.

> Some cities have funded improved access to public transportation for physically handicapped passengers. Because of budget constraints, our city chose to fund after-school programs rather than transportation programs. As a result, citizens have begun to question how funds are distributed and why certain programs are more important than others.

Some of the paragraph's improvements do not involve choice and must be fixed in any revision. The hyphen in *after-school programs* is necessary; a noun must be substituted for the pronoun *these* in the last sentence; and the question mark in the second sentence must be changed to a period.

GRAMMAR CHECKERS can help with some but by no means all of the sentence-level problems in a typical draft. Many problems — such as faulty parallelism and misplaced modifiers — require an understanding of grammatical structure that computer programs lack. Such problems often slip right past the grammar checker. Even when the grammar checker makes a suggestion for revision, it is your responsibility as the writer to decide whether the suggestion is more effective than your original.

Proofreading

After revising and editing, you are ready to prepare the final manuscript. (See 6a for guidelines.) Make sure to allow yourself enough time for proofreading — the final and most important step in manuscript preparation.

Proofreading is a special kind of reading: a slow and methodical search for misspellings, typographical mistakes, and omitted words or word endings. Such errors can be difficult to spot in your own work because you may read what you intended to write, not what is actually on the page. To fight this tendency, try proofreading out loud, articulating each word as it is actually written. You might also try proofreading your sentences in reverse order, a strategy that takes your attention away from the meanings you intended and forces you to think about surface features instead.

Although proofreading may be dull, it is crucial. Errors strewn throughout an essay are distracting and annoying. If the writer doesn't care about this piece of writing, thinks the reader, why should I? A carefully proofread essay, however, sends a positive message: It shows that you value your writing and respect your readers.

> **SPELL CHECKERS** are much more reliable than grammar checkers, but they too must be used with caution. Many typographical errors (such as *quiet* for *quite*) and misused words (such as *effect* for *affect*) slip past the spell checker because it flags only words not found in its dictionary.

Student Essay

Matt Watson, who wrote "Hooked on Credit Cards" (pp. 35–39), was responding to the following assignment.

> In an essay of 500–1,000 words, discuss a significant problem facing today's college students. Assume that your audience consists of general readers, not simply college students.
>
> If you use any sources, document them with in-text citations and a list of works cited in MLA style (see section 55 in *Rules for Writers*).

When he received the assignment, Watson considered several possibilities before settling on the topic of credit cards. He already knew something about the topic because his older sister had run up large credit card bills while in college and was working hard to pay them off. Because the assignment required him to *discuss* a problem, he decided that a good strategy would be to identify a *how* or *why* question to answer.

To get started on his paper, Watson interviewed his sister over the phone and then typed the following ideas into his computer.

easy to get hooked on credit cards and run up huge debts

Why do credit card companies try to sign up students? Aren't we a

bad risk? But they must be profiting, or they'd stop. High interest rates.

advertisements for credit cards appear all over campus and on the Web

using plastic doesn't seem like spending money

tactics used by the companies--offering low interest rates at first,
setting high credit limits, allowing a revolving balance

What happens to students who get in debt but don't have parents
who can bail them out?

After he listed these ideas, Watson realized that what puz-
zled him most was why credit card companies would put so
many resources into soliciting students in spite of their poor
credit profiles. He decided that his purpose would be to answer
this question for himself and his audience. He wrote his first
draft quickly, focusing more on ideas than on grammar, style,
and mechanics. Then he made some additions and deletions
and fixed a few typos before submitting the draft for peer review in a networked classroom. Here is the draft he submitted,
together with the most helpful comments he received from
classmates. The peer reviewers were asked to comment on
global issues — audience appeal, focus, organization, content,
and point of view — and to ignore any problems with grammar
and punctuation.

ROUGH DRAFT

Good question. Seems like there might be more to the answer than you've written here. That is, why are these companies trying to hook us? (Mark)

Some students do have jobs. (Sara)

The assignment asks for a general audience; your thesis shouldn't be about "us." (Sara)

Shouldn't your thesis also explain *how* the companies hook students? (Tim)

Hooked on Credit Cards

Credit card companies love to extend credit
to college students. You see ads for these cards
on campus bulletin boards and also on the Web.
Why do companies market their product to a population that has no job and lacks a substantial
credit history? They seem to be trying to hook us
on their cards; unfortunately many of us do get
hooked on a cycle of spending that leads to
financial ruin.

Good point. I never thought of it that way. (Sara)

Maybe you could also mention the solicitors who show up during orientation. (Mark)

This sentence sounds less formal than the rest of your essay. (Tim)

I like this example. (Mark)

Why not give us some numbers here? Just how low and how high? (Sara)

The shift to "you" seems odd. (Sara)

Maybe you could search LexisNexis for some statistical information. (Mark)

This paragraph seems sort of skimpy. (Tim)

This would be more convincing if you provided some evidence to back up your claim. (Mark)

Banks require applicants for a loan to demonstrate a good credit history and some evidence of a source of income, but credit card companies don't. On campus, students are bombarded with offers of preapproved credit cards. Then there are the Web sites. Sites with lots of student traffic are plastered with banner ads like this one: "To get a credit card, you need to establish credit. To establish credit, you need a credit card. Stop the vicious cycle! Apply for our student MasterCard."

Credit card companies often entice students with low interest rates, then they jack up the rates later. A student may not think about the cost of interest. That new stereo or back-to-school wardrobe can get pretty expensive at 17.9% interest if it's compounded over several months. Would you have bought that $600 item if you knew it would end up costing you $900?

Most cards allow the holder to keep a revolving balance, which means that they don't have to pay the whole bill, they just pay a minimum amount. The minimum is usually not too much, but a young person may be tempted to keep running up debt. The companies also give students an unrealistically high credit limit. I've heard of undergraduates who had a limit as high as $4,000.

Card companies make money not just from high interest rates. Often they charge fees for late payments. I've heard of penalties for going over the credit limit too.

Professor Mills won't like your shifts to "you" and "I" here. (Sara)

Often students discover too late that they are thoroughly trapped. Some drop out of school, others graduate and then can't find a good job because they have a poor credit rating. There are psychological problems too. Your parents may bail you out of debt, but you'll probably feel guilty. On a Web site, I read that two students felt so bad they committed suicide.

Also, he wants us to cite our sources. (Sara)

Your paper focuses on the tactics that the companies use, but your conclusion doesn't mention them. (Tim)

Credit cards are a part of life these days, and everyone is probably wise to have a charge account for emergencies. But every college student must take a hard look at their financial picture. The very things that make those cards so convenient and easy to use can lead to a mountain of debt that will take years to pay off.

After rereading his draft and considering the feedback from his classmates, Watson realized that he needed to develop his thesis further. He thought that the question about what credit card companies gain by hooking students was a good one, and he decided that his paper would be stronger if he could answer it. He decided to work on expanding his explanation of both why and how credit card companies market cards to students.

Watson also decided that he needed more evidence to back up his claims about how credit card companies hook students. He located several Web sites with relevant information and rejected those that were obviously promotional. He relied on sites sponsored by two reputable organizations, the student loan provider Nellie Mae and the Consumer Federation of America.

In his next draft, Watson reworked his introduction to explain why credit card companies profit from students who have no steady source of income. Then he strengthened his content by supplying more facts. While adding facts, he discovered ways to improve the organization. He also adjusted his point of view so that his essay would be appropriate for a general audience, not just for other students. When he was more or less satisfied with the paper as a whole, he worked to polish his sentences. Watson's final draft begins on the next page.

Watson 1

Matt Watson

Professor Mills

English 101

12 March 2001

Hooked on Credit Cards

Credit card companies love to extend credit to college students, especially those just out of high school. Ads for credit cards line campus bulletin boards, flash across commercial Web sites for students, and get stuffed into shopping bags at college bookstores. Why do the companies market their product so vigorously to a population that lacks a substantial credit history and often has no steady source of income? The answer is that significant profits can be earned through high interest rates and assorted penalties and fees. By granting college students liberal lending arrangements, credit card companies often hook them on a cycle of spending that can ultimately lead to financial ruin.

Whereas banks require applicants for a loan to demonstrate a good credit history and some evidence of an income flow, credit card companies make no such demands on students. On campus, students find themselves bombarded with offers of preapproved cards--and not just on flyers pinned to bulletin boards. Many campuses allow credit card vendors to

Introduction orients readers and ends with the thesis.

Introduction poses a question to engage readers and lead them to the thesis.

Thesis announces the writer's main point.

Clear topic sentences guide readers through the body of the paper.

Watson 2

solicit applications during orientation week. In addition
to offering preapproved cards, these vendors often give
away T-shirts or CDs to entice students to apply. Students
are bombarded on the Web as well. Sites with heavy
student traffic are emblazoned with banner ads like this
one: "To get a credit card, you need to establish credit.
To establish credit, you need a credit card. Stop the
vicious cycle! Apply for our student MasterCard."

Body paragraphs are developed with details and examples.

   Credit card companies often entice students with
low "teaser" interest rates of 13% and later raise those
rates to 18% or even higher. Others charge high rates up
front, trusting that students won't read the fine print.
Some young people don't think about the cost of interest, let alone the cost of interest compounding month
after month. That back-to-school wardrobe can get pretty
expensive at 17.9% interest compounded over several
months. A $600 trip to Fort Lauderdale is not such a
bargain when in the long run it costs $900 or more.

Transition serves as a bridge between paragraphs.

Summary of the source is in the student's own words.

   In addition to charging high interest rates, credit
card companies try to maximize the amount of interest
generated. One tactic is to extend an unreasonably
high credit limit to students. According to Nellie Mae
statistics, in 1998 undergraduates were granted an
average credit limit of $3,683; for graduate students,
the figure jumped to $15,721. Nearly 10% of the
students in the Nellie Mae study carried balances
near or exceeding these credit limits (Blair).

Source is docu- mented with an MLA in-text citation.

Watson 3

Another tactic is to allow students to maintain a revolving balance. A revolving balance permits the debtor to pay only part of a current bill, often an amount just a little larger than the accumulated interest. The indebted student is tempted to keep on charging, paying a minimum amount every month, because there aren't any immediate consequences to doing so.

Once a student is hooked on a cycle of debt, the companies profit even further by assessing a variety of fees and penalties. According to a press release issued by Consumer Action and the Consumer Federation of America, many credit card companies charge late fees and "over the limit" penalties as high as $29 per month. In addition, grace periods are often shortened to ensure that late fees kick in earlier. Many companies also raise interest rates for those who fail to pay on time or who exceed the credit limit. Those "penalty" rates can climb as high as 25% (1-2).

Writer cites a Web article from a reputable source.

Often students discover too late that they are thoroughly hooked. The results can be catastrophic. Some students are forced to drop out of school and take low-paying full-time jobs. Others, once they graduate, have difficulty landing good jobs because of their poor credit rating. Many students suffer psychologically as well. Even those who have parents willing to bail them out of debt often experience a great deal

Watson 4

of anxiety and guilt. Two students recently grew so stressed by their accumulating debt that they committed suicide (Consumer Federation of Amer. 3).

Conclusion echoes the writer's main idea.

Credit cards are a part of life these days, and there is nothing wrong with having one or two of them. Before signing up for a particular card, however, college students should take the time to read the fine print and do some comparison shopping. Students also need to learn to resist the many seductive offers that credit card companies extend to them once they have signed up. Students who can't "just say no" to temptations such as high credit limits and revolving balances could well become hooked on a cycle of debt from which there is no easy escape.

Watson 5

Works Cited

Blair, Alan D. "A High Wire Act: Balancing Student Loan

and Credit Card Debt." *Credit World* 86.2 (1997):

15-17. *Business Source Premier*. Web. 4 Mar. 2001.

Consumer Action and Consumer Federation of America.

"Card Issuers Hike Fees and Rates to Bolster

Profits." *Consumer Federation of America*.

Consumer Federation of Amer., 5 Nov. 1998.

Web. 4 Mar. 2001.

Consumer Federation of America. "Credit Card Debt

Imposes Huge Costs on Many College

Students." *Consumer Federation of America*.

Consumer Federation of Amer., 8 June 1999.

Web. 4 Mar. 2001.

Works cited page
follows MLA format.

4

Build effective paragraphs.

Except for special-purpose paragraphs, such as introductions and conclusions (see 2a and 2c), paragraphs are clusters of information supporting an essay's main point (or advancing a story's action). Aim for paragraphs that are clearly focused, well developed, organized, coherent, and neither too long nor too short for easy reading.

4a Focus on a main point.

A paragraph should be unified around a main point. The point should be clear to readers, and all sentences in the paragraph should relate to it.

Stating the main point in a topic sentence

As readers move into a paragraph, they need to know where they are — in relation to the whole essay — and what to expect in the sentences to come. A good topic sentence, a one-sentence summary of the paragraph's main point, acts as a signpost pointing in two directions: backward toward the thesis of the essay and forward toward the body of the paragraph.

Like a thesis sentence (see 1c and 2a), a topic sentence is more general than the material supporting it. Usually the topic sentence (italicized in the following example) comes first in the paragraph.

> *All living creatures manage some form of communication.* The dance patterns of bees in their hive help to point the way to distant flower fields or announce successful foraging. Male stickleback fish regularly swim upside-down to indicate outrage in a courtship contest. Male deer and lemurs mark territorial ownership by rubbing their own body secretions on boundary stones or trees. Everyone has seen a frightened dog put his tail between his legs and run in panic. We, too, use gestures, expressions, postures, and movement to give our words point. [Italics added.]
> — Olivia Vlahos, *Human Beginnings*

Sometimes the topic sentence is introduced by a transitional sentence linking it to earlier material. In the following paragraph, the topic sentence has been delayed to allow for a transition.

> But flowers are not the only source of spectacle in the wilderness. *An opportunity for late color is provided by the berries of wildflowers, shrubs, and trees.* Baneberry presents its tiny white flowers in spring but in late summer bursts forth with clusters of red berries. Bunchberry, a ground-cover plant, puts out red berries in the fall, and the red berries of wintergreen last from autumn well into the winter. In California, the bright red, fist-sized clusters of Christmas berries can be seen growing beside highways for up to six months of the year. [Italics added.]
> —James Crockett et al., *Wildflower Gardening*

Occasionally the topic sentence may be withheld until the end of the paragraph — but only if the earlier sentences hang together so well that readers perceive their direction, if not their exact point. The opening sentences of the following paragraph state facts, so they are supporting material rather than topic sentences, but they strongly suggest a central idea. The topic sentence at the end is hardly a surprise.

> Tobacco chewing starts as soon as people begin stirring. Those who have fresh supplies soak the new leaves in water and add ashes from the hearth to the wad. Men, women, and children chew tobacco and all are addicted to it. Once there was a shortage of tobacco in Ḳaobawä's village and I was plagued for a week by early morning visitors who requested permission to collect my cigarette butts in order to make a wad of chewing tobacco. Normally, if anyone is short of tobacco, he can request a share of someone else's already chewed wad, or simply borrow the entire wad when its owner puts it down somewhere. *Tobacco is so important to them that their word for "poverty" translates as "being without tobacco."* [Italics added.]
> —Napoleon A. Chagnon, *Yanomamö: The Fierce People*

You will find that some professional writers, especially journalists and informal essayists, do not always use clear topic sentences. In college writing, however, topic sentences are often necessary for clarifying the lines of an argument or reporting the research in a field. In business writing, topic sentences (along with headings) are essential, since readers often scan for information.

Sticking to the point

Sentences that do not support the topic sentence destroy the unity of a paragraph. If the paragraph is otherwise well focused, such offending sentences can simply be deleted or perhaps moved elsewhere. In the following paragraph describing the inadequate facilities in a high school, the information about the chemistry instructor (in italics) is clearly off the point.

> As the result of tax cuts, the educational facilities of Lincoln High School have reached an all-time low. Some of the books date back to 1990 and have long since shed their covers. The few computers in working order must share one printer. The lack of lab equipment makes it necessary for four or five students to work at one table, with most watching rather than performing experiments. *Also, the chemistry instructor left to have a baby at the beginning of the semester, and most of the students don't like the substitute.* As for the furniture, many of the upright chairs have become recliners, and the desk legs are so unbalanced that they play seesaw on the floor. [Italics added.]

Sometimes the solution for a disunified paragraph is not as simple as deleting or moving material. Writers often wander into uncharted territory because they cannot think of enough evidence to support a topic sentence. Feeling that it is too soon to break into a new paragraph, they move on to new ideas for which they have not prepared the reader. When this happens, the writer is faced with a choice: Either find more evidence to support the topic sentence or adjust the topic sentence to mesh with the evidence that is available.

EXERCISE 4–1 Underline the topic sentence in the following paragraph and cross out any material that does not clarify or develop the central idea.

> Quilt making has served as an important means of social, political, and artistic expression for women. In the nineteenth century, quilting circles provided one of the few opportunities for women to forge social bonds outside of their families. Once a week or more, they came together to sew as well as trade small talk, advice, and news. They used dyed cotton fabrics much like the fabrics quilters use today; surprisingly, quilters' basic materials haven't changed that much over the years. Sometimes the women joined their efforts in the support of a political cause, making quilts that would be raffled to raise money for temper-

¶

ance societies, hospitals for sick and wounded soldiers, and the fight against slavery. Quilt making also afforded women a means of artistic expression at a time when they had few other creative outlets. Within their socially acceptable roles as homemakers, many quilters subtly pushed back at the restrictions placed on them by experimenting with color, design, and technique.

ON THE WEB > dianahacker.com/rules
Writing exercises > E-ex 4–1

4b Develop the main point.

Though an occasional short paragraph is fine, particularly if it functions as a transition or emphasizes a point, a series of brief paragraphs suggests inadequate development. How much development is enough? That varies, depending on the writer's purpose and audience.

For example, when she wrote a paragraph attempting to convince readers that it is impossible to lose fat quickly, health columnist Jane Brody knew that she would have to present a great deal of evidence because many dieters want to believe the opposite. She did *not* write:

> When you think about it, it's impossible to lose — as many diets suggest — 10 pounds of *fat* in ten days, even on a total fast. Even a moderately active person cannot lose so much weight so fast. A less active person hasn't a prayer.

This three-sentence paragraph is too skimpy to be convincing. But the paragraph that Brody wrote contains enough evidence to convince even skeptical readers.

> When you think about it, it's impossible to lose — as many . . . diets suggest — 10 pounds of *fat* in ten days, even on a total fast. A pound of body fat represents 3,500 calories. To lose 1 pound of fat, you must expend 3,500 more calories than you consume. Let's say you weigh 170 pounds and, as a moderately active person, you burn 2,500 calories a day. If your diet contains only 1,500 calories, you'd have an energy deficit of 1,000 calories a day. In a week's time that would add up to a 7,000-calorie deficit, or 2 pounds of real fat. In ten days, the accumulated deficit would represent nearly 3 pounds of lost body fat. Even if you ate nothing at all for ten days and maintained your usual level of activity, your caloric deficit would add up to 25,000 calories. . . . At 3,500 calories per pound of fat, that's still only 7 pounds of lost fat.
> — Jane Brody, *Jane Brody's Nutrition Book*

4c Choose a suitable pattern of organization.

Although paragraphs (and indeed whole essays) may be patterned in any number of ways, certain patterns of organization occur frequently, either alone or in combination: examples and illustrations, narration, description, process, comparison and contrast, analogy, cause and effect, classification and division, and definition. There is nothing particularly magical about these patterns (sometimes called *methods of development*). They simply reflect some of the ways in which we think.

Examples and illustrations

Examples, perhaps the most common pattern of development, are appropriate whenever the reader might be tempted to ask, "For example?" Though examples are just selected instances, not a complete catalog, they are enough to suggest the truth of many topic sentences, as in the following paragraph.

> Normally my parents abided scrupulously by "The Budget," but several times a year Dad would dip into his battered black strongbox and splurge on some irrational, totally satisfying luxury. Once he bought over a hundred comic books at a flea market, doled out to us thereafter at the tantalizing rate of two a week. He always got a whole flat of pansies, Mom's favorite flower, for us to give her on Mother's Day. One day a boy stopped at our house selling fifty-cent raffle tickets on a sailboat and Dad bought every ticket the boy had left — three books' worth.
> — Connie Hailey, student

Illustrations are extended examples, frequently presented in story form. Because they require several sentences apiece, they are used more sparingly than examples. When well selected, however, they can be a vivid and effective means of developing a point. The writer of the following paragraph uses illustrations to demonstrate that Harriet Tubman, famous conductor on the underground railroad for escaping slaves, was a genius at knowing how and when to retreat.

> Part of [Harriet Tubman's] strategy of conducting was, as in all battle-field operations, the knowledge of how and when to retreat. Numerous allusions have been made to her moves when she suspected that she was in danger. When she feared the party was closely pursued, she would take it for a time on a train

southward bound. No one seeing Negroes going in this direction would for an instant suppose them to be fugitives. Once on her return she was at a railroad station. She saw some men reading a poster and she heard one of them reading it aloud. It was a description of her, offering a reward for her capture. She took a southbound train to avert suspicion. At another time when Harriet heard men talking about her, she pretended to read a book which she carried. One man remarked, "This can't be the woman. The one we want can't read or write." Harriet devoutly hoped the book was right side up.

— Earl Conrad, *Harriet Tubman*

Narration

A paragraph of narration tells a story or part of a story. Narrative paragraphs are usually arranged in chronological order, but they may also contain flashbacks, interruptions that take the story back to an earlier time. The following paragraph, from Jane Goodall's *In the Shadow of Man*, recounts one of the author's experiences in the African wild.

One evening when I was wading in the shallows of the lake to pass a rocky outcrop, I suddenly stopped dead as I saw the sinuous black body of a snake in the water. It was all of six feet long, and from the slight hood and the dark stripes at the back of the neck I knew it to be a Storm's water cobra — a deadly reptile for the bite of which there was, at that time, no serum. As I stared at it an incoming wave gently deposited part of its body on one of my feet. I remained motionless, not even breathing, until the wave rolled back into the lake, drawing the snake with it. Then I leaped out of the water as fast as I could, my heart hammering.

— Jane Goodall, *In the Shadow of Man*

Description

A descriptive paragraph sketches a portrait of a person, place, or thing by using concrete and specific details that appeal to one or more of our senses — sight, sound, smell, taste, and touch. Consider, for example, the following description of the grasshopper invasions that devastated the midwestern landscape in the late 1860s.

They came like dive bombers out of the west. They came by the millions with the rustle of their wings roaring overhead. They came in waves, like the rolls of the sea, descending with a terrifying speed, breaking now and again like a mighty surf. They came with the force of a williwaw and they formed a huge, ominous, dark brown cloud that eclipsed the sun. They dipped and touched earth, hitting objects and people like hailstones. But they were not hail. These were *live* demons. They popped, snapped, crackled, and roared. They were dark brown, an inch or longer in length, plump in the middle and tapered at the ends. They had transparent wings, slender legs, and two black eyes that flashed with a fierce intelligence.

— Eugene Boe, "Pioneers to Eternity"

Process

A process paragraph is structured in chronological order. A writer may choose this pattern either to describe how something is made or done or to explain to readers, step by step, how to do something. The following paragraph describes what happens when water freezes.

In school we learned that with few exceptions the solid phase of matter is more dense than the liquid phase. Water, alone among common substances, violates this rule. As water begins to cool, it contracts and becomes more dense, in a perfectly typical way. But about four degrees above the freezing point, something remarkable happens. It ceases to contract and begins expanding, becoming less dense. At the freezing point the expansion is abrupt and drastic. As water turns to ice, it adds about one-eleventh to its liquid volume.

— Chet Raymo, "Curious Stuff, Water and Ice"

Here is a paragraph explaining how to perform a "roll cast," a popular fly-fishing technique.

Begin by taking up a suitable stance, with one foot slightly in front of the other and the rod pointing down the line. Then begin a smooth, steady draw, raising your rod hand to just above shoulder height and lifting the rod to the 10:30 or 11:00 position. This steady draw allows a loop of line to form between the rod top and the water. While the line is still moving, raise the rod slightly, then punch it rapidly forward and down. The rod is now flexed and under maximum compression, and the line follows its path, bellying out slightly behind you and coming off the water close to your feet. As you power the rod down through the 3:00 position, the belly of line will roll forward. Follow through smoothly so that the line unfolds and straightens above the water.

— *The Dorling Kindersley Encyclopedia of Fishing*

Comparison and contrast

To compare two subjects is to draw attention to their similarities, although the word *compare* also has a broader meaning that includes a consideration of differences. To contrast is to focus only on differences.

Whether a paragraph stresses similarities or differences, it may be patterned in one of two ways. The two subjects may be presented one at a time, as in the following paragraph of contrast.

> So Grant and Lee were in complete contrast, representing two diametrically opposed elements in American life. Grant was the modern man emerging; beyond him, ready to come on the stage, was the great age of steel and machinery, of crowded cities and a restless, burgeoning vitality. Lee might have ridden down from the old age of chivalry, lance in hand, silken banner fluttering over his head. Each man was the perfect champion of his cause, drawing both his strengths and his weaknesses from the people he led.
>
> — Bruce Catton, "Grant and Lee: A Study in Contrasts"

Or a paragraph may proceed point by point, treating the two subjects together, one aspect at a time. The following paragraph uses the point-by-point method to contrast the writer's academic experiences in an American high school with those in an Irish convent.

> Strangely enough, instead of being academically inferior to my American high school, the Irish convent was superior. In my class at home, *Love Story* was considered pretty heavy reading, so imagine my surprise at finding Irish students who could recite passages from *War and Peace*. In high school we complained about having to study *Romeo and Juliet* in one semester, whereas in Ireland we simultaneously studied *Macbeth* and Dickens's *Hard Times*, in addition to writing a composition a day in English class. In high school, I didn't even begin algebra until the ninth grade, while at the convent seventh graders (or their Irish equivalent) were doing calculus and trigonometry.
>
> — Margaret Stack, student

Analogy

Analogies draw comparisons between items that appear to have little in common. Writers turn to analogies for a variety of reasons: to make the unfamiliar seem familiar, to provide a concrete understanding of an abstract topic, to argue a point, or to provoke fresh thoughts or changed feelings about a subject. In the following paragraph, physician Lewis Thomas draws an analogy between the behavior of ants and that of humans.

> Ants are so much like human beings as to be an embarrassment. They farm fungi, raise aphids as livestock, launch armies into wars, use chemical sprays to alarm and confuse enemies, capture slaves. The families of weaver ants engage in child labor, holding their larvae like shuttles to spin out the thread that sews the leaves together for their fungus gardens. They exchange information ceaselessly. They do everything but watch television.
> — Lewis Thomas, "On Societies as Organisms"

Although analogies can be a powerful tool for illuminating a subject, they should be used with caution in arguments. Just because two things may be alike in one respect, we cannot conclude that they are alike in all respects. (See "false analogy," p. 374.)

Cause and effect

When causes and effects are a matter of argument, they are too complex to be reduced to a simple pattern (see p. 374). However, if a writer wishes merely to describe a cause-and-effect relationship that is generally accepted, then the effect may be stated in the topic sentence, with the causes listed in the body of the paragraph.

> The fantastic water clarity of the Mount Gambier sinkholes results from several factors. The holes are fed from aquifers holding rainwater that fell decades — even centuries — ago, and that has been filtered through miles of limestone. The high level of calcium that limestone adds causes the silty detritus from dead plants and animals to cling together and settle quickly to the bottom. Abundant bottom vegetation in the shallow sinkholes also helps bind the silt. And the rapid turnover of water prohibits stagnation.
> — Hillary Hauser, "Exploring a Sunken Realm in Australia"

Or the paragraph may move from cause to effects, as in this paragraph from a student paper on the effects of the industrial revolution on American farms.

> The rise of rail transport in the nineteenth century forever changed American farming — for better and for worse. Farmers who once raised crops and livestock to sustain just their own

families could now make a profit by selling their goods in towns and cities miles away. These new markets improved the living standard of struggling farm families and encouraged them to seek out innovations that would increase their profits. On the downside, the competition fostered by the new markets sometimes created hostility among neighboring farm families where there had once been a spirit of cooperation. Those farmers who couldn't compete with their neighbors left farming forever, facing poverty worse than they had ever known.

— Chris Mileski, student

Classification and division

Classification is the grouping of items into categories according to some consistent principle. For example, an elementary school teacher might classify children's books according to their level of difficulty, but a librarian might group them by subject matter. The principle of classification that a writer chooses ultimately depends on the purpose of the classification. The following paragraph classifies species of electric fish.

Scientists sort electric fishes into three categories. The first comprises the strongly electric species like the marine electric rays or the freshwater African electric catfish and South American electric eel. Known since the dawn of history, these deliver a punch strong enough to stun a human. In recent years, biologists have focused on a second category: weakly electric fish in the South American and African rivers that use tiny voltages for communication and navigation. The third group contains sharks, nonelectric rays, and catfish, which do not emit a field but possess sensors that enable them to detect the minute amounts of electricity that leak out of other organisms.

— Anne and Jack Rudloe, "Electric Warfare: The Fish That Kill with Thunderbolts"

Division takes one item and divides it into parts. As with classification, division should be made according to some consistent principle. The following passage describes the components that make up a baseball.

Like the game itself, a baseball is composed of many layers. One of the delicious joys of childhood is to take apart a baseball and examine the wonders within. You begin by removing the red cotton thread and peeling off the leather cover — which comes from the hide of a Holstein cow and has been tanned, cut, printed, and punched with holes. Beneath the cover is a thin layer of cotton string, followed by several hundred yards of woolen yarn, which makes up the bulk of the ball. Finally, in the middle is a rubber ball, or "pill," which is a little smaller than a golf ball. Slice into the rubber and you'll find the ball's heart—a cork core. The cork is from Portugal, the rubber from southeast Asia, the covers are American, and the balls are assembled in Costa Rica.

—Dan Gutman, *The Way Baseball Works*

Definition

A definition puts a word or concept into a general class and then provides enough details to distinguish it from others in the same class. In the following paragraph, the writer defines *envy* as a special kind of desire.

> Envy is so integral and so painful a part of what animates behavior in market societies that many people have forgotten the full meaning of the word, simplifying it into one of the synonyms of desire. It is that, which may be why it flourishes in market societies: democracies of desire, they might be called, with money for ballots, stuffing permitted. But envy is more or less than desire. It begins with an almost frantic sense of emptiness inside oneself, as if the pump of one's heart were sucking on air. One has to be blind to perceive the emptiness, of course, but that's just what envy is, a selective blindness. *Invidia*, Latin for envy, translates as "non-sight," and Dante has the envious plodding along under cloaks of lead, their eyes sewn shut with leaden wire. What they are blind to is what they have, God-given and humanly nurtured, in themselves.　　　　　—Nelson W. Aldrich Jr., *Old Money*

4d Make paragraphs coherent.

When sentences and paragraphs flow from one to another without discernible bumps, gaps, or shifts, they are said to be coherent. Coherence can be improved by strengthening the ties between old information and new. A number of techniques for strengthening those ties are detailed in this section.

Linking ideas clearly

Readers expect to learn a paragraph's main point in a topic sentence early in the paragraph. Then, as they move into the body of the paragraph, they expect to encounter specific details, facts, or examples that support the topic sentence — either directly or indirectly. In the following paragraph, all of the sentences following the topic sentence directly support it.

> A passenger list of the early years [of the Orient Express] would read like a *Who's Who of the World*, from art to politics. Sarah Bernhardt and her Italian counterpart Eleonora Duse used the train to thrill the stages of Europe. For musicians there were Toscanini and Mahler. Dancers Nijinsky and Pavlova were there, while lesser performers like Harry Houdini and the girls of the Ziegfeld Follies also rode the rails. Violinists were allowed to practice on the train, and occasionally one might see trapeze artists hanging like bats from the baggage racks.
> — Barnaby Conrad III, "Train of Kings"

If a sentence does not support the topic sentence directly, readers expect it to support another sentence in the paragraph and therefore to support the topic sentence indirectly. The following paragraph begins with a topic sentence. The italicized sentences are direct supports, and the rest of the sentences are indirect supports.

> Though the open-space classroom works for many children, it is not practical for my son, David. *First, David is hyperactive.* When he was placed in an open-space classroom, he became distracted and confused. He was tempted to watch the movement going on around him instead of concentrating on his own work. *Second, David has a tendency to transpose letters and numbers, a tendency that can be overcome only by individual attention from the instructor.* In the open classroom he was moved from teacher to teacher, with each one responsible for a different subject. No single teacher worked with David long enough to diagnose the problem, let alone help him with it. *Finally, David is not a highly motivated learner.* In the open classroom, he was graded "at his own level," not by criteria for a certain grade. He could receive a B in reading and still be a grade level behind, because he was doing satisfactory work "at his own level." [Italics added.]
> — Margaret Smith, student

Repeating key words

Repetition of key words is an important technique for gaining coherence. To prevent repetitions from becoming dull, you can use variations of a key word (*hike, hiker, hiking*), pronouns referring to the word (*gamblers . . . they*), and synonyms (*run, spring, race, dash*). In the following paragraph describing plots among indentured servants in the seventeenth century, historian Richard Hofstadter binds sentences together by repeating the key word *plots* and echoing it with a variety of synonyms (which are italicized).

> *Plots* hatched by several servants to run away together occurred mostly in the plantation colonies, and the few recorded servant *uprisings* were entirely limited to those colonies. Virginia had been forced from its very earliest years to take stringent steps against *mutinous plots,* and severe punishments for *such behavior* were recorded. Most servant *plots* occurred in the seventeenth century: a contemplated *uprising* was nipped in the bud in York County in 1661; apparently led by some left-wing offshoots of the *Great Rebellion*, servants *plotted* an *insurrection* in Gloucester County in 1663, and four leaders were condemned and executed; some discontented servants apparently joined *Bacon's Rebellion* in the 1670's. In the 1680's the planters became newly apprehensive of discontent among the servants "owing to their great necessities and want of clothes," and it was feared they would *rise up* and *plunder* the storehouses and ships; in 1682 there were plant-cutting *riots* in which servants and laborers, as well as some planters, took part. [Italics added.]
> — Richard Hofstadter, *America at 1750*

Using parallel structures

Parallel structures are frequently used within sentences to underscore the similarity of ideas (see 9). They may also be used to bind together a series of sentences expressing similar information. In the following passage describing folk beliefs, anthropologist Margaret Mead presents similar information in parallel grammatical form.

> Actually, almost every day, even in the most sophisticated home, something is likely to happen that evokes the memory of some old folk belief. The salt spills. A knife falls to the floor. Your nose tickles. Then perhaps, with a slightly embarrassed smile, the person who spilled the salt tosses a pinch over his left shoulder. Or someone recites the old rhyme, "Knife falls, gentleman calls." Or as you rub your nose you think, That means a letter. I wonder who's writing?
> — Margaret Mead, "New Superstitions for Old"

Maintaining consistency

Coherence suffers whenever a draft shifts confusingly from one point of view to another or from one verb tense to another. (See 13.) In addition, coherence can suffer when new information is introduced with the subject of each sentence. As a rule, a sentence's subject should echo a subject or object in the previous sentence.

The following rough-draft paragraph is needlessly hard to read because so few of the sentences' subjects are tied to earlier subjects or objects. The subjects appear in italics.

> *One* goes about trapping in this manner. At the very outset *one* acquires a "trapping" state of mind. A *library* of books must be read, and preferably *someone* with experience should educate the novice. *Preparing* for the first expedition takes several steps. The *purchase* of traps is first. A *pair* of rubber gloves, waterproof *boots*, and the grubbiest *clothes* capable of withstanding human use come next to outfit the trapper for his adventure. Finally, the *decision* has to be made on just what kind of animals to seek, what sort of bait to use, and where to place the traps. [Italics added.]

Although the writer repeats a number of key words, such as *trapping*, the paragraph seems disconnected because new information is introduced with the subject of each sentence.

To improve the paragraph, the writer used the first-person pronoun as the subject of every sentence. The revision is much easier to read.

> *I* went about trapping in this manner. To acquire a "trapping" state of mind, *I* read a library of books and talked at length with an experienced trapper, my father. Then *I* purchased the traps and outfitted myself by collecting a pair of rubber gloves, waterproof boots, and the grubbiest clothes capable of withstanding human use. Finally, *I* decided just what kinds of animals to seek, what sort of bait to use, and where to place my traps. [Italics added.]
> — John Clyde Thatcher, student

Notice that Thatcher combined some of his original sentences. By doing so, he was able to avoid excessive repetitions of the pronoun *I*. Notice, too, that he varied his sentence openings (most sentences do not begin with *I*) so that readers are not likely to find the repetitions tiresome.

Providing transitions

Transitions are bridges between what has been read and what is about to be read. Transitions help readers move from sentence to sentence; they also alert readers to more global connections of ideas—those between paragraphs or even larger blocks of text.

> **ACADEMIC ENGLISH** Choose transitions carefully and vary them appropriately. For instance, avoid using a transition that signals a logical relationship (such as *therefore*) if no clear logical relationship exists. Each transition has a different meaning; if you do not use an appropriate signal, you might confuse your reader.
>
> ▶ Although taking eight o'clock classes may seem unappealing,
>
>   *For example,*
>   coming to school early has its advantages. ~~Moreover,~~ students
>   ^
>   who arrive early typically avoid the worst traffic and find
>
>   the best parking spaces.

SENTENCE-LEVEL TRANSITIONS   Certain words and phrases signal connections between (or within) sentences. Frequently used transitions are included in the chart on page 55.

Skilled writers use transitional expressions with care, making sure, for example, not to use *consequently* when *also* would be more precise. They are also careful to select transitions with an appropriate tone, perhaps preferring *so* to *thus* in an informal piece, *in summary* to *in short* for a scholarly essay.

In the following paragraph, taken from an argument that dinosaurs had the "'right-sized' brains for reptiles of their body size," biologist Stephen Jay Gould uses transitions (italicized) with skill.

> I don't wish to deny that the flattened, minuscule head of largebodied Stegosaurus houses little brain from our subjective, top-heavy perspective, *but* I do wish to assert that we should not expect more of the beast. *First of all*, large animals have relatively smaller brains than related, small animals. The correlation of brain size with body size among kindred animals (all reptiles, all mammals, *for example*) is remarkably regular. *As* we move from small to large animals, from mice to elephants or small lizards to Komodo dragons, brain size increases, *but* not so fast as body

Common transitions

TO SHOW ADDITION and, also, besides, further, furthermore, in addition, moreover, next, too, first, second

TO GIVE EXAMPLES for example, for instance, to illustrate, in fact, specifically

TO COMPARE also, in the same manner, similarly, likewise

TO CONTRAST but, however, on the other hand, in contrast, nevertheless, still, even though, on the contrary, yet, although

TO SUMMARIZE OR CONCLUDE in short, in summary, in conclusion, to sum up, therefore

TO SHOW TIME after, as, before, next, during, later, finally, meanwhile, then, when, while, immediately

TO SHOW PLACE OR DIRECTION above, below, beyond, nearby, opposite, close, to the left

TO INDICATE LOGICAL RELATIONSHIP if, so, therefore, consequently, thus, as a result, for this reason, because, since

size. *In other words*, bodies grow faster than brains, *and* large animals have low ratios of brain weight to body weight. *In fact*, brains grow only about two-thirds as fast as bodies. *Since* we have no reason to believe that large animals are consistently stupider than their smaller relatives, we must conclude that large animals require relatively less brain to do as well as smaller animals. *If* we do not recognize this relationship, we are likely to underestimate the mental power of very large animals, dinosaurs *in particular*. [Italics added.]

— Stephen Jay Gould, "Were Dinosaurs Dumb?"

ON THE WEB > dianahacker.com/rules
Writing exercises > E-ex 4–2

PARAGRAPH-LEVEL TRANSITIONS Paragraph-level transitions usually link the *first* sentence of a new paragraph with the *first* sentence of the previous paragraph. In other words, the topic sentences signal global connections.

Look for opportunities to allude to the subject of a previous paragraph (as summed up in its topic sentence) in the topic sentence of the next one. In his essay "Little Green Lies," Jonathan H.

Alder uses this strategy in the following topic sentences, which appear in a passage describing the benefits of plastic packaging.

> Consider aseptic packaging, the synthetic packaging for the "juice boxes" so many children bring to school with their lunch. One criticism of aseptic packaging is that it is nearly impossible to recycle, yet on almost every other count, aseptic packaging is environmentally preferable to the packaging alternatives. Not only do aseptic containers not require refrigeration to keep their contents from spoiling, but their manufacture requires less than one-10th the energy of making glass bottles.
>
> What is true for juice boxes is also true for other forms of synthetic packaging. The use of polystyrene, which is commonly (and mistakenly) referred to as "Styrofoam," can reduce food waste dramatically due to its insulating properties. (Thanks to these properties, polystyrene cups are much preferred over paper for that morning cup of coffee.) Polystyrene also requires significantly fewer resources to produce than its paper counterpart.

TRANSITIONS BETWEEN BLOCKS OF TEXT   In long essays, you will need to alert readers to connections between blocks of text more than one paragraph long. You can do this by inserting transitional sentences or short paragraphs at key points in the essay. Here, for example, is a transitional paragraph from a student research paper. It announces that the first part of the paper has come to a close and the second part is about to begin.

> Although the great apes have demonstrated significant language skills, one central question remains: Can they be taught to use that uniquely human language tool we call grammar, to learn the difference, for instance, between "ape bite human" and "human bite ape"? In other words, can an ape create a sentence?

Another strategy to help readers move from one block of text to another is to insert headings in your essay. Headings, which usually sit above blocks of text, allow you to announce a new topic boldly, without the need for subtle transitions. (See 5b.)

4e   If necessary, adjust paragraph length.

Most readers feel comfortable reading paragraphs that range between one hundred and two hundred words. Shorter paragraphs force too much starting and stopping, and longer ones strain readers' attention span. There are exceptions to this guideline, however. Paragraphs longer than two hundred words frequently appear in scholarly writing, where they suggest seriousness and depth. Paragraphs shorter than one hundred words occur in newspapers because of narrow columns; in informal essays to quicken the pace; and in business writing and Web sites, where readers routinely skim for main ideas.

In an essay, the first and last paragraphs will ordinarily be the introduction and the conclusion. These special-purpose paragraphs are likely to be shorter than the paragraphs in the body of the essay. Typically, the body paragraphs will follow the essay's outline: one paragraph per point in short essays, a group of paragraphs per point in longer ones. Some ideas require more development than others, however, so it is best to be flexible. If an idea stretches to a length unreasonable for a paragraph, you should divide the paragraph, even if you have presented comparable points in the essay in single paragraphs.

Paragraph breaks are not always made for strictly logical reasons. Writers use them for the following reasons as well.

REASONS FOR BEGINNING A NEW PARAGRAPH

- to mark off the introduction and conclusion
- to signal a shift to a new idea
- to indicate an important shift in time or place
- to emphasize a point (by placing it at the beginning or the end, not in the middle, of a paragraph)
- to highlight a contrast
- to signal a change of speakers (in dialogue)
- to provide readers with a needed pause
- to break up text that looks too dense

Beware of using too many short, choppy paragraphs, however. Readers want to see how your ideas connect, and they become irritated when you break their momentum by forcing them to pause every few sentences. Here are some reasons you might have for combining some of the paragraphs in a rough draft.

REASONS FOR COMBINING PARAGRAPHS

- to clarify the essay's organization
- to connect closely related ideas
- to bind together text that looks too choppy

Document Design

The term *document* is broad enough to describe anything you might write in a college class, in the business world, and in everyday life. How you design a document (format it for the printed page or for a computer screen) will affect how readers respond to it.

5

Become familiar with the principles of document design.

Good document design promotes readability, but what *readability* means depends on your purpose and audience and perhaps on other elements of your writing situation, such as your subject, length restrictions, or any other specific requirements (see the checklists on pp. 3 and 61). All of your design choices — layout, word processing options such as margins and fonts, headings, and lists — should be made in light of your writing situation. Likewise, different types of visuals — tables, charts, and images — can support your writing if they are used appropriately.

5a Select appropriate format options.

Similar types of documents share similar design features. Taken together, these features — layout, margins and line spacing, alignment, fonts, and font styles — form an appearance that helps to guide readers.

Layout

Most readers have set ideas about how different kinds of documents should look. Advertisements, for example, have a distinctive appearance, as do newsletters, flyers, brochures, and menus. Instructors have expectations about how a college paper should look (see 6). Employers too expect documents such as letters, résumés, memos, and e-mail messages to be presented in standard ways (see 7).

Planning a document: Purpose and audience checklist

- What is the purpose of your document? How can your document design help you achieve this purpose?

- Who are your readers? What are their expectations?

- What format is required? What format options — layout, margins, line spacing, alignment, and fonts — will readers expect?

- How can you use visuals — charts, graphs, tables, images — to help you convey information?

Unless you have a compelling reason to stray from convention, it's best to choose a document layout that conforms to your readers' expectations. If you're not sure what readers expect, look at examples of the kind of document you are producing.

Margins and line spacing

Margins help control the look of a page. For most academic and business documents, leave a margin of one to one and a half inches on all sides. These margins create a visual frame for the text and provide room for annotations, such as an instructor's comments or an editor's suggestions. Tight margins generally make a page crowded and difficult to read.

Most manuscripts in progress are double-spaced to allow room for editing. Final copy is often double-spaced as well, since single-spacing is less inviting to read. If you are unsure about margin and spacing requirements for your document, check with your instructor or consult documents similar to the one you are writing.

At times, the advantages of wide margins and double-spaced lines are offset by other considerations. For example, most business and technical documents are single-spaced, with double-spacing between paragraphs, to save paper and promote quick scanning. Your document's purpose and context should determine appropriate margins and line spacing.

SINGLE-SPACED, UNFORMATTED   **DOUBLE-SPACED, FORMATTED**

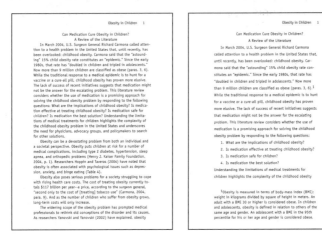

Alignment

Word processing programs allow you to align text and visuals on a page in four ways:

LEFT-ALIGNED	**RIGHT-ALIGNED**	**CENTERED**	**JUSTIFIED**

Most academic and business documents are left-aligned for easy reading.

Fonts

If you have a choice, select a font that fits your writing situation in an easy-to-read size (usually 10 to 12 points). Although off-beat fonts may seem attractive, they slow readers down and can distract them from your ideas. For example, using comic sans, a font with a handwritten, childish feel, can make an essay seem too informal or unpolished, regardless of how well it's written. Fonts that are easy to read and appropriate for college and workplace documents include the following.

Arial	Tahoma
Courier	Times New Roman
Garamond	**Verdana**
Georgia	

Font styles

Font styles — such as **boldface**, *italics*, and underlining — can be useful for calling attention to parts of a document. On the whole, it is best to use restraint when selecting styles. Applying too many different styles within a document can result in busy-looking pages and may confuse readers.

TIP: Never write a document in all capital or all lowercase letters. Doing so can frustrate or annoy readers. Although some readers have become accustomed to instant messages and e-mails that omit capital letters entirely, their absence makes a message difficult to read.

5b Use headings when appropriate.

You will have little need for headings in short essays, especially if you use paragraphing and clear topic sentences to guide readers. In more complex documents, however, such as research papers, grant proposals, business reports, and Web sites, headings can be a useful visual cue for readers.

Headings help readers see at a glance the organization of a document. If more than one level of heading is used, the headings also indicate the hierarchy of ideas — as they do throughout this book.

Headings serve a number of functions, depending on the needs of different readers. When readers are simply looking up information, headings will help them find it quickly. When readers are scanning, hoping to pick up the gist of things, headings will guide them. Even when readers are committed enough to read every word, headings can help them preview a document before they begin reading.

TIP: While headings can be useful, they cannot substitute for transitions between paragraphs. Keep this in mind as you write college essays.

Phrasing headings

Headings should be as brief and as informative as possible. Certain styles of headings — the most common being *-ing* phrases, noun phrases, questions, and imperative sentences — work better for some purposes, audiences, and subjects than others.

Whatever style you choose, use it consistently. Headings on the same level of organization should be written in parallel structure (see 9), as in the following examples from a report, a history textbook, a financial brochure, and a nursing manual, respectively.

-*ING* HEADINGS

Safeguarding the earth's atmosphere

Charting the path to sustainable energy

Conserving global forests

NOUN PHRASE HEADINGS

The economics of slavery

The sociology of slavery

The psychological effects of slavery

QUESTIONS AS HEADINGS

How do I buy shares?

How do I redeem shares?

What is the history of the fund's performance?

IMPERATIVE SENTENCES AS HEADINGS

Ask the patient to describe current symptoms.

Take a detailed medical history.

Record the patient's vital signs.

Placing and formatting headings

Headings on the same level of organization should be placed and formatted in a consistent way. If you have more than one level of heading, you might center your first-level headings and make them boldface; then you might make the second-level headings left-aligned and italicized, like this:

First-level heading

Second-level heading

A college paper with headings typically has only one level, and the headings are often centered, as in the sample paper on pages 515–19. Business memos often include headings. Important headings can be highlighted by using white space around them. Less important headings can be downplayed by using less white space or by running them into the text.

5c Use lists to guide readers.

Lists are easy to read or scan when they are displayed rather than run into your text. You might choose to display the following kinds of lists:

- steps in a process
- materials needed for a project
- parts of an object
- advice or recommendations
- items to be discussed
- criteria for evaluation (as in checklists)

Lists should usually be introduced with an independent clause followed by a colon (*All mammals share the following five characteristics:*). Periods are not used after items in a list unless the items are complete sentences. Lists are most readable when they are presented in parallel grammatical form (see 9).

If the order of items is not important, use bullets (circles or squares) or dashes to draw readers' eyes to a list. If you are describing a sequence or a set of steps, number your list with arabic numerals (1, 2, 3) followed by periods.

Although lists can be useful visual cues, don't overdo them. Too many will clutter a document.

5d Add visuals to supplement your text.

Visuals can convey information concisely and powerfully. Charts, graphs, and tables, for example, can simplify complex numerical information. Images — including photographs and diagrams — often express an idea more vividly than words can. With access to the Internet, digital photography, and word processing or desktop publishing software, you can download or create your own visuals to enhance your document. If you download a visual, you must credit your source (see 51).

Choosing appropriate visuals

Use visuals to supplement your writing, not to substitute for it. Always consider how a visual supports your purpose and how your audience might respond to it. A student writing about electronic surveillance in the workplace, for example, used a cartoon to illustrate her point about employees' personal use of the Internet at work (see 56b). Another student, writing about treatments for childhood obesity, created a table to display data she had found in two different sources and discussed in her paper (see 61b).

As you draft and revise a document, choose carefully the visuals that support your main point, and avoid overloading your text with too many images. The chart on pages 68–69 describes eight types of visuals and their purposes.

Placing and labeling visuals

A visual may be placed in the text of a document, near a discussion to which it relates, or it can be put in an appendix, labeled, and referred to in the text.

Placing visuals in the text of a document can be tricky. Usually you will want the visual to appear close to the sentences that relate to it, but page breaks won't always allow this placement. At times you may need to insert the visual at a later point and tell readers where it can be found; sometimes you can make the text flow around the visual. No matter where you place a visual, refer to it in your text. Don't expect visuals to speak for themselves.

Most of the visuals you include in a document will require some sort of label. A label, which is typically placed above or below the visual, should be brief but descriptive. Most com-

VISUAL WITH A SOURCE CREDITED

Fig. 6.

Postal Service Size, by Number of Employees

	Among the Global 500			Among US Companies	
Rank	Company	Employees as of 2002	Rank	Company	Employees as of 2002
1	Wal-Mart Stores	1,300,000	1	Wal-Mart Stores	1,300,000
2	China National Petroleum	1,146,194	2	**US Postal Service**	**854,376**
3	Sinopec	917,000	3	McDonald's	413,000
4	**US Postal Service**	**854,376**	4	United Parcel Service	360,000
5	Agricultural Bank of China	490,999	5	Ford Motor	350,321
6	Siemens	426,000	6	General Motors	350,000
7	McDonald's	413,000	7	Intl. Business Machines	315,889
8	Ind. & Comm. Bank of China	405,000	8	General Electric	315,000
9	Carrefour	396,662	9	Target	306,000
10	Compass Group	392,352	10	Home Depot	300,000
11	China Telecomm	365,778	11	Kroger	289,000
12	DaimlerChrysler	365,571	12	Sears Roebuck	289,000
13	United Parcel Service	360,000	13	Tyco International	267,000
14	Ford Motor	350,321	14	Citigroup	252,500
15	General Motors	350,000	15	Verizon Communications	229,497

Source: Number of employees rankings by *Fortune Magazine*, April 14, 2003.

monly, a visual is labeled with the word "Figure" or the abbreviation "Fig.," followed by a number: *Fig. 4.* Sometimes a title might be included to explain how the visual relates to the text: *Fig. 4. Voter turnout by age.*

Using visuals responsibly

Most word processing and spreadsheet software will allow you to produce your own visuals. If you create a chart, a table, or a graph using information from your research, you must cite the source of the information even though the visual is your own. The table at the top of this page credits the source of its data.

If you download a photograph from the Web or scan an image from a magazine or book, you must credit the person or organization that created it, just as you would cite any other source you use in a college paper (see 51). If your document is written for publication outside the classroom, you will need to request permission to use any visual you borrow.

Guidelines for using visuals vary by academic discipline. See 56a and 61a for guidelines in English and humanities and in social sciences, respectively.

Choosing visuals to suit your purpose

Pie chart

Pie charts compare a part or parts to the whole. The parts are displayed as segments of the pie, represented as percentages of the whole (which is always 100 percent).

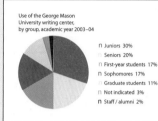

Line graph

Line graphs highlight trends over a period of time or compare numerical data.

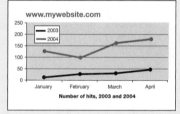

Bar graph

Bar graphs can be used for the same purpose as line graphs. This bar graph displays the same data as in the line graph above.

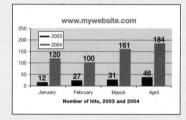

Table

Tables organize complicated numerical information into a digestible format.

Prices of daily doses of AIDS drugs ($US)

Drug	Brazil	Uganda	Côte d'Ivoire	US
3TC (Lamuvidine)	1.66	3.28	2.95	8.70
ddC (Zalcitabine)	0.24	4.17	3.75	8.80
Didanosine	2.04	5.26	3.48	7.25
Efavirenz	6.96	n/a	6.41	13.13
Indinavir	10.32	12.79	9.07	14.93
Nelfinavir	4.14	4.45	4.39	6.47
Nevirapine	5.04	n/a	n/a	8.48
Saquinavir	6.24	7.37	5.52	6.50
Stavudine	0.56	6.19	4.10	9.07
ZDV/3TC	1.44	7.34	n/a	18.78
Zidovudine	1.08	4.34	2.43	10.12

Source: UNAIDS, 2000

Photograph

Photographs vividly depict people, scenes, or objects discussed in a text.

Diagram

Diagrams, useful in scientific and technical writing, concisely illustrate processes, structures, or interactions.

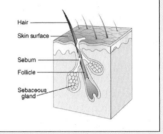

Map

Maps indicate distances, historical information, or demographics.

Flowchart

Flowcharts show structures or steps in a process. (Also see p. 158.)

6

Use standard academic formatting.

Instructors have certain expectations about how a college paper should look. If your instructor provides guidelines for formatting an essay, report, or research paper, you should follow them. Otherwise, use the manuscript format that is recommended for your academic discipline.

6a Use the manuscript format required by your academic discipline.

In most English and humanities classes, you will be asked to use the MLA (Modern Language Association) format. In most social science classes, such as psychology and sociology, and in most health fields, you will be asked to use APA (American Psychological Association) format. See 6b and 60e, respectively, for more details.

6b Follow MLA format for most composition papers.

The sample on pages 71–72 illustrates MLA format. For more detailed MLA manuscript guidelines and a sample research paper, see 56.

7

Use standard business formatting.

This section provides guidelines for preparing business letters, résumés, and memos. For a more detailed discussion of these and other business documents — proposals, reports, executive summaries, and so on — consult a business writing textbook or look at current examples at the organization for which you are writing.

MLA ESSAY FORMAT

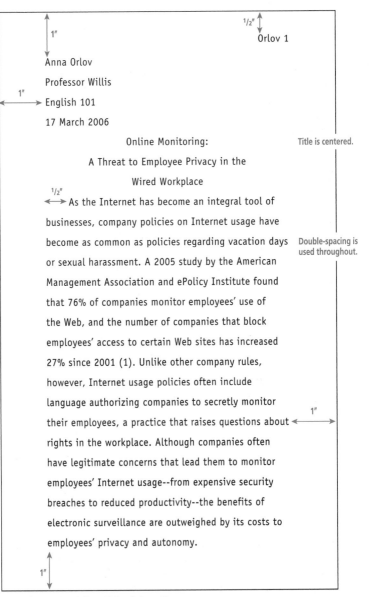

Orlov 1

Anna Orlov

Professor Willis

English 101

17 March 2006

Online Monitoring: Title is centered.

A Threat to Employee Privacy in the

Wired Workplace

As the Internet has become an integral tool of

businesses, company policies on Internet usage have

become as common as policies regarding vacation days   Double-spacing is
used throughout.

or sexual harassment. A 2005 study by the American

Management Association and ePolicy Institute found

that 76% of companies monitor employees' use of

the Web, and the number of companies that block

employees' access to certain Web sites has increased

27% since 2001 (1). Unlike other company rules,

however, Internet usage policies often include

language authorizing companies to secretly monitor

their employees, a practice that raises questions about

rights in the workplace. Although companies often

have legitimate concerns that lead them to monitor

employees' Internet usage--from expensive security

breaches to reduced productivity--the benefits of

electronic surveillance are outweighed by its costs to

employees' privacy and autonomy.

Marginal annotations indicate MLA-style formatting.

MLA ESSAY FORMAT (*continued*)

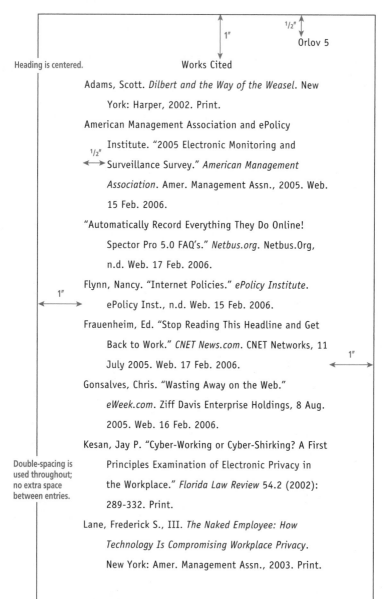

Heading is centered.

1"

1/2"

Orlov 5

Works Cited

Adams, Scott. *Dilbert and the Way of the Weasel*. New York: Harper, 2002. Print.

American Management Association and ePolicy Institute. "2005 Electronic Monitoring and Surveillance Survey." *American Management Association*. Amer. Management Assn., 2005. Web. 15 Feb. 2006.

"Automatically Record Everything They Do Online! Spector Pro 5.0 FAQ's." *Netbus.org*. Netbus.Org, n.d. Web. 17 Feb. 2006.

Flynn, Nancy. "Internet Policies." *ePolicy Institute*. ePolicy Inst., n.d. Web. 15 Feb. 2006.

Frauenheim, Ed. "Stop Reading This Headline and Get Back to Work." *CNET News.com*. CNET Networks, 11 July 2005. Web. 17 Feb. 2006.

Gonsalves, Chris. "Wasting Away on the Web." *eWeek.com*. Ziff Davis Enterprise Holdings, 8 Aug. 2005. Web. 16 Feb. 2006.

Kesan, Jay P. "Cyber-Working or Cyber-Shirking? A First Principles Examination of Electronic Privacy in the Workplace." *Florida Law Review* 54.2 (2002): 289-332. Print.

Lane, Frederick S., III. *The Naked Employee: How Technology Is Compromising Workplace Privacy*. New York: Amer. Management Assn., 2003. Print.

1/2"

1"

1"

Double-spacing is used throughout; no extra space between entries.

7a Use established conventions for business letters.

In writing a business letter, be direct, clear, and courteous, but do not hesitate to be firm if necessary. State your purpose or request at the beginning of the letter and include only relevant information in the body. By being as direct and concise as possible, you show that you value your reader's time.

For the format of the letter, stick to established business conventions. The following sample business letter is typed in what is known as *full block* style. Paragraphs are not indented

BUSINESS LETTER IN FULL BLOCK STYLE

LatinoVoice

March 16, 2006 ——————— Date

Jonathan Ross
Managing Editor
Latino World Today ——————— Inside
2971 East Oak Avenue   address
Baltimore, MD 21201

Dear Mr. Ross: ——————— Salutation

Thank you very much for taking the time yesterday to speak to the University of Maryland's Latino Club. A number of students have told me that they enjoyed your presentation and found your job search suggestions to be extremely helpful.

As I mentioned to you when we first scheduled your appearance, the club publishes a monthly newsletter, *Latino Voice*. Our purpose is to share up-to-date information and expert advice with members of the university's Latino population. Considering how much students benefited from your talk, I would like to publish excerpts from it in our newsletter.

Body — I have taken the liberty of transcribing parts of your presentation and organizing them into a question-and-answer format for our readers. When you have a moment, would you mind looking through the enclosed article and letting me know if I may have your permission to print it? I would be happy, of course, to make any changes or corrections that you request. I'm hoping to include this article in our next newsletter, so I would need your response by April 4.

Once again, Mr. Ross, thank you for sharing your experiences with us. You gave an informative and entertaining speech, and I would love to be able to share it with the students who couldn't hear it in person.

Sincerely, ——————— Close

Jeffrey Richardson
——————— Signature
Jeffrey Richardson
Associate Editor

Enc.

210 Student Center University of Maryland **College Park MD 20742**

and are typed single-spaced, with double-spacing between them. This style is usually preferred when the letter is typed on letterhead stationery, as in the example.

Below the signature, aligned at the left, you may include the abbreviation *Enc.* to indicate that something is enclosed with the letter or the abbreviation *cc* followed by a colon and the name of someone who is receiving a copy of the letter.

7b Write effective résumés and cover letters.

An effective résumé gives relevant information in a clear and concise form. You may be asked to produce a traditional résumé, a scannable résumé, or a Web résumé. The cover letter gives a prospective employer a reason to look at your résumé. The trick is to present yourself in a favorable light without including unnecessary details and wasting your reader's time.

COVER LETTERS When you send out your résumé, always include a cover letter that introduces yourself, states the position you seek, and tells where you learned about it. The letter should also highlight past experiences that qualify you for the position and emphasize what you can do for the employer (not what the job will do for you). End the letter with a suggestion for a meeting, and tell your prospective employer when you will be available.

TRADITIONAL RÉSUMÉS Traditional résumés are produced on paper, and they are screened by people, not by computers. Because screeners may face stacks of applications, they often spend very little time looking at each résumé. Therefore, you will need to make your résumé as reader-friendly as possible. Here are a few guidelines:

- Limit your résumé to one page if possible, two pages at the most. (If your résumé is longer than a page, repeat your name at the top of the second page.)
- Organize your information into clear categories — Education, Experience, and so on.
- Present the information in each category in reverse chronological order to highlight your most recent accomplishments.

TRADITIONAL RÉSUMÉ

Jeffrey Richardson

121 Knox Road, #6
College Park, MD 20740
301–555–2651
jrichardson@jrichardson.localhost

OBJECTIVE	To obtain an editorial internship with a magazine
EDUCATION Fall 2003– present	University of Maryland • BA expected in June 2007 • Double major: English and Latin American studies • GPA: 3.7 (on a 4-point scale)
EXPERIENCE Fall 2005– present	Associate editor, *Latino Voice*, newsletter of Latino Club • Assign and edit feature articles • Coordinate community outreach
Fall 2004– present	Photo editor, *The Diamondback*, college paper • Shoot and print photographs • Select and lay out photographs and other visuals
Summer 2005	Intern, *The Globe,* Fairfax, Virginia • Wrote stories about local issues and personalities • Interviewed political candidates • Edited and proofread copy • Coedited "The Landscapes of Northern Virginia: A Photoessay"
Summers 2004, 2005	Tutor, Fairfax County ESL Program • Tutored Latino students in English as a Second Language • Trained new tutors
ACTIVITIES	Photographers' Workshop, Latino Club
PORTFOLIO	Available at http://jrichardson.localhost/jrportfolio.htm
REFERENCES	Available upon request

- Use bulleted lists or some other simple, clear visual device to organize information.
- Use strong, active verbs to emphasize your accomplishments. (Use present-tense verbs, such as *manage*, for current activities and past-tense verbs, such as *managed*, for past activities.)

SCANNABLE RÉSUMÉS Scannable résumés might be submitted on paper, by e-mail, or through an online employment service. The prospective employer scans and searches the résumé electronically; a database matches keywords in the employer's job description with keywords in the résumé. A human screener then looks through the résumés filtered out by the database matching.

A scannable résumé must be very simply formatted so that the scanner can accurately pick up its content. In general, follow these guidelines when preparing a scannable résumé:

- Include a Keywords section that lists words likely to be searched by a scanner. (Use nouns such as *manager,* not verbs such as *manage* or *managed.*)

- Use standard résumé headings (for example, Education, Experience, References).

- Avoid special characters, graphics, or font styles such as boldface or italics.

- Avoid formatting features such as tabs, indents, columns, or tables.

WEB RÉSUMÉS Posting your résumé on a Web site is an easy way to provide prospective employers with recent information about your employment goals and accomplishments. Web résumés allow you to present details about yourself without overwhelming your readers. Most guidelines for traditional résumés apply to Web résumés, but if you choose to post your résumé to your personal Web site, consider the following guidelines.

- Keep the opening screen of your Web site (home page) simple and concise. Provide a clear link to your résumé and to any other relevant pages, such as an electronic portfolio.

- Consider including an HTML version and a downloadable/printable version (a PDF file, for instance) of your résumé.

- Include identifying information — your name, address, and phone number and a link to your e-mail address — at the top of your résumé page.

- Always list the date that you last updated the résumé.

ON THE WEB > **dianahacker.com/rules**
Additional resources > Links Library > Document design

7c Write clear and concise memos.

Usually brief and to the point, a memo reports information, makes a request, or recommends an action. The format of a memo, which varies from company to company, is designed for easy distribution, quick reading, and efficient filing.

BUSINESS MEMO

Commonwealth Press

MEMORANDUM

February 28, 2007

To: Production, promotion, and editorial assistants

cc: Stephen Chapman

From: Helen Brown

Subject: New computers for staff

We will receive the new personal computers next week for the assistants in production, promotion, and editorial. In preparation, I would like you to take part in a training program and to rearrange your work areas to accommodate the new equipment.

Training Program

A computer consultant will teach in-house workshops on how to use our spreadsheet program. If you have already tried the program, be prepared to discuss any problems you have encountered.

Workshops for our three departments will be held in the training room at the following times:

- Production: Wednesday, March 7, 10:00 a.m. to 2:00 p.m.
- Promotion: Friday, March 9, 10:00 a.m. to 2:00 p.m.
- Editorial: Monday, March 12, 10:00 a.m. to 2:00 p.m.

Lunch will be provided in the cafeteria. If you cannot attend, please let me know by March 3.

Allocation and Setup

To give everyone access to a computer, we will set up the new computers as follows: two in the assistants' workspace in production; two in the area outside the conference room for the promotion assistants; and two in the library for the editorial assistants.

Assistants in all three departments should see me before the end of the week to discuss preparation of the spaces for the new equipment.

Most memos display the date, the name of the recipient, the name of the sender, and the subject on separate lines at the top. Many companies have preprinted forms for memos, and some word processing programs have memo templates. Memos also may be distributed via e-mail to be read on-screen.

The subject line of a memo, on paper or in e-mail, should describe the topic as clearly and concisely as possible, and the introductory paragraph should get right to the point. In addition, the body of the memo should be well organized and easy to skim. To promote skimming, use headings where possible and display any items that deserve special attention by setting them off from the text — in a list, for example, or in boldface. A sample memo appears on page 77.

7d Write effective e-mail messages.

E-mail is fast replacing regular mail in the business world and in most people's personal lives. Especially in business and academic contexts, you will want to show readers that you value their time. Your message may be just one of many that your readers have to wade through. Here are some strategies for writing effective e-mails:

- Fill in the subject line with a meaningful, concise subject to help readers sort through messages and set priorities.
- Put the most important part of your message at the beginning so it will be seen on the first screen.
- For long, detailed messages, consider providing a summary at the beginning.
- Write concisely, and keep paragraphs fairly short, especially if your audience is likely to read your message on the screen.
- Avoid writing in all capital letters or all lowercase letters, a practice that is easy on the writer but hard on the reader.
- Use an appropriate tone when writing e-mail in academic or business settings.
- Check with the original sender before forwarding e-mail messages.
- Use formatting such as boldface and italics and special characters sparingly; not all e-mail systems handle such elements consistently.
- Proofread for typos and obvious errors that are likely to slow down or annoy readers.

Clarity

8

Prefer active verbs.

As a rule, choose an active verb and pair it with a subject that names the person or thing doing the action. Active verbs express meaning more emphatically and vigorously than their weaker counterparts — forms of the verb *be* or verbs in the passive voice. Verbs in the passive voice lack strength because their subjects receive the action instead of doing it. Forms of the verb *be* (*be, am, is, are, was, were, being, been*) lack vigor because they convey no action.

Although passive verbs and the forms of *be* have legitimate uses, if an active verb can carry your meaning, use it.

PASSIVE	The pumps *were destroyed* by a surge of power.
BE VERB	A surge of power *was* responsible for the destruction of the pumps.
ACTIVE	A surge of power *destroyed* the pumps.

Even among active verbs, some are more active — and therefore more vigorous and colorful — than others. Carefully selected verbs can energize a piece of writing.

▶ The goalie crouched low, ~~reached~~ *swept* out his stick, and ~~sent~~ *hooked* the

rebound away from the mouth of the net.

GRAMMAR CHECKERS are fairly good at flagging passive verbs, such as *is used*. However, because passive verbs are sometimes appropriate, you — not the computer program — must decide whether to change a verb from passive to active. Grammar checkers tend to suggest revisions only when the passive sentence contains a *by* phrase (*Carbon dating is used by scientists to determine an object's approximate age*). Occasionally they make inappropriate suggestions for revision (*Scientists to determine an object's approximate age use carbon dating*). Only you can determine the most sensible word order for your sentence.

ACADEMIC ENGLISH Although you may be tempted to avoid the passive voice completely, keep in mind that it is preferred in some writing situations, especially in scientific writing. For appropriate uses of the passive voice, see 8a; for advice about forming the passive, see 28c.

8a Use the active voice unless you have a good reason for choosing the passive.

In the active voice, the subject does the action; in the passive voice, the subject receives the action (see also 63c). Although both voices are grammatically correct, the active voice is usually more effective because it is simpler and more direct.

> **ACTIVE** Hernando *caught* the fly ball.
>
> **PASSIVE** The fly ball *was caught* by Hernando.

In passive sentences, the actor (in this case Hernando) frequently disappears from the sentence: *The fly ball was caught.*

In most cases, you will want to emphasize the actor, so you should use the active voice. To replace a passive verb with an active alternative, make the actor the subject of the sentence.

> *A bolt of lightning struck the transformer.*
> ▶ The transformer was struck by a bolt of lightning.
>   ^

The active verb (*struck*) makes the point more forcefully than the passive verb (*was struck*).

> *The settlers stripped the land of timber before realizing*
> ▶ The land was stripped of timber before the settlers realized
>   ^
>
> the consequences of their actions.

The revision emphasizes the actors (*settlers*) by naming them in the subject.

> *The contractor removed the*
> ▶ The debris was removed from the construction site.
>   ^

When an actor does not appear in a passive-voice sentence, the writer must decide on an appropriate subject, in this case *The contractor*.

Appropriate uses of the passive

The passive voice is appropriate if you wish to emphasize the receiver of the action or to minimize the importance of the actor.

APPROPRIATE PASSIVE	Many native Hawaiians *are forced* to leave their beautiful beaches to make room for hotels and condominiums.
APPROPRIATE PASSIVE	As the time for harvest approaches, the tobacco plants *are sprayed* with a chemical to retard the growth of suckers.

The writer of the first sentence wished to emphasize the receiver of the action, *Hawaiians*. The writer of the second sentence wished to focus on the tobacco plants, not on the people spraying them.

In much scientific writing, the passive voice properly emphasizes the experiment or process being described, not the researcher.

APPROPRIATE PASSIVE	The solution *was heated* to the boiling point, and then it *was reduced* in volume by 50 percent.

ON THE WEB > **dianahacker.com/rules**
Language Debates > Passive voice

8b Replace *be* verbs that result in dull or wordy sentences.

Not every *be* verb needs replacing. The forms of *be* (*be, am, is, are, was, were, being, been*) work well when you want to link a subject to a noun that clearly renames it or to an adjective that describes it: *History is a bucket of ashes. Scoundrels are always sociable.* And when used as helping verbs before present participles (*is flying, are disappearing*) to express ongoing action, *be* verbs are fine: *Derrick was plowing the field when his wife went into labor.* (See 28a.)

If using a *be* verb makes a sentence needlessly dull and wordy, however, consider replacing it. Often a phrase following the verb will contain a word (such as *violation*) that suggests a more vigorous, active alternative (*violate*).

> *violate*
> Burying nuclear waste in Antarctica would ~~be in violation of~~
>   ^
>
> an international treaty.

Violate is less wordy and more vigorous than *be in violation of.*

> *resisted*
> When Rosa Parks ~~was resistant to~~ giving up her seat on the
>   ^
>
> bus, she became a civil rights hero.

Resisted is stronger than *was resistant to.*

EXERCISE 8–1   Revise any weak, unemphatic sentences by replacing *be* verbs or passive verbs with active alternatives and, if necessary, by naming in the subject the person or thing doing the action. Some sentences are emphatic; do not change them. Revisions of lettered sentences appear in the back of the book. Example:

> *The ranger doused the campfire before giving us*
> ~~The campfire was doused by the ranger before we were given~~
>   ^
>
> a ticket for unauthorized use of a campsite.

a. The Prussians were victorious over the Saxons in 1745.
b. The entire operation is managed by Ahmed, the producer.
c. The sea kayaks were awkwardly paddled by the video game programmers.
d. At the crack of rocket and mortar blasts, I jumped from the top bunk and landed on my buddy below, who was crawling on the floor looking for his boots.
e. There were shouting protesters on the courthouse steps.

1. A strange sound was made in the willow tree by the monkey that had escaped from the zoo.
2. Her letter was in acknowledgment of the student's participation in the literacy program.
3. The bomb bay doors rumbled open, and freezing air whipped through the plane.
4. The work of Paul Oakenfold and Sandra Collins was influential in my choice of music for my audition.
5. The only responsibility I was given by my parents was putting gas in the brand-new Volkswagen GTI they bought me my senior year.

ON THE WEB > dianahacker.com/rules
Grammar exercises > Clarity > E-ex 8–1 to 8–3

9

Balance parallel ideas.

If two or more ideas are parallel, they are easier to grasp when expressed in parallel grammatical form. Single words should be balanced with single words, phrases with phrases, clauses with clauses.

A kiss can be a comma, a question mark, or an exclamation point.
                                            — Mistinguett

This novel is not to be tossed lightly aside, but to be hurled with great force.
                                            — Dorothy Parker

In matters of principle, stand like a rock; in matters of taste, swim with the current.
                                            — Thomas Jefferson

Writers often use parallelism to create emphasis. (See p. 119.)

> **GRAMMAR CHECKERS** only occasionally flag faulty parallelism. Because the programs cannot assess whether ideas are parallel in grammatical form, they fail to catch the faulty parallelism in sentences such as this: *In my high school, boys were either jocks, preppies, or studied constantly.*

9a Balance parallel ideas in a series.

Readers expect items in a series to appear in parallel grammatical form. When one or more of the items violate readers' expectations, a sentence will be needlessly awkward.

▶ Children who study music also learn confidence, coordination,
      creativity.
    and ~~they are creative.~~
        ^

The revision presents all of the items as nouns.

▶ Hooked on romance novels, I learned that there is nothing

having
more important than being rich, looking good, and ~~to have~~ a
⌃
good time.

The revision uses *-ing* forms for all items in the series.

▶ After assuring us that he was sober, Sam drove down the
went through
middle of the road, ran one red light, and two stop signs.
⌃
The revision adds a verb to make the three items parallel:
drove…, ran…, went through….

NOTE: In headings and lists, aim for as much parallelism as the content allows. (See 5b and 5c.)

9b Balance parallel ideas presented as pairs.

When pairing ideas, underscore their connection by expressing them in similar grammatical form. Paired ideas are usually connected in one of these ways:

- with a coordinating conjunction such as *and, but,* or *or*
- with a pair of correlative conjunctions such as *either…or* or *not only…but also*
- with a word introducing a comparison, usually *than* or *as*

Parallel ideas linked with coordinating conjunctions

Coordinating conjunctions (*and, but, or, nor, for, so,* and *yet*) link ideas of equal importance. When those ideas are closely parallel in content, they should be expressed in parallel grammatical form.

▶ At Lincoln High School, vandalism can result in suspension
expulsion
or even ~~being expelled~~ from school.
⌃
The revision balances the nouns *suspension* and *expulsion.*

▶ Many states are reducing property taxes for home owners

extending
and ~~extend~~ financial aid in the form of tax credits to renters.
  ^

The revision balances the verb *reducing* with the verb *extending*.

Parallel ideas linked with correlative conjunctions

Correlative conjunctions come in pairs: *either...or, neither ...nor, not only...but also, both...and, whether...or*. Make sure that the grammatical structure following the second half of the pair is the same as that following the first half.

▶ Thomas Edison was not only a prolific inventor but also ~~was~~

a successful entrepreneur.

The words *a prolific inventor* follow *not only*, so *a successful entrepreneur* should follow *but also*. Repeating *was* creates an unbalanced effect.

to
▶ The clerk told me either to change my flight or take the train.
                                                    ^

To change my flight, which follows *either*, should be balanced with *to take the train*, which follows *or*.

Comparisons linked with than or as

In comparisons linked with *than* or *as*, the elements being compared should be expressed in parallel grammatical structure.

to ground
▶ It is easier to speak in abstractions than ~~grounding~~ one's
                                              ^
thoughts in reality.

▶ Mother could not persuade me that giving is as much a joy as
receiving.
~~to receive.~~
^

To speak in abstractions is balanced with *to ground one's thoughts in reality*. *Giving* is balanced with *receiving*.

NOTE: Comparisons should also be logical and complete. (See 10c.)

9c Repeat function words to clarify parallels.

Function words such as prepositions (*by, to*) and subordinating conjunctions (*that, because*) signal the grammatical nature of the word groups to follow. Although they can sometimes be omitted, include them whenever they signal parallel structures that might otherwise be missed by readers.

▶ Business owners are motivated to mark down prices when

when
sales slump in the month before a major holiday or the
 ^

competition introduces new products or discounts.

EXERCISE 9–1 Edit the following sentences to correct faulty parallelism. Revisions of lettered sentences appear in the back of the book. Example:

Rowena began her workday by pouring a cup of coffee and
checking
~~checked~~ her e-mail.
 ^

a. Police dogs are used for finding lost children, tracking criminals, and the detection of bombs and illegal drugs.
b. Hannah told her rock-climbing partner that she bought a new harness and of her desire to climb Otter Cliffs.
c. It is more difficult to sustain an exercise program than starting one.
d. During basic training, I was not only told what to do but also what to think.
e. Jan wanted to drive to the wine country or at least Sausalito.

1. Activities on Wednesday afternoons include fishing trips, dance lessons, and computers.
2. Arriving at Lake Powell in a thunderstorm, the campers found it safer to remain in their cars than setting up their tents.
3. The streets were not only too steep but also were too narrow for anything other than pedestrian traffic.
4. More digital artists in the show are from the South Shore than the North Shore.
5. To load her toolbox, Anika the Clown gathered hats of different sizes, put in two tubes of face paint, arranged a bundle of extra-long straws, added a bag of colored balloons, and a battery-powered hair dryer.

ON THE WEB > **dianahacker.com/rules**
    Grammar exercises > Clarity > E-ex 9–1 to 9–3

10

Add needed words.

Do not omit words necessary for grammatical or logical completeness. Readers need to see at a glance how the parts of a sentence are connected.

> **ESL** Languages sometimes differ in the need for certain words. In particular, be alert for missing articles, verbs, subjects, or expletives. See 29, 30a, and 30b.

> **GRAMMAR CHECKERS** do not flag the vast majority of missing words. They can, however, catch some missing verbs (see 27e). Although they can flag some missing articles (*a, an,* and *the*), they often suggest that an article is missing when in fact it is not. (See also 29.)

10a Add words needed to complete compound structures.

In compound structures, words are often omitted for economy: *Tom is a man who means what he says and* [*who*] *says what he means.* Such omissions are perfectly acceptable as long as the omitted words are common to both parts of the compound structure.

If the shorter version defies grammar or idiom because an omitted word is not common to both parts of the compound structure, the word must be put back in.

▶ Some of the regulars are acquaintances whom we see at work
    who
or live in our community.
  ^

The word *who* must be included because *whom . . . live in our community* is not grammatically correct.

         accepted
▶ Mayor Davis never has and never will accept a bribe.
          ^

Has . . . accept is not grammatically correct.

                      in
▶ Many South Pacific islanders still believe and live by ancient
                      ^

laws.

Believe . . . by is not idiomatic in English. (For a list of common idioms, see 18d.)

10b Add the word *that* if there is any danger of misreading without it.

If there is no danger of misreading, the word *that* may be omitted when it introduces a subordinate clause. *The value of a principle is the number of things* [*that*] *it will explain.* Occasionally, however, a sentence might be misread without *that*.

                      that
▶ Looking out the family room window, Sarah saw her favorite
                      ^

tree, which she had climbed so often as a child, was gone.

Sarah didn't see the tree; she saw that the tree was gone. The word *that* tells readers to expect a clause, not just *tree,* as the direct object of *saw.*

10c Add words needed to make comparisons logical and complete.

Comparisons should be made between items that are alike. To compare unlike items is illogical and distracting.

▶ The forests of North America are much more extensive than
those of
Europe.
^

Forests must be compared with forests.

Our   *graduate at a higher rate*
▶ ~~The graduation rate of our~~ student athletes ~~is higher~~ than
          ^   ^

the rest of the student population.

A rate cannot be logically compared to a population. The writer could revise the sentence by inserting *that of* after *than,* but the preceding revision is more concise.

▶ Some say that Ella Fitzgerald's renditions of Cole Porter's
                    singer's.
songs are better than any other ~~singer.~~
                    ^

Ella Fitzgerald's renditions cannot be logically compared with a singer. The revision uses the possessive form *singer's,* with the word *renditions* implied.

Sometimes the word *other* must be inserted to make a comparison logical.

           other
▶ Jupiter is larger than any planet in our solar system.
                ^

Jupiter cannot be larger than itself.

Sometimes the word *as* must be inserted to make a comparison grammatically complete.

           as
▶ The city of Lowell is as old, if not older than, the city of
                ^

Lawrence.

The construction *as old* is not complete without a second *as: as old as . . . the city of Lawrence.*

Finally, comparisons should be complete enough to ensure clarity. The reader should understand what is being compared.

INCOMPLETE	Brand X is less salty.
COMPLETE	Brand X is less salty than Brand Y.

Also, comparisons should leave no ambiguity for readers. In the following sentence, two interpretations are possible.

AMBIGUOUS	Ken helped me more than my roommate.
CLEAR	Ken helped me more than *he helped* my roommate.
CLEAR	Ken helped me more than my roommate *did*.

10d Add the articles *a*, *an*, and *the* where necessary for grammatical completeness.

Articles are sometimes omitted in recipes and other instructions that are meant to be followed while they are being read. Such omissions are inappropriate, however, in nearly all other forms of writing, whether formal or informal.

▶ Blood can be drawn only by *a* doctor or by *an* authorized person who has been trained in *the* procedure.

It is not always necessary to repeat articles with paired items: *We bought a computer and printer.* However, if one of the items requires *a* and the other requires *an*, both articles must be included.

▶ We bought a computer and *an* antivirus program.

ESL Articles can cause special problems for speakers of English as a second language. See 29.

EXERCISE 10–1 Add any words needed for grammatical or logical completeness in the following sentences. Revisions of lettered sentences appear in the back of the book. Example:

The officer feared *that* the prisoner would escape.

a. A good source of vitamin C is a grapefruit or orange.
b. The women entering VMI can expect haircuts as short as the male cadets.
c. The driver went to investigate, only to find one of the new tires had blown.
d. The graphic designers are interested and knowledgeable about producing posters for the balloon race.
e. Reefs are home to more species than any ecosystem in the sea.

1. Very few black doctors were allowed to serve in the Civil War, and their qualifications had to be higher than white doctors.
2. Producers of violent video games are not capable or interested in regulating themselves.
3. Vassily likes mathematics more than his teacher.
4. The inspection team saw many historic buildings had been damaged by the earthquake.
5. American English has borrowed more words from Spanish than from any language.

ON THE WEB > dianahacker.com/rules
Grammar exercises > Clarity > E-ex 10–1 and 10–2

11

Untangle mixed constructions.

A mixed construction contains parts that do not sensibly fit together. The mismatch may be a matter of grammar or of logic.

> **GRAMMAR CHECKERS** can flag *is when, is where,* and *reason . . . is because* constructions (11c), but they fail to identify nearly all other mixed constructions, including sentences as tangled as this one: *Depending on our method of travel and our destination determines how many suitcases we are allowed to pack.*

11a Untangle the grammatical structure.

Once you head into a sentence, your choices are limited by the range of grammatical patterns in English. (See 63 and 64.) You cannot begin with one grammatical plan and switch without warning to another.

MIXED	For most drivers who have a blood alcohol content of .05 percent double their risk of causing an accident.
REVISED	For most drivers who have a blood alcohol content of .05 percent, the risk of causing an accident is doubled.
REVISED	Most drivers who have a blood alcohol content of .05 percent double their risk of causing an accident.

The writer began with a long prepositional phrase that was destined to be a modifier but then tried to press it into service as the subject of the sentence. A prepositional phrase cannot serve as the subject of a sentence. If the sentence is to begin with the prepositional phrase, the writer must finish the sentence with a subject and verb (*risk . . . is doubled*). The writer who wishes to stay with the original verb (*double*) must head into the sentence another way: *Most drivers. . . .*

▶ *Being*
~~When an employee is~~ promoted without warning can be
     ^

alarming.

The adverb clause *When an employee is promoted without warning* cannot serve as the subject of the sentence. The revision replaces the adverb clause with a gerund phrase, a word group that can function as the subject. (See 64b and 64c.)

▶ Although the United States is one of the wealthiest nations

in the world, ~~but~~ more than twelve million of our children

live in poverty.

The *Although* clause is subordinate, so it cannot be linked to an independent clause with the coordinating conjunction *but*.

Occasionally a mixed construction is so tangled that it defies grammatical analysis. When this happens, back away from the sentence, rethink what you want to say, and then say it again as clearly as you can.

| MIXED | In the whole-word method children learn to recognize entire words rather than by the phonics method in which they learn to sound out letters and groups of letters. |
| REVISED | The whole-word method teaches children to recognize entire words; the phonics method teaches them to sound out letters and groups of letters. |

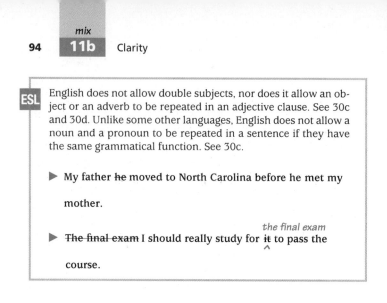

mix

ESL English does not allow double subjects, nor does it allow an object or an adverb to be repeated in an adjective clause. See 30c and 30d. Unlike some other languages, English does not allow a noun and a pronoun to be repeated in a sentence if they have the same grammatical function. See 30c.

▶ My father ~~he~~ moved to North Carolina before he met my

mother.

the final exam
▶ ~~The final exam~~ I should really study for ~~it~~ to pass the

course.

11b Straighten out the logical connections.

The subject and the predicate should make sense together; when they don't, the error is known as *faulty predication.*

Tiffany
▶ We decided that ~~Tiffany's welfare~~ would not be safe living

with her mother.

Tiffany, not her welfare, may not be safe.

double personal exemption for the
▶ Under the revised plan, the elderly/ ~~who now receive a double~~

~~personal exemption,~~ will be abolished.

The exemption, not the elderly, will be abolished.

An appositive and the noun to which it refers should be logically equivalent. When they are not, the error is known as *faulty apposition.*

Tax accounting,
▶ ~~The tax accountant,~~ a very lucrative field, requires intelligence

and patience.

The tax accountant is a person, not a field.

11c Avoid *is when, is where,* and *reason . . . is because* constructions.

In formal English, many readers object to *is when, is where,* and *reason . . . is because* constructions on either grammatical or logical grounds. Grammatically, the verb *is* (as well as *are, was,* and *were*) should be followed by a noun that renames the subject or by an adjective that describes it, not by an adverb clause beginning with *when, where,* or *because.* (See 63b and 64b.) Logically, the words *when, where,* and *because* suggest relations of time, place, and cause — relations that do not always make sense with *is, was,* or *were.*

▶ Anorexia nervosa is ~~where people,~~ *a disorder suffered by people who,* believing they are too fat,

diet to the point of starvation.

Anorexia nervosa is a disorder, not a place.

▶ ~~The reason~~ I missed the exam ~~is~~ because my motorcycle

broke down.

The writer might have changed *because* to *that* (*The reason I missed the exam is that my motorcycle broke down*), but the preceding revision is more concise.

EXERCISE 11–1 Edit the following sentences to untangle mixed constructions. Revisions of lettered sentences appear in the back of the book. Example:

~~By keeping~~ *Keeping* your wrists relaxed while rowing will help you

avoid injury.

a. Using surgical gloves is a precaution now worn by dentists to prevent contact with patients' blood and saliva.
b. A physician, the career my brother is pursuing, requires at least ten years of challenging work.
c. The reason the pharaohs had bad teeth was because tiny particles of sand found their way into Egyptian bread.
d. Recurring bouts of flu among team members set a record for number of games forfeited.

e. In this box contains the key to your future.

1. Early diagnosis of prostate cancer is often curable.
2. Depending on our method of travel and our destination determines how many suitcases we are allowed to pack.
3. Dyslexia is where people have a learning disorder that impairs reading ability.
4. Even though Ellen had heard French spoken all her life, yet she could not write it.
5. In understanding artificial intelligence code is a critical skill for computer game designers.

ON THE WEB > dianahacker.com/rules
Grammar exercises > Clarity > E-ex 11–1 and 11–2

12

Repair misplaced and dangling modifiers.

Modifiers, whether they are single words, phrases, or clauses, should point clearly to the words they modify. As a rule, related words should be kept together.

GRAMMAR CHECKERS can flag split infinitives, such as *to carefully and thoroughly sift* (12d). However, they don't alert you to other misplaced modifiers (*I only ate three radishes*) or dangling modifiers, including danglers like this one: *When a young man, my mother enrolled me in tap dance classes, hoping I would become the next Savion Glover.*

12a Put limiting modifiers in front of the words they modify.

Limiting modifiers such as *only, even, almost, nearly,* and *just* should appear in front of a verb only if they modify the verb: *At first, I couldn't even touch my toes, much less grasp them.* If they limit the meaning of some other word in the sentence, they should be placed in front of that word.

▶ Lasers ~~only~~ destroy the target, leaving the surrounding
   only
   ^

healthy tissue intact.

Only limits the meaning of *the target,* not *destroy.*

▶ The turtle ~~only~~ makes progress when it sticks its neck out.
                only
                ^

Only limits the meaning of the *when* clause.

When the limiting modifier *not* is misplaced, the sentence
usually suggests a meaning the writer did not intend.

▶ In the United States in 1860, all black southerners were ~~not~~
                                                      not
                                                      ^

slaves.

The original sentence says that no black southerners were slaves.
The revision makes the writer's real meaning clear: Some (but not
all) black southerners were slaves.

12b Place phrases and clauses so that readers can see at a glance what they modify.

Although phrases and clauses can appear at some distance
from the words they modify, make sure your meaning is clear.
When phrases or clauses are oddly placed, absurd misreadings
can result.

MISPLACED   The soccer player returned to the clinic where he
            had undergone emergency surgery in 2004 in a
            limousine sent by Adidas.

REVISED   Traveling in a limousine sent by Adidas, the soccer
            player returned to the clinic where he had under-
            gone emergency surgery in 2004.

The revision corrects the false impression that the soccer
player underwent emergency surgery in a limousine.

> *On the walls*
> ~~There~~ are many pictures of comedians who have performed
> ^
> at Gavin's. ~~on the walls.~~
> ^

The comedians weren't performing on the walls; the pictures were on the walls.

> *150-pound,*
> The robber was described as a six-foot-tall man with a heavy
> ^
> mustache. ~~weighing 150 pounds.~~
> ^

The robber, not the mustache, weighed 150 pounds. The revision makes this clear.

Occasionally the placement of a modifier leads to an ambiguity, in which case two revisions will be possible, depending on the writer's intended meaning.

AMBIGUOUS	The exchange students we met for coffee occasionally questioned us about our latest slang.
CLEAR	The exchange students we occasionally met for coffee questioned us about our latest slang.
CLEAR	The exchange students we met for coffee questioned us occasionally about our latest slang.

In the original version, it was not clear whether the meeting or the questioning happened occasionally. The revisions eliminate the ambiguity.

12c Move awkwardly placed modifiers.

As a rule, a sentence should flow from subject to verb to object, without lengthy detours along the way. When a long adverbial element separates a subject from its verb, a verb from its object, or a helping verb from its main verb, the result is often awkward.

> *A*   *Hong Kong*
> ~~Hong Kong,~~ after more than 150 years of British rule, was
> ^   ^
> transferred back to Chinese control in 1997.

There is no reason to separate the subject, *Hong Kong,* from the verb, *was transferred,* with a long phrase.

EXCEPTION: Occasionally a writer may choose to delay a verb or an object to create suspense. In the following passage, for example, Robert Mueller inserts the *after* phrase between the subject *women* and the verb *walk* to heighten the dramatic effect.

> I asked a Burmese why women, after centuries of following their men, now walk ahead. He said there were many unexploded land mines since the war.   — Robert Mueller

---

ESL English does not allow an adverb to appear between a verb and its object. See 30f.

> *easily*
> ▶ Yolanda lifted ~~easily~~ the fifty-pound weight.
>   ^

12d Avoid split infinitives when they are awkward.

An infinitive consists of *to* plus a verb: *to think, to breathe, to dance.* When a modifier appears between *to* and the verb, an infinitive is said to be "split": *to carefully balance, to completely understand.*

When a long word or a phrase appears between the parts of the infinitive, the result is usually awkward.

> *If possible, the*
> ▶ ~~The~~ patient should try to ~~if possible~~ avoid going up stairs.
>   ^

Attempts to avoid split infinitives can result in equally awkward sentences. When alternative phrasing sounds unnatural, most experts allow — and even encourage — splitting the infinitive.

AWKWARD	We decided actually to enforce the law.
BETTER	We decided to actually enforce the law.

At times, neither the split infinitive nor its alternative sounds particularly awkward. In such situations, you may want to unsplit the infinitive, especially in formal writing.

> ▶ Nursing students learn to ~~accurately~~ record a patient's
>   *accurately.*
>   vital signs/
>   ^

ON THE WEB > **dianahacker.com/rules**
Language Debates > Split infinitives

EXERCISE 12–1 Edit the following sentences to correct misplaced or awkwardly placed modifiers. Revisions of lettered sentences appear in the back of the book. Example:

> *in a telephone survey*
> **Answering questions can be annoying. ~~in a telephone survey.~~**
>   ^   ^

a. Our English professor asked us to very carefully reread the sonnet, looking for subtleties we had missed on a first reading.
b. The monarch arrived in a gold carriage at the gate pulled by four white horses.
c. Rhonda and Sam almost talked all night about her surgery.
d. A coolhunter is a person who can find in the unnoticed corners of modern society the next wave of fashion.
e. All geese do not fly beyond Narragansett for the winter.

1. Carlos sat solemnly and didn't even smile once during the comedy.
2. Angelie wrote about collecting peacock feathers with her uncle David in her class notebook.
3. Several recent studies have encouraged heart patients to more carefully watch their cholesterol levels.
4. The garden's centerpiece is a huge sculpture that was carved by three women called *Walking in Place.*
5. The old Marlboro ads depicted a man on a horse smoking a cigarette.

ON THE WEB > **dianahacker.com/rules**
Electronic grammar exercises > E-ex 12–1 and 12–2

12e Repair dangling modifiers.

A dangling modifier fails to refer logically to any word in the sentence. Dangling modifiers are easy to repair, but they can be hard to recognize, especially in your own writing.

Recognizing dangling modifiers

Dangling modifiers are usually word groups (such as verbal phrases) that suggest but do not name an actor. When a sentence opens with such a modifier, readers expect the subject of the next clause to name the actor. If it doesn't, the modifier dangles.

► *When the driver opened*
~~Opening~~ the window to let out a huge bumblebee, the car
   ^

accidentally swerved into an oncoming car.

► After completing seminary training, ~~women's~~ *women were often denied* access to the
                                                  ^

priesthood. ~~was often denied.~~
            ^

The car didn't open the window; the driver did. The women (not
their access to the priesthood) complete the training.

The following sentences illustrate four common kinds of
dangling modifiers.

DANGLING   *Deciding to join the navy,* the recruiter enthusiasti-
               cally pumped Joe's hand. [Participial phrase]

DANGLING   *Upon entering the doctor's office,* a skeleton
               caught my attention. [Preposition followed by
               a gerund phrase]

DANGLING   *To please the children,* some fireworks were set off a
               day early. [Infinitive phrase]

DANGLING   *Though only sixteen,* UCLA accepted Martha's
               application. [Elliptical clause with an understood
               subject and verb]

These dangling modifiers falsely suggest that the recruiter decided to join the navy, that the skeleton entered the doctor's office, that the fireworks intended to please the children, and that
UCLA is only sixteen years old.

Although most readers will understand the writer's intended meaning in such sentences, the inadvertent humor can
be distracting, and it can make the writer appear foolish.

Repairing dangling modifiers

To repair a dangling modifier, you can revise the sentence in
one of two ways:

1. Name the actor in the subject of the sentence, or
2. name the actor in the modifier.

Depending on your sentence, one of these revision strategies may be more appropriate than the other.

ACTOR NAMED IN SUBJECT

▶ Upon entering the doctor's office, a skeleton. *I noticed* ~~caught my~~
  ~~attention.~~

▶ To please the children, some fireworks *we set off* ~~were set off~~ a day early.

ACTOR NAMED IN MODIFIER

▶ *When Joe decided* ~~Deciding~~ to join the navy, the recruiter enthusiastically
  pumped ~~Joe's~~ *his* hand.

▶ Though only sixteen, UCLA accepted *Martha was* ~~Martha's~~ *her* application.

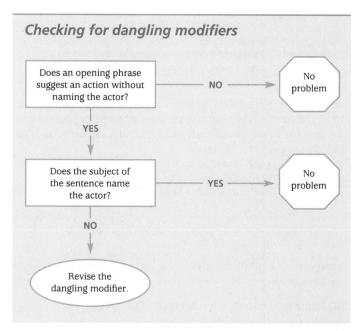

Checking for dangling modifiers

Does an opening phrase suggest an action without naming the actor? —— **NO** ——▶ No problem

↓ **YES**

Does the subject of the sentence name the actor? —— **YES** ——▶ No problem

↓ **NO**

Revise the dangling modifier.

NOTE: You cannot repair a dangling modifier just by moving it. Consider, for example, the sentence about the skeleton. If you put the modifier at the end of the sentence (*A skeleton caught my attention upon entering the doctor's office*), you are still suggesting — absurdly, of course — that the skeleton entered the office. The only way to avoid the problem is to put the word *I* in the sentence, either as the subject or in the modifier.

▶ Upon entering the doctor's office, a skeleton. ~~caught my~~ *I noticed*

~~attention.~~

▶ ~~Upon entering~~ the doctor's office, a skeleton caught my *As I entered*

attention.

ON THE WEB > dianahacker.com/rules
Language Debates > Dangling modifiers

EXERCISE 12–2 Edit the following sentences to correct dangling modifiers. Most sentences can be revised in more than one way. Revisions of lettered sentences appear in the back of the book. Example:

To acquire a degree in almost any field, two science courses. *a student must complete*

~~must be completed.~~

a. At the age of ten, my parents took me on my first balloon ride.
b. To replace the gear mechanism, attached is a form to order the part by mail.
c. Nestled in the cockpit, the pounding of the engine was muffled only slightly by my helmet.
d. After studying polymer chemistry, computer games seemed less complex to Phuong.
e. When a young man, my mother enrolled me in tap dance classes, hoping I would become the next Savion Glover.

1. While working as a ranger in Everglades National Park, a Florida panther crossed the road in front of my truck one night.
2. By following this new procedure, our mailing costs will be reduced significantly.
3. Serving as president of the missionary circle, one of Grandmother's duties is to raise money for the church.

4. After buying an album by Ali Farka Toure, the rich and rolling rhythms of Malian music made more sense to Silas.
5. Understanding the high-tech needs of drivers, the Volkswagen Phaeton has an innovative dashboard design.

ON THE WEB > **dianahacker.com/rules**
Grammar exercises > Clarity > E-ex 12–3 and 12–4

13

Eliminate distracting shifts.

GRAMMAR CHECKERS usually do not flag shifts in point of view or in verb tense, mood, or voice. Even obvious errors, like the following shift in tense, slip right past the grammar checker: *My three-year-old fell into the pool and to my surprise she swims to the shallow end.*

Sometimes grammar checkers mark a shift from direct to indirect question or quotation but do not make any suggestions for revision. You must decide where the structure is faulty and determine how to fix it.

13a Make the point of view consistent in person and number.

The point of view of a piece of writing is the perspective from which it is written: first person (*I* or *we*), second person (*you*), or third person (*he, she, it, one,* or *they*).

The *I* (or *we*) point of view, which emphasizes the writer, is a good choice for informal letters and writing based primarily on personal experience. The *you* point of view, which emphasizes the reader, works well for giving advice or explaining how to do something. The third-person point of view, which emphasizes the subject, is appropriate in formal academic and professional writing.

Writers who are having difficulty settling on an appropriate point of view sometimes shift confusingly from one to another. The solution is to choose a suitable perspective and then stay with it.

▶ One week our class met in a junkyard to practice rescuing a

victim trapped in a wrecked car. We learned to dismantle the
                                                        We   *our*
car with the essential tools. ~~You~~ were graded on ~~your~~ speed
                           ^   ^
       our
and ~~your~~ skill in extricating the victim.
       ^

The writer should have stayed with the *we* point of view. *You* is inappropriate because the writer is not addressing readers directly. *You* should not be used in a vague sense meaning "anyone." (See 23d.)

You need
▶ ~~One needs~~ a password and a credit card number to access
  ^
this database. You can retrieve any number of articles and

will be billed at an hourly rate.

You is an appropriate choice because the writer is giving advice directly to readers.

Police officers are
▶ ~~A police officer is~~ often criticized for always being there when
  ^
they aren't needed and never being there when they are.

Although the writer might have changed *they* to *he or she* (to match the singular *officer*), the revision in the plural is more concise. (See also 17f and 22a.)

EXERCISE 13–1 Edit the following paragraph to eliminate distracting shifts in point of view (person and number).

When online dating first became available, many people thought that it would simplify romance. We believed that you could type in a list of criteria — sense of humor, college education, green eyes, good job — and a database would select the perfect mate. Thousands of people signed up for services and filled out their profiles, confident that true love was only a few mouse clicks away. As it turns out, however, virtual dating is no easier than traditional dating. I still have to contact the people I find, exchange e-mails and phone calls, and meet him in the real world. Although a database might produce a list of possibilities and screen out obviously undesirable people, you can't predict

chemistry. More often than not, people who seem perfect online just don't click in person. Electronic services do help a single person expand their pool of potential dates, but it's no substitute for the hard work of romance.

13b Maintain consistent verb tenses.

Consistent verb tenses clearly establish the time of the actions being described. When a passage begins in one tense and then shifts without warning and for no reason to another, readers are distracted and confused.

▶ There was no way I could fight the current and win. Just as I
was losing hope, a stranger ~~jumps~~ *jumped* off a passing boat and ~~swims~~ *swam*
toward me.

Writers often encounter difficulty with verb tenses when writing about literature. Because fictional events occur outside the time frames of real life, the past tense and the present tense may seem equally appropriate. The literary convention, however, is to describe fictional events consistently in the present tense.

▶ The scarlet letter is a punishment sternly placed upon Hester's
breast by the community, and yet it ~~was~~ *is* an extremely fanciful
and imaginative product of Hester's own needlework.

EXERCISE 13–2   Edit the following paragraphs to eliminate distracting shifts in tense.

The English colonists who settled in Massachusetts received assistance at first from the local Indian tribes, but by 1675 there had been friction between the English and the Indians for many years. On June 20 of that year, Metacomet, whom the colonists called Philip, leads the Wampanoag tribe in the first of a series of attacks on the colonial settlements. The war, known today as King Philip's War, rages on for over a year and leaves three thousand Indians and six hundred colonists dead. Metacomet's attempt to retain power in his native land failed. Finally he too is killed, and the victorious colonists sell his wife and children into slavery.

The Indians did not leave records of their unfortunate encounters with the English settlers, but the settlers recorded some of their experiences at the hands of the Indians. One of the few accounts to survive was written by a captured colonist, Mrs. Mary Rowlandson. She is a minister's wife who is kidnapped by an Indian war party and held captive for eleven weeks in 1676. Her history, *A Narrative of the Captivity and Restoration of Mrs. Mary Rowlandson,* tells the story of her experiences with the Wampanoags. Although it did not paint a completely balanced picture of the Indians, Rowlandson's narrative, which is considered a classic early American text, showed its author to be a keen observer of life in an Indian camp.

13c Make verbs consistent in mood and voice.

Unnecessary shifts in the mood of a verb can be as distracting as needless shifts in tense. There are three moods in English: the *indicative*, used for facts, opinions, and questions; the *imperative*, used for orders or advice; and the *subjunctive*, used in certain contexts to express wishes or conditions contrary to fact (see 28e).

The following passage shifts confusingly from the indicative to the imperative mood.

▶ The officers advised us against allowing anyone into our

homes without proper identification. A̶l̶s̶o̶,̶ *They also suggested that we* alert neighbors to

our vacation schedules.

Since the writer's purpose was to report the officers' advice, the revision puts both sentences in the indicative.

A verb may be in either the active voice (with the subject doing the action) or the passive voice (with the subject receiving the action). (See 8a.) If a writer shifts without warning from one to the other, readers may be left wondering why.

▶ When the tickets are ready, the travel agent notifies the

          lists each ticket

  client/, ~~Each ticket is then listed~~ on a daily register form, and

files

  a copy of the itinerary. ~~is filed.~~

The passage began in the active voice (*agent notifies*) and then switched to the passive (*ticket is listed, copy is filed*). Because the active voice is clearer and more direct, the writer changed all the verbs to the active voice.

13d Avoid sudden shifts from indirect to direct questions or quotations.

An indirect question reports a question without asking it: *We asked whether we could visit Mimo.* A direct question asks directly: *Can we visit Mimo?* Sudden shifts from indirect to direct questions are awkward. In addition, sentences containing such shifts are impossible to punctuate because indirect questions must end with a period and direct questions must end with a question mark. (See 38b.)

▶ I wonder whether Karla knew of the theft and, if so, ~~did~~

  whether she reported

  ~~she report~~ it to the police/.

The revision poses both questions indirectly. The writer could also ask both questions directly: *Did Karla know of the theft and, if so, did she report it to the police?*

An indirect quotation reports someone's words without quoting word-for-word: *Annabelle said that she is a Virgo.* A direct quotation presents the exact words of a speaker or writer, set off with quotation marks: *Annabelle said, "I am a Virgo."* Unannounced shifts from indirect to direct quotations are distracting and confusing, especially when the writer fails to insert the necessary quotation marks, as in the following example.

                      asked me not to

▶ Mother said that she would be late for dinner and ~~please do~~

                   came

  ~~not~~ leave for choir practice until Dad ~~comes~~ home.

The revision reports all of the mother's words. The writer could also quote directly: *Mother said, "I will be late for dinner. Please do not leave for choir practice until Dad comes home."*

EXERCISE 13–3 Edit the following sentences to eliminate distracting shifts. Revisions of lettered sentences appear in the back of the book. Example:

> For many first-year engineering students, adjusting to
>
> rigorous courses can be so challenging that ~~you~~ *they* sometimes
>
> feel overwhelmed.

a. A courtroom lawyer has more than a touch of theater in their blood.
b. The interviewer asked if we had brought our proof of birth and citizenship and did we bring our passports.
c. The reconnaissance scout often has to make fast decisions and use sophisticated equipment to keep their team from detection.
d. After the animators finish their scenes, the production designer arranges the clips according to the storyboard. Synchronization notes must also be made for the sound editor and the composer.
e. Madame Defarge is a sinister figure in Dickens's *A Tale of Two Cities*. On a symbolic level, she represents fate; like the Greek Fates, she knitted the fabric of individual destiny.

1. Everyone should protect yourself from the sun, especially on the first day of extensive exposure.
2. Our neighbors told us that the island was being evacuated because of the coming storm. Also, take the northern route to the mainland.
3. Rescue workers put water on her face and lifted her head gently onto a pillow. Finally, she opens her eyes.
4. In my first tai chi class, the sensei asked if I had ever done yoga stretches and did I have good balance.
5. The artist has often been seen as a threat to society, especially when they refuse to conform to conventional standards of taste.

ON THE WEB > dianahacker.com/rules
Grammar exercises > Clarity > E-ex 13–1 to 13–4

14

Emphasize key ideas.

Within each sentence, emphasize your point by expressing it in the subject and verb of an independent clause, the words that receive the most attention from readers (see 14a–14e).

Within longer stretches of prose, you can draw attention to ideas deserving special emphasis by using a variety of techniques, often involving an unusual twist or some element of surprise (see 14f).

14a Coordinate equal ideas; subordinate minor ideas.

When combining two or more ideas in one sentence, you have two choices: coordination or subordination. Choose coordination to indicate that the ideas are equal or nearly equal in importance. Choose subordination to indicate that one idea is less important than another.

GRAMMAR CHECKERS do not catch the problems with coordination and subordination discussed in this section. Not surprisingly, computer programs have no way of sensing the relative importance of ideas.

Coordination

Coordination draws attention equally to two or more ideas. To coordinate single words or phrases, join them with a coordinating conjunction or with a pair of correlative conjunctions (see 62g). To coordinate independent clauses — word groups that could each stand alone as a sentence — join them with a comma and a coordinating conjunction or with a semicolon:

, and	, but	, or	, nor
, for	, so	, yet	;

The semicolon is often accompanied by a conjunctive adverb such as *moreover, furthermore, therefore,* or *however* or by a transitional phrase such as *for example, in other words,* or *as a matter of fact.* (For a longer list, see p. 111.)

Assume, for example, that your intention is to draw equal attention to the following two ideas.

Grandmother lost her sight. Her hearing sharpened.

To coordinate these ideas, you can join them with a comma

Using coordination to combine sentences of equal importance

1. Consider using a comma and a coordinating conjunction. (See 32a.)

, and	, but	, or	, nor
, for	, so	, yet	

▶ In Orthodox Jewish funeral ceremonies, the shroud is a simple linen

        and the

  vestment/. ~~The~~ coffin is plain wood with no adornment.

2. Consider using a semicolon and a conjunctive adverb or transitional phrase. (See 34b.)

also	in addition	now
as a result	in fact	of course
besides	in other words	on the other hand
consequently	in the first place	otherwise
finally	meanwhile	still
for example	moreover	then
for instance	nevertheless	therefore
furthermore	next	thus
however		

                moreover, she

▶ Alicia scored well on the SAT/. ~~She also~~ had excellent grades and a

  record of community service.

3. Consider using a semicolon alone. (See 34a.)

                in

▶ In youth we learn/. ~~In~~ age we understand.

and the coordinating conjunction *but* or with a semicolon and the conjunctive adverb *however*.

> Grandmother lost her sight, but her hearing sharpened.

> Grandmother lost her sight; however, her hearing sharpened.

It is important to choose a coordinating conjunction or conjunctive adverb appropriate to your meaning. In the preceding example, the two ideas contrast with one another, calling for *but* or *however*.

Subordination

To give unequal emphasis to two or more ideas, express the major idea in an independent clause and place any minor ideas in subordinate clauses or phrases. (For specific subordination strategies, see the chart on p. 113.)

Deciding which idea to emphasize is not a matter of right and wrong but is determined by the meaning you intend. Consider the two ideas about Grandmother's sight and hearing.

> Grandmother lost her sight. Her hearing sharpened.

If your purpose is to stress your grandmother's acute hearing rather than her blindness, subordinate the idea about her blindness.

> *As Grandmother lost her sight,* her hearing sharpened.

To focus on your grandmother's growing blindness, subordinate the idea about her hearing.

> *Though her hearing sharpened,* Grandmother gradually lost her sight.

14b Combine choppy sentences.

Short sentences demand attention, so you should use them primarily for emphasis. Too many short sentences, one after the other, make for a choppy style.

If an idea is not important enough to deserve its own sentence, try combining it with a sentence close by. Put any minor ideas in subordinate structures such as phrases or subordinate clauses. (See 64.)

▶ We keep our use of insecticides to a minimum. ~~We are~~
  because we

  concerned about their effect on the environment.

> A minor idea is now expressed in a subordinate clause beginning with *because.*

▶ The Chesapeake and Ohio Canal, is a 184-mile waterway

  constructed in the 1800s. ~~It~~ was a major source of

  transportation for goods during the Civil War.

Using subordination to combine sentences of unequal importance

1. Consider putting the less important idea in a subordinate clause beginning with one of the following words. (See 64b.)

after	before	that	which
although	even though	unless	while
as	if	until	who
as if	since	when	whom
because	so that	where	whose

► ~~My~~ *When my* son asked his grandmother to chaperone the class
trip~~.~~*/* ~~She~~ *she* was thrilled.

► My sister owes much of her recovery to a yoga program~~.~~*/* ~~She~~ *that she* began
~~the program~~ three years ago.

2. Consider putting the less important idea in an appositive phrase. (See 64d.)

► Karate*,* ~~is~~ a discipline based on the philosophy of nonviolence~~.~~*/,*
~~It~~ teaches the art of self-defense.

3. Consider putting the less important idea in a participial phrase. (See 64c.)

► ~~I noticed~~ *Noticing* that smoke had filled the backyard~~.~~*/,* I ran out to see
where it was coming from.

A minor idea is now expressed in an appositive phrase (*a 184-mile waterway constructed in the 1800s*).

► ~~Sister Consilio was~~ *E*nveloped in a black robe with only her
face and hands visible~~.~~*/,* ~~She~~ *Sister Consilio* was an imposing figure.

A minor idea is now expressed in a participial phrase beginning with *Enveloped.*

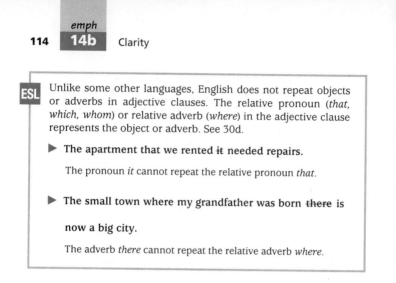

ESL Unlike some other languages, English does not repeat objects or adverbs in adjective clauses. The relative pronoun (*that, which, whom*) or relative adverb (*where*) in the adjective clause represents the object or adverb. See 30d.

▶ The apartment that we rented ~~it~~ needed repairs.

The pronoun *it* cannot repeat the relative pronoun *that*.

▶ The small town where my grandfather was born ~~there~~ is

now a big city.

The adverb *there* cannot repeat the relative adverb *where*.

Although subordination is ordinarily the most effective technique for combining short, choppy sentences, coordination is appropriate when the ideas are equal in importance.

▶ The hospital decides when patients sleep/, ~~It~~ dictates when

    and
they eat/, ~~It~~ tells them when they may be with family.

Equivalent ideas are expressed as parallel elements of a compound predicate: *decides . . . dictates . . . tells.*

EXERCISE 14–1 Combine the following sentences by subordinating minor ideas or by coordinating ideas of equal importance. You must decide which ideas are minor because the sentences are given out of context. Revisions of lettered sentences appear in the back of the book. Example:

Agnes, ~~was another girl I worked with/, She~~ was a hyperac-

tive child.

a. The X-Men comic books and Japanese woodcuts of kabuki dancers were part of Marlena's research project on popular culture. They covered the tabletop and the chairs.
b. Our waitress was costumed in a kimono. She had painted her face white. She had arranged her hair in an upswept lacquered beehive.
c. Students can apply for a spot in the foundation's leadership pro-

gram. The program teaches thinking and communication skills.

d. Shore houses were flooded up to the first floor. Beaches were washed away. Brant's Lighthouse was swallowed by the sea.

e. Laura Thackray is an engineer at Volvo Car Corporation. She designed a pregnant crash-test dummy. She addressed women's safety needs.

1. I noticed that the sky was glowing orange and red. I bent down to crawl into the bunker.

2. The Market Inn is located on North Wharf. It doesn't look very impressive from the outside. The food, however, is excellent.

3. He walked up to the pitcher's mound. He dug his toe into the ground. He swung his arm around backward and forward. Then he threw the ball and struck the batter out.

4. Eryn and Maeve have decided to start a business. They have known each other since kindergarten. They will renovate homes for people with disabilities.

5. The first football card set was released by the Goudey Gum Company in 1933. The set featured only three football players. They were Red Grange, Bronko Nagurski, and Knute Rockne.

ON THE WEB > dianahacker.com/rules
Grammar exercises > Clarity > E-ex 14–1 and 14–2

14c Avoid ineffective or excessive coordination.

Coordinate structures are appropriate only when you intend to draw the reader's attention equally to two or more ideas: *Professor Sakellarios praises loudly, and she criticizes softly.* If one idea is more important than another — or if a coordinating conjunction does not clearly signal the relation between the ideas — you should subordinate the less important idea.

> **INEFFECTIVE** Closets were taxed as rooms, and most colonists stored their clothes in chests or clothes presses.
>
> **IMPROVED** Because closets were taxed as rooms, most colonists stored their clothes in chests or clothes presses.

The revision subordinates the less important idea (*closets were taxed as rooms*) by putting it in a subordinate clause. Notice that the subordinating conjunction *Because* signals the relation between the ideas more clearly than the coordinating conjunction *and*.

Because it is so easy to string ideas together with *and*, writers often rely too heavily on coordination in their rough drafts. The cure for excessive coordination is simple: As you revise, look for opportunities to tuck minor ideas into subordinate clauses or phrases.

> *When*
> ▶ Jason walked over to his new Mini Cooper, ~~and~~ he saw that
> ^
> its windshield had been smashed.

The minor idea has become a subordinate clause beginning with *When*.

> *noticing*
> ▶ My uncle, ~~noticed~~ my frightened look, ~~and~~ told me that
> ^ ^
> Grandma had to feel my face because she was blind.

The less important idea has become a participial phrase modifying the noun *uncle*.

> *After four hours,*
> ▶ ~~Four hours went by, and~~ a rescue truck finally arrived, but by
> ^
> that time we had been evacuated in a helicopter.

Three independent clauses were excessive. The least important idea has become a prepositional phrase.

EXERCISE 14–2 In the following sentences, ideas have been coordinated (joined with a coordinating conjunction or a semicolon). Restructure the sentences by subordinating minor ideas. You must decide which ideas are minor because the sentences are given out of context. Revisions of lettered sentences appear in the back of the book. Example:

> *where they*
> The crew team finally returned to shore, ~~and~~ had a party on
> ^
> *to celebrate*
> the beach ~~and celebrated~~ the start of the season.
> ^

a. These particles are known as "stealth liposomes," and they can hide in the body for a long time without detection.
b. Irena is a competitive gymnast and majors in biochemistry; her goal is to apply her athletic experience and her science degree to a career in sports medicine.

c. Students, textile workers, and labor unions have loudly protested sweatshop abuses, so apparel makers have been forced to examine their labor practices.

d. IRC (Internet Relay Chat) was developed in a European university; it was created as a way for a group of graduate students to talk about projects from their dorm rooms.

e. The cafeteria's new menu has an international flavor, and it includes everything from enchiladas and pizza to pad thai and sauerbraten.

1. Victor switched on his remote-control lawn mower, and it began to shudder and emit clouds of smoke.

2. Iguanas are dependent on ultraviolet rays from the sun, so in the winter months they must be put under ultraviolet-coated lights that can be purchased at most pet stores.

3. The Civil War Trust was founded in 1991; it spearheads a nationwide campaign to protect America's Civil War battlefields.

4. We did not expect to receive so many large orders so quickly, and we are short on inventory.

5. I am certain that Mother spread her love equally among all her children, but she had a way of making each of us feel special in our own way.

14d Do not subordinate major ideas.

If a sentence buries its major idea in a subordinate construction, readers may not give the idea enough attention. Express the major idea in an independent clause and subordinate any minor ideas.

▶ Lanie, who now walks with the help of braces ^*had polio as a child,*^ ~~. had polio as a child.~~

The writer wanted to focus on Lanie's ability to walk, but the original sentence buried this information in an adjective clause. The revision puts the major idea in an independent clause and tucks the less important idea into an adjective clause (*who had polio as a child*).

▶ ^*As*^ I was driving home from my new job, heading down Ranchitos Road, ~~when~~ my car suddenly overheated.

The writer wanted to emphasize that the car overheated, not the fact of driving home. The revision expresses the major idea in an independent clause, the less important idea in an adverb clause (*As I was driving home from my new job*).

14e Do not subordinate excessively.

In attempting to avoid short, choppy sentences, writers sometimes go to the opposite extreme, putting more subordinate ideas into a sentence than its structure can bear. If a sentence collapses of its own weight, occasionally it can be restructured. More often, however, such sentences must be divided.

▶ Our job is to stay between the stacker and the tie machine
                                 If they do,
  to see if the newspapers jam/. ~~in which case~~ we pull the

  bundles off and stack them on a skid, because otherwise

  they would back up in the stacker.

EXERCISE 14–3 In each of the following sentences, the idea that the writer wished to emphasize is buried in a subordinate construction. Restructure each sentence so that the independent clause expresses the major idea and lesser ideas are subordinated. Revisions of lettered sentences appear in the back of the book. Example:

> *Although*
> Catherine has weathered many hardships, ~~although~~ she has
>
> rarely become discouraged. [*Emphasize that Catherine has*
>
> *rarely become discouraged.*]

a. Gina worked as an aide for the relief agency, distributing food and medical supplies. [*Emphasize distributing food and medical supplies.*]
b. Janbir spent every Saturday learning tabla drumming, noticing with each hour of practice that his memory for complex patterns was growing stronger. [*Emphasize Janbir's memory.*]
c. The rotor hit, gouging a hole about an eighth of an inch deep in my helmet. [*Emphasize that the rotor gouged a hole in the helmet.*]
d. My grandfather, who raised his daughters the old-fashioned way, was born eighty years ago in Puerto Rico. [*Emphasize how the grandfather raised his daughters.*]

   e. The Narcan reversed the depressive effect of the drug, saving the patient's life. [*Emphasize that the patient's life was saved.*]

  1. Fatima, who studied Persian miniature painting after college, majored in early childhood education. [*Emphasize Fatima's studies after college.*]

  2. I was losing consciousness when my will to live kicked in. [*Emphasize the will to live.*]

  3. Using a sliding compound miter saw, the carpenter made intricate edges on the cabinets. [*Emphasize the carpenter's use of the saw.*]

  4. Ernie was experimenting with origami to solve some tricky manufacturing problems when he decided to leave engineering and become an artist. [*Emphasize Ernie's decision.*]

  5. As the undulating waves glinted in the sun, the paddlers synchronized their strokes. [*Emphasize the brightness of the waves.*]

ON THE WEB > dianahacker.com/rules
Grammar exercises > Clarity > E-ex 14–3

14f Experiment with techniques for gaining special emphasis.

By experimenting with certain techniques, usually involving some element of surprise, you can draw attention to ideas that deserve special emphasis. Use such techniques sparingly, however, or they will lose their punch. The writer who tries to emphasize everything ends up emphasizing nothing.

Using sentence endings for emphasis

You can highlight an idea simply by withholding it until the end of a sentence. The technique works something like a punch line. In the following example, the sentence's meaning is not revealed until its very last word.

> The only completely consistent people are the dead.
> — Aldous Huxley

Using parallel structure for emphasis

Parallel grammatical structure draws special attention to paired ideas or to items in a series. (See 9.) When parallel ideas are paired, the emphasis falls on words that underscore comparisons or contrasts, especially when they occur at the end of a phrase or clause.

We must *stop talking* about the *American dream* and *start listening*
to the *dreams of Americans.*   — Reubin Askew

In a parallel series, the emphasis falls at the end, so it is
generally best to end with the most dramatic or climactic item
in the series.

Sister Charity enjoyed passing out writing punishments: translate
the Ten Commandments into Latin, type a thousand-word essay
on good manners, copy the New Testament with a quill pen.
                                                        — Marie Visosky, student

Using an occasional short sentence for emphasis

Too many short sentences in a row will fast become monotonous (see 14b), but an occasional short sentence, when played
off against longer sentences in the same passage, will draw attention to an idea.

The great secret, known to internists and learned early in
marriage by internists' wives [or husbands], but still hidden
from the general public, is that most things get better by themselves. Most things, in fact, are better by morning.
                                                        — Lewis Thomas

15

Provide some variety.

When a rough draft is filled with too many same-sounding sentences, try injecting some variety — as long as you can do so
without sacrificing clarity or ease of reading.

> **GRAMMAR CHECKERS** are of little help with sentence variety. It
> takes a human ear to know when and why sentence variety is
> needed.
>   Some programs tell you when you have used the same
> word to open several sentences, but sometimes it is a good idea
> to do so — if you are trying to highlight parallel ideas, for ex-
> ample (see p. 52).

15a Vary your sentence openings.

Most sentences in English begin with the subject, move to the verb, and continue to the object, with modifiers tucked in along the way or put at the end. For the most part, such sentences are fine. Put too many of them in a row, however, and they become monotonous.

Adverbial modifiers, being easily movable, can often be inserted ahead of the subject. Such modifiers might be single words, phrases, or clauses.

▶ *Eventually a*
A few drops of sap ~~eventually~~ began to trickle into the bucket.

Like most adverbs, *eventually* does not need to appear close to the verb it modifies (*began*).

▶ *Just as the sun was coming up, a*
A pair of black ducks flew over the pond. ~~just as the sun was coming up.~~

The adverb clause, which modifies the verb *flew,* is as clear at the beginning of the sentence as it is at the end.

Adjectives and participial phrases can frequently be moved to the beginning of a sentence without loss of clarity.

▶ *Dejected and withdrawn,*
Edward, ~~dejected and withdrawn,~~ nearly gave up his search for a job.

▶ *John and I*
~~John and I,~~ anticipating a peaceful evening, sat down at the campfire to brew a cup of coffee.

TIP: When beginning a sentence with an adjective or a participial phrase, make sure that the subject of the sentence names the person or thing described in the introductory phrase. If it doesn't, the phrase will dangle. (See 12e.)

15b Use a variety of sentence structures.

A writer should not rely too heavily on simple sentences and compound sentences, for the effect tends to be both monotonous and choppy. (See 14b and 14c.) Too many complex or compound-complex sentences, however, can be equally monotonous. If your style tends to one or the other extreme, try to achieve a better mix of sentence types. For a discussion of sentence types, see 65a.

15c Try inverting sentences occasionally.

A sentence is inverted if it does not follow the normal subject-verb-object pattern (see 63c). Many inversions sound artificial and should be avoided except in the most formal contexts. But if an inversion sounds natural, it can provide a welcome touch of variety.

> *Opposite the produce section is a*
> ▶ ̶A̶ refrigerated case of mouth-watering cheeses; ̶i̶s̶ ̶o̶p̶p̶o̶s̶i̶t̶e̶
> ̶t̶h̶e̶ ̶p̶r̶o̶d̶u̶c̶e̶ ̶s̶e̶c̶t̶i̶o̶n̶;̶ a friendly attendant will cut off just the
> amount you want.

The revision inverts the normal subject-verb order by moving the verb, *is,* ahead of its subject, *case.*

> *Set at the top two corners of the stage were huge*
> ▶ ̶H̶u̶g̶e̶ lavender hearts outlined in bright white lights. ̶w̶e̶r̶e̶ ̶s̶e̶t̶
> ̶a̶t̶ ̶t̶h̶e̶ ̶t̶o̶p̶ ̶t̶w̶o̶ ̶c̶o̶r̶n̶e̶r̶s̶ ̶o̶f̶ ̶t̶h̶e̶ ̶s̶t̶a̶g̶e̶.̶

In the revision the subject, *hearts,* appears after the verb, *were set.* Notice that the two parts of the verb are also inverted — and separated from one another — without any awkwardness or loss of meaning.

EXERCISE 15–1   Edit the following paragraph to increase sentence variety.

   Making architectural models is a skill that requires patience and precision. It is an art that illuminates a design. Architects come up with a grand and intricate vision. Draftspersons convert that vision into blueprints. The model maker follows the blueprints. The model maker builds a miniature version of the structure. Modelers can work in traditional materials like wood and clay and paint. Modelers can work in newer materials like Styrofoam and liquid polymers. Some modelers still use cardboard, paper, and glue. Other modelers prefer glue guns, deformable plastic, and thin aluminum and brass wire. The modeler may seem to be making a small mess in the early stages of model building. In the end the modeler has completed a $^1/_{100}$-scale structure. Architect Rem Koolhaas has insisted that plans reveal the logic of a design. He has argued that models expose the architect's vision. The model maker's art makes vision real.

16

Tighten wordy sentences.

Long sentences are not necessarily wordy, nor are short sentences always concise. A sentence is wordy if it can be tightened without loss of meaning.

> **GRAMMAR CHECKERS** flag wordy constructions only occasionally. They sometimes alert you to common redundancies, such as *true fact,* but they overlook more redundancies than they catch. They may miss empty or inflated phrases, such as *in my opinion* and *in order that,* and they rarely identify sentences with needlessly complex structures. Grammar checkers are very good, however, at flagging and suggesting revisions for wordy constructions beginning with *there is* and *there are.*

16a Eliminate redundancies.

Redundancies such as *cooperate together, close proximity, basic essentials,* and *true fact* are a common source of wordiness. There is no need to say the same thing twice.

▶ Twenty-somethings are often ~~thought of or~~ stereotyped as

apathetic even though many are active in political and

service groups.

▶ Daniel ~~is now employed~~ at a private rehabilitation center
   ^works^
~~working~~ as a registered physical therapist.

Though modifiers ordinarily add meaning to the words
they modify, occasionally they are redundant.

▶ Sylvia ~~very hurriedly~~ scribbled her name, address, and phone

number on a greasy napkin.

▶ Joel was determined ~~in his mind~~ to lose weight.

The words *scribbled* and *determined* already contain the notions
suggested by the modifiers *very hurriedly* and *in his mind.*

16b Avoid unnecessary repetition of words.

Though words may be repeated deliberately, for effect, repetitions will seem awkward if they are clearly unnecessary. When
a more concise version is possible, choose it.

▶ Our fifth patient, in room six, is a mentally ill. ~~patient.~~
   ^

▶ The best teachers help each student to ~~become a better~~
   ^grow^

~~student~~ both academically and emotionally.

16c Cut empty or inflated phrases.

An empty phrase can be cut with little or no loss of meaning.
Common examples are introductory word groups that apologize or hedge: *in my opinion, I think that, it seems that, one must
admit that,* and so on.

▶ ~~In my opinion,~~ our current immigration policy is misguided.
   ^O^

Readers understand without being told that they are hearing the
writer's opinion.

Inflated phrases can be reduced to a word or two without loss of meaning.

INFLATED	CONCISE
along the lines of	like
as a matter of fact	in fact
at all times	always
at the present time	now, currently
at this point in time	now, currently
because of the fact that	because
by means of	by
by virtue of the fact that	because
due to the fact that	because
for the purpose of	for
for the reason that	because
have the ability to	be able to, can
in light of the fact that	because
in order to	to
in spite of the fact that	although, though
in the event that	if
in the final analysis	finally
in the nature of	like
in the neighborhood of	about
until such time as	until

▶ We will file the appropriate papers ~~in the event that~~ *if* we are

unable to meet the deadline.

16d Simplify the structure.

If the structure of a sentence is needlessly indirect, try simplifying it. Look for opportunities to strengthen the verb.

▶ The CEO claimed that because of volatile market conditions

she could not ~~make an~~ estimate ~~of~~ the company's future

profits.

The verb *estimate* is more vigorous and concise than *make an estimate of*.

The colorless verbs *is, are, was,* and *were* frequently generate excess words.

> *monitors and balances*
> ▶ Eduartina ~~is responsible for monitoring and balancing~~ the
>   ^
>
> budgets for travel, contract services, and personnel.

The revision is more direct and concise. Actions originally appearing in subordinate structures have become verbs replacing *is*.

The expletive constructions *there is* and *there are* (or *there was* and *there were*) can also generate excess words. The same is true of expletive constructions beginning with *it*. (See 63c.)

>   A
> ▶ ~~There is~~ Another module ~~that~~ tells the story of Charles
>   ^
>
> Darwin and introduces the theory of evolution.

>   A   *must*
> ▶ ~~It is imperative that~~ All police officers follow strict
>   ^   ^
>
> procedures when apprehending a suspect.

Expletive constructions do have legitimate uses, however. For example, they are appropriate when a writer has a good reason for delaying the subject. (See 63c.)

Finally, verbs in the passive voice may be needlessly indirect. When the active voice expresses your meaning as well, use it. (See 8a.)

> *our coaches have recruited*
> ▶ All too often, athletes with marginal academic skills, ~~have~~
>   ^   ^
>
> ~~been recruited by our coaches.~~

16e Reduce clauses to phrases, phrases to single words.

Word groups functioning as modifiers can often be made more compact. Look for any opportunities to reduce clauses to phrases or phrases to single words.

▶ We took a side trip to Monticello, ~~which was~~ the home of

Thomas Jefferson.

silk
▶ For her birthday we gave Jess a stylish vest, ~~made of~~

~~silk.~~
    ^   ^

EXERCISE 16–1   Edit the following sentences for wordiness. Revisions
of lettered sentences appear in the back of the book. Example:

even though
The Wilsons moved into the house ~~in spite of the fact that~~
                                   ^

the back door was only ten yards from the train tracks.

a. Martin Luther King Jr. was a man who set a high standard for future leaders to meet.
b. Arlene has been deeply in love with cooking since she was little
   and could first peek over the edge of a big kitchen tabletop.
c. In my opinion, Bloom's race for the governorship is a futile
   exercise.
d. It is pretty important in being a successful graphic designer to
   have technical knowledge and at one and the same moment an
   eye for color and balance.
e. Your task will be the deliverance of correspondence to employees
   in every building.

1. Seeing the barrels, the driver immediately slammed on his brakes.
2. A really well-stocked bookshelf should have classical literature on
   it as well as important modern works of the current day.
3. China's enormously huge work population has an effect on the
   global world of high-tech manufacturing of things.
4. A typical autocross course consists of at least two straightaways,
   and the rest of the course is made up of numerous slaloms and
   several sharp turns.
5. At breakfast time, Mehrdad always started his day with canta-
   loupe, lemon yogurt, and black coffee.

ON THE WEB > **dianahacker.com/rules**
Grammar exercises > Clarity > E-ex 16–1 to 16–3

Choose appropriate language.

Language is appropriate when it suits your subject, engages your audience, and blends naturally with your own voice.

To some extent, your choice of language will be governed by the conventions of the genre in which you are writing. When in doubt about the conventions of a particular genre — lab reports, informal essays, business memos, and so on — look at models written by experts in the field.

17a Stay away from jargon.

Jargon is specialized language used among members of a trade, profession, or group. Use jargon only when readers will be familiar with it; even then, use it only when plain English will not do as well.

Sentences filled with jargon are likely to be long and lumpy. To revise such sentences, you must rewrite them, usually in fewer words.

> **JARGON**   For years the indigenous body politic of South Africa attempted to negotiate legal enfranchisement without result.

> **REVISED**   For years the indigenous people of South Africa negotiated in vain for the right to vote.

Though a political scientist might feel comfortable with the original version, jargon such as *body politic* and *legal enfranchisement* is needlessly complicated for ordinary readers.

Broadly defined, jargon includes puffed-up language designed more to impress readers than to inform them. The following are common examples from business, government, higher education, and the military, with plain English translations in parentheses.

ameliorate (improve)	exit (leave)
commence (begin)	facilitate (help)
components (parts)	factor (consideration, cause)
endeavor (try)	impact (v.) (affect)

indicator (sign)
optimal (best, most favorable)
parameters (boundaries, limits)
peruse (read, look over)

prior to (before)
utilize (use)
viable (workable)

Sentences filled with jargon are hard to read, and they are often wordy as well.

▶ All ~~employees functioning in the capacity of~~ work-study
          must prove that they are currently enrolled.
  students ~~are required to give evidence of current enrollment.~~

        begin
▶ Mayor Summers will ~~commence~~ his term of office by

  improving   *poor neighborhoods.*
  ~~ameliorating~~ living conditions in ~~economically deprived zones.~~

17b Avoid pretentious language, most euphemisms, and "doublespeak."

Hoping to sound profound or poetic, some writers embroider their thoughts with large words and flowery phrases, language that in fact sounds pretentious. Pretentious language is so ornate and often so wordy that it obscures the thought that lies beneath.

                            difficult
▶ We ~~mere mortals~~ often find ~~that~~ it ~~requires cerebral exertion~~

  face   *harsh*
  to ~~confront~~ the ~~virtually unendurable~~ reality that we all

  die.
  ~~ultimately perish from this life.~~

Related to pretentious language are euphemisms, nice-sounding words or phrases substituted for words thought to sound harsh or ugly. Like pretentious language, euphemisms are wordy and indirect. Unlike pretentious language, they are sometimes appropriate. It is our social custom, for example, to use euphemisms when speaking or writing about excretion (*I have to go to the bathroom*), sexual intercourse (*They did not sleep together until they were married*), and the like. We may also use euphemisms out of concern for someone's feelings.

Telling parents, for example, that their daughter is "unmotivated" is more sensitive than saying she's lazy. Tact or politeness, then, can justify an occasional euphemism.

Most euphemisms, however, are needlessly evasive or even deceitful. Like pretentious language, they obscure the intended meaning.

EUPHEMISM	PLAIN ENGLISH
adult entertainment	pornography
preowned automobile	used car
economically deprived	poor
selected out	fired
negative savings	debts
strategic withdrawal	retreat or defeat
revenue enhancers	taxes
chemical dependency	drug addiction
downsize	lay off
correctional facility	prison

The term *doublespeak* applies to any deliberately evasive or deceptive language, including euphemisms. Doublespeak is especially common in politics, where missiles are named "Peacekeepers," airplane crashes are termed "uncontrolled contact with the ground," and a military retreat is called "tactical redeployment." Business also gives us its share of doublespeak. When the manufacturer of a pacemaker writes that its product "may result in adverse health consequences in pacemaker-dependent patients as a result of sudden 'no output' failure," it takes an alert reader to grasp the message: The pacemakers might suddenly stop functioning and cause a heart attack or even death.

> **GRAMMAR CHECKERS** rarely identify jargon and only occasionally flag pretentious language. Sometimes they flag language that is acceptable in academic writing. You should be alert to your own use of jargon and pretentious language and simplify it whenever possible. If your grammar checker continually questions language that is appropriate in an academic setting, check to see whether you can set it to a formal style level.

EXERCISE 17–1 Edit the following sentences to eliminate jargon, pretentious or flowery language, euphemisms, and doublespeak. You may need to make substantial changes in some sentences. Revisions of lettered sentences appear in the back of the book. Example:

After two weeks in the legal department, Sue has ~~worked~~ ^*mastered*^

~~into~~ the routine,^*office*^ ~~of the office,~~ and her ~~functional and self-~~^*performance has*^

~~management skills have~~ exceeded all expectations.

a. In my youth, my family was under the constraints of difficult material circumstances.
b. In order that I may increase my expertise in the area of delivery of services to clients, I feel that participation in this conference will be beneficial.
c. Have you ever been accused of flagellating a deceased equine?
d. Governmentally sanctioned investigations into the continued value of after-school programs have begun to indicate a perceived need in the public realm at large.
e. Passengers should endeavor to finalize the customs declaration form prior to exiting the aircraft.

1. We learned that the mayor had been engaging in a creative transfer of city employees' pension funds.
2. After a cursory examination of brand-new research materials on textiles, Patricia and the members of her team made the decision to engage in a series of visits to fashion manufacturers in the local vicinity.
3. The nurse announced that there had been a negative patient-care outcome due to a therapeutic misadventure on the part of the surgeon.
4. A generally leisurely pace at the onset of tai chi exercises can yield a variety of beneficial points within a short period of time.
5. The bottom line is that the company is experiencing a negative cash flow.

ON THE WEB > dianahacker.com/rules
Grammar exercises > Clarity > E-ex 17–1

17c Avoid obsolete and invented words.

Although dictionaries list obsolete words such as *recomfort* and *reechy,* these words are not appropriate for current use. Invented words (also called *neologisms*) are too recently created to be part of standard English. Many invented words fade out of use without becoming standard. *Bling* and *technobabble* are neologisms that may not last. *Printout* and *flextime* are no longer neologisms; they have become standard English. Avoid using invented words in formal writing unless they are given in the dictionary as standard or unless no other word expresses your meaning.

17d In most contexts, avoid slang, regional expressions, and nonstandard English.

Slang is an informal and sometimes private vocabulary that expresses the solidarity of a group such as teenagers, hip-hop musicians, or football fans; it is subject to more rapid change than standard English. For example, the slang teenagers use to express approval changes every few years; *cool, groovy, neat, awesome, phat,* and *sweet* have replaced one another within the last three decades. Sometimes slang becomes so widespread that it is accepted as standard vocabulary. *Jazz,* for example, started out as slang but is now generally accepted to describe a style of music.

Although slang has a certain vitality, it is a code that not everyone understands, and it is very informal. Therefore, it is inappropriate in most writing.

▶ If we don't begin studying for the final, a whole semester's
      will be wasted.
   work ~~is going down the tubes.~~
        ^

                                              disgust you.
▶ The government's "filth" guidelines for food will ~~gross you out.~~
                                                        ^

Regional expressions are common to a group in a geographical area. *Let's talk with the bark off* (for *Let's speak frankly*) is an expression in the southern United States, for example. Regional expressions have the same limitations as slang and are therefore inappropriate in most writing.

▶ John was four blocks from the house before he remembered
      turn on
   to ~~cut~~ the headlights. ~~on.~~
      ^   ^

▶ I'm not ~~for~~ sure, but I think the dance has been postponed.

Standard English is the language used in all academic, business, and professional fields. Nonstandard English is spoken by people with a common regional or social heritage. Although nonstandard English may be appropriate when spoken within a close group, it is out of place in most formal and informal writing.

▶ The counselor ~~have~~ *has* so many problems in her own life that she ~~don't~~ *doesn't* know how to advise anyone else.

If you speak a nonstandard dialect, try to identify the ways in which your dialect differs from standard English. Look especially for the following features of nonstandard English, which commonly cause problems in writing.

Misuse of verb forms such as *began* and *begun* (See 27a.)

Omission of *-s* endings on verbs (See 27c.)

Omission of *-ed* endings on verbs (See 27d.)

Omission of necessary verbs (See 27e.)

Double negatives (See 26d.)

17e Choose an appropriate level of formality.

In deciding on a level of formality, consider both your subject and your audience. Does the subject demand a dignified treatment, or is a relaxed tone more suitable? Will readers be put off if you assume too close a relationship with them, or might you alienate them by seeming too distant?

For most college and professional writing, some degree of formality is appropriate. In a letter applying for a job, for example, it is a mistake to sound too breezy and informal.

TOO INFORMAL	I'd like to get that technician job you've got in the paper.
MORE FORMAL	I would like to apply for the technician position listed in the *Peoria Journal Star*.

Informal writing is appropriate for private letters, personal e-mail and instant messages, and business correspondence between close associates. Like spoken conversation, it allows contractions (*don't, I'll*) and colloquial words (*kids, buddy*). Vocabulary and sentence structure are rarely complex.

In choosing a level of formality, above all be consistent. When a writer's voice shifts from one level of formality to another, readers receive mixed messages.

▶ Bob's pitching lesson ~~commenced~~ *began* with his famous sucker
 ^

 which he threw
pitch, ~~implemented~~ as a slow ball coming behind a fast windup.
 ^

Formal words such as *commenced* and *implemented* clash with appropriate informal terms such as *sucker pitch* and *fast windup*.

> ✓ **GRAMMAR CHECKERS** rarely flag slang and informal language. They do, however, flag contractions. If your ear tells you that a contraction such as *isn't* or *doesn't* strikes the right tone, stay with it.

17f Avoid sexist language.

Sexist language is language that stereotypes or demeans men or women, usually women. Using nonsexist language is a matter of courtesy — of respect for and sensitivity to the feelings of others.

Recognizing sexist language

Some sexist language is easy to recognize because it reflects genuine contempt for women: referring to a woman as a "chick," for example, or calling a lawyer a "lady lawyer," or saying in an advertisement, "If our new sports car were a lady, it would get its bottom pinched."

Other forms of sexist language are less blatant. The following practices, while they may not result from conscious sexism, reflect stereotypical thinking: referring to nurses as women and doctors as men, using different conventions when naming or identifying women and men, or assuming that all of one's readers are men.

STEREOTYPICAL LANGUAGE

After the nursing student graduates, *she* must face a difficult state board examination. [Not all nursing students are women.]

Running for city council are Jake Stein, an attorney, and *Mrs. Cynthia Jones, a professor of English and *mother of three*. [The title *Mrs.* and the phrase *mother of three* are irrelevant.]

Wives of senior government officials are required to report any gifts they receive that are valued at more than $100. [Not all senior government officials are men.]

Still other forms of sexist language result from outmoded traditions. The pronouns *he, him,* and *his,* for instance, were traditionally used to refer generically to persons of either sex.

GENERIC *HE* OR *HIS*

When a physician is harassed by managed care professionals, *he* may be tempted to leave the profession.

A journalist is stimulated by *his* deadline.

Today, however, such usage is widely viewed as sexist because it excludes women and encourages sex-role stereotyping— the view that men are somehow more suited than women to be doctors, journalists, and so on.

Like the pronouns *he, him,* and *his,* the nouns *man* and *men* were once used indefinitely to refer to persons of either sex. Current usage demands gender-neutral terms for references to both men and women.

INAPPROPRIATE	APPROPRIATE
chairman	chairperson, moderator, chair, head
clergyman	member of the clergy, minister, pastor
congressman	member of Congress, representative, legislator
fireman	firefighter
foreman	supervisor
mailman	mail carrier, postal worker, letter carrier
(to) man	to operate, to staff
mankind	people, humans
manpower	personnel

INAPPROPRIATE	APPROPRIATE
policeman	police officer
salesman	salesperson, sales associate, salesclerk
weatherman	weather forecaster, meteorologist
workman	worker, laborer

GRAMMAR CHECKERS are good at flagging obviously sexist terms, such as *mankind* and *fireman,* but they do not flag language that might be demeaning to women (*woman doctor*) or stereotypical (referring to assistants as women and lawyers as men, for instance). They also have no way of identifying the generic use of *he* or *his* (*An obstetrician is available to his patients at all hours*). You must use your common sense to tell when a word or a construction is offensive.

ON THE WEB > dianahacker.com/rules
Language Debates > Sexist language

Revising sexist language

When revising sexist language, be sparing in your use of the wordy constructions *he or she* and *his or her*. Although these constructions are fine in small doses, they become awkward when repeated throughout an essay. A better revision strategy is to write in the plural; yet another strategy is to recast the sentence so that the problem does not arise.

SEXIST

When a physician is harassed by managed care professionals, *he* may be tempted to leave the profession.

A good designer chooses *her* projects carefully.

ACCEPTABLE BUT WORDY

When a physician is harassed by managed care professionals, *he or she* may be tempted to leave the profession.

A good designer chooses *his or her* projects carefully.

BETTER: USING THE PLURAL

When *physicians* are harassed by managed care professionals, *they* may be tempted to leave the profession.

Good designers choose *their* projects carefully.

BETTER: RECASTING THE SENTENCE

When harassed by managed care professionals, a *physician* may be tempted to leave the profession.

A good designer chooses projects carefully.

For more examples of these revision strategies, see 22.

EXERCISE 17–2 Edit the following sentences to eliminate sexist language or sexist assumptions. Revisions of lettered sentences appear in the back of the book. Example:

> *Scholarship athletes*   *their*
> A scholarship athlete must be as concerned about his
>   ^   ^
>   *they are*   *their*
> academic performance as he is about his athletic
>   ^   ^
>
> performance.

a. Mrs. Geralyn Farmer, who is the mayor's wife, is the chief surgeon at University Hospital. Dr. Paul Green is her assistant.
b. Every applicant wants to know how much he will make.
c. An elementary school teacher should understand the concept of nurturing if she intends to be a success.
d. Every student of high-tech architecture picks his favorite when he studies such inspirational architects as Renzo Piano and Zaha Hadid.
e. If man does not stop polluting his environment, mankind will destroy the Earth.

1. A fireman often spends his off-duty time giving fire safety presentations in local schools.
2. The chairman for the new program in digital art is Ariana Tamlin, an accomplished portrait painter, computer programmer, and cookie baker.
3. In the gubernatorial race, Lena Weiss, a defense lawyer and mother of two, easily defeated Harvey Tower, an architect.
4. Recent military history has shown that lady combat pilots are as skilled, reliable, and resourceful as men.
5. An emergency room head nurse must know how to use sophisticated digital equipment if she is to keep track of all her patients' data and guide her medical team.

ON THE WEB > dianahacker.com/rules
Grammar exercises > Clarity > E-ex 17–2

17g Revise language that may offend groups of people.

Obviously it is impolite to use offensive terms such as *Polack*, *redneck*, and *crippled*. But biased language can take more subtle forms. Because language evolves over time, names once thought acceptable may become offensive. When describing groups of people, choose names that the groups currently use to describe themselves.

▶ North Dakota takes its name from the ~~Indian~~ *Lakota* word meaning

   "friend" or "ally."

▶ Many ~~Oriental~~ *Asian* immigrants have recently settled in our small

   town in Tennessee.

Negative stereotypes (such as "drives like a teenager" or "haggard as an old crone") are of course offensive. But you should avoid stereotyping a person or a group even if you believe your generalization to be positive.

▶ It was no surprise that Greer, ~~a Chinese American,~~ *an excellent math and science student,* was

   selected for the honors chemistry program.

18

Find the exact words.

Two reference works (or their online equivalents) will help you find words to express your meaning exactly: a good dictionary, such as *The American Heritage Dictionary* or *Merriam-Webster's Collegiate Dictionary,* and a book of synonyms and antonyms, such as *Roget's International Thesaurus.*

> **GRAMMAR CHECKERS** flag some nonstandard idioms, such as *comply to,* but few clichés. They do not identify commonly confused words, such as *principal* and *principle* or misused word forms, such as *significance* and *significant.* You must be alert for such words and use your dictionary if you are unsure of the correct form. Grammar checkers are of little help with the other problems discussed in 18: choosing words with appropriate connotations, using concrete language, and using figures of speech appropriately.

18a Select words with appropriate connotations.

In addition to their strict dictionary meanings (or *denotations*), words have *connotations,* emotional colorings that affect how readers respond to them. The word *steel* denotes "made of or resembling commercial iron that contains carbon," but it also calls up a cluster of images associated with steel, such as the sensation of touching it. These associations give the word its connotations — cold, smooth, unbending.

If the connotation of a word does not seem appropriate for your purpose, your audience, or your subject matter, you should change the word. When a more appropriate synonym does not come quickly to mind, consult a dictionary or a thesaurus.

> *slender*
▶ The model was ~~skinny~~ and fashionable.

> The connotation of the word *skinny* is too negative.

> *sweat*
▶ As I covered the boats with marsh grass, the ~~perspiration~~ I

> had worked up made the cold morning air seem even colder.

> The term *perspiration* is too dainty for the context, which suggests vigorous exercise.

18b Prefer specific, concrete nouns.

Unlike general nouns, which refer to broad classes of things, specific nouns point to definite and particular items. *Film,* for example, names a general class, *fantasy film* names a narrower class, and *Lord of the Rings: Return of the King* is more specific still. Other examples: *team, football team, Denver Broncos; music, symphony, Beethoven's Ninth.*

Unlike abstract nouns, which refer to qualities and ideas (*justice, beauty, realism, dignity*), concrete nouns point to immediate, often sensory experience and to physical objects (*steeple, asphalt, lilac, stone, garlic*).

Specific, concrete nouns express meaning more vividly than general or abstract ones. Although general and abstract language is sometimes necessary to convey your meaning, ordinarily prefer specific, concrete alternatives.

▶ The senator spoke about the challenges of the future:

 pollution, dwindling resources, and terrorism.
 ~~the environment and world peace.~~
 ^

Nouns such as *thing, area, aspect, factor,* and *individual* are especially dull and imprecise.

 rewards.
▶ A career in city planning offers many ~~things.~~
 ^

 experienced technician.
▶ Try pairing a trainee with an ~~individual with technical~~
 ^
 ~~experience.~~

18c Do not misuse words.

If a word is not in your active vocabulary, you may find yourself misusing it, sometimes with embarrassing consequences. When in doubt, check the dictionary.

 climbing
▶ The fans were ~~migrating~~ up the bleachers in search of seats.
 ^

 avail.
▶ Mrs. Johnson tried to fight but to no ~~prevail.~~
 ^

 permeated
▶ The Internet has so ~~diffused~~ our culture that it touches all
 ^
 segments of society.

Be especially alert for misused word forms — using a noun such as *absence, significance,* or *persistence,* for example, when your meaning requires the adjective *absent, significant,* or *persistent.*

    persistent
▶ Most dieters are not ~~persistence~~ enough to make a permanent
                             ^

change in their eating habits.

EXERCISE 18-1 Edit the following sentences to correct misused words. Revisions of lettered sentences appear in the back of the book. Example:

                                   all-absorbing.
The training required for a ballet dancer is ~~all-absorbent.~~
                                         ^

a. We regret this delay; thank you for your patients.
b. Ada's plan is to require education and experience to prepare herself for a position as property manager.
c. Tiger Woods, the penultimate competitor, has earned millions of dollars just in endorsements.
d. Many people take for granite that public libraries have up-to-date networked computer systems.
e. The affect of Gao Xinjian's novels on Chinese exiles is hard to gauge.

1. Waste, misuse of government money, security and health violations, and even pilfering have become major dilemmas in some government agencies.
2. Designers of handheld devices know that changes in ambience temperatures can damage the tiny circuit boards.
3. Grand Isle State Park is surrounded on three sides by water.
4. The Old World nuance of the restaurant intrigued us.
5. The person who complained to the human resources manager wishes to remain unanimous.

ON THE WEB > dianahacker.com/rules
    Grammar exercises > Clarity > E-ex 18–1

18d   Use standard idioms.

Idioms are speech forms that follow no easily specified rules. The English say "Maria went *to hospital,*" an idiom strange to

American ears, which are accustomed to hearing *the* in front of *hospital*. Native speakers of a language seldom have problems with idioms, but prepositions sometimes cause trouble, especially when they follow certain verbs and adjectives. When in doubt, consult a dictionary.

UNIDIOMATIC	IDIOMATIC
abide with (a decision)	abide by (a decision)
according with	according to
agree to (an idea)	agree with (an idea)
angry at (a person)	angry with (a person)
capable to	capable of
comply to	comply with
desirous to	desirous of
different than (a person or thing)	different from (a person or thing)
intend on doing	intend to do
off of	off
plan on doing	plan to do
preferable than	preferable to
prior than	prior to
superior than	superior to
sure and	sure to
try and	try to
type of a	type of

ESL Because idioms follow no particular rules, you must learn them individually. You may find it helpful to keep a list of idioms that you frequently encounter in conversation and in reading. For idiomatic combinations of adjectives and prepositions (such as *afraid of*), see 31c. For idiomatic combinations of verbs and prepositions (such as *search for*), see 31d.

EXERCISE 18–2 Edit the following sentences to eliminate errors in the use of idiomatic expressions. If a sentence is correct, write "correct" after it. Answers to lettered sentences appear in the back of the book. Example:

We agreed to abide ~~with~~ *by* the decision of the judge.

a. Queen Anne was so angry at Sarah Churchill that she refused to see her again.
b. Jean-Pierre's ambitious travel plans made it impossible for him to comply with the graduate program's residency requirement.

c. The parade moved off of the street and onto the beach.
d. The frightened refugees intend on making the dangerous trek across the mountains.
e. What type of a wedding are you planning?

1. Be sure and report on the danger of releasing genetically engineered bacteria into the atmosphere.
2. Why do you assume that embezzling bank assets is so different than robbing the bank?
3. The wilderness guide seemed capable to show us where the trail of petroglyphs was located.
4. In Evan's cautious mind, packing his own parachute seemed preferable to letting an indifferent teenager fold all that silk and cord into a small pack.
5. Andrea plans on joining the Peace Corps after graduation.

ON THE WEB > **dianahacker.com/rules**
Grammar exercises > Clarity > E-ex 18–2

18e Do not rely heavily on clichés.

The pioneer who first announced that he had "slept like a log" no doubt amused his companions with a fresh and unlikely comparison. Today, however, that comparison is a cliché, a saying that has lost its dazzle from overuse. No longer can it surprise.

To see just how dully predictable clichés are, put your hand over the right-hand column in the following list and then finish the phrases on the left.

cool as a	cucumber
beat around	the bush
blind as a	bat
busy as a	bee, beaver
crystal	clear
dead as a	doornail
out of the frying pan and	into the fire
light as a	feather
like a bull	in a china shop
playing with	fire
nutty as a	fruitcake
selling like	hotcakes
starting out at the bottom	of the ladder
water under the	bridge
white as a	sheet, ghost
avoid clichés like the	plague

The cure for clichés is frequently simple: Just delete them. When this won't work, try adding some element of surprise. One student, for example, who had written that she had butterflies in her stomach, revised her cliché like this:

> If all of the action in my stomach is caused by butterflies, there must be a horde of them, with horseshoes on.

The image of butterflies wearing horseshoes is fresh and unlikely, not dully predictable like the original cliché.

ON THE WEB > dianahacker.com/rules
Language Debates > Clichés

18f Use figures of speech with care.

A figure of speech is an expression that uses words imaginatively (rather than literally) to make abstract ideas concrete. Most often, figures of speech compare two seemingly unlike things to reveal surprising similarities.

In a *simile,* the writer makes the comparison explicitly, usually by introducing it with *like* or *as: By the time cotton had to be picked, Grandfather's neck was as red as the clay he plowed.* In a *metaphor,* the *like* or *as* is omitted, and the comparison is implied. For example, in the Old Testament Song of Solomon, a young woman compares the man she loves to a fruit tree: "With great delight I sat in his shadow, and his fruit was sweet to my taste."

Although figures of speech are useful devices, writers sometimes use them without thinking through the images they evoke. The result is sometimes a *mixed metaphor,* the combination of two or more images that don't make sense together.

▶ Crossing Utah's salt flats in his new convertible, my father flew
    at jet speed.
    ~~under a full head of steam.~~
    ^

Flew suggests an airplane, while *under a full head of steam* suggests a steamboat or a train. To clarify the image, the writer should stick with one comparison or the other.

▶ Our office decided to put all controversial issues on a

back burner ~~in a holding pattern~~ until the annual meeting

was over.

Here the writer is mixing stoves and airplanes. Simply deleting one of the images corrects the problem.

EXERCISE 18–3 Edit the following sentences to replace worn-out expressions and clarify mixed figures of speech. Revisions of lettered sentences appear in the back of the book. Example:

the color drained from his face.

When he heard about the accident, ~~he turned white as a~~

~~sheet.~~

a. John stormed into the room like a bull in a china shop.
b. Some people insist that they'll always be there for you, even when they haven't been before.
c. The Cubs easily beat the Mets, who were in the soup early in the game today at Wrigley Field.
d. We ironed out the sticky spots in our relationship.
e. My mother accused me of beating around the bush when in fact I was just talking off the top of my head.

1. Patricia was used to burning the candle at both ends to get her assignments done.
2. No matter how many books he reads, André can never seem to quench his hunger for knowledge.
3. In an era of cutbacks and outsourcing, the best high-tech workers discover that being a jack of all trades is a solid gold key to continued success.
4. There are too many cooks in the broth at corporate headquarters.
5. Juanita told Kyle that keeping skeletons in the closet would be playing with fire.

ON THE WEB > dianahacker.com/rules
Grammar exercises > Clarity > E-ex 18–3

Grammar

19

Repair sentence fragments.

A sentence fragment is a word group that pretends to be a sentence. Sentence fragments are easy to recognize when they appear out of context, like these:

> When the cat leaped onto the table.

> Running for the bus.

> And immediately popped their flares and life vests.

When fragments appear next to related sentences, however, they are harder to spot.

> We had just sat down to dinner. When the cat leaped onto the table.

> I tripped and twisted my ankle. Running for the bus.

> The pilots ejected from the burning plane, landing in the water not far from the ship. And immediately popped their flares and life vests.

Recognizing sentence fragments

To be a sentence, a word group must consist of at least one full independent clause. An independent clause has a subject and a verb, and it either stands alone or could stand alone.

To test whether a word group is a complete sentence or a fragment, use the flowchart on page 149. By using the flowchart, you can see exactly why *When the cat leaped onto the table* is a fragment: It has a subject (*cat*) and a verb (*leaped*), but it begins with a subordinating word (*When*). *Running for the bus* is a fragment because it lacks a subject and a verb (*Running* is a verbal, not a verb). *And immediately popped their flares and life vests* is a fragment because it lacks a subject. (See also 64b and 64c.)

Test for fragments

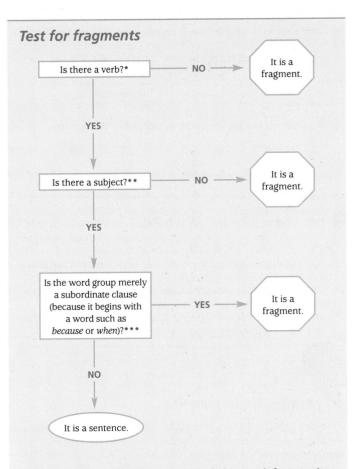

* Do not mistake verbals for verbs. A verbal is a verb form (such as *walking, to act*) that does not function as a verb of a clause. (See 64c.)
** The subject of a sentence may be *you,* understood. (See 63a.)
*** A sentence may open with a subordinate clause, but the sentence must also include an independent clause. (See 19a and 65a.)

If you find any fragments, try one of these methods of revision:

1. Attach the fragment to a nearby sentence.
2. Turn the fragment into a sentence.

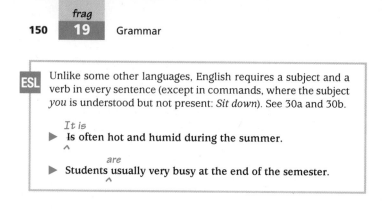

ESL Unlike some other languages, English requires a subject and a verb in every sentence (except in commands, where the subject *you* is understood but not present: *Sit down*). See 30a and 30b.

▶ *It is*
Is often hot and humid during the summer.
  ^

▶ Students usually very busy at the end of the semester.
        are
           ^

GRAMMAR CHECKERS can flag as many as half of the sentence fragments in a sample; but that means, of course, that they miss half or more of them. If fragments are a serious problem for you, you will still need to proofread for them.

Sometimes the grammar checker will identify "false positives," sentences that it flags but that are not fragments. For example, a grammar checker flagged this complete sentence as a possible fragment: *I bent down to crawl into the bunker.* When a program spots a possible fragment, you should check to see if it is really a fragment by using the flowchart on page 149.

Repairing sentence fragments

You can repair most fragments in one of two ways: Either pull the fragment into a nearby sentence or turn the fragment into a sentence.

▶ We had just sat down to dinner./ When the cat leaped onto
                                when
        ^
the table.

▶ I tripped and twisted my ankle. Running for the bus.
  Running for the bus,
  ^

▶ The pilots ejected from the burning plane, landing in the
water not far from the ship. And immediately popped their
                             They
                               ^
flares and life vests.

19a Attach fragmented subordinate clauses or turn them into sentences.

A subordinate clause is patterned like a sentence, with both a subject and a verb, but it begins with a word that marks it as subordinate. The following words commonly introduce subordinate clauses.

after	even though	so that	when	whom
although	how	than	where	whose
as	if	that	whether	why
as if	in order that	though	which	
because	rather than	unless	while	
before	since	until	who	

Subordinate clauses function within sentences as adjectives, as adverbs, or as nouns. They cannot stand alone. (See 64b.)

Most fragmented clauses beg to be pulled into a sentence nearby.

▶ Americans have come to fear the West Nile virus/ ~~Because~~ *because*

it is transmitted by the common mosquito.

Because introduces a subordinate clause. (For punctuation of a subordinate clause appearing at the end of a sentence, see 33f.)

▶ Although we seldom get to see wildlife in the city/, ~~At~~ *at* the zoo

we can still find some of our favorites.

Although introduces a subordinate clause. (For punctuation of subordinate clauses appearing at the beginning of a sentence, see 32b.)

If a fragmented clause cannot be attached to a nearby sentence or if you feel that attaching it would be awkward, try turning the clause into a sentence. The simplest way to do this is to delete the opening word or words that mark it as subordinate.

▶ Population increases and uncontrolled development are

taking a deadly toll on the environment. ~~So that in~~ *In* many

parts of the world, fragile ecosystems are collapsing.

19b Attach fragmented phrases or turn them into sentences.

Like subordinate clauses, phrases function within sentences as adjectives, as adverbs, or as nouns. They cannot stand alone. Fragmented phrases are often prepositional or verbal phrases; sometimes they are appositives, words or word groups that re-name nouns or pronouns. (See 64a, 64c, and 64d.)

Often a fragmented phrase may simply be pulled into a nearby sentence.

▶ The archaeologists worked slowly/, ~~Examining~~ and labeling
  examining
  ^

  every pottery shard they uncovered.

  The word group beginning with *Examining* is a verbal phrase.

▶ Mary is suffering from agoraphobia/, ~~A~~ fear of the outside world.
  a
  ^

  A fear of the outside world is an appositive renaming the noun *agoraphobia*. (For punctuation of appositives, see 32e.)

If a fragmented phrase cannot be pulled into a nearby sentence effectively, turn the phrase into a sentence. You may need to add a subject, a verb, or both.

▶ In the training session, Jamie explained how to access our
  new database. ~~Also~~ how to submit expense reports and
  She also taught us
  ^

  request vendor payments.

  The revision turns the fragmented phrase into a sentence by adding a subject and a verb.

19c Attach other fragmented word groups or turn them into sentences.

Other word groups that are commonly fragmented include parts of compound predicates, lists, and examples introduced by *such as, for example,* or similar expressions.

Parts of compound predicates

A predicate consists of a verb and its objects, complements, and modifiers (see 63b). A compound predicate includes two or more predicates joined by a coordinating conjunction such as *and, but,* or *or.* Because the parts of a compound predicate have the same subject, they should appear in the same sentence.

▶ The woodpecker finch of the Galápagos Islands carefully

and
selects a twig of a certain size and shape/ ~~And~~ then uses this

tool to pry out grubs from trees.

Notice that no comma appears between the parts of a compound predicate. (See 33a.)

Lists

When a list is mistakenly fragmented, it can often be attached to a nearby sentence with a colon or a dash. (See 35a and 39a.)

▶ It has been said that there are only three indigenous

musical
American art forms/: ~~Musical~~ comedy, jazz, and soap

opera.

Sometimes terms like *especially, namely, like,* and *such as* introduce fragmented lists. Such fragments can usually be attached to the preceding sentence.

▶ In the twentieth century, the South produced some

such
great American writers/, ~~Such~~ as Flannery O'Connor,

William Faulkner, Alice Walker, Tennessee Williams, and

Thomas Wolfe.

Examples introduced by for example, in addition, *or similar expressions*

Other expressions that introduce examples or explanations can lead to unintentional fragments. Although you may begin a sentence with some of the following words or phrases, make sure that what follows has a subject and a verb.

also	for example	mainly
and	for instance	or
but	in addition	that is

The easiest solution is often to turn the fragment into a sentence.

▶ If Eric doesn't get his way, he goes into a fit of rage. For

example, ~~lying~~ *he lies* on the floor screaming or ~~opening~~ *opens* the cabinet

doors and then ~~slamming~~ *slams* them shut.

The writer corrected this fragment by adding a subject — *he* — and substituting verbs for the verbals *lying, opening,* and *slamming.*

▶ Janine shoveled her elderly neighbors' driveway. ~~Also~~ *She also* brought

in their mail and shopped for groceries.

19d Exception: Occasionally a fragment may be used deliberately, for effect.

Skilled writers occasionally use sentence fragments for the following special purposes.

FOR EMPHASIS	Following the dramatic Americanization of their children, even my parents grew more publicly confident. *Especially my mother.* — Richard Rodriguez
TO ANSWER A QUESTION	Are these new drug tests 100 percent reliable? *Not in the opinion of most experts.*
AS TRANSITION	*And now the opposing arguments.*

EXCLAMATIONS   *Not again!*

IN ADVERTISING   *Fewer carbs. Improved taste.*

Although fragments are sometimes appropriate, writers and readers do not always agree on when they are appropriate. That's why you will find it safer to write in complete sentences.

EXERCISE 19–1   Repair any fragment by attaching it to a nearby sentence or by rewriting it as a complete sentence. If a word group is correct, write "correct" after it. Revisions of lettered sentences appear in the back of the book. Example:

One Greek island that should not be missed is Mykonos/, A

vacation spot for Europeans and a playground for the rich

and famous.

a. Listening to the CD her sister had sent, Mia was overcome with a mix of emotions. Happiness, homesickness, nostalgia.
b. Cortés and his soldiers were astonished when they looked down from the mountains and saw Tenochtitlán, The magnificent capital of the Aztecs.
c. Although my spoken Spanish is not very good, I can read the language with ease. - if 2nd 1st no comma b/c can stand alone
d. There are several reasons for not eating meat. One reason being is that dangerous chemicals are used throughout the various stages of meat production.
e. To learn how to sculpt beauty from everyday life. This is my intention in studying art and archaeology.

1. The panther lay motionless behind the rock, Waiting silently for its prey.
2. Mother loved to play all our favorite games, Canasta, Monopoly, hide-and-seek, and even kick-the-can. including
3. With machetes, the explorers cut their way through the tall grasses to the edge of the canyon. Then they began to lay out the tapes for the survey. Correct
4. The owners of the online grocery store rented a warehouse in the Market district, An area catering to small businesses.
5. If a woman from the desert tribe showed anger toward her husband, she was whipped in front of the whole village. And shunned by the rest of the women.

EXERCISE 19–2 Repair each fragment in the following passage by attaching it to a sentence nearby or by rewriting it as a complete sentence.

Browsing the Web has become a way of life, but some people think it is destroying a way of life. That we will never recover. Our grandparents and parents feared that the age of television — starting with *Howdy Doody* and progressing through MTV and *America's Next Top Model* — would create generations of viewers who were content to sit for hours and hours. Passively watching images flit before their eyes. Cable television now offers far more passive entertainment than previous generations could ever have imagined. Hundreds of channels and an endless supply of round-the-clock programming. The World Wide Web has the potential to top even cable television's reach. Making access to information easy and available to people anywhere in the world at any time.

One major risk that our grandparents and parents feared is still an issue today. In a culture based on images, the written word may become an endangered species. As our brains eventually adapt to greater and greater levels of stimulation. Will we continue to be able to focus on a page of print? Before we send out too many alarms, however, we should remember that the World Wide Web is based more on words than television ever was. There is some evidence that those who spend time browsing the Web are doing more, not less, reading. Unlike TV viewers. Some Web surfers prefer to run their eyes over the words on the screen. An activity that is, after all, reading. Others download information and read the printouts. While it is true that television has reduced our nation's level of literacy, the World Wide Web could well advance it. Only the future will tell.

ON THE WEB > dianahacker.com/rules
Grammar exercises > Grammar > E-ex 19–1 to 19–3

20

Revise run-on sentences.

Run-on sentences are independent clauses that have not been joined correctly. An independent clause is a word group that can stand alone as a sentence. (See 65a.) When two independent clauses appear in one sentence, they must be joined in one of these ways:

- with a comma and a coordinating conjunction (*and, but, or, nor, for, so, yet*)
- with a semicolon (or occasionally with a colon or a dash)

Recognizing run-on sentences

There are two types of run-on sentences. When a writer puts no mark of punctuation and no coordinating conjunction between independent clauses, the result is called a *fused sentence.*

┌─────────── INDEPENDENT CLAUSE ───────────┐┌───────
FUSED   Air pollution poses risks to all humans it can be

─── INDEPENDENT CLAUSE ───┐
deadly for asthma sufferers.

A far more common type of run-on sentence is the *comma splice* — two or more independent clauses joined with a comma but without a coordinating conjunction. In some comma splices, the comma appears alone.

COMMA   Air pollution poses risks to all humans, it can be
SPLICE   deadly for asthma sufferers.

In other comma splices, the comma is accompanied by a joining word that is *not* a coordinating conjunction. There are only seven coordinating conjunctions in English: *and, but, or, nor, for, so*, and *yet.* Notice that all of these words are short — only two or three letters long.

COMMA   Air pollution poses risks to all humans, however, it can
SPLICE   be deadly for asthma sufferers.

However is a transitional expression, not a coordinating conjunction (see 20b).

To review your writing for possible run-on sentences, use the flowchart on page 158.

ON THE WEB > dianahacker.com/rules
   Language Debates > Comma splices

Recognizing run-on sentences

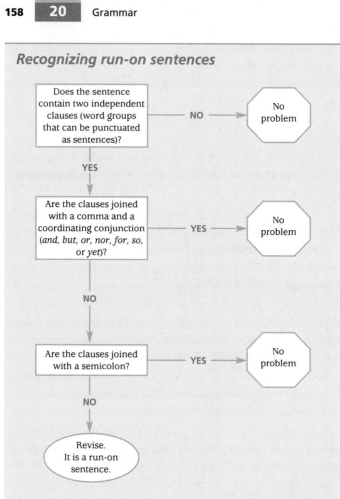

```
┌─────────────────────┐
│ Does the sentence   │
│ contain two         │         ┌──────────┐
│ independent clauses │── NO ──▶ │   No     │
│ (word groups that   │         │ problem  │
│ can be punctuated   │         └──────────┘
│ as sentences)?      │
└─────────────────────┘
          │ YES
          ▼
┌─────────────────────┐
│ Are the clauses     │
│ joined with a comma │         ┌──────────┐
│ and a coordinating  │── YES ─▶ │   No     │
│ conjunction (and,   │         │ problem  │
│ but, or, nor, for,  │         └──────────┘
│ so, or yet)?        │
└─────────────────────┘
          │ NO
          ▼
┌─────────────────────┐
│ Are the clauses     │         ┌──────────┐
│ joined with a       │── YES ─▶ │   No     │
│ semicolon?          │         │ problem  │
└─────────────────────┘         └──────────┘
          │ NO
          ▼
    ╭──────────────╮
    │   Revise.    │
    │ It is a run-on│
    │  sentence.   │
    ╰──────────────╯
```

If you find an error, choose an effective method of revision. See 20a–20d for revision strategies.

GRAMMAR CHECKERS flag fewer than half the run-on sentences in a sample. They usually suggest a semicolon as a method of revision, but you can consult 20a–20d for other revision strategies that might be more suitable in a particular situation. If you have repeated problems with run-ons, the flowchart on this page will help you identify them.

Revising run-on sentences

To revise a run-on sentence, you have four choices:

1. Use a comma and a coordinating conjunction (*and, but, or, nor, for, so, yet*).

   ▶ Air pollution poses risks to all humans, *but* it can be deadly

   for asthma sufferers.

2. Use a semicolon (or, if appropriate, a colon or a dash). A semicolon may be used alone; it can also be accompanied by a transitional expression.

   ▶ Air pollution poses risks to all humans*/;* it can be deadly

   for asthma sufferers.

   ▶ Air pollution poses risks to all humans*/ ; however,* it can be deadly for

   asthma sufferers.

3. Make the clauses into separate sentences.

   ▶ Air pollution poses risks to all humans*/. It* ~~it~~ can be deadly for

   asthma sufferers.

4. Restructure the sentence, perhaps by subordinating one of the clauses.

   ▶ *Although air* ~~Air~~ pollution poses risks to all humans, it can be deadly for

   asthma sufferers.

One of these revision techniques usually works better than the others for a particular sentence. The fourth technique, the one requiring the most extensive revision, is often the most effective.

20a Consider separating the clauses with a comma and a coordinating conjunction.

There are seven coordinating conjunctions in English: *and, but, or, nor, for, so,* and *yet.* When a coordinating conjunction joins independent clauses, it is usually preceded by a comma. (See 32a.)

> ▶ The paramedic asked where I was hurt, as soon as I told him, *and*
>
> he cut up the leg of my favorite pair of jeans.

> ▶ Many government officials privately admit that the polygraph *yet*
>
> is unreliable, ~~however,~~ they continue to use it as a security
>
> measure.

However is a transitional expression, not a coordinating conjunction, so it cannot be used with only a comma to join independent clauses. (See also 20b.)

20b Consider separating the clauses with a semicolon (or, if appropriate, with a colon or a dash).

When the independent clauses are closely related and their relation is clear without a coordinating conjunction, a semicolon is an acceptable method of revision. (See 34a.)

> ▶ Tragedy depicts the individual confronted with the fact
>
> of death,; comedy depicts the adaptability of human
>
> society.

A semicolon is required between independent clauses that have been linked with a transitional expression (such as *however, therefore, moreover, in fact,* or *for example*). For a longer list, see 34b.

▶ Handheld PDAs are gaining in popularity/; however, they are

not nearly as popular as cell phones.

▶ Everyone in my outfit had a specific job/; as a matter of fact,

most of the officers had three or four duties.

If the first independent clause introduces the second or if the second clause summarizes or explains the first, a colon or a dash may be an appropriate method of revision. (See 35b and 39a.) In formal writing, the colon is usually preferred to the dash.

             : This
▶ Nuclear waste is hazardous ~~this~~ is an indisputable fact.

▶ The female black widow spider is often a widow of her own

        --
making/ she has been known to eat her partner after mating.

If the first independent clause introduces a quoted sentence, a colon is an appropriate method of revision.

▶ Feminist writer and scholar Carolyn Heilbrun has this to

say about the future/: "Today's shocks are tomorrow's

conventions."

20c Consider making the clauses into separate sentences.

▶ Why should we spend money on expensive space
          We
exploration/? we have enough underfunded programs here

on Earth.

Since one independent clause is a question and the other is a statement, they should be separate sentences.

▶ I gave the necessary papers to the police officer. ~~then~~ he said *Then*

I would have to accompany him to the police station, where

a counselor would talk with me and call my parents.

Because the second independent clause is quite long, a sensible revision is to use separate sentences.

NOTE: When two quoted independent clauses are divided by explanatory words, make each clause its own sentence.

▶ "It's always smart to learn from your mistakes," quipped my

supervisor/. "~~it's~~ even smarter to learn from the mistakes of *"It's*

others."

20d Consider restructuring the sentence, perhaps by subordinating one of the clauses.

If one of the independent clauses is less important than the other, turn it into a subordinate clause or phrase. (For more about subordination, see 14, especially the chart on p. 113.)

▶ One of the most famous advertising slogans is Wheaties

cereal's "Breakfast of Champions," ~~it~~ was penned *which*

in 1933.

▶ ~~Many~~ scholars dismiss the abominable snowman of the Hima- *Although many*

layas as a myth, others claim it may be a kind of ape.

▶ Mary McLeod Bethune, ~~was~~ the seventeenth child of former

slaves, ~~she~~ founded the National Council of Negro Women in

1935.

Minor ideas in these sentences are now expressed in subordinate clauses or phrases.

EXERCISE 20–1   Revise any run-on sentences using the method of revision suggested in brackets. Revisions of lettered sentences appear in the back of the book. Example:

Because
Orville had been obsessed with his weight as a teenager, he
^
rarely ate anything sweet. [*Restructure the sentence.*]

a. The city had one public swimming pool,~~it~~ *that* stayed packed with children all summer long. [*Restructure the sentence.*]
b. The building is being renovated, ~~therefore~~ *so* at times we have no heat, water, or electricity. [*Use a comma and a coordinating conjunction.*]
c. The view was not what the travel agent had described, where were the rolling hills, the fields of poppies, and the shimmering rivers? [*Make two sentences.*]
d. All those gnarled equations looked like toxic insects; maybe I was going to have to rethink my major. [*Use a semicolon.*]
e. City officials told FEMA they had good reason to fear a major earthquake; most of the business district was built on landfill. [*Use a colon.*]   *because*

1. The car was hardly worth trading, the frame was twisted and the block was warped. [*Restructure the sentence.*]
2. The next time an event is canceled because of bad weather, don't blame the meteorologist, *B*lame nature. [*Make two sentences.*]
3. *Since* Ray was fluent in American Sign Language, he could sign as easily as he could speak. [*Restructure the sentence.*] *no since*
4. Susanna arrived with a stack of her latest hats, she hoped the gift shop would place a big winter order. [*Restructure the sentence.*]
5. There was one major reason for John's wealth: his grandfather had been a multimillionaire. [*Use a colon.*]

EXERCISE 20–2   Revise any run-on sentences using a technique that you find effective. If a sentence is correct, write "correct" after it. Revisions of lettered sentences appear in the back of the book. Example:

Crossing so many time zones on an eight-hour flight, I knew

but
I would be tired when I arrived, ~~however,~~ I was too excited
^

to sleep on the plane.

a. Wind power for the home is a supplementary source of energy, it can be combined with electricity, gas, or solar energy.   *Since*

b. Aidan viewed Sofia Coppola's *Lost in Translation* three times, ~~then~~ *and* he wrote a paper describing the film as the work of a mysterious modern painter.

c. In the Middle Ages, the streets of London were dangerous places; it was safer to travel by boat along the Thames. *correct*

d. "He's not drunk," I said. "He's in a state of diabetic shock."

e. Are you able to endure boredom, isolation, and potential violence? then the army may well be the adventure for you.

1. Death Valley National Monument, located in southern California and Nevada, is one of the hottest places on Earth. temperatures there have soared as high as 134 degrees Fahrenheit.

2. Anamaria opened the boxes crammed with toys; out sprang griffins, dragons, and phoenixes.

3. Subatomic physics is filled with strange and marvelous particles, *inclu...* tiny bodies of matter that shiver, wobble, pulse, and flatten to no thickness at all.

4. As his first major project, Frederick Law Olmsted designed New York City's Central Park, one of the most beautiful urban spaces in the United States. *correct*

5. The neurosurgeon explained that the medication could have one side effect; it might cause me to experience temporary memory loss.

ON THE WEB > dianahacker.com/rules
Grammar exercises > Grammar > E-ex 20–1 to 20–3

21

Make subjects and verbs agree.

Native speakers of standard English know by ear that *he talks, she has,* and *it doesn't* (not *he talk, she have,* and *it don't*) are standard subject-verb combinations. For such speakers, problems with subject-verb agreement arise only in certain tricky situations, which are detailed in 21b–21k.

If you don't trust your ear — perhaps because you speak English as a second language or because you speak or hear nonstandard English in your community — you will need to learn the standard forms explained in 21a. Even if you do trust your ear, take a look at 21a to see what "subject-verb agreement" means.

21a Consult this section for standard subject-verb combinations.

In the present tense, verbs agree with their subjects in number (singular or plural) and in person (first, second, or third). The present-tense ending -s (or -es) is used on a verb if its subject is third-person singular; otherwise the verb takes no ending. Consider, for example, the present-tense forms of the verbs *love* and *try*, given at the beginning of the following chart.

Subject-verb agreement at a glance

Present-tense forms of *love* and *try* (typical verbs)

	SINGULAR		PLURAL	
FIRST PERSON	I	love	we	love
SECOND PERSON	you	love	you	love
THIRD PERSON	he/she/it	loves	they	love

	SINGULAR		PLURAL	
FIRST PERSON	I	try	we	try
SECOND PERSON	you	try	you	try
THIRD PERSON	he/she/it	tries	they	try

Present-tense forms of *have*

	SINGULAR		PLURAL	
FIRST PERSON	I	have	we	have
SECOND PERSON	you	have	you	have
THIRD PERSON	he/she/it	has	they	have

Present-tense forms of *do*

	SINGULAR		PLURAL	
FIRST PERSON	I	do/don't	we	do/don't
SECOND PERSON	you	do/don't	you	do/don't
THIRD PERSON	he/she/it	does/doesn't	they	do/don't

Present-tense and past-tense forms of *be*

	SINGULAR		PLURAL	
FIRST PERSON	I	am/was	we	are/were
SECOND PERSON	you	are/were	you	are/were
THIRD PERSON	he/she/it	is/was	they	are/were

The verb *be* varies from this pattern; unlike any other verb, it has special forms in *both* the present and the past tense. These forms appear at the end of the chart.

If you aren't confident that you know the standard forms, use the charts on page 165 and this page as you proofread for subject-verb agreement. Also see 27c on -s endings.

When to use the -s (or -es) form of a present-tense verb

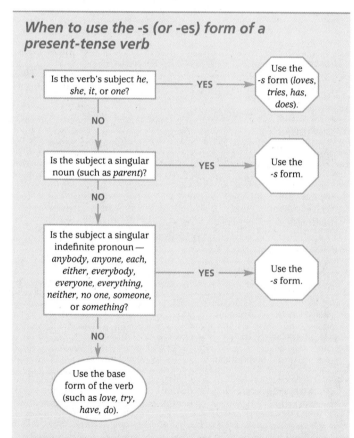

Is the verb's subject *he, she, it,* or *one*? — YES → Use the -s form (*loves, tries, has, does*).

NO ↓

Is the subject a singular noun (such as *parent*)? — YES → Use the -s form.

NO ↓

Is the subject a singular indefinite pronoun — *anybody, anyone, each, either, everybody, everyone, everything, neither, no one, someone,* or *something*? — YES → Use the -s form.

NO ↓

Use the base form of the verb (such as *love, try, have, do*).

EXCEPTION: Choosing the correct present-tense form of *be* (*am, is,* or *are*) is not quite so simple. See the chart on the previous page for both present- and past-tense forms of *be*.

ESL TIP: Do not use the -s form of a verb that follows a modal or another helping verb such as *can, must,* or *should.* (See 28b.)

GRAMMAR CHECKERS are fairly good at flagging subject-verb agreement problems. They occasionally flag a correct sentence, usually because they misidentify the subject, the verb, or both. Sometimes they miss an agreement problem because they don't recognize a pronoun's antecedent. In the following sentence, for example, the grammar checker did not detect that *eggs* is the antecedent of *which*: *Some animal rights groups oppose eating eggs, which comes from animals.* Because *eggs* is plural, the correct verb is *come.*

21b Make the verb agree with its subject, not with a word that comes between.

Word groups often come between the subject and the verb. Such word groups, usually modifying the subject, may contain a noun that at first appears to be the subject. By mentally stripping away such modifiers, you can isolate the noun that is in fact the subject.

The *samples* on the tray in the lab *need* testing.

▶ High levels of air pollution causes damage to the respiratory

tract.

The subject is *levels,* not *pollution.* Strip away the phrase *of air pollution* to hear the correct verb: *levels cause.*

has
▶ The slaughter of pandas for their pelts ~~have~~ caused the
^

panda population to decline drastically.

The subject is *slaughter,* not *pandas* or *pelts.*

NOTE: Phrases beginning with the prepositions *as well as, in addition to, accompanied by, together with,* and *along with* do not make a singular subject plural.

was
▶ The governor as well as his press secretary ~~were~~ shot.
^

To emphasize that two people were shot, the writer could use *and* instead: *The governor and his press secretary were shot.*

21c Treat most subjects joined with *and* as plural.

A subject with two or more parts is said to be compound. If the parts are connected by *and,* the subject is nearly always plural.

Leon and Jan often *jog* together.

▶ Jill's natural ability and her desire to help others has led to a

career in the ministry.

have

Ability and desire is a plural subject, so its verb should be *have*.

EXCEPTIONS: When the parts of the subject form a single unit or when they refer to the same person or thing, treat the subject as singular.

Strawberries and cream was a last-minute addition to the menu.

Sue's friend and adviser was surprised by her decision.

When a compound subject is preceded by *each* or *every,* treat it as singular.

Each tree, shrub, and vine needs to be sprayed.

Every car, truck, and van is required to pass inspection.

This exception does not apply when a compound subject is followed by *each*: *Alan and Marcia each have different ideas.*

21d With subjects joined with *or* or *nor* (or with *either . . . or* or *neither . . . nor*), make the verb agree with the part of the subject nearer to the verb.

A driver's *license* or credit *card is* required.

A driver's *license* or two credit *cards are* required.

▶ If an infant or a child are having difficulty breathing, seek

is

medical attention immediately.

were
▶ Neither the lab assistant nor the students w̶a̶s̶ able to down-
                                               ^

load the information.

The verb must be matched with the part of the subject closer to it: *child is* in the first sentence, *students were* in the second.

NOTE: If one part of the subject is singular and the other is plural, put the plural one last to avoid awkwardness.

21e Treat most indefinite pronouns as singular.

Indefinite pronouns are pronouns that do not refer to specific persons or things. The following commonly used indefinite pronouns are singular.

anybody	each	everyone	nobody	somebody
anyone	either	everything	no one	someone
anything	everybody	neither	nothing	something

Many of these words appear to have plural meanings, and they are often treated as plural in casual speech. In formal written English, however, they are nearly always treated as singular.

Everyone on the team *supports* the coach.

has
▶ Each of the furrows h̶a̶v̶e̶ been seeded.
                      ^

                                                        was
▶ Everybody who signed up for the snowboarding trip w̶e̶r̶e̶
                                                     ^

taking lessons.

The subjects of these sentences are *Each* and *Everybody*. These indefinite pronouns are third-person singular, so the verbs must be *has* and *was*.

A few indefinite pronouns (*all, any, none, some*) may be singular or plural depending on the noun or pronoun they refer to.

Some of our *luggage was* lost. *None* of his *advice makes* sense.

Some of the *rocks are* slippery. *None* of the *eggs were* broken.

NOTE: When the meaning of *none* is emphatically "not one," *none* may be treated as singular: *None* [meaning "Not one"] *of the eggs was broken.* However, some experts advise using *not one* instead: *Not one of the eggs was broken.*

ON THE WEB > dianahacker.com/rules
  Language Debates > *none*

21f Treat collective nouns as singular unless the meaning is clearly plural.

Collective nouns such as *jury, committee, audience, crowd, class, troop, family,* and *couple* name a class or a group. In American English, collective nouns are nearly always treated as singular: They emphasize the group as a unit. Occasionally, when there is some reason to draw attention to the individual members of the group, a collective noun may be treated as plural. (Also see 22b.)

SINGULAR   The *class respects* the teacher.

PLURAL   The *class are* debating among themselves.

To underscore the notion of individuality in the second sentence, many writers would add a clearly plural noun such as *members: The class members are debating among themselves.*

▶ The board of trustees ~~meet~~ *meets* in Denver twice a year.

  The board as a whole meets; there is no reason to draw attention to its individual members.

▶ A young couple ~~was~~ *were* arguing about politics while holding hands.

  The meaning is clearly plural. Only individuals can argue and hold hands.

NOTE: The phrase *the number* is treated as singular, *a number* as plural.

SINGULAR   *The number* of school-age children *is* declining.

PLURAL   *A number* of children *are* attending the wedding.

NOTE: In general, when fractions or units of measurement are used with a singular noun, treat them as singular; when they are used with a plural noun, treat them as plural.

SINGULAR   *Three-fourths* of the pie *has* been eaten.

SINGULAR   Twenty *inches* of wallboard *was* covered with mud.

PLURAL   *One-fourth* of the drivers *were* drunk.

PLURAL   Five *pounds* of ostrich feathers *were* used to make the scarf.

21g Make the verb agree with its subject even when the subject follows the verb.

Verbs ordinarily follow subjects. When this normal order is reversed, it is easy to become confused. Sentences beginning with *there is* or *there are* (or *there was* or *there were*) are inverted; the subject follows the verb.

There *are* surprisingly few *children* in our neighborhood.

▶ There ~~was~~ [were] a social worker and a crew of twenty volunteers at
                 ^

the scene of the accident.

The subject, *worker and crew,* is plural, so the verb must be *were.*

Occasionally you may decide to invert a sentence for variety or effect. When you do so, check to make sure that your subject and verb agree.

▶ At the back of the room ~~is~~ [are] a small aquarium and an enormous
                              ^

terrarium.

The subject, *aquarium and terrarium,* is plural, so the verb must be *are.* If the correct sentence seems awkward, begin with the subject: *A small aquarium and an enormous terrarium are at the back of the room.*

21h Make the verb agree with its subject, not with a subject complement.

One basic sentence pattern in English consists of a subject, a linking verb, and a subject complement: *Jack is a securities lawyer.* Because the subject complement names or describes the subject, it is sometimes mistaken for the subject. (See 63b on subject complements.)

> *are*
> A tent and a sleeping bag ~~is~~ the required equipment for all
>
> campers.

Tent and bag is the subject, not *equipment.*

> *is*
> A major force in today's economy ~~are~~ women — as earners,
>
> consumers, and investors.

Force is the subject, not *women.* If the corrected version seems awkward, make *women* the subject: *Women are a major force in today's economy — as earners, consumers, and investors.*

21i *Who, which,* and *that* take verbs that agree with their antecedents.

Like most pronouns, the relative pronouns *who, which,* and *that* have antecedents, nouns or pronouns to which they refer. Relative pronouns used as subjects of subordinate clauses take verbs that agree with their antecedents. (See 64b.)

Take a *suit that travels* well.

Constructions such as *one of the students who* (or *one of the things that*) cause problems for writers. Do not assume that the antecedent must be *one.* Instead, consider the logic of the sentence.

> Our ability to use language is one of the things that sets us
>
> apart from animals.

The antecedent of *that* is *things*, not *one*. Several things set us apart from animals.

When the word *only* comes before *one*, you are safe in assuming that *one* is the antecedent of the relative pronoun.

▶ Veronica was the only one of the first-year Spanish students

was
who ~~were~~ fluent enough to apply for the exchange program.
  ^

The antecedent of *who* is *one*, not *students*. Only one student was fluent enough.

ON THE WEB > **dianahacker.com/rules**
Language Debates > *one of those who* (or *that*)

21j Words such as *athletics, economics, mathematics, physics, politics, statistics, measles,* and *news* are usually singular, despite their plural form.

is
▶ Politics ~~are~~ among my mother's favorite pastimes.
  ^

EXCEPTION: Occasionally some of these words, especially *economics, mathematics, politics,* and *statistics,* have plural meanings: *Office politics often sway decisions about hiring and promotion. The economics of the building plan are prohibitive.*

21k Titles of works, company names, words mentioned as words, and gerund phrases are singular.

describes
▶ *Lost Cities* ~~describe~~ the discoveries of many ancient
  ^
civilizations.

specializes
▶ Delmonico Brothers ~~specialize~~ in organic produce and
  ^
additive-free meats.

▶ *Controlled substances* ~~are~~ **is** a euphemism for illegal drugs.

A gerund phrase consists of an *-ing* verb form followed by any objects, complements, or modifiers (see 64c). Treat gerund phrases as singular.

▶ *Encountering busy signals* ~~are~~ **is** troublesome to our clients, so we have hired two new switchboard operators.

EXERCISE 21–1 Underline the subject (or compound subject) and then select the verb that agrees with it. (If you have difficulty identifying the subject, consult 63a.) Answers to lettered sentences appear in the back of the book. Example:

<u>Everyone</u> in the telecom focus group (has/have) experienced problems with cell phones.

a. Your friendship over the years and your support (has/have) meant a great deal to us.
b. Shelters for teenage runaways (offers/offer) a wide variety of services.
c. The main source of income for Trinidad (is/are) oil and pitch.
d. The chances of your being promoted (is/are) excellent.
e. There (was/were) a Yu-Gi-Oh! card and a quirky haiku stuck to the refrigerator.

1. Neither the professor nor his assistants (was/were) able to solve the mystery of the eerie glow in the laboratory.
2. Many hours at the driving range (has/have) led us to design golf balls with GPS locators in them.
3. Discovered in the soil of our city garden (was/were) a button dating from the Civil War and three marbles dating from the turn of the twentieth century.
4. Every year, during the midsummer festival, the smoke of village bonfires (fills/fill) the sky.
5. The story performers (was/were) surrounded by children and adults eager to see magical tales.

EXERCISE 21–2 Edit the following sentences to eliminate problems with subject-verb agreement. If a sentence is correct, write "correct"

after it. Answers to lettered sentences appear in the back of the book.
Example:

> *were*
> Jack's first days in the infantry ~~was~~ grueling.
> ^

a. One of the main reasons for elephant poaching are the profits received from selling the ivory tusks.
b. Not until my interview with Dr. Hwang were other possibilities opened to me.
c. A number of students in the seminar was aware of the importance of joining the discussion.
d. Batik cloth from Bali, blue and white ceramics from Delft, and a bocce ball from Turin has made Angelie's room the talk of the dorm.
e. The board of directors, ignoring the wishes of the neighborhood, has voted to allow further development.

1. Measles is a contagious childhood disease.
2. Adorning a shelf in the lab is a Vietnamese figurine, a set of Korean clay gods, and an American plastic village.
3. The presence of certain bacteria in our bodies is one of the factors that determines our overall health.
4. Sheila is the only one of the many applicants who has the ability to step into this job.
5. Neither the explorer nor his companions was ever seen again.

ON THE WEB > **dianahacker.com/rules**
Grammar exercises > Grammar > E-ex 21–1 to 21–3

22

Make pronouns and antecedents agree.

A pronoun is a word that substitutes for a noun. (See 62b.) Many pronouns have antecedents, nouns or pronouns to which they refer. A pronoun and its antecedent agree when they are both singular or both plural.

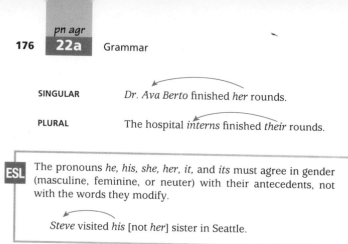

SINGULAR   *Dr. Ava Berto* finished *her* rounds.

PLURAL   The hospital *interns* finished *their* rounds.

ESL The pronouns *he, his, she, her, it,* and *its* must agree in gender (masculine, feminine, or neuter) with their antecedents, not with the words they modify.

> *Steve* visited *his* [not *her*] sister in Seattle.

GRAMMAR CHECKERS do not flag problems with pronoun-antecedent agreement. It takes a human eye to see that a plural pronoun, such as *their*, does not agree with a singular noun, such as *logger*, in a sentence like this: *The logger in the Northwest relies on the old forest growth for their living.*

When grammar checkers do flag agreement problems, they often suggest (correctly) substituting the singular phrase *his or her* for the plural pronoun *their*. For other revision strategies that avoid the wordy *his or her* construction, see the chart on page 178.

22a Do not use plural pronouns to refer to singular antecedents.

Writers are frequently tempted to use plural pronouns to refer to two kinds of singular antecedents: indefinite pronouns and generic nouns.

Indefinite pronouns

Indefinite pronouns refer to nonspecific persons or things. Even though some of the following indefinite pronouns may seem to have plural meanings, treat them as singular in formal English.

anybody	each	everyone	nobody	somebody
anyone	either	everything	no one	someone
anything	everybody	neither	nothing	something

In class *everyone* performs at *his or her* [not *their*] own fitness level.

When a plural pronoun refers mistakenly to a singular indefinite pronoun, you can usually choose one of three options for revision:

1. Replace the plural pronoun with *he or she* (or *his or her*).
2. Make the antecedent plural.
3. Rewrite the sentence so that no agreement problem exists.

▶ When someone has been drinking, ~~they are~~ *he or she is* likely to speed.

▶ When someone ~~has~~ been drinking, they are likely to speed. *drivers have*

▶ When someone has been drinking, ~~they are~~ *is* likely to speed. *A driver who*

Because the *he or she* construction is wordy, often the second or third revision strategy is more effective. Be aware that the traditional use of *he* (or *his*) to refer to persons of either sex is widely considered sexist. (See 17f.)

Generic nouns

A generic noun represents a typical member of a group, such as a typical student, or any member of a group, such as any lawyer. Although generic nouns may seem to have plural meanings, they are singular.

Every *runner* must train rigorously if *he or she wants* [not *they want*] to excel.

When a plural pronoun refers mistakenly to a generic noun, you will usually have the same three revision options as mentioned at the top of this page for indefinite pronouns.

▶ A medical student must study hard if ~~they want~~ *he or she wants* to

succeed.

Medical students
▶ ~~A medical student~~ must study hard if they want to

succeed.
  ^

▶ A medical student must study hard ~~if they want~~ to

succeed.

ON THE WEB > **dianahacker.com/rules**
Language Debates > Pronoun-antecedent agreement

Choosing a revision strategy that avoids sexist language

Because many readers object to sexist language, avoid the use of *he, him,* and *his* to refer to both men and women. Also try to be sparing in your use of the wordy expressions *he or she* and *his or her.* Where possible, seek out more graceful alternatives.

Use an occasional *he or she* (or *his or her*).

his or her
▶ In our office, everyone works at ~~their~~ own pace.
               ^

Make the antecedent plural.

Employees
▶ ~~An employee~~ on extended leave may continue their life
  ^

insurance.

Recast the sentence.

▶ The amount of annual leave a federal worker may

accrue depends on ~~their~~ length of service.

  A
▶ ~~If~~ a child ~~is~~ born to parents who are both bipolar~~/ they~~
  ^
  has
have a high chance of being bipolar.
  ^

22b Treat collective nouns as singular unless the meaning is clearly plural.

Collective nouns such as *jury, committee, audience, crowd, class, troop, family, team,* and *couple* name a class or a group. Ordinarily the group functions as a unit, so the noun should be treated as singular; if the members of the group function as individuals, however, the noun should be treated as plural. (See also 21f.)

AS A UNIT   The *committee* granted *its* permission to build.

AS INDIVIDUALS   The *committee* put *their* signatures on the document.

When treating a collective noun as plural, many writers prefer to add a clearly plural antecedent such as *members* to the sentence: *The members of the committee put their signatures on the document.*

> *its*
> ▶ The jury has reached ~~their~~ decision.

There is no reason to draw attention to the individual members of the jury, so *jury* should be treated as singular. Notice also that the writer treated the noun as singular when choosing the verb *has,* so for consistency the pronoun must be *its.*

22c Treat most compound antecedents connected by *and* as plural.

Jill and John moved to Luray, where *they* built a cabin.

22d With compound antecedents connected by *or* or *nor* (or by *either . . . or* or *neither . . . nor*), make the pronoun agree with the nearer antecedent.

Either *Bruce* or *Tom* should receive first prize for *his* poem.

Neither the *mouse* nor the *rats* could find *their* way through the maze.

NOTE: If one of the antecedents is singular and the other plural, as in the second example, put the plural one last to avoid awkwardness.

EXCEPTION: If one antecedent is male and the other female, do not follow the traditional rule. The sentence *Either Bruce or Elizabeth should receive first prize for her short story* makes no sense. The best solution is to recast the sentence: *The prize for best short story should go to Bruce or Elizabeth*.

EXERCISE 22–1 Edit the following sentences to eliminate problems with pronoun-antecedent agreement. Most of the sentences can be revised in more than one way, so experiment before choosing a solution. If a sentence is correct, write "correct" after it. Revisions of lettered sentences appear in the back of the book. Example:

> *Recruiters*
> ~~The recruiter~~ may tell the truth, but there is much that they
> choose not to tell.

a. Every presidential candidate must appeal to a wide variety of ethnic and social groups if they want to win the election.

b. David lent his motorcycle to someone who allowed their friend to use it.

c. The aerobics teacher motioned for everyone to move their arms in wide, slow circles.

d. The parade committee was unanimous in its decision to allow all groups and organizations to join the festivities.

e. The applicant should be bilingual if they want to qualify for this position.

1. If a driver refuses to take a blood or breath test, he or she will have their licenses suspended for six months.

2. Why should anyone learn a second language? One reason is to sharpen their minds.

3. The Department of Education issued new guidelines for school security. They were trying to anticipate problems and avert disaster.

4. Seven qualified Hispanic agents applied, each hoping for a career move that would let them use their language and cultural training on more than just translations.

5. If anyone notices any suspicious activity, they should report it to the police.

EXERCISE 22–2   Edit the following paragraph to eliminate problems with pronoun-antecedent agreement or sexist language.

A common practice in businesses is to put each employee in their own cubicle. A typical cubicle resembles an office, but their walls don't reach the ceiling. Many office managers feel that a cubicle floor plan has its advantages. Cubicles make a large area feel spacious. In addition, they can be moved around so that each new employee can be accommodated in his own work area. Of course, the cubicle model also has problems. The typical employee is not as happy with a cubicle as they would be with a traditional office. Also, productivity can suffer. Neither a manager nor a frontline worker can ordinarily do their best work in a cubicle because of noise and lack of privacy. Each worker can hear his neighbors tapping on computer keyboards, making telephone calls, and muttering under their breath.

ON THE WEB > dianahacker.com/rules
Grammar exercises > Grammar > E-ex 22–1 to 22–3

23

Make pronoun references clear.

Pronouns substitute for nouns; they are a kind of shorthand. In a sentence like *After Andrew intercepted the ball, he kicked it as hard as he could,* the pronouns *he* and *it* substitute for the nouns *Andrew* and *ball.* The word a pronoun refers to is called its *antecedent.*

GRAMMAR CHECKERS do not flag problems with faulty pronoun reference. Although a computer program can identify pronouns, it has no way of knowing which words, if any, they refer to. For example, grammar checkers miss the fact that the pronoun *it* has an ambiguous reference in the following sentence: *The thief stole the woman's purse and her car and then destroyed it.* Did the thief destroy the purse or the car? It takes human judgment to realize that readers might be confused.

23a Avoid ambiguous or remote pronoun reference.

Ambiguous pronoun reference occurs when a pronoun could refer to two possible antecedents.

> *The pitcher broke when Gloria set it*
> ▶ ~~When Gloria set the pitcher~~ on the glass-topped table~~/. it~~
>   ^   ^
> ~~broke.~~

> *"You have*
> ▶ Tom told James, ~~that he had~~ won the lottery.*"*
>   ^   ^

What broke — the table or the pitcher? Who won the lottery — Tom or James? The revisions eliminate the ambiguity.

Remote pronoun reference occurs when a pronoun is too far away from its antecedent for easy reading.

> ▶ After the court ordered my ex-husband to pay child support,
>
> he refused. Approximately eight months later, we were back
>
> in court. This time the judge ordered him to make payments
>
> directly to the Support and Collections Unit, which would in
>
> turn pay me. For the first six months I received regular pay-
>
> *my ex-husband*
> ments, but then they stopped. Again he was summoned to
>   ^
>
> appear in court; he did not respond.

The pronoun *he* was too distant from its antecedent, *ex-husband*, which appeared several sentences earlier.

23b Generally, avoid broad reference of *this, that, which,* and *it.*

For clarity, the pronouns *this, that, which,* and *it* should ordinarily refer to specific antecedents rather than to whole ideas or sentences. When a pronoun's reference is needlessly broad, either replace the pronoun with a noun or supply an antecedent to which the pronoun clearly refers.

▶ More and more often, especially in large cities, we are finding

our fate

ourselves victims of serious crimes. We learn to accept ~~this~~
                                                          ^

with minor gripes and groans.

For clarity the writer substituted a noun (*fate*) for the pronoun *this,* which referred broadly to the idea expressed in the preceding sentence.

▶ Romeo and Juliet were both too young to have acquired

a fact

much wisdom, which accounts for their rash actions.
            ^

The writer added an antecedent (*fact*) that the pronoun *which* clearly refers to.

23c Do not use a pronoun to refer to an implied antecedent.

A pronoun should refer to a specific antecedent, not to a word that is implied but not present in the sentence.

the braids

▶ After braiding Ann's hair, Sue decorated ~~them~~ with ribbons.
                                            ^

The pronoun *them* referred to Ann's braids (implied by the term *braiding*), but the word *braids* did not appear in the sentence.

Modifiers, such as possessives, cannot serve as antecedents. A modifier may strongly imply the noun that the pronoun might logically refer to, but it is not itself that noun.

Mary Gordon

▶ In ~~Mary Gordon's~~ *The Shadow Man,* ~~she~~ writes about her
                                        ^

father's mysterious and startling past.

The pronoun *she* cannot refer logically to the possessive modifier *Mary Gordon's.* The revision substitutes the noun *Mary Gordon* for the pronoun *she,* thereby eliminating the problem.

ON THE WEB > **dianahacker.com/rules**
Language Debates > Possessives as antecedents

23d Avoid the indefinite use of *they, it,* and *you*.

Do not use the pronoun *they* to refer indefinitely to persons who have not been specifically mentioned. *They* should always refer to a specific antecedent. If no antecedent appears in the sentence, you may need to substitute a noun for the pronoun.

▶ In 2001, ~~they~~ shut down all government agencies
   Congress
   ^

   for more than a month until the budget crisis was finally

   resolved.

The word *it* should not be used indefinitely in constructions such as *It is said on television . . .* or *In the article it says that. . . .*

▶ ~~In the~~ encyclopedia ~~it~~ states that male moths can smell
   The
   ^

   female moths from several miles away.

The pronoun *you* is appropriate when the writer is addressing the reader directly: *Once you have kneaded the dough, let it rise in a warm place.* Except in informal contexts, however, the indefinite *you* (meaning "anyone in general") is inappropriate.

▶ Ms. Pickersgill's *Guide to Etiquette* stipulates that you should
   a guest
   ^

   not arrive at a party too early, leave too late, or drink too much

   wine.

The writer could have replaced *you* with *one,* but in American English the pronoun *one* can seem stilted.

ON THE WEB > **dianahacker.com/rules**
Language Debates > *you*

23e To refer to persons, use *who, whom,* or *whose,* not *which* or *that.*

In most contexts, use *who, whom,* or *whose* to refer to persons, *which* or *that* to refer to animals or things. *Which* is reserved only for animals or things, so it is impolite to use it to refer to persons.

> whom
> ▶ All thirty-two women in the study, half of ~~which~~ were
> ^
> unemployed for more than six months, reported higher
>
> self-esteem after job training.

Although *that* is sometimes used to refer to persons, many readers will find such references dehumanizing. It is more polite to use a form of *who* — a word reserved only for people.

> who
> ▶ Fans wondered how an out-of-shape old man ~~that~~ walked
> ^
> with a limp could play football.

NOTE: Occasionally *whose* may be used to refer to animals and things to avoid the awkward *of which* construction.

> whose
> ▶ A local school, ~~the~~ name ~~of which~~ will be in tomorrow's
> ^
> paper, has received the Governor's Gold Medal for outstand-
>
> ing community service.

ON THE WEB > dianahacker.com/rules
Language Debates > *who* versus *which* or *that*

EXERCISE 23–1   Edit the following sentences to correct errors in pronoun reference. In some cases you will need to decide on an antecedent that the pronoun might logically refer to. Revisions of lettered sentences appear in the back of the book. Example:

Following the breakup of AT&T, many other companies began

to offer long-distance phone service. ~~This~~ *The competition* has led to lower

long-distance rates.

a. They say that an engineering student should have hands-on experience with dismantling and reassembling machines.
b. She had decorated her living room with posters from chamber music festivals. This led her date to believe that she was interested in classical music. Actually she preferred rock.
c. In Ethiopia, you don't need much property to be considered well-off.
d. Marianne told Jenny that she was worried about her mother's illness.
e. Though Lewis cried for several minutes after scraping his knee, eventually it subsided.

1. Our German conversation group is made up of six people, three of which I had never met before.
2. Many people believe that the polygraph test is highly reliable if you employ a licensed examiner.
3. Parent involvement is high at Mission San Jose High School. They participate in many committees and activities that affect all aspects of school life.
4. Because of Paul Robeson's outspoken attitude toward fascism, he was labeled a Communist.
5. In the report it points out that lifting the ban on Compound 1080 would prove detrimental, possibly even fatal, to the bald eagle.

ON THE WEB > dianahacker.com/rules
Grammar exercises > Grammar > E-ex 23–1 to 23–3

24

Distinguish between pronouns such as *I* and *me*.

The personal pronouns in the following chart change what is known as *case form* according to their grammatical function in a sentence. Pronouns functioning as subjects (or subject complements) appear in the *subjective* case; those functioning as objects appear in the *objective* case; and those showing ownership appear in the *possessive* case.

	SUBJECTIVE CASE	OBJECTIVE CASE	POSSESSIVE CASE
SINGULAR	I	me	my
	you	you	your
	he/she/it	him/her/it	his/her/its
PLURAL	we	us	our
	you	you	your
	they	them	their

Pronouns in the subjective and objective cases are frequently confused. Most of the rules in this section specify when to use one or the other of these cases (*I* or *me, he* or *him,* and so on). Section 24g explains a special use of pronouns and nouns in the possessive case.

> GRAMMAR CHECKERS sometimes flag incorrect pronouns and suggest using the correct form: *I* or *me, he* or *him, she* or *her, we* or *us, they* or *them.* A grammar checker correctly flagged *we* in the following sentence and advised using *us* instead: *I say it is about time for we parents to revolt.* Grammar checkers miss more incorrect pronouns than they catch, however, and their suggestions for revision are sometimes off the mark. A grammar checker caught the error in the following sentence: *I am a little jealous that my dog likes my neighbor more than I.* But instead of suggesting changing the final *I* to *me* (. . . *more than me*), it suggested adding *do* (. . . *more than I do*), which does not fit the meaning of the sentence.

24a Use the subjective case (*I, you, he, she, it, we, they*) for subjects and subject complements.

When personal pronouns are used as subjects, ordinarily your ear will tell you the correct pronoun. Problems sometimes arise, however, with compound word groups containing a pronoun, so it is not always safe to trust your ear.

▶ Joel ran away from home because his stepfather and ~~him~~ *he*

had argued.

His stepfather and he is the subject of the verb *had argued*. If we strip away the words *his stepfather and,* the correct pronoun becomes clear: *he had argued* (not *him had argued*).

When a pronoun is used as a subject complement (a word following a linking verb), your ear may mislead you, since the incorrect form is frequently heard in casual speech. (See "subject complement," 63b.)

▶ During the Lindbergh trial, Bruno Hauptmann repeatedly

denied that the kidnapper was ~~him~~. *he.*

If *kidnapper was he* seems too stilted, rewrite the sentence: *During the Lindbergh trial, Bruno Hauptmann repeatedly denied that he was the kidnapper.*

24b Use the objective case (*me, you, him, her, it, us, them*) for all objects.

When a personal pronoun is used as a direct object, an indirect object, or the object of a preposition, ordinarily your ear will lead you to the correct pronoun. When an object is compound, however, you may occasionally become confused.

▶ Janice was indignant when she realized that the salesclerk

was insulting her mother and ~~she~~. *her.*

Her mother and her is the direct object of the verb *was insulting.* Strip away the words *her mother and* to hear the correct pronoun: *was insulting her* (not *was insulting she*).

▶ The most traumatic experience for her father and ~~I~~ occurred *me*

long after her operation.

Her father and me is the object of the preposition *for.* Strip away the words *her father and* to test for the correct pronoun: *for me* (not *for I*).

When in doubt about the correct pronoun, some writers try to avoid making the choice by using a reflexive pronoun such as *myself*. Such evasions are nonstandard, even though they are used by some educated persons.

> The Indian cab driver gave my husband and ~~myself~~ some

  me
  ^

> good tips on traveling in New Delhi.

> *My husband and me* is the indirect object of the verb *gave*. For correct uses of *myself*, see the Glossary of Usage.

ON THE WEB > **dianahacker.com/rules**
Language Debates > *myself*

24c Put an appositive and the word to which it refers in the same case.

Appositives are noun phrases that rename nouns or pronouns. A pronoun used as an appositive has the same function (usually subject or object) as the word(s) it renames.

> The top strategists, Dr. Bell and ~~me,~~ could not agree on a

  I,
  ^

> plan.

> The appositive *Dr. Bell and I* renames the subject, *strategists*. Test: *I could not agree* (not *me could not agree*).

> The reporter interviewed only two witnesses, the bicyclist

> and ~~I.~~

  me.
  ^

> The appositive *the bicyclist and me* renames the direct object, *witnesses*. Test: *interviewed me* (not *interviewed I*).

24d Following *than* or *as,* choose the pronoun that expresses your meaning.

When a comparison begins with *than* or *as,* your choice of a pronoun will depend on your intended meaning. Consider the difference in meaning between the following sentences.

My husband likes football more than I.

My husband likes football more than me.

Finish each sentence mentally and its meaning becomes clear: *My husband likes football more than I [do]. My husband likes football more than [he likes] me.*

▶ Even though he is sometimes ridiculed by the other boys,

they.

Nathan is much better off than ~~them~~.
  ^

They is the subject of the verb *are*, which is understood: *Nathan is much better off than they [are]*. If the correct English seems too formal, you can always add the verb.

▶ We respected no other candidate for the city council as

her.

much as ~~she~~.
  ^

This sentence means that we respected no other candidate as much as *we respected her. Her* is the direct object of the understood verb *respected*.

24e For *we* or *us* before a noun, choose the pronoun that would be appropriate if the noun were omitted.

We

▶ ~~Us~~ tenants would rather fight than move.
  ^

us

▶ Management is short-changing ~~we~~ tenants.
  ^

No one would say *Us would rather fight than move* or *Management is short-changing we.*

24f Use the objective case for subjects and objects of infinitives.

An infinitive is the word *to* followed by the base form of a verb. (See 64c.) Subjects of infinitives are an exception to the rule that subjects must be in the subjective case. Whenever an infinitive has a subject, it must be in the objective case. Objects of infinitives also are in the objective case.

>   *me*   *her*
> ▶ Ms. Wilson asked John and ~~I~~ to drive the senator and ~~she~~ to
>
> the airport.

John and me is the subject of the infinitive *to drive; senator and her* is the direct object of the infinitive.

24g Use the possessive case to modify a gerund.

A pronoun that modifies a gerund or a gerund phrase should appear in the possessive case (*my, our, your, his, her, its, their*). A gerund is a verb form ending in *-ing* that functions as a noun. Gerunds frequently appear in phrases, in which case the whole gerund phrase functions as a noun. (See 64c.)

>   *your*
> ▶ The chances of ~~you~~ being hit by lightning are about two
>
> million to one.

Your modifies the gerund phrase *being hit by lightning.*

Nouns as well as pronouns may modify gerunds. To form the possessive case of a noun, use an apostrophe and an *-s* (*victim's*) or just an apostrophe (*victims'*). (See 36a.)

>   *aristocracy's*
> ▶ The old order in France paid a high price for the ~~aristocracy~~
>
> exploiting the lower classes.

The possessive noun *aristocracy's* modifies the gerund phrase *exploiting the lower classes.*

Gerund phrases should not be confused with participial phrases, which function as adjectives, not as nouns: *We saw Brenda driving a yellow convertible.* Here *driving a yellow convertible* is a participial phrase modifying the noun *Brenda.* (See 64c.)

Sometimes the choice between the objective or the possessive case conveys a subtle difference in meaning:

We watched *them* dancing.

We watched *their* dancing.

In the first sentence the emphasis is on the people; *dancing* is a participle modifying the pronoun *them*. In the second sentence the emphasis is on the dancing; *dancing* is a gerund, and *their* is a possessive pronoun modifying the gerund.

NOTE: Do not use the possessive if it creates an awkward effect. Try to reword the sentence instead.

AWKWARD	The president agreed to the applications' being reviewed by a faculty committee.
REVISED	The president agreed that the applications could be reviewed by a faculty committee.
REVISED	The president agreed that a faculty committee could review the applications.

ON THE WEB > dianahacker.com/rules
Language Debates > Possessive before a gerund

EXERCISE 24–1 Edit the following sentences to eliminate errors in case. If a sentence is correct, write "correct" after it. Answers to lettered sentences appear in the back of the book. Example:

> Grandfather cuts down trees for neighbors much younger
>
> *he.*
> than ~~him.~~
>   ^

a. Rick applied for the job even though he heard that other candidates were more experienced than he.
b. The volleyball team could not believe that the coach was she.
c. She appreciated him telling the truth in such a difficult situation.
d. The director has asked you and I to draft a proposal for a new recycling plan.
e. Five close friends and myself rented a station wagon, packed it with food, and drove two hundred miles to Mardi Gras.

1. The squawk of the brass horns nearly overwhelmed us oboe and bassoon players.
2. Ushio, the last rock climber up the wall, tossed Teri and she the remaining pitons and carabiners.
3. The programmer realized that her and the interface designers were creating an entirely new Web application.
4. My desire to understand classical music was aided by me working as an usher at Symphony Hall.

5. The shower of sinking bricks caused he and his diving partner to race away from the collapsing seawall.

EXERCISE 24–2   Choose the correct pronoun in each set of parentheses.

We may blame television for the number of products based on characters in children's TV shows — from Big Bird to Sponge-Bob — but in fact merchandising that capitalizes on a character's popularity started long before television. Raggedy Ann began as a child's rag doll, and a few years later books about (she / her) and her brother, Raggedy Andy, were published. A cartoonist named Johnny Gruelle painted a cloth face on a family doll and applied for a patent in 1915. Later Gruelle began writing and illustrating stories about Raggedy Ann, and in 1918 (he / him) and a publisher teamed up to publish the books and sell the dolls. He was not the only one to try to sell products linked to children's stories. Beatrix Potter published the first of many Peter Rabbit picture books in 1902, and no one was better than (she / her) at making a living from spin-offs. After Peter Rabbit and Benjamin Bunny became popular, Potter began putting pictures of (they / them) and their little animal friends on merchandise. Potter had fans all over the world, and she understood (them / their) wanting to see Peter Rabbit not only in books but also on teapots and plates and lamps and other furnishings for the nursery. Potter and Gruelle, like countless others before and since, knew that entertaining children could be a profitable business.

ON THE WEB > dianahacker.com/rules
Grammar exercises > Grammar > E-ex 24–1 and 24–2

25

Distinguish between *who* and *whom*.

The choice between *who* and *whom* (or *whoever* and *whomever*) occurs primarily in subordinate clauses and in questions. *Who* and *whoever,* subjective-case pronouns, are used for subjects and subject complements. *Whom* and *whomever,* objective-case pronouns, are used for objects.

An exception to this general rule occurs when the pronoun functions as the subject of an infinitive (see 25c). See also 24f.

> **GRAMMAR CHECKERS** catch misuses of *who* and *whom* (*whoever* and *whomever*) only about half the time. A grammar checker flagged the incorrect use of *whomever* in the sentence *Daniel donates money to whomever needs it*, recognizing that *whoever* is required as the subject of the verb *needs*. But it did not flag the incorrect use of *who* in this sentence: *My cousin Sylvie, who I am teaching to fly a kite, watches us every time we compete.*

25a In subordinate clauses, use *who* and *whoever* for subjects or subject complements, *whom* and *whomever* for all objects.

When *who* and *whom* (or *whoever* and *whomever*) introduce subordinate clauses, their case is determined by their function *within the clause they introduce.* To choose the correct pronoun, isolate the subordinate clause and then decide how the pronoun functions within it. (See "subordinate clauses," 64b.)

In the following two examples, the pronouns *who* and *whoever* function as the subjects of the clauses they introduce.

▶ First prize goes to the runner ~~whom~~ *who* collects the most points.

The subordinate clause is *who collects the most points.* The verb of the clause is *collects,* and its subject is *who.*

▶ He tells the story of his narrow escape to ~~whomever~~ *whoever* will listen.

The writer selected the pronoun *whomever,* thinking that it was the object of the preposition *to.* However, the object of the preposition is the entire subordinate clause *whoever will listen.* The verb of the clause is *will listen,* and the subject of the verb is *whoever.*

Who occasionally functions as a subject complement in a subordinate clause. Subject complements occur with linking verbs (usually *be, am, is, are, was, were, being,* and *been*). (See 63b.)

▶ From your social security number, anyone can find out

   who
   ~~whom~~ you are.
   ^

The subordinate clause is *who you are.* Its subject is *you,* and its subject complement is *who.*

When functioning as an object in a subordinate clause, *whom* (or *whomever*) appears out of order, before both the subject and the verb. To choose the correct pronoun, you must mentally restructure the clause.

                                  whom
▶ You will work with our senior traders, ~~who~~ you will meet
                                     ^

later.

The subordinate clause is *whom you will meet later.* The subject of the clause is *you* and the verb is *will meet. Whom* is the direct object of the verb. The correct choice becomes clear if you mentally restructure the clause: *you will meet whom.*

When functioning as the object of a preposition in a subordinate clause, *whom* is often separated from its preposition.

         whom
▶ The tutor ~~who~~ I was assigned to was very supportive.
        ^

Whom is the object of the preposition *to.* In this sentence, the writer might choose to drop *whom: The tutor I was assigned to was very supportive.*

NOTE: Inserted expressions such as *they know, I think,* and *she says* should be ignored in determining whether to use *who* or *whom.*

▶ All of the show-offs, bullies, and tough guys in school

                            who
want to take on a big guy ~~whom~~ they know will not
                            ^

hurt them.

Who is the subject of *will hurt,* not the object of *know.*

25b In questions, use *who* and *whoever* for subjects, *whom* and *whomever* for all objects.

When *who* and *whom* (or *whoever* and *whomever*) are used to open questions, their case is determined by their function within the question. In the following example, *who* functions as the subject of the question.

> *Who*
> ▶ ~~Whom~~ was responsible for creating that computer virus?
>   ^
> *Who* is the subject of the verb *was*.

When *whom* functions as the object of a verb or the object of a preposition in a question, it appears out of normal order. To choose the correct pronoun, you must mentally restructure the question.

> *Whom*
> ▶ ~~Who~~ did the Democratic Party nominate in 1992?
>   ^
> *Whom* is the direct object of the verb *did nominate*. This becomes clear if you restructure the question: *The Democratic Party did nominate whom in 1992?*

> *Whom*
> ▶ ~~Who~~ did you enter into the contract with?
>   ^
> *Whom* is the object of the preposition *with*, as is clear if you recast the question: *You did enter into the contract with whom?*

25c Use *whom* for subjects or objects of infinitives.

An infinitive is the word *to* followed by the base form of a verb. (See 64c.) Subjects of infinitives are an exception to the rule that subjects must be in the subjective case. Whenever an infinitive has a subject, it must be in the objective case. Objects of infinitives also are in the objective case.

>   *whom*
> ▶ On the subject of health care, I don't know ~~who~~ to believe.
>   ^

NOTE: In spoken English, *who* is frequently used when the correct *whom* sounds too stuffy. Even educated speakers are likely to say *Who* [not *Whom*] *did Joe replace?* Although some readers will accept such constructions in informal written English, it is safer to use *whom* in formal English: *Whom did Joe replace?*

ON THE WEB > dianahacker.com/rules
   Language Debates > *who* versus *whom*

EXERCISE 25–1   Edit the following sentences to eliminate errors in the use of *who* and *whom* (or *whoever* and *whomever*). If a sentence is correct, write "correct" after it. Answers to lettered sentences appear in the back of the book. Example:

> *whom*
> What is the address of the artist ~~who~~ Antonio hired?
>   ^

 a. The roundtable featured scholars who I had never heard of.
 b. Arriving late for rehearsal, we had no idea who was supposed to dance with whom.
 c. Whom did you support in the last presidential election?
 d. Daniel donates money to whomever needs it.
 e. So many singers came to the audition that Natalia had trouble deciding who to select for the choir.

 1. My cousin Sylvie, who I am teaching to fly a kite, watches us every time we compete.
 2. Who decided to research the history of Hungarians in New Brunswick?
 3. According to the Greek myth, the Sphinx devoured those who could not answer her riddles.
 4. The people who ordered their medications from Canada were retirees whom don't have health insurance.
 5. Who did the committee select?

ON THE WEB > dianahacker.com/rules
   Grammar exercises > Grammar > E-ex 25–1 and 25–2

26

Choose adjectives and adverbs with care.

Adjectives ordinarily modify nouns or pronouns; occasionally they function as subject complements following linking verbs. Adverbs modify verbs, adjectives, or other adverbs. (See 62d and 62e.)

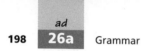

Many adverbs are formed by adding *-ly* to adjectives (*normal, normally; smooth, smoothly*). But don't assume that all words ending in *-ly* are adverbs or that all adverbs end in *-ly*. Some adjectives end in *-ly* (*lovely, friendly*) and some adverbs don't (*always, here, there*). When in doubt, consult a dictionary.

> **ESL** In English, adjectives are not pluralized to agree with the words they modify: *The red [not reds] roses were a wonderful surprise.*

> **GRAMMAR CHECKERS** can flag a number of problems with adjectives and adverbs: some misuses of *bad* or *badly* and *good* or *well*; some double comparisons, such as *more meaner*; some absolute comparisons, such as *most unique*; and some double negatives, such as *can't hardly*. However, the programs miss more problems than they find. Programs ignored errors like these: *could have been handled more professional* and *hadn't been bathed regular.*

26a Use adverbs, not adjectives, to modify verbs, adjectives, and adverbs.

When adverbs modify verbs (or verbals), they nearly always answer the question When? Where? How? Why? Under what conditions? How often? or To what degree? When adverbs modify adjectives or other adverbs, they usually qualify or intensify the meaning of the word they modify. (See 62e.)

Adjectives are often used incorrectly in place of adverbs in casual or nonstandard speech.

▶ The arrangement worked out ~~perfect~~ *perfectly* for everyone.

▶ The manager must see that the office runs ~~smooth~~ *smoothly* and ~~efficient.~~ *efficiently*.

The adverb *perfectly* modifies the verb *worked out*; the adverbs *smoothly* and *efficiently* modify the verb *runs*.

▶ In the early 1970s, chances for survival of the bald eagle

      really

looked ~~real~~ slim.

      ^

Only adverbs can be used to modify adjectives or other adverbs. *Really* intensifies the meaning of the adjective *slim*.

NOTE: The incorrect use of the adjective *good* in place of the adverb *well* to modify a verb is especially common in casual and nonstandard speech. Use *well,* not *good,* to modify a verb in your writing.

                          well

▶ We were glad that Sanya had done ~~good~~ on the CPA exam.

                                   ^

The adverb *well* should be used to modify the verb *had done.*

The word *well* is an adjective, however, when it means "healthy," "satisfactory," or "fortunate."

    I feel very well today.

    All is well.

    It is just as well.

ESL The placement of adverbs varies from language to language. Unlike some languages, English does not allow an adverb between a verb (*poured*) and its direct object (*the liquid*). See 30f.

                               slowly

▶ In the last stage of our experiment, we poured ~~slowly~~ the

                                     ^

    liquid into the container.

26b Use adjectives, not adverbs, as subject complements.

A subject complement follows a linking verb and completes the meaning of the subject. (See 63b.) When an adjective functions as a subject complement, it describes the subject.

    Justice is *blind.*

Problems can arise with verbs such as *smell, taste, look,* and *feel,* which sometimes, but not always, function as linking verbs. If the word following one of these verbs describes the subject, use an adjective; if it modifies the verb, use an adverb.

ADJECTIVE	The detective looked *cautious.*
ADVERB	The detective looked *cautiously* for fingerprints.

The adjective *cautious* describes the detective; the adverb *cautiously* modifies the verb *looked.*

Linking verbs suggest states of being, not actions. Notice, for example, the different meanings of *looked* in the preceding examples. To look cautious suggests the state of being cautious; to look cautiously is to perform an action in a cautious way.

▶ The lilacs in our backyard smell especially ~~sweetly~~ *sweet* this year.

▶ Lori looked ~~well~~ *good* in her new go-go boots.

The verbs *smell* and *looked* suggest states of being, not actions. Therefore, they should be followed by adjectives, not adverbs. (Contrast with action verbs: *We smelled the flowers. Lori looked for her go-go boots.*)

When the verb *feel* refers to the state of a person's health or emotions, it is a linking verb and should be followed by an adjective.

▶ We felt ~~badly~~ *bad* upon hearing of your grandmother's death.

Another adjective, such as *saddened,* could be used in place of *bad.*

ON THE WEB > **dianahacker.com/rules**
Language Debates > *bad* versus *badly*

26c Use comparatives and superlatives with care.

Most adjectives and adverbs have three forms: the positive, the comparative, and the superlative.

POSITIVE	COMPARATIVE	SUPERLATIVE
soft	softer	softest
fast	faster	fastest
careful	more careful	most careful
bad	worse	worst
good	better	best

Comparative versus superlative

Use the comparative to compare two things, the superlative to compare three or more.

▶ Which of these two low-carb drinks is ~~best~~?
  better?

▶ Though Shaw and Jackson are impressive, Hobbs is the ~~more~~ qualified of the three candidates running for mayor.
  most

Form of comparatives and superlatives

To form comparatives and superlatives of most one- and two-syllable adjectives, use the endings *-er* and *-est*: *smooth, smoother, smoothest; easy, easier, easiest*. With longer adjectives, use *more* and *most* (or *less* and *least* for downward comparisons): *exciting, more exciting, most exciting; helpful, less helpful, least helpful*.

Some one-syllable adverbs take the endings *-er* and *-est* (*fast, faster, fastest*), but longer adverbs and all of those ending in *-ly* form the comparative and superlative with *more* and *most* (or *less* and *least*).

The comparative and superlative forms of the following adjectives and adverbs are irregular: *good, better, best; well, better, best; bad, worse, worst; badly, worse, worst*.

▶ The Kirov is the ~~talentedest~~ ballet company we have seen.
  most talented

▶ Lloyd's luck couldn't have been ~~worser~~ than David's.
  worse

Double comparatives or superlatives

Do not use double comparatives or superlatives. When you have added *-er* or *-est* to an adjective or adverb, do not also use *more* or *most* (or *less* or *least*).

▶ Of all her family, Julia is the ~~most~~ happiest about the move.

▶ All the polls indicated that Gore was more ~~likelier~~ *likely* to win

than Bush.

Absolute concepts

Avoid expressions such as *more straight, less perfect, very round,* and *most unique.* Either something is unique or it isn't. It is illogical to suggest that absolute concepts come in degrees.

▶ That is the most ~~unique~~ *unusual* wedding gown I have ever seen.

▶ The painting would have been even more ~~priceless~~ *valuable* had it

been signed.

ON THE WEB > dianahacker.com/rules
Language Debates > Absolute concepts such as *unique*

26d Avoid double negatives.

Standard English allows two negatives only if a positive meaning is intended: *The orchestra was not unhappy with its performance.* Double negatives used to emphasize negation are nonstandard.

Negative modifiers such as *never, no,* and *not* should not be paired with other negative modifiers or with negative words such as *neither, none, no one, nobody,* and *nothing.*

▶ Management is not doing ~~nothing~~ *anything* to see that the trash is

picked up.

The double negative *not . . . nothing* is nonstandard.

The modifiers *hardly, barely,* and *scarcely* are considered negatives in standard English, so they should not be used with negatives such as *not, no one,* or *never.*

▶ Maxine is so weak she ~~can't~~ *can* hardly climb stairs.

EXERCISE 26–1 Edit the following sentences to eliminate errors in the use of adjectives and adverbs. If a sentence is correct, write "correct" after it. Answers to lettered sentences appear in the back of the book. Example:

> We weren't surprised by how ~~good~~ *well* the sidecar racing team
>
> flowed through the tricky course.

a. Did you do good on last week's chemistry exam?
b. With the budget deadline approaching, our office hasn't hardly had time to handle routine correspondence.
c. Some flowers smell surprisingly bad.
d. The customer complained that he hadn't been treated nice.
e. Of all my relatives, Uncle Roberto is the most cleverest.

1. When you answer the phone, speak clear and courteous.
2. Who was more upset about the loss? Was it the coach or the quarterback or the owner of the team?
3. To a novice skateboarder, even a basic move like the ollie seems real challenging.
4. After checking how bad I had been hurt, my sister dialed 911.
5. If the college's Web page had been updated more regular, students would have learned about the new course offerings.

ON THE WEB > **dianahacker.com/rules**
    Grammar exercises > Grammar > E-ex 26–1 and 26–2

27

Choose appropriate verb forms, tenses, and moods in standard English.

In nonstandard English, spoken by those who share a regional or cultural heritage, verb forms sometimes differ from those of standard English. In writing, use standard English verb forms unless you are quoting nonstandard speech or using nonstandard forms for literary effect. (See 17d.)

Except for the verb *be,* all verbs in English have five forms. The following list shows the five forms and provides a sample sentence in which each might appear.

BASE FORM	Usually I (*walk, ride*).
PAST TENSE	Yesterday I (*walked, rode*).
PAST PARTICIPLE	I have (*walked, ridden*) many times before.
PRESENT PARTICIPLE	I am (*walking, riding*) right now.
-S FORM	He/she/it (*walks, rides*) regularly.

Both the past-tense and past-participle forms of regular verbs end in *-ed* (*walked, walked*). Irregular verbs form the past tense and past participle in other ways (*rode, ridden*).

The verb *be* has eight forms instead of the usual five: *be, am, is, are, was, were, being, been.*

> **GRAMMAR CHECKERS** sometimes flag misused irregular verbs in sentences, such as *I had drove the car to school* and *Lucia seen the movie already.* But you cannot rely on grammar checkers to identify problems with irregular verbs — they miss about twice as many errors as they find.

27a Choose standard English forms of irregular verbs.

For all regular verbs, the past-tense and past-participle forms are the same (ending in *-ed* or *-d*), so there is no danger of confusion. This is not true, however, for irregular verbs, such as the following.

BASE FORM	PAST TENSE	PAST PARTICIPLE
go	went	gone
fight	fought	fought
fly	flew	flown

The past-tense form always occurs alone, without a helping verb. It expresses action that occurred entirely in the past: *I rode to work yesterday. I walked to work last Tuesday.* The past participle is used with a helping verb. It forms the perfect tenses with *has, have,* or *had*; it forms the passive voice with *be, am, is, are, was, were, being,* or *been.* (See 62c for a complete list of helping verbs and 27f for a survey of tenses.)

| PAST TENSE | Last July, we *went* to Paris. |
| HELPING VERB + PAST PARTICIPLE | We *have gone* to Paris twice. |

The list of common irregular verbs beginning at the bottom of this page will help you distinguish between past tense and past participle. Choose the past-participle form if the verb in your sentence requires a helping verb; choose the past-tense form if the verb does not require a helping verb.

>   *saw*
> Yesterday we ~~seen~~ an unidentified flying object.
>   ^

The past-tense form *saw* is required because there is no helping verb.

>   *stolen*
> The truck was apparently ~~stole~~ while the driver ate lunch.
>   ^

>   *fallen*
> By Friday, the stock market had ~~fell~~ two hundred points.
>   ^

Because of the helping verbs, the past-participle forms are required: *was stolen, had fallen.*

When in doubt about the standard English forms of irregular verbs, consult the following list or look up the base form of the verb in the dictionary, which also lists any irregular forms. (If no additional forms are listed in the dictionary, the verb is regular, not irregular.)

Common irregular verbs

BASE FORM	PAST TENSE	PAST PARTICIPLE
arise	arose	arisen
awake	awoke, awaked	awaked, awoke
be	was, were	been
beat	beat	beaten, beat
become	became	become
begin	began	begun
bend	bent	bent
bite	bit	bitten, bit
blow	blew	blown
break	broke	broken
bring	brought	brought
build	built	built
burst	burst	burst
buy	bought	bought
catch	caught	caught
choose	chose	chosen

→

BASE FORM	PAST TENSE	PAST PARTICIPLE
cling	clung	clung
come	came	come
cost	cost	cost
deal	dealt	dealt
dig	dug	dug
dive	dived, dove	dived
do	did	done
drag	dragged	dragged
draw	drew	drawn
dream	dreamed, dreamt	dreamed, dreamt
drink	drank	drunk
drive	drove	driven
eat	ate	eaten
fall	fell	fallen
fight	fought	fought
find	found	found
fly	flew	flown
forget	forgot	forgotten, forgot
freeze	froze	frozen
get	got	gotten, got
give	gave	given
go	went	gone
grow	grew	grown
hang (suspend)	hung	hung
hang (execute)	hanged	hanged
have	had	had
hear	heard	heard
hide	hid	hidden
hurt	hurt	hurt
keep	kept	kept
know	knew	known
lay (put)	laid	laid
lead	led	led
lend	lent	lent
let (allow)	let	let
lie (recline)	lay	lain
lose	lost	lost
make	made	made
prove	proved	proved, proven
read	read	read
ride	rode	ridden
ring	rang	rung
rise (get up)	rose	risen
run	ran	run
say	said	said
see	saw	seen
send	sent	sent

BASE FORM	PAST TENSE	PAST PARTICIPLE
set (place)	set	set
shake	shook	shaken
shoot	shot	shot
shrink	shrank	shrunk
sing	sang	sung
sink	sank	sunk
sit (be seated)	sat	sat
slay	slew	slain
sleep	slept	slept
speak	spoke	spoken
spin	spun	spun
spring	sprang	sprung
stand	stood	stood
steal	stole	stolen
sting	stung	stung
strike	struck	struck, stricken
swear	swore	sworn
swim	swam	swum
swing	swung	swung
take	took	taken
teach	taught	taught
throw	threw	thrown
wake	woke, waked	waked, woken
wear	wore	worn
wring	wrung	wrung
write	wrote	written

27b Distinguish among the forms of *lie* and *lay*.

Writers and speakers frequently confuse the various forms of *lie* (meaning "to recline or rest on a surface") and *lay* (meaning "to put or place something"). *Lie* is an intransitive verb; it does not take a direct object: *The tax forms lie on the table.* The verb *lay* is transitive; it takes a direct object: *Please lay the tax forms on the table.* (See 63b.)

In addition to confusing the meaning of *lie* and *lay*, writers and speakers are often unfamiliar with the standard English forms of these verbs.

BASE FORM	PAST TENSE	PAST PARTICIPLE	PRESENT PARTICIPLE
lie	lay	lain	lying
lay	laid	laid	laying

> *lay*
> Sue was so exhausted that she l̶a̶i̶d̶ down for a nap.
>   ^

The past-tense form of *lie* ("to recline") is *lay*.

> *lain*
> The patient had l̶a̶i̶d̶ in an uncomfortable position all night.
>   ^

The past-participle form of *lie* ("to recline") is *lain*. If the correct English seems too stilted, recast the sentence: *The patient had been lying in an uncomfortable position all night.*

> *laid*
> The prosecutor l̶a̶y̶ the pistol on a table close to the jurors.
>   ^

The past-tense form of *lay* ("to place") is *laid*.

> *lying*
> Letters dating from the Civil War were l̶a̶y̶i̶n̶g̶ in the corner of
>   ^
> the chest.

The present participle of *lie* ("to rest on a surface") is *lying*.

ON THE WEB > dianahacker.com/rules
Language Debates > *lie* versus *lay*

EXERCISE 27–1 Edit the following sentences to eliminate problems with irregular verbs. If a sentence is correct, write "correct" after it. Answers to lettered sentences appear in the back of the book. Example:

> *saw*
> Was it you I s̶e̶e̶n̶ last night at the concert?
>   ^

a. When I get the urge to exercise, I lay down until it passes.
b. Grandmother had drove our new SUV to the sunrise church service on Savage Mountain, so we were left with the station wagon.
c. A pile of dirty rags was laying at the bottom of the stairs.
d. How did the computer know that the gamer had went from the room with the blue ogre to the hall where the gold was heaped?
e. Abraham Lincoln took good care of his legal clients; the contracts he drew for the Illinois Central Railroad could never be broke.

1. The burglar must have gone immediately upstairs, grabbed what looked good, and took off.
2. Have you ever dreamed that you were falling from a cliff or flying through the air?

3. Tomás reached for the pen, signed the title page of his novel, and then laid the book on the table for the first customer in line.
4. In her junior year, Cindy run the 440-yard dash in 51.1 seconds.
5. Larry claimed that he had drank a bad soda, but Esther suspected the truth.

ON THE WEB > **dianahacker.com/rules**
Grammar exercises > Grammar > E-ex 27–1

27c Use *-s* (or *-es*) endings on present-tense verbs that have third-person singular subjects.

All singular nouns (*child, tree*) and the pronouns *he, she,* and *it* are third-person singular; indefinite pronouns such as *everyone* and *neither* are also third-person singular. When the subject of a sentence is third-person singular, its verb takes an *-s* or *-es* ending in the present tense. (See also 21.)

	SINGULAR		PLURAL	
FIRST PERSON	I	know	we	know
SECOND PERSON	you	know	you	know
THIRD PERSON	he/she/it	knows	they	know
	child	knows	parents	know
	everyone	knows		

In nonstandard speech, the *-s* ending required by standard English is sometimes omitted.

▶   *drives*
My cousin ~~drive~~ to Cape Cod every weekend in the summer.
     ^

▶   *turns*   *dissolves*   *eats*
Sulfur dioxide ~~turn~~ leaves yellow, ~~dissolve~~ marble, and ~~eat~~
           ^   ^   ^

away iron and steel.

The subjects *cousin* and *sulfur dioxide* are third-person singular, so the verbs must end in *-s*.

TIP: Do not add the *-s* ending to the verb if the subject is not third-person singular.

The writers of the following sentences, knowing they sometimes dropped *-s* endings from verbs, overcorrected by adding the endings where they don't belong.

▶ I prepares program specifications and logic diagrams.

The writer mistakenly concluded that the -s ending belongs on present-tense verbs used with *all* singular subjects, not just *third-person* singular subjects. The pronoun *I* is first-person singular, so its verb does not require the -s.

▶ The dirt floors requires continual sweeping.

The writer mistakenly thought that the -s ending on the verb indicated plurality. The -s goes on present-tense verbs used with third-person *singular* subjects.

Has *versus* have

In the present tense, use *has* with third-person singular subjects; all other subjects require *have.*

	SINGULAR		PLURAL	
FIRST PERSON	I	have	we	have
SECOND PERSON	you	have	you	have
THIRD PERSON	he/she/it	has	they	have

In some dialects, *have* is used with all subjects. But standard English requires *has* for third-person singular subjects.

                                            has
▶ This respected musician almost always ~~have~~ a message to

convey in his work.

                                     has
▶ As for the retirement income program, it ~~have~~ finally been

established.

The subjects *musician* and *it* are third-person singular, so the verb should be *has* in each case.

TIP: Do not use *has* if the subject is not third-person singular. The writers of the following sentences were aware that they often wrote *have* when standard English requires *has.* Here they are using what appears to them to be the "more correct" form, but in an inappropriate context.

> *have*
> My business law classes ~~has~~ helped me to understand more
>   ^
about contracts.

> *have*
> I ~~has~~ much to be thankful for.
>   ^

The subjects of these sentences — *classes* and *I* — are third-person plural and first-person singular, so standard English requires *have*. *Has* is used with third-person singular subjects only.

Does *versus* do *and* doesn't *versus* don't

In the present tense, use *does* and *doesn't* with third-person singular subjects; all other subjects require *do* and *don't*.

	SINGULAR		PLURAL	
FIRST PERSON	I	do/don't	we	do/don't
SECOND PERSON	you	do/don't	you	do/don't
THIRD PERSON	he/she/it	does/doesn't	they	do/don't

> *doesn't*
> Grandfather really ~~don't~~ have a place to call home.
>   ^

> *Does*
> ~~Do~~ she know the correct procedure for setting up the
> ^
experiment?

Grandfather and *she* are third-person singular, so the verbs should be *doesn't* and *does*.

Am, is, *and* are; was *and* were

The verb *be* has three forms in the present tense (*am, is, are*) and two in the past tense (*was, were*). Use *am* and *was* with first-person singular subjects; use *is* and *was* with third-person singular subjects. With all other subjects, use *are* and *were*.

	SINGULAR		PLURAL	
FIRST PERSON	I	am/was	we	are/were
SECOND PERSON	you	are/were	you	are/were
THIRD PERSON	he/she/it	is/was	they	are/were

▶ Judy wanted to borrow Tim's notes, but she ~~were~~ *was* too shy to

ask for them.

The subject *she* is third-person singular, so the verb should be *was*.

▶ Did you think you ~~was~~ *were* going to drown?

The subject *you* is second-person singular, so the verb should be *were*.

GRAMMAR CHECKERS are fairly good at catching missing *-s* endings on verbs and some misused *-s* forms of the verb, consistently flagging errors such as *The training session take place later today* and *The careful camper learn to feel the signs of a coming storm.* (See the grammar checker advice on p. 167 for more information about subject-verb agreement.)

27d Do not omit *-ed* endings on verbs.

Speakers who do not fully pronounce *-ed* endings sometimes omit them unintentionally in writing. Failure to pronounce *-ed* endings is common in many dialects and in informal speech even in standard English. In the following frequently used words and phrases, for example, the *-ed* ending is not always fully pronounced.

advised	developed	prejudiced	supposed to
asked	fixed	pronounced	used to
concerned	frightened	stereotyped	

When a verb is regular, both the past tense and the past participle are formed by adding *-ed* to the base form of the verb.

Past tense

Use an *-ed* or *-d* ending to express the past tense of regular verbs. The past tense is used when the action occurred entirely in the past.

▶ Over the weekend, Ed ~~fix~~ his brother's skateboard and tuned
         fixed
        ^

up his mother's 1977 Cougar.

▶ Last summer, my counselor ~~advise~~ me to ask my chemistry
                        advised
                         ^

instructor for help.

Past participles

Past participles are used in three ways: (1) following *have, has,* or
had to form one of the perfect tenses; (2) following *be, am, is,
are, was, were, being,* or *been* to form the passive voice; and (3) as
adjectives modifying nouns or pronouns. The perfect tenses are
listed on page 216, and the passive voice is discussed in 8a. For a
discussion of participles functioning as adjectives, see 64c.

▶ Robin has ~~ask~~ me to go to California with her.
      asked
       ^

Has asked is present perfect tense (*have* or *has* followed by a past
participle).

▶ Though it is not a new phenomenon, domestic violence is
   publicized
 ~~publicize~~ more frequently than before.
 ^

Is publicized is a verb in the passive voice (a form of *be* followed by
a past participle).

▶ All aerobics classes end in a cool-down period to stretch
   tightened
 ~~tighten~~ muscles.
 ^

The past participle *tightened* functions as an adjective modifying
the noun *muscles*.

GRAMMAR CHECKERS flag missing *-ed* endings on verbs more
often than not. Unfortunately, they often suggest an *-ing* ending (*passing*) rather than the missing *-ed* ending (*passed*), as in
the following sentence: *The law was pass last week.*

27e Do not omit needed verbs.

Although standard English allows some linking verbs and helping verbs to be contracted, at least in informal contexts, it does
not allow them to be omitted.

Linking verbs, used to link subjects to subject complements, are frequently a form of *be: be, am, is, are, was, were,
being, been.* (See 63b.) Some of these forms may be contracted
(*I'm, she's, we're, you're, they're*), but they should not be omitted
altogether.

▶ When we quiet in the evening, we can hear crickets in the woods.
  ^are^

▶ Alvin a man who can defend himself.
  ^is^

Helping verbs, used with main verbs, include forms of *be,
do,* and *have* or the words *can, will, shall, could, would, should,
may, might,* and *must.* (See 62c.) Some helping verbs may be
contracted (*he's leaving, we'll celebrate, they've been told*), but
they should not be omitted altogether.

▶ We been in Chicago since last Thursday.
  ^have^

▶ Do you know someone who be good for the job?
  ^would^

ESL Some languages do not require a linking verb between a subject and its complement. English, however, requires a verb in
every sentence. See 30a.

▶ Every night, I read a short book to my daughter. When I
  ^am^

   too busy, my husband reads to her.

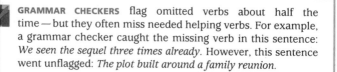

GRAMMAR CHECKERS flag omitted verbs about half the
time — but they often miss needed helping verbs. For example,
a grammar checker caught the missing verb in this sentence:
We seen the sequel three times already. However, this sentence
went unflagged: *The plot built around a family reunion.*

EXERCISE 27–2 Edit the following sentences to eliminate problems with -s and -ed verb forms and with omitted verbs. If a sentence is correct, write "correct" after it. Answers to lettered sentences appear in the back of the book. Example:

> _covers_
> The Pell Grant sometimes ~~cover~~ the student's full tuition.
> ^

a. The glass sculptures of the Swan Boats was prominent in the brightly lit lobby.
b. Visitors to the glass museum were not suppose to touch the exhibits.
c. Our church has all the latest technology, even a close-circuit television.
d. Christos didn't know about Marlo's promotion because he never listens. He always talking.
e. Most psychologists agree that no one performs well under stress.

1. Have there ever been a time in your life when you were too depressed to get out of bed?
2. My days in this department have taught me to do what I'm told without asking questions.
3. We have change our plan and are waiting out the storm before leaving.
4. Winter training for search-and-rescue divers consist of building up a tolerance to icy water temperatures.
5. How would you feel if a love one had been a victim of a crime like this?

ON THE WEB > dianahacker.com/rules
Grammar exercises > Grammar > E-ex 27–2

27f Choose the appropriate verb tense.

Tenses indicate the time of an action in relation to the time of the speaking or writing about that action.

The most common problem with tenses — shifting confusingly from one tense to another — is discussed in 13. Other problems with tenses are detailed in this section, after the following survey of tenses.

GRAMMAR CHECKERS do not flag most problems with tense discussed in this section: special uses of the present tense, use of past versus past perfect, and sequence of tenses.

Survey of tenses

Tenses are classified as present, past, and future, with simple, perfect, and progressive forms for each.

The simple tenses indicate relatively simple time relations. The simple present tense is used primarily for actions occurring at the time of the speaking or for actions occurring regularly. The simple past tense is used for actions completed in the past. The simple future tense is used for actions that will occur in the future. In the following table, the simple tenses are given for the regular verb *walk*, the irregular verb *ride*, and the highly irregular verb *be*.

SIMPLE PRESENT

SINGULAR		PLURAL	
I	walk, ride, am	we	walk, ride, are
you	walk, ride, are	you	walk, ride, are
he/she/it	walks, rides, is	they	walk, ride, are

SIMPLE PAST

SINGULAR		PLURAL	
I	walked, rode, was	we	walked, rode, were
you	walked, rode, were	you	walked, rode, were
he/she/it	walked, rode, was	they	walked, rode, were

SIMPLE FUTURE

I, you, he/she/it, we, they	will walk, ride, be

More complex time relations are indicated by the perfect tenses. A verb in one of the perfect tenses (a form of *have* plus the past participle) expresses an action that was or will be completed at the time of another action.

PRESENT PERFECT

I, you, we, they	have walked, ridden, been
he/she/it	has walked, ridden, been

PAST PERFECT

I, you, he/she/it, we, they	had walked, ridden, been

FUTURE PERFECT

I, you, he/she/it, we, they	will have walked, ridden, been

The simple and perfect tenses just discussed have progressive forms that describe actions in progress. A progressive verb consists of a form of *be* followed by a present participle. The progressive forms are not normally used with mental activity verbs such as *believe, know,* and *think.*

PRESENT PROGRESSIVE

I	am walking, riding, being
he/she/it	is walking, riding, being
you, we, they	are walking, riding, being

PAST PROGRESSIVE

| I, he/she/it | was walking, riding, being |
| you, we, they | were walking, riding, being |

FUTURE PROGRESSIVE

| I, you, he/she/it, we, they | will be walking, riding, being |

PRESENT PERFECT PROGRESSIVE

| I, you, we, they | have been walking, riding, being |
| he/she/it | has been walking, riding, being |

PAST PERFECT PROGRESSIVE

| I, you, he/she/it, we, they | had been walking, riding, being |

FUTURE PERFECT PROGRESSIVE

| I, you, he/she/it, we, they | will have been walking, riding, being |

Special uses of the present tense

Use the present tense when expressing general truths, when writing about literature, and when quoting, summarizing, or paraphrasing an author's views.

General truths or scientific principles should appear in the present tense, unless such principles have been disproved.

>   *revolves*
> ▶ Galileo taught that the earth ~~revolved~~ around the sun.
>   ^

Since Galileo's teaching has not been discredited, the verb should be in the present tense. The following sentence, however, is acceptable: *Ptolemy taught that the sun revolved around the earth.*

When writing about a work of literature, you may be tempted to use the past tense. The convention, however, is to describe fictional events in the present tense.

> In Masuji Ibuse's *Black Rain*, a child ~~reached~~ for a pomegranate
>   ^ *reaches*
> in his mother's garden, and a moment later he ~~was~~ dead,
>   ^ *is*
> killed by the blast of the atomic bomb.

When you are quoting, summarizing, or paraphrasing the author of a nonliterary work, use present-tense verbs such as *writes, reports, asserts,* and so on. This convention is usually followed even when the author is dead (unless a date or the context specifies the time of writing).

> Baron Bowan of Colwood ~~wrote~~ that "a metaphysician is one
>   ^ *writes*
> who goes into a dark cellar at midnight without a light, looking
>
> for a black cat that is not there."

EXCEPTION: When you are documenting a paper with the APA (American Psychological Association) style of in-text citations, use past-tense verbs such as *reported* or *demonstrated* or present perfect verbs such as *has reported* or *has demonstrated.*

> E. Wilson (1994) reported that positive reinforcement alone was a less effective teaching technique than a mixture of positive reinforcement and constructive criticism.

The past perfect tense

The past perfect tense consists of a past participle preceded by *had* (*had worked, had gone*). This tense is used for an action already completed by the time of another past action or for an action already completed at some specific past time.

> Everyone *had spoken* by the time I arrived.

> Everyone *had spoken* by 10:00 a.m.

Writers sometimes use the simple past tense when they should use the past perfect.

▶ We built our cabin high on a pine knoll, forty feet above an

had been

abandoned quarry that ~~was~~ flooded in 1920 to create a lake.
^

The building of the cabin and the flooding of the quarry both occurred in the past, but the flooding was completed before the time
of building.

had
▶ By the time dinner was served, the guest of honor left.
^

The past perfect tense is needed because the action of leaving was
already completed at a specific past time (when dinner was served).

Some writers tend to overuse the past perfect tense. Do not
use the past perfect if two past actions occurred at the same
time.

▶ When we arrived in Paris, Pauline ~~had~~ met us at the train

station.

Sequence of tenses with infinitives and participles

An infinitive is the base form of a verb preceded by *to*. (See
64c.) Use the present infinitive to show action at the same time
as or later than the action of the verb in the sentence.

raise
▶ The club had hoped to ~~have raised~~ a thousand dollars by April 1.
^

The action expressed in the infinitive (*to raise*) occurred later than
the action of the sentence's verb (*had hoped*).

Use the perfect form of an infinitive (*to have* followed by
the past participle) for an action occurring earlier than that of
the verb in the sentence.

have joined
▶ Dan would like to ~~join~~ the navy, but he did not pass the physical.
^

The liking occurs in the present; the joining would have occurred
in the past.

Like the tense of an infinitive, the tense of a participle is
governed by the tense of the sentence's verb. Use the present

participle (ending in *-ing*) for an action occurring at the same time as that of the sentence's verb.

> Hiking the Appalachian Trail in early spring, we spotted many wildflowers.

Use the past participle (such as *given* or *helped*) or the present perfect participle (*having* plus the past participle) for an action occurring before that of the verb.

> *Discovered* off the coast of Florida, the *Atocha* yielded many treasures.

> *Having worked* her way through college, Lee graduated debt-free.

27g Use the subjunctive mood in the few contexts that require it.

There are three moods in English: the *indicative,* used for facts, opinions, and questions; the *imperative,* used for orders or advice; and the *subjunctive,* used in certain contexts to express wishes, requests, or conditions contrary to fact. Of these moods, only the subjunctive causes problems for writers.

Forms of the subjunctive

In the subjunctive mood, present-tense verbs do not change form to indicate the number and person of the subject (see 21). Instead, the subjunctive uses the base form of the verb (*be, drive, employ*) with all subjects.

> It is important that you *be* [not *are*] prepared for the interview.

> We asked that she *drive* [not *drives*] more slowly.

Also, in the subjunctive mood, there is only one past-tense form of *be*: *were* (never *was*).

> If I *were* [not *was*] you, I'd proceed more cautiously.

Uses of the subjunctive

The subjunctive mood appears only in a few contexts: in contrary-to-fact clauses beginning with *if* or expressing a wish; in *that* clauses following verbs such as *ask, insist, recommend, request,* and *suggest*; and in certain set expressions.

IN CONTRARY-TO-FACT CLAUSES BEGINNING WITH *IF* When a subordinate clause beginning with *if* expresses a condition contrary to fact, use the subjunctive mood.

▶ If I ~~was~~ a member of Congress, I would vote for that bill.
   were

▶ We could be less cautious if Jake ~~was~~ more trustworthy.
   were

The verbs in these sentences express conditions that do not exist: The writer is not a member of Congress, and Jake is not trustworthy.

Do not use the subjunctive mood in *if* clauses expressing conditions that exist or may exist.

If Dana *wins* the contest, she will leave for Barcelona in June.

IN CONTRARY-TO-FACT CLAUSES EXPRESSING A WISH In formal English, the subjunctive is used in clauses expressing a wish or desire; in informal speech, however, the indicative is more common.

FORMAL   I wish that Dr. Vaughn *were* my professor.

INFORMAL   I wish that Dr. Vaughn *was* my professor.

IN *THAT* CLAUSES FOLLOWING VERBS SUCH AS *ASK, INSIST, REQUEST,* AND *SUGGEST* Because requests have not yet become reality, they are expressed in the subjunctive mood.

▶ Professor Moore insists that her students ~~are~~ on time.
   be

▶ We recommend that Lambert ~~files~~ form 1050 soon.
   file

IN CERTAIN SET EXPRESSIONS The subjunctive mood, once more widely used, remains in certain set expressions: *Be that as it may, as it were, far be it from me,* and so on.

GRAMMAR CHECKERS only sometimes flag problems with the subjunctive mood. What they catch is very spotty, so you must be alert to the correct uses of the subjunctive in your own writing.

EXERCISE 27-3 Edit the following sentences to eliminate errors in verb tense or mood. If a sentence is correct, write "correct" after it. Answers to lettered sentences appear in the back of the book. Example:

> *had been*
> After the path ~~was~~ plowed, we were able to walk through the park.
>   ^

a. The palace of Knossos in Crete is believed to have been destroyed by fire around 1375 BCE.

b. Watson and Crick discovered the mechanism that controlled inheritance in all life: the workings of the DNA molecule.

c. When Hitler decided to kill the Jews in 1941, did he know that Himmler and his SS had mass murder in mind since 1938?

d. Tonight's concert begins at 9:30. If it were earlier, I'd consider going.

e. As soon as my aunt applied for the position of pastor, the post was filled by an inexperienced seminary graduate who had been so hastily snatched that his mortarboard was still in midair.

1. Don Quixote, in Cervantes's novel, was an idealist ill suited for life in the real world.

2. Visiting the technology museum inspired the high school seniors and had reminded them that science could be fun.

3. I would like to have been on the *Mayflower* but not to have lived through the first winter.

4. When the director yelled "Action!" I forgot my lines, even though I practiced my part every waking hour for three days.

5. If midday naps were a regular practice in American workplaces, employees would be far more productive.

ON THE WEB > dianahacker.com/rules
Grammar exercises > Grammar > E-ex 27–3

ESL Challenges

This section of *Rules for Writers* is primarily for multilingual writers. You may find this section helpful if you learned English as a second language (ESL) or if you speak a language other than English with your friends and family.

ON THE WEB > **dianahacker.com/rules**
ESL help

28

Verbs

Both native and nonnative speakers of English encounter the following challenges with verbs, which are treated elsewhere in this book:

> making subjects and verbs agree (21)
>
> using irregular verb forms (27a)
>
> leaving off verb endings (27c, 27d)
>
> choosing the correct verb tense (27f)
>
> avoiding inappropriate uses of the passive voice (8a)

This section focuses on the major challenges that verbs can cause for multilingual writers.

28a Use the appropriate verb form and tense.

This section offers a brief review of English verb forms and tenses. See the chart on pages 233–35 for an overview of verb usage. For additional help, see 27f and 62c.

Basic verb forms

Every main verb in English has five forms, which are used to create all of the verb tenses in standard English. The chart at the top of page 225 shows these forms for the regular verb *help* and the irregular verbs *give* and *be*. (*Be* has the six forms listed in the chart as well as *am* and *are*, used in the present tense. See 27a for a list of common irregular verbs.)

Basic verb forms

VERB FORM	REGULAR VERB *HELP*	IRREGULAR VERB *GIVE*	IRREGULAR VERB *BE*
BASE FORM	help	give	be
PAST TENSE	helped	gave	was, were
PAST PARTICIPLE	helped	given	been
PRESENT PARTICIPLE	helping	giving	being
-S FORM	helps	gives	is

Simple tenses for general facts, states of being, habitual actions

SIMPLE PRESENT (BASE FORM OR *-S* FORM)   Simple present tense shows general facts, constant states, or habitual or repetitive actions. It is also used for scheduled future events. (For uses of the present tense in writing about literature, see p. 217.)

> We *donate* to a different charity each year.
>
> The sun *rises* in the east and *sets* in the west.
>
> The plane *leaves* tomorrow at 6:30 p.m.

SIMPLE PAST (BASE FORM + *-ED* OR *-D* OR IRREGULAR FORM)   Simple past tense expresses actions that happened at a specific time or during a specific period in the past. It can also show states of being and repetitive actions that have ended. It is often accompanied by a word (such as *ago* or *yesterday*) or a phrase (*in 1902, last year*) that indicates a specific past time. (See 27a for irregular past-tense forms.)

> She *drove* to Montana three years ago.
>
> When I *was* young, I usually *walked* to school with my sister.

SIMPLE FUTURE (*WILL* + BASE FORM)   Simple future tense expresses actions that will happen at some time in the future as well as promises or predictions of future events.

> I *will call* you next week.

Simple progressive forms for continuing actions

PRESENT PROGRESSIVE (*AM, IS, ARE* + PRESENT PARTICIPLE) Present progressive verbs show actions that are in progress at the present time but are not expected to remain constant or to continue indefinitely. Present progressive forms of verbs such as *leave*, *go*, *come*, and *move* are also used to express future actions.

> Carlos *is building* his house on a cliff overlooking the ocean.

> We *are going* to the circus tomorrow.

PAST PROGRESSIVE (*WAS, WERE* + PRESENT PARTICIPLE) Past progressive verbs express actions that were in progress at a specific past time. They often indicate a continuing action that was interrupted by another action. The past progressive form *was going to* or *were going to* is used for past plans that did not happen.

> Roy *was driving* a brand-new red Corvette yesterday.

> When my roommate walked in, we *were planning* her party.

> We *were going to* spend spring break in Florida, but we went to New York instead.

FUTURE PROGRESSIVE (*WILL* + *BE* + PRESENT PARTICIPLE) Future progressive verbs show actions that will be in progress at a certain time in the future.

> Naomi *will be flying* home tomorrow.

TIP: Certain verbs are not usually used in the progressive sense in English. In general, these verbs express a state of being or mental activity, not a dynamic action. Common examples are *appear, believe, belong, contain, have, hear, know, like, need, see, seem, taste, think, understand,* and *want.*

>   *want*
> ▶ I ~~am wanting~~ to see August Wilson's *Gem of the Ocean.*
>   ^

Some of these verbs, however, have special uses in which progressive forms are normal (*We are thinking about going to the Bahamas*). You should note exceptions as you encounter them.

Perfect tenses for actions that happened or will happen before another time

PRESENT PERFECT (*HAVE, HAS* + PAST PARTICIPLE) Present perfect tense expresses actions that began in the past and continue to the present or actions that happened at an unspecific time in the past.

> An-Mei *has* not *spoken* Chinese since she was a child.

> My parents *have traveled* to South Africa twice.

PAST PERFECT (*HAD* + PAST PARTICIPLE) The past perfect tense conveys actions that began in the past and continued to a more recent past time. It is also used for an action that happened at an unspecific time before another past event. (For uses of the past perfect in conditional sentences, see 28e.)

> By the time Hakan was fifteen, he *had* already *learned* to drive.

> I *had* just *finished* the test when the professor announced that time was up.

FUTURE PERFECT (*WILL* + *HAVE* + PAST PARTICIPLE) The future perfect tense expresses actions that will be completed before or at a specified future time.

> By the time I graduate, I *will have taken* five composition classes.

Perfect progressive forms for continuous past actions before another time

PRESENT PERFECT PROGRESSIVE (*HAVE, HAS* + *BEEN* + PRESENT PARTICIPLE) Present perfect progressive verbs express continuous actions that began in the past and continue to the present.

> My sister *has been living* in Oregon since 2001.

PAST PERFECT PROGRESSIVE (*HAD* + *BEEN* + PRESENT PARTICIPLE) Past perfect progressive verbs convey actions that began and continued in the past until some other past action.

> By the time I moved to Georgia, I *had been supporting* myself for five years.

FUTURE PERFECT PROGRESSIVE (*WILL* + *HAVE* + *BEEN* + PRESENT PARTICIPLE) Future perfect progressive verbs indicate actions that are or will be in progress before a specified time in the future.

By the time we reach the register, we *will have been waiting* in line for two full hours.

EXERCISE 28–1 Revise any sentences to correct errors in verb forms and verb tenses. You may need to look at the list in 27a to determine the correct form of some irregular verbs. Answers to lettered sentences appear in the back of the book. Example:

$$\text{The meeting } \overset{begins}{\underset{\wedge}{\cancel{begin}}} \text{ tonight at 7:30.}$$

a. In the past, tobacco companies deny any connection between smoking and health problems.
b. There is nothing in the world that TV has not touch on.
c. I am wanting to register for a summer tutoring session.
d. By the end of the year, the state will have test 139 birds for avian flu.
e. The benefits of eating fruits and vegetables have been promoting by health care providers.

1. By the time he was twelve years old, Mozart had compose an entire opera.
2. A serious accident was happened at the corner of Main Street and First Avenue last night.
3. My family has been gone to Sam's restaurant ever since we moved to this neighborhood.
4. I have ate Thai food only once before.
5. The bear is appearing to be sedated.

ON THE WEB > dianahacker.com/rules
Grammar exercises > ESL challenges > E-ex 28–1

28b Use the base form of the verb after a modal.

A modal verb — *can, could, may, might, must, shall, should, will,* or *would* — is used with the base form of a verb to show certainty, necessity, or possibility. Modals do not change form to indicate tense. For a summary of modals and their meanings, see the chart beginning on page 229. (Along with forms of *have, do,* and *be,* modals are also called *helping verbs.* See 62c.)

▶ My cousin will send~~s~~ us photographs from her wedding when she returns from Portugal.

speak
▶ We could ~~spoke~~ Portuguese when we were young.
     ^

TIP: Do not use *to* in front of a main verb that follows a modal.

▶ Gina can ~~to~~ drive us home from the party if we miss the last

subway train.

For the use of modals in conditional sentences, see 28e.

Modals and their meanings

Can

■ General ability (present)

> Valerie *can sing.*
> Jorge *can run* the marathon faster than his brother.

■ Informal requests or permission

> *Can* you *tell* me where the bookstore is?
> You *can borrow* my calculator until Wednesday.

Could

■ General ability (past)

> Hilit *could speak* three languages when she was only five years old.

■ Polite, informal requests or suggestions

> *Could* you *give* me that pen?

May

■ Formal requests or permission

> *May* I *use* your pen?

> Students *may park* only in the yellow zone.

■ Possibility

> I *may try* to finish my homework tonight, or I *may wake up* early and finish it tomorrow.

→

Modals and their meanings (continued)

Might

■ Possibility

The population of New Delhi *might reach* thirteen million by 2010.

Must

■ Necessity (present or future)

To be effective, welfare-to-work programs *must provide* access to job training.

■ Strong possibility or near certainty (present or past)

Amy doesn't look well this morning. She *must be* sick. [She is probably sick.]

I *must have left* my wallet at home. [I probably left my wallet at home.]

Should

■ Suggestions or advice

Frank *should join* student government.

You *should drink* plenty of water every day.

■ Obligations or duties

The government *should protect* the rights of citizens.

■ Expectations

The books *should arrive* soon. [We expect the books to arrive soon.]

Will

■ Certainty

If you don't leave now, you *will be* late.

■ Requests

Will you *help* me study for my history test?

■ Promises and offers

I *will arrange* the carpool.

→

NOTE: *Shall* traditionally was the modal used with *I* or *we* in place of *will*. It is now used mainly for polite requests or in very formal contexts (*Shall I call you soon?*).

Would

■ Polite requests

> *Would* you *help* me carry these books?
>
> I *would like* some coffee. [Polite for *want*.]

■ Habitual or repeated actions (past)

> Whenever I needed help with sewing, I *would call* my aunt.

EXERCISE 28–2 Edit the following sentences to correct errors in the use of verb forms with modals. If a sentence is correct, write "correct" after it. Answers to lettered sentences appear in the back of the book. Example:

> We should ~~to~~ order pizza for dinner.

a. A major league pitcher can to throw a baseball over ninety-five miles per hour.
b. The writing center tutors will helps you to revise your essay.
c. A reptile must adjusted its body temperature to its environment.
d. In some states, individuals may renew a driver's license online or in person.
e. My uncle, a caricature artist, could sketched a face in less than two minutes.

1. Working more than twelve hours a day might to contribute to insomnia, according to researchers.
2. A wasp will carry its immobilized prey back to the nest.
3. Hikers should not wandered too far from the trail.
4. Should we continued to submit hard copies of our essays?
5. Surgery may to cure patients with carpal tunnel syndrome.

ON THE WEB > **dianahacker.com/rules**
Grammar exercises > ESL challenges > E-ex 28–2

28c Use a form of *be* with the past participle to write a verb in the passive voice.

When a sentence is written in the passive voice, the subject receives the action instead of doing it. (See 63c.)

```
       ┌─────S─────┐ ┌──V──┐
```
The control group was given a placebo.

Melissa *was taken* to the hospital.

To form the passive voice, use a form of *be* — *am, is, are, was, were, being, be,* or *been* — followed by the past participle of the main verb.

>   *written*
> ▶ *Dreaming in Cuban* was ~~writing~~ by Cristina García.

The past participle *written*, not the present participle *writing*, must be used following *was* (the past tense of *be*) in the passive voice.

>   *be*
> ▶ Senator Dixon will defeated.

The passive voice requires a form of *be* before the past participle.

>   *teased.*
> ▶ The child was being ~~tease.~~

The past participle *teased*, not the base form *tease*, must be used with *was being* to form the passive voice.

For details on forming the passive in various tenses, consult the chart on pages 233–35. (For appropriate uses of the passive voice, see 8a.)

TIP: Only transitive verbs, those that take direct objects, may be used in the passive voice. Intransitive verbs such as *occur, happen, sleep, die, become,* and *fall* are not used in the passive. (See 63b.)

> ▶ The accident ~~was~~ happened suddenly.

>   *fell*
> ▶ The kittens ~~were fallen~~ from the tree.

Verbs at a glance

Simple tenses

	ACTIVE VOICE	PASSIVE VOICE
Simple present • general facts • states of being • habitual, repetitive actions	Base form or -s form College students often *study* late at night.	*am, is, are* + past participle Breakfast *is served* daily at 8:00.
Simple past • completed past actions • facts or states of being in the past	Base form + -ed or -d or irregular form The storm *destroyed* their property.	*was, were* + past participle He *was punished* for being late.
Simple future • future actions, promises, or predictions	*will* + base form I *will exercise* tomorrow.	*will be* + past participle The governor *will be elected* next week.

Simple progressive forms

	ACTIVE VOICE	PASSIVE VOICE
Present progressive • actions in progress at the present time • future actions (with *leave, go, come, move,* etc.)	*am, is, are* + present participle The students *are taking* an exam in Room 105. I *am leaving* tomorrow morning.	*am, is, are* + being + past participle Dinner *is being served* now. Jo *is being moved* to a new class next month.
Past progressive • actions in progress at a specific time in the past	*was, were* + present participle They *were swimming* when the storm struck.	*was, were* + being + past participle We thought we *were being followed*.

→

ESL

Verbs at a glance (continued)

	ACTIVE VOICE	PASSIVE VOICE
Future progressive • actions in progress at a specific time in the future	*will* + *be* + present participle Brad *will be cooking* when his parents arrive.	[Future progressive is usually not used in the passive voice.]

Perfect tenses

	ACTIVE VOICE	PASSIVE VOICE
Present perfect • repetitive or constant actions that began in the past and continue to the present • actions that happened at an unknown or unspecific time in the past	*has, have* + past participle I *have loved* cats since I was a child. Steph *has visited* Wales three times.	*has, have* + *been* + past participle Wars *have been fought* throughout history.
Past perfect • actions that began or occurred before another time in the past	*had* + past participle She *had* just *crossed* the street when the runaway car plowed into the building.	*had* + *been* + past participle He *had been given* all the hints he needed to complete the puzzle.
Future perfect • actions that will be completed before or at a specific future time	*will* + *have* + past participle By the end of this year, I *will have seen* three concerts.	[Future perfect is usually not used in the passive voice.]

→

Perfect progressive forms

ACTIVE VOICE

**Present perfect
progressive**

- continuous actions
  that began in the
  past and continue
  to the present

has, have + *been* + present participle

My sister *has been trying* to get a job in
Boston for five years.

**Past perfect
progressive**

- actions that began
  and continued in the
  past until some
  other past action

had + *been* + present participle

By the time I entered high school, I *had
been taking* piano lessons for eight
years.

**Future perfect
progressive**

- actions that are or
  will be in progress
  before a specified
  future time

will + *have* + *been* + present
participle

When Carol is eighty years old, she *will
have been living* in Vermont for sixty-
two years.

28d To make negative verb forms, add *not* in the appropriate place.

If the verb is the simple present or past tense of *be* (*am, is, are,
was, were*), add *not* after the verb.

Mario *is not* a member of the club.

For simple present-tense verbs other than *be*, use *do* or
does plus *not* before the base form of the verb. (For the correct
use of *do* and *does*, see the chart in 21a.)

▶ Mariko ~~no~~ *does not* want more dessert.

▶ Mariko does not want~~s~~ more dessert.

For simple past-tense verbs other than *be*, use *did* plus *not*
before the base form of the verb.

plant
▶ They did not ~~planted~~ corn this year.
     ^

In a verb phrase consisting of one or more helping verbs and a present or past participle (_is watching, were living, has played, could have been driven_), use the word _not_ after the first helping verb.

not
▶ Inna should have ~~not~~ gone dancing last night.
        ^

not
▶ Bonnie is ~~no~~ singing this weekend.
      ^

NOTE: The word _not_ can be contracted to _n't_ when used with some forms of _be_ (_is, are, was, were_) and with other helping verbs and modals. Use _isn't_ for _is not_, _don't_ for _do not_, _doesn't_ for _does not_, _shouldn't_ for _should not_, and so on. _Won't_ is the contracted form of _will not_. The contracted form of _am not_, used only in questions, is _aren't_.

English allows only one negative in an independent clause to express a negative idea; using more than one is an error known as a _double negative_ (see also 26d). Double negatives can be corrected by eliminating one of the two negative words or by replacing one of them with an article or another noun marker such as _any_.

▶ I don't have ~~no~~ homework this weekend.

any
▶ We could not find ~~no~~ books about the history of our school.
           ^

_a_
▶ The smoke detector doesn't have ~~no~~ battery in it.
                 ^

28e In a conditional sentence, choose verb tenses according to the type of condition expressed in the sentence.

Conditional sentences contain two clauses: a subordinate clause (usually starting with _if, when,_ or _unless_) and an independent clause. The subordinate clause (sometimes called the _if_ or _unless_ clause) states the condition or cause; the independent clause states the result or effect.

Verb tenses in conditional sentences usually express the nature of the condition rather than the time of an action or event. Present tenses typically express factual or true conditions, and past tenses typically express speculative or imaginary conditions.

Three kinds of conditional sentences are discussed in this section: factual, predictive, and speculative. In each example, the subordinate clause is marked SUB, and the independent clause is marked IND.

Factual

Factual conditional sentences express factual relationships. If the relationship is a scientific truth, use the present tense in both clauses.

> ┌──── SUB ────┐ ┌─IND─┐
> If water *cools* to 32°, it *freezes*.

If the sentence describes a condition that is (or was) habitually true, use the same tense in both clauses.

> ┌──────── SUB ────────┐ ┌──────── IND ────────┐
> When Sue *jogs* along the canal, her dog *runs* ahead of her.

> ┌──────── SUB ────────┐ ┌──IND──┐
> Whenever the coach *asked* for help, I *volunteered*.

Predictive

Predictive conditional sentences are used to predict the future or to express future plans or possibilities. To form a predictive sentence, use a present-tense verb in the subordinate clause; in the independent clause, use the modal *will*, *can*, *may*, *should*, or *might* plus the base form of the verb.

> ┌──── SUB ────┐ ┌──────── IND ────────┐
> If you *practice* regularly, your tennis game *should improve*.

> ┌──────── IND ────────┐ ┌──── SUB ────┐
> We *will lose* our remaining wetlands unless we *act* now.

TIP: In all types of conditional sentences (factual, predictive, and speculative), *if* or *unless* clauses do not use the modal verb *will*.

> passes
> ▶ If Jenna ~~will pass~~ her history test, she will graduate this year.
>   ^

Speculative

Speculative conditional sentences, sometimes called *unreal conditionals*, show unlikely, contrary-to-fact, or impossible conditions. To show distance from truth or reality, English uses past or past perfect tense in the *if* clause, even for conditions in the present and future.

UNLIKELY POSSIBILITIES   If the condition is possible but unlikely in the present or future, use the past tense in the subordinate clause; in the independent clause, use *would, could,* or *might* plus the base form of the verb.

┌──────SUB──────┐ ┌────── IND ──────┐
If I *won* the lottery, I *would travel* to Egypt.

The writer does not expect to win the lottery. Because this is a possible but unlikely present or future situation, the subordinate clause uses the past tense.

CONDITIONS CONTRARY TO FACT   In conditions that are currently unreal or contrary to fact, use the past-tense verb *were* (not *was*) in the *if* clause for all subjects. (See 27g for more details.)

>   *were*
> ▶ If I ~~was~~ president, I would make children's issues a priority.
>   ^

The writer is not president, so *were* is correct in the *if* clause.

EVENTS THAT DID NOT HAPPEN   In a conditional sentence that speculates about an event that did not happen or was impossible in the past, use the past perfect tense in the *if* clause; in the independent clause, use *would have, could have,* or *might have* with the past participle. (See also past perfect tense, p. 227.)

┌──────SUB──────┐ ┌────── IND ──────┐
If I *had saved* enough money, I *would have visited* Senegal last year.

The writer did not save enough money and did not travel to Senegal. This sentence shows a possibility that did not happen.

┌──────────SUB──────────┐ ┌─── IND ───┐
If Aunt Grace *had been* alive for your graduation, she *would have*
├───────────┐
been very proud.

Aunt Grace was not alive at the time of the graduation. This sentence shows an impossible situation in the past.

EXERCISE 28–3 Edit the following conditional sentences for problems with verbs. In some cases, more than one revision is possible. Suggested revisions of lettered sentences appear in the back of the book. Example:

> *had*
> If I ~~have~~ time, I would study both French and Russian next
>   ^
>
> semester.

a. The electrician might have discovered the broken circuit if she went through the modules one at a time.
b. If Verena wins a scholarship, she would go to graduate school.
c. Whenever there is a fire in our neighborhood, everybody came out to watch.
d. Sarah will take the paralegal job unless she would get a better offer.
e. If I live in Budapest with my cousin Szusza, she would teach me Hungarian cooking.

1. If the science fiction festival starts Monday, we wouldn't need to plan entertainment for our visitors.
2. If everyone has voted in the last election, the results would have been very different.
3. The tenants will not pay the rent unless the landlord fixed the furnace.
4. When dark gray clouds appeared on a hot summer afternoon, a thunderstorm often follows.
5. Our daughter would have drowned if Officer Blake didn't risk his life to save her.

ON THE WEB > **dianahacker.com/rules**
  Grammar exercises > ESL challenges > E-ex 28–3

28f Become familiar with verbs that may be followed by gerunds or infinitives.

A gerund is a verb form that ends in *-ing* and is used as a noun: *sleeping, dreaming.* (See 64c.) An infinitive is the word *to* plus the base form of the verb: *to sleep, to dream.* The word *to* is not a preposition in this use but an infinitive marker.

A few verbs may be followed by either a gerund or an infinitive; others may be followed by a gerund but not by an infinitive; still others may be followed by an infinitive but not by a gerund.

Verb + gerund or infinitive (no change in meaning)

The following commonly used verbs may be followed by a gerund or an infinitive, with little or no difference in meaning:

begin	hate	love
continue	like	start

I love *skiing*. I love *to ski*.

Verb + gerund or infinitive (change in meaning)

With a few verbs, the choice of a gerund or an infinitive changes the meaning dramatically:

forget	remember	stop	try

She stopped *speaking* to Lucia. [She no longer spoke to Lucia.]

She stopped *to speak* to Lucia. [She paused so that she could speak to Lucia.]

Verb + gerund

These verbs may be followed by a gerund but not by an infinitive:

admit	enjoy	postpone	resist
appreciate	escape	practice	risk
avoid	finish	put off	suggest
deny	imagine	quit	tolerate
discuss	miss	recall	

Bill enjoys *playing* [not *to play*] the piano.

Jamie quit *smoking*.

Verb + infinitive

These verbs may be followed by an infinitive but not by a gerund:

agree	expect	need	refuse
ask	help	offer	wait
beg	hope	plan	want
claim	manage	pretend	wish
decide	mean	promise	would like

Jill has offered *to water* [not *watering*] the plants while we are away.

Joe finally managed *to find* a parking space.

The man refused *to join* the rebellion.

A few of these verbs may be followed either by an infinitive directly or by a noun or pronoun plus an infinitive:

ask	help	promise	would like
expect	need	want	

We asked *to speak* to the congregation.

We asked *Rabbi Abrams to speak* to our congregation.

Alex expected *to get* the lead in the play.

Ira expected *Alex to get* the lead in the play.

Verb + noun or pronoun + infinitive

With certain verbs in the active voice, a noun or pronoun must come between the verb and the infinitive that follows it. The noun or pronoun usually names a person who is affected by the action.

advise	convince	order	tell
allow	encourage	persuade	urge
cause	have ("own")	remind	warn
command	instruct	require	

              V   N ⌈INF⌉

The class encouraged Luis to tell the story of his escape.

The counselor *advised Haley to take* four courses instead of five.

Professor Howlett *instructed us to write* our names on the left side of the paper.

Verb + noun or pronoun + unmarked infinitive

An unmarked infinitive is an infinitive without *to*. A few verbs (often called *causative verbs*) may be followed by a noun or pronoun and an unmarked infinitive.

have ("cause")	help	let ("allow")	make ("force")

Jorge *had the valet park* his car.

► Please let me ~~to~~ pay for the tickets.

► Frank made me ~~to~~ carry his book for him.

NOTE: *Help* can be followed by a noun or pronoun and either an unmarked or a marked infinitive: *Emma helped Brian wash the dishes. Emma helped Brian to wash the dishes.*

EXERCISE 28–4   Form sentences by adding gerund or infinitive constructions to the following sentence openings. In some cases, more than one kind of construction may be possible. Possible answers to lettered items appear in the back of the book. Example:

> **Please remind** *your sister to call me.*
>   ^

a. I enjoy
b. The tutor told Samantha
c. The team hopes
d. Ricardo and his brothers miss
e. The babysitter let

1. Pollen makes
2. The club president asked
3. Next summer we plan
4. My supervisor intends
5. Please stop

ON THE WEB > dianahacker.com/rules
    Grammar exercises > ESL challenges > E-ex 28–4

29

Articles and types of nouns

Articles (*a, an, the*) are part of a category of words known as *noun markers* or *determiners*. Standard English uses noun markers to help identify the nouns that follow. In addition to articles, noun markers include

- possessive nouns, such as *Elena's* (See 36a.)
- possessive pronoun/adjectives: *my, your, his, her, its, our, their* (See 62b.)
- demonstrative pronoun/adjectives: *this, that, these, those* (See 62b.)
- quantifiers: *all, any, each, either, every, few, many, more, most, much, neither, several, some,* and so on (See 29e.)
- numbers: *one, two,* and so on

29a Be familiar with articles and other noun markers.

Articles and other noun markers always appear before nouns. If you use an adjective with a noun, put the article before the adjective.

       ART N
Felix is reading a book about mythology.

       ART ADJ N
We took an exciting trip to Alaska last summer.

In most cases, do not use an article with another noun marker, such as *Natalie's* or *this*.

▶ When did you buy ~~the~~ this round pine table?

▶ ~~The~~ Natalie's older brother lives in Wisconsin.

EXCEPTION: Expressions like *a few, the most,* and *all the* are exceptions. Also see 29e.

Did you bring *all the books* with you?

We got *the most snow* ever in January.

29b Understand the different types of nouns.

To choose an appropriate article for a noun, you must first determine whether the noun is common or proper, specific or general, count or noncount, and singular or plural.

Types of articles

Indefinite articles

Indefinite articles (*a, an*) are used with nouns that are not specific. See 29d.

a   *A* means "one" or "one among many." Use *a* before a consonant sound: *a banana, a tree, a picture, a hand, a happy child.*

an   *An* also means "one" or "one among many." Use *an* before a vowel sound: *an eggplant, an occasion, an uncle, an hour, an honorable person.*

NOTE: Words beginning with *h* and *u* can have either a consonant sound (*a hand, a happy baby, a university, a union*) or a vowel sound (*an hour, an honorable person, an umbrella, an uncle*). (See also *a, an* in the Glossary of Usage.)

Definite article

The definite article (*the*) is used with specific nouns. See 29c.

the   *The* makes nouns specific; it does not refer to a number or amount. Use *the* with one or more than one specific thing: *the newspaper, the soldiers.*

Common or proper

Common nouns name general persons, places, things, or ideas. Proper nouns, which are marked in English with capital letters, name specific persons, places, things, or ideas. (See also 45.)

- common: religion, student, country
- proper: Hinduism, Philip, Vietnam

Specific (definite) or general (indefinite)

Specific or definite nouns represent persons, places, things, or ideas that can be identified within a group of nouns of the same type. General or indefinite nouns represent whole categories in general; they can also name nonspecific persons, places, things, or ideas that represent a group.

SPECIFIC   The *students* in Professor Martin's class should study harder. [The specific students in the class]

GENERAL	*Students* should study. [All students, students in general]
SPECIFIC	The *airplane* carrying Senator Chen took off at 1:30. [The specific airplane carrying the senator]
GENERAL	The *airplane* has made commuting between major cities easy. [All airplanes as a category of transportation]

Count or noncount

Count nouns refer to persons, places, things, or ideas that can be counted. Only count nouns have plural forms. Noncount nouns refer to things or abstract ideas that cannot be counted or made plural.

- count: *one girl, two girls; one city, three cities; one goose, four geese; one philosophy, five philosophies*
- noncount: *water, silver, air, furniture, patience, knowledge*

Some nouns can be used in both a count and a noncount sense.

COUNT	**NONCOUNT**
I'll have *a coffee*.	I'll have *coffee*.
There are many *democracies* in the world.	We learned that *democracy* originated in ancient Greece.

Some nouns (such as *advice* and *information*) may be countable in some languages but not in English. If you do not know whether a noun is count or noncount, refer to the chart on page 246 or consult an ESL dictionary.

Singular or plural

Singular nouns represent one person, place, thing, or idea; plural nouns represent more than one. Only count nouns can be made plural. (For more information on forming plural nouns, see 43c.)

- singular: *backpack, country, woman, achievement*
- plural: *backpacks, countries, women, achievements*

GRAMMAR CHECKERS rarely flag missing or misused articles. They cannot distinguish when *a* or *an* is appropriate and when *the* is correct, nor can they tell when an article is missing.

Commonly used noncount nouns

Food and drink

beef, bread, butter, candy, cereal, cheese, cream, meat, milk, pasta, rice, salt, sugar, water, wine

Nonfood substances

air, cement, coal, dirt, gasoline, gold, paper, petroleum, plastic, rain, silver, snow, soap, steel, wood, wool

Abstract nouns

advice, anger, beauty, confidence, courage, employment, fun, happiness, health, honesty, information, intelligence, knowledge, love, poverty, satisfaction, wealth

Other

biology (and other areas of study), clothing, equipment, furniture, homework, jewelry, luggage, machinery, mail, money, news, poetry, pollution, research, scenery, traffic, transportation, violence, weather, work

NOTE: A few noncount nouns can also be used as count nouns: *You can't buy love. He had two loves: music and archery.*

29c Use *the* with most specific common nouns.

The definite article *the* is used with most nouns — both count and noncount — that the reader can identify specifically. Usually the identity will be clear to the reader for one of the following reasons.

1. The noun has been previously mentioned.

▶ A truck cut in front of our van. When ^*the* truck skidded a few seconds

   later, we almost crashed into it.

   The article *A* is used before *truck* when the noun is first mentioned. When the noun is mentioned again, it needs the article *the* because readers can now identify which truck skidded.

2. A phrase or clause following the noun restricts its identity.

> *the*
> ► Bryce warned me that computer on his desk had just
>   ^
>
> crashed.

The phrase *on his desk* identifies the specific computer.

NOTE: Descriptive adjectives do not necessarily make a noun specific. A specific noun is one that readers can identify within a group of nouns of the same type.

>   *a*
> ► If I win the lottery, I will buy ~~the~~ brand-new bright red sports car.
>   ^

The reader cannot identify which specific brand-new bright red sports car the writer will buy. Even though *car* has many adjectives in front of it, it is a general noun in this sentence.

3. A superlative adjective such as *best* or *most intelligent* makes the noun's identity specific. (See also 26c on comparatives and superlatives.)

>   *the*
> ► Our petite daughter dated tallest boy in her class.
>   ^

The superlative *tallest* makes the noun *boy* specific. Although there might be several tall boys, only one boy can be the tallest.

4. The noun describes a unique person, place, or thing.

>   *the*
> ► During an eclipse, one should not look directly at sun.
>   ^

There is only one sun in our solar system, so its identity is clear.

5. The context or situation makes the noun's identity clear.

>   *the*
> ► Please don't slam door when you leave.
>   ^

Both the speaker and the listener know which door is meant.

6. The noun is singular and refers to a scientific class or category of items (most often animals, musical instruments, and inventions).

>   *The assembly*
> ► ~~Assembly~~ line transformed manufacturing in America.
>   ^

The writer is referring to the assembly line as an invention.

Choosing articles for common nouns

This chart summarizes the most frequent uses of articles with common nouns. For help choosing articles with proper nouns, see 29g.

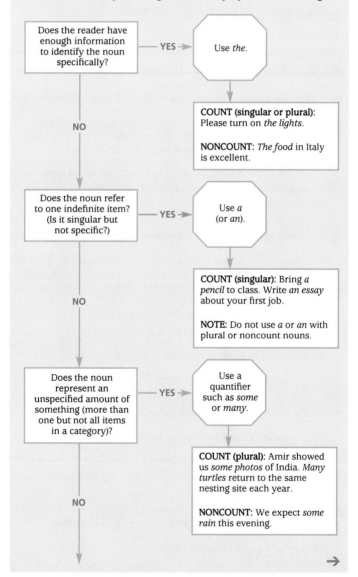

Does the reader have enough information to identify the noun specifically? — YES → Use *the*.

COUNT (singular or plural): Please turn on *the lights*.

NONCOUNT: *The food* in Italy is excellent.

NO ↓

Does the noun refer to one indefinite item? (Is it singular but not specific?) — YES → Use *a* (or *an*).

COUNT (singular): Bring *a pencil* to class. Write *an essay* about your first job.

NOTE: Do not use *a* or *an* with plural or noncount nouns.

NO ↓

Does the noun represent an unspecified amount of something (more than one but not all items in a category)? — YES → Use a quantifier such as *some* or *many*.

COUNT (plural): Amir showed us *some photos* of India. *Many turtles* return to the same nesting site each year.

NONCOUNT: We expect *some rain* this evening.

NO ↓

→

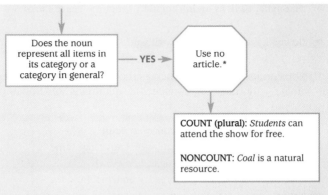

Does the noun represent all items in its category or a category in general? — **YES** → Use no article.*

COUNT (plural): *Students* can attend the show for free.

NONCOUNT: *Coal* is a natural resource.

*A singular count noun is occasionally used with *the* to refer to all items in a class or a specific category. See 29f.

29d Use *a* (or *an*) with common singular count nouns that refer to "one" or "any."

If a count noun refers to one unspecific item (not a whole category), use the indefinite article *a* (or *an*). *A* and *an* usually mean "one among many" but can also mean "any one."

▶ My English professor asked me to bring ^*a*^ dictionary to class.

The noun *dictionary* refers to "one unspecific dictionary" or "any dictionary."

▶ We want to rent ^*an*^ apartment close to the lake.

The noun *apartment* refers to "any apartment close to the lake," not a specific apartment.

29e Use a quantifier such as *some* or *more*, not *a* (or *an*), with a noncount noun to express an approximate amount.

Do not use *a* (or *an*) with noncount nouns. Also do not use numbers or words such as *several* or *many* because they must be used with plural nouns, and noncount nouns do not have plural forms.

▶ Dr. Snyder gave us ~~an~~ information about the Peace Corps.

▶ Do you have ~~many~~ money with you?

You can use quantifiers such as the following to suggest approximate amounts or nonspecific quantities of noncount nouns.

QUANTIFIER	NONCOUNT NOUN
a little	salt, rain, knowledge, time
any	sugar, homework
enough	bread, wood, money
less	meat, violence
more	coffee, information
much (*or* a lot of)	snow, pollution
plenty of	paper, lumber
some	tea, news, work

▶ Claudia's mother told her that she had ~~a~~ news that
      some

would surprise her.

29f Do not use articles with nouns that refer to all of something or something in general.

When a noncount noun refers to all of its type or to a concept in general, it is not marked with an article.

▶ ~~The kindness~~ is a virtue.
      Kindness

The noun represents kindness in general; it does not represent a specific type of kindness.

▶ In some parts of the world, ~~the~~ rice is preferred to all other grains.

The noun *rice* represents rice in general, not a specific type or serving of rice.

In most cases, when you use a count noun to represent a general category, make the noun plural. Do not use unmarked singular count nouns to represent whole categories.

> *Fountains are*
> ~~Fountain is~~ an expensive element of landscape design.
>   ^

Fountains is a count noun that represents fountains in general.

EXCEPTION: In some cases, *the* can be used with singular count nouns to represent a class or specific category: *The American alligator is no longer listed as an endangered species.* Also see number 6 in 29c.

29g   Do not use articles with most singular proper nouns. Use *the* with most plural proper nouns.

Since singular proper nouns are already specific, they typically do not need an article: *Prime Minister Blair, Jamaica, Lake Huron, Mount Etna.*

There are, however, many exceptions. In most cases, if the proper noun consists of a common noun with modifiers (adjectives or an *of* phrase), use *the* with the proper noun.

>   *the*
> ▶ We visited Great Wall of China last year.
>   ^

>   *the*
> ▶ Rob wants to be a translator for Central Intelligence Agency.
>   ^

The is used with most plural proper nouns: *the McGregors, the Bahamas, the Finger Lakes, the United States.*

Geographical names create problems because there are so many exceptions to the rules. When in doubt, consult the chart on page 252, check a dictionary, or ask a native speaker.

EXERCISE 29–1   Edit the following sentences for proper use of articles and nouns. If a sentence is correct, write "correct" after it. Answers to lettered sentences appear in the back of the book. Example:

> ~~The~~ Josefina's dance routine was flawless.

a. Doing volunteer work often brings a satisfaction.
b. As I looked out the window of the plane, I could see the Cape Cod.
c. Melina likes to drink her coffees with lots of cream.
d. Recovering from abdominal surgery requires patience.
e. I completed the my homework assignment quickly.

Using the *with geographical nouns*

When to omit *the*

streets, squares, parks	Ivy Street, Union Square, Denali National Park
cities, states, counties	Miami, New Mexico, Bee County
most countries, continents	Italy, Nigeria, China, South America, Africa
bays, single lakes	Tampa Bay, Lake Geneva
single mountains, islands	Mount Everest, Crete

When to use *the*

country names with *of* phrase	the United States (of America), the People's Republic of China
large regions, deserts	the East Coast, the Sahara
peninsulas	the Iberian Peninsula, the Sinai Peninsula
oceans, seas, gulfs	the Pacific Ocean, the Dead Sea, the Persian Gulf
canals and rivers	the Panama Canal, the Amazon
mountain ranges	the Rocky Mountains, the Alps
groups of islands	the Solomon Islands

1. The attorney argued that her client should receive a money for emotional suffering.
2. Please check to see if there is a mail in the mailbox.
3. The Times Square in New York City is known for its billboards and theaters.
4. A cement is one of the components in concrete.
5. I took all the boys on the roller coaster after lunch.

EXERCISE 29–2 Articles have been omitted from the following story, adapted from *Zen Flesh, Zen Bones,* compiled by Paul Reps. Insert the articles *a, an,* and *the* where English requires them and be prepared to explain the reasons for your choices.

Moon Cannot Be Stolen

Ryokan, who was Zen master, lived simple life in little hut at foot of mountain. One evening thief visited hut only to discover there was nothing in it to steal.

Ryokan returned and caught him. "You may have come long way to visit me," he told prowler, "and you should not return empty-handed. Please take my clothes as gift." Thief was bewildered. He took Ryokan's clothes and slunk away. Ryokan sat naked, watching moon. "Poor fellow," he mused. "I wish I could give him this beautiful moon."

ON THE WEB > **dianahacker.com/rules**
Grammar exercises > ESL challenges > E-ex 29–1 and 29–2

30

Sentence structure

Although their structure can vary widely, sentences in English generally flow from subject to verb to object or complement: *Bears eat fish.* This section focuses on the major challenges that multilingual students face when writing sentences in English. For more details on the parts of speech and how they work together to form sentences, consult sections 62–65.

30a Use a linking verb between a subject and its complement.

Some languages, such as Russian and Turkish, do not use linking verbs (*is, are, was, were*) between subjects and complements (nouns or adjectives that rename or describe the subject). Every English sentence, however, must include a verb. For more on linking verbs, see 27e.

> Jim _∧intelligent. *is*

> Many streets in San Francisco _∧very steep. *are*

30b Include a subject in every sentence.

Some languages, such as Spanish and Japanese, do not require a subject in every sentence. Every English sentence, however, needs a subject. An exception is commands, in which the subject *you* is understood but not present (*Give to the poor*).

▶ Your aunt is very energetic. ~~Seems~~ young for her age.
   She seems

The word *it* is used as the subject of a sentence describing the weather or temperature, stating the time, indicating distance, or suggesting an environmental fact.

▶ ~~Is~~ raining in the valley and snowing in the mountains.
   It is

▶ In July, ~~is~~ very hot in Arizona.
   it

▶ ~~Is~~ 9:15 a.m.
   It is

▶ ~~Is~~ three hundred miles to Chicago.
   It is

▶ ~~Gets~~ noisy in our dorm on weekends.
   It gets

In most English sentences, the subject appears before the verb. Some sentences, however, are inverted: The subject comes after the verb. In these sentences, a placeholder called an *expletive* (*there* or *it*) often comes before the verb.

EXP V ┌──── S ────┐   ┌──── S ────┐ V
There are many people here today. (Many people are here today.)

▶ ~~Is~~ an apple in the refrigerator.
   There is

▶ As you know, ~~many~~ religious sects in India.
   there are

Notice that the verb agrees with the subject that follows it: *apple is, sects are.* (See 21g.)

In inverted sentences that have an infinitive (*to work*) or a noun clause (*that she is intelligent*) as the subject, the placeholder *it* is needed to open the sentence. *It* is followed by a linking verb (*is, was, seems,* and so on), an adjective, and then the subject. (See 64b and 64c.)

EXP V   ┌── S ──┐   ┌── S ──┐ V
It is important to study daily. (To study daily is important.)

> ⟨It is⟩
▶ ~~Is~~ healthy to eat fruit and grains.
  ^

> ⟨It is⟩
▶ ~~Is~~ clear that we must change our approach.
  ^

TIP: The words *here* and *there* are not used as subjects. When they mean "in this place" (*here*) or "in that place" (*there*), they are adverbs, not nouns.

> ⟨It⟩ ⟨there.⟩
▶ I just returned from a vacation in Japan. ~~There~~ is very beautiful⟨.⟩
  ^ ^

> ⟨This school⟩ ⟨that school⟩
▶ ~~Here~~ offers a master's degree in physical therapy; ~~there~~ has
  ^ ^

only a bachelor's program.

GRAMMAR CHECKERS can flag some sentences with a missing expletive, or placeholder (*there* or *it*), but they often misdiagnose the problem, suggesting that if a sentence opens with a word such as *Is* or *Are,* it may need a question mark at the end. Consider this sentence, which a grammar checker flagged as requiring a question mark: *Are two grocery stores on Elm Street.* The sentence is missing the placeholder *there*, whether it is phrased as a question or as a statement: *There are two grocery stores on Elm Street. Are there two grocery stores on Elm Street?*

30c Do not use both a noun and a pronoun to perform the same grammatical function in a sentence.

English does not allow a subject to be repeated in its own clause.

▶ The doctor ~~she~~ advised me to cut down on salt.

▶ Andrea ~~she~~ is late all the time.

The pronoun *she* cannot repeat the subject, *doctor*, in the first sentence or the subject, *Andrea*, in the second.

Do not add a pronoun even when a word group comes between the subject and the verb.

▶ The watch that had been lost on vacation ~~it~~ was in my

backpack.

The pronoun *it* cannot repeat the subject, *watch.*

Some languages allow "topic fronting," or placing a word or phrase (a "topic") at the beginning of a sentence and following it with an independent clause that explains something about the topic. This form is not allowed in English.

             ┌─ TOPIC ─┐ ┌──── IND CLAUSE ────┐
INCORRECT   The seeds I planted them last fall.

The pronoun *them* repeats the "topic," *the seeds.* The sentence can be revised by replacing *them* with *the seeds.*

            the seeds
▶ ~~The seeds~~ I planted ~~them~~ last fall.
                      ^

30d Do not repeat an object or an adverb in an adjective clause.

Adjective clauses begin with relative pronouns (*who, whom, whose, which, that*) or relative adverbs (*when, where*). Relative pronouns usually serve as subjects or objects in the clauses they introduce; another word in the clause cannot serve the same function. Relative adverbs should not be repeated by other adverbs later in the clause.

                  ┌──────── ADJ CLAUSE ────────┐
The cat ran under the car that was parked on the street.

▶ The cat ran under the car that ~~it~~ was parked on the street.

The relative pronoun *that* is the subject of the adjective clause, so the pronoun *it* cannot be added as the subject.

▶ Myrna enjoyed the investment seminars that she attended ~~them~~

last week.

The relative pronoun *that* is the object of the verb *attended.* The pronoun *them* cannot also serve as object.

Sometimes the relative pronoun is understood but not present in the sentence. In such cases, do not add another word with the same function as the omitted pronoun.

▶ **Myrna enjoyed the investment seminars she attended ~~them~~**

last week.

The relative pronoun *that* is understood even though it is not present in the sentence.

If the clause begins with a relative adverb, do not use another adverb with the same meaning later in the clause.

▶ **The office where I work ~~there~~ is one hour from the city.**

The adverb *there* cannot repeat the relative adverb *where*.

GRAMMAR CHECKERS usually fail to mark sentences with repeated subjects or objects. One program flagged some sentences with repeated subjects, such as this one: *The yarn that she ordered it will arrive next Monday.* But the program misdiagnosed the problem and did not recognize that *it* repeats the subject, *yarn*.

EXERCISE 30–1 In the following sentences, add needed subjects or expletives and delete any repeated subjects, objects, or adverbs. Answers to lettered sentences appear in the back of the book. Example:

The new geology professor is the one whom we saw ~~him~~ on

TV this morning.

a. Are some cartons of ice cream in the freezer.
b. I don't use the subway because am afraid.
c. The prime minister she is the most popular leader in my country.
d. We tried to get in touch with the same manager whom we spoke to him earlier.
e. Recently have been a number of earthquakes in Turkey.

1. We visited an island where several ancient ruins are being excavated there.
2. In this city is difficult to find a high-paying job.

3. Beginning knitters they are often surprised that their fingers are sore at first.
4. Is a banyan tree in our backyard.
5. The CD that teaches Italian for opera lovers it was stolen from my backpack.

ON THE WEB > **dianahacker.com/rules**
Grammar exercises > ESL challenges > E-ex 30–1

30e Do not mix *although* or *because* with other linking words that serve the same purpose in a sentence.

A word group that begins with *although* cannot be linked to a word group that begins with *but* or *however* (both words have the same meaning as *although*). Similarly, a word group that begins with *because* cannot be linked to a word group that begins with *so* or *therefore*.

If you want to keep *although* or *because,* drop the other linking word.

▶ Although the sales figures look impressive, ~~but~~ the company is

losing money.

▶ Because finance laws are not always enforced, ~~therefore~~

investing in the former Soviet Union can be very risky.

If you want to keep the other linking word, omit *although* or *because.*

Finance
▶ ~~Because finance~~ laws are not always enforced,/; therefore,

investing in the former Soviet Union can be very risky.

The
▶ ~~Although the~~ sales figures look impressive, but the company is

losing money.

For advice about using commas and semicolons with linking words, see 32a and 34b.

30f Do not place an adverb between a verb and its direct object.

Adverbs modifying verbs can appear in various positions:

- at the beginning or end of the sentence

  Slowly, we drove along the rain-slick road.

  Mother wrapped the gift *carefully*.

- before or after the verb

  Martin *always* wins our tennis matches.

  Christina is *rarely* late for our lunch dates.

- between a helping verb and a main verb

  My daughter has *often* spoken of you.

  The election results were being *closely* followed by analysts.

However, an adverb cannot appear between a verb and its direct object.

▶ Mother wrapped ~~carefully~~ the gift. *(carefully)*

The adverb *carefully* may be placed at the beginning or at the end of this sentence or before the verb, *wrapped*. It cannot appear after the verb because the verb is followed by a direct object, *the gift*.

EXERCISE 30–2 Edit the following sentences for proper sentence structure. If a sentence is correct, write "correct" after it. Answers to lettered sentences appear in the back of the book. Example:

She peeled ~~slowly~~ the banana. *(slowly.)*

a. Although freshwater freezes at 32 degrees Fahrenheit, however ocean water freezes at 28 degrees Fahrenheit.
b. Because we switched Internet service providers, so our e-mail address has changed.
c. The competitor mounted confidently his skateboard.
d. My sister performs well the *legong*, a Balinese dance.
e. Because product development is behind schedule, we will have to launch the product next spring.

1. The teller counted methodically the stack of one-dollar bills.
2. I gasped when I saw the lightning strike repeatedly the barn.
3. Although hockey is traditionally a winter sport, but many towns offer skills programs all year long.
4. Because salmon can survive in both freshwater and salt water, so they are classified as anadromous fish.
5. A surveyor determines precisely the boundaries of a piece of property.

ON THE WEB > **dianahacker.com/rules**
Grammar exercises > ESL challenges > E-ex 30–2

30g Distinguish between present participles and past participles used as adjectives.

Both present and past participles may be used as adjectives. The present participle always ends in *-ing.* Past participles usually end in *-ed, -d, -en, -n,* or *-t.* (See 27a.)

PRESENT PARTICIPLES   confusing, speaking, boring

PAST PARTICIPLES   confused, spoken, bored

Like all other adjectives, participles can come before nouns; they also can follow linking verbs, in which case they describe the subject of the sentence. (See 63b.)

ADJ   N
It was a depressing movie.

V   ADJ
The movie was depressing.

The *confused tourists* stared at the map.

The *tourists* were *confused* by the map.

Use a present participle to describe a person or thing *causing or stimulating an experience.*

The *boring lecture* put us to sleep. [The lecture caused boredom; it didn't experience it.]

Use a past participle to describe a person or thing *undergoing an experience.*

The *audience* was *bored* by the lecture. [The audience experienced boredom; it didn't cause boredom.]

Choosing the present or past participle

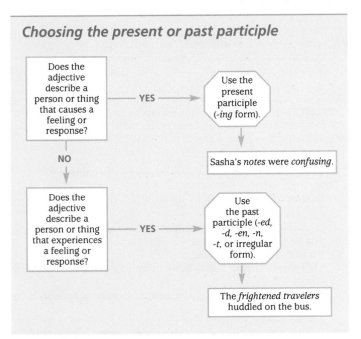

Does the adjective describe a person or thing that causes a feeling or response? —— YES ——> Use the present participle (*-ing* form).

NO

Sasha's *notes* were *confusing.*

Does the adjective describe a person or thing that experiences a feeling or response? —— YES ——> Use the past participle (*-ed, -d, -en, -n, -t,* or irregular form).

The *frightened travelers* huddled on the bus.

Participles that describe emotions or mental states often cause the most confusion.

▶ Our hike was ~~exhausted.~~ *exhausting.*

Exhausting describes how the hike made us feel.

▶ The ~~exhausting~~ hikers reached camp at sunset. *exhausted*

Exhausted describes how the hikers felt.

The chart at the top of this page can help you use these participles correctly.

annoying/annoyed	exhausting/exhausted
boring/bored	fascinating/fascinated
confusing/confused	frightening/frightened
depressing/depressed	satisfying/satisfied
exciting/excited	surprising/surprised

> **GRAMMAR CHECKERS** do not flag problems with present and past participles used as adjectives. Not surprisingly, the programs have no way of knowing the meaning a writer intends.

EXERCISE 30–3   Edit the following sentences for proper use of present and past participles. If a sentence is correct, write "correct" after it. Answers to lettered sentences appear in the back of the book. Example:

excited
Danielle and Monica were very ~~exciting~~ to be going to a
                                      ^

Broadway show for the first time.

a. Listening to everyone's complaints all day was irritated.
b. The long flight to Singapore was exhausted.
c. His skill at chess is amazing.
d. After a great deal of research, the scientist made a fascinated discovery.
e. That blackout was one of the most frightened experiences I've ever had.

1. I couldn't concentrate on my homework because I was distracted.
2. The directions to the new board game seem extremely complicating.
3. How interested are you in visiting Civil War battlefields?
4. The aerial view of the devastated villages was depressing.
5. Even after the lecturer went over the main points again, the students were still confusing.

ON THE WEB > dianahacker.com/rules
Grammar exercises > ESL challenges > E-ex 30–3

30h Place cumulative adjectives in an appropriate order.

Adjectives usually come before the nouns they modify and may also come after linking verbs. (See 62d, 62e, and 63b.)

ADJ N   V ADJ
Janine wore a new necklace. Janine's necklace was new.

Cumulative adjectives, which cannot be joined by the word *and* or separated by commas, must come in a particular order.

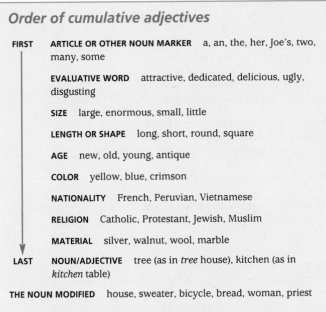

Order of cumulative adjectives

FIRST **ARTICLE OR OTHER NOUN MARKER**   a, an, the, her, Joe's, two, many, some

         EVALUATIVE WORD   attractive, dedicated, delicious, ugly, disgusting

         SIZE   large, enormous, small, little

         LENGTH OR SHAPE   long, short, round, square

         AGE   new, old, young, antique

         COLOR   yellow, blue, crimson

         NATIONALITY   French, Peruvian, Vietnamese

         RELIGION   Catholic, Protestant, Jewish, Muslim

         MATERIAL   silver, walnut, wool, marble

LAST   **NOUN/ADJECTIVE**   tree (as in *tree* house), kitchen (as in *kitchen* table)

THE NOUN MODIFIED   house, sweater, bicycle, bread, woman, priest

     My long green wool coat is in the attic.

     Ana's collection includes *four small antique silver* coins.

If you use cumulative adjectives before a noun, see the chart at the top of this page. The chart is only a guide; don't be surprised if you encounter exceptions. (See also 33d.)

▶ My dorm room has only a small desk and a ~~plastic red smelly~~ *smelly red plastic*

chair.

▶ Nice weather, ~~blue clear~~ *clear blue* water, and ancient monuments attract

many people to Italy.

EXERCISE 30–4 Using the chart at the top of this page, arrange the following modifiers and nouns in their proper order. Answers to lettered items appear in the back of the book. Example:

two new French racing bicycles
new, French, two, bicycles, racing

a. woman, young, an, Vietnamese, attractive
b. dedicated, a, priest, Catholic
c. old, her, sweater, blue, wool
d. delicious, Joe's, Scandinavian, bread
e. many, boxes, jewelry, antique, beautiful

1. oval, nine, brass, lamps, miniature
2. several, yellow, tulips, tiny
3. the, tree, gingko, yellow, ancient, Mongolian
4. courtyard, a, square, small, brick
5. charming, restaurants, Italian, several

ON THE WEB > dianahacker.com/rules
Grammar exercises > ESL challenges > E-ex 30–4

31

Prepositions and idiomatic expressions

31a Become familiar with prepositions that show time and place.

The most frequently used prepositions in English are *at, by, for, from, in, of, on, to,* and *with.* Prepositions can be difficult to master because the differences among them are subtle and idiomatic. The chart on page 265 is limited to three troublesome prepositions that show time and place: *at, on,* and *in.*

Not every possible use is listed in the chart, so don't be surprised when you encounter exceptions and idiomatic uses that you must learn one at a time. For example, in English we ride *in* a car but *on* a bus, plane, train, or subway.

▶ My first class starts ~~on~~ *at* 8:00 a.m.

▶ The farmers go to market ~~in~~ *on* Wednesday.

▶ I want to work at one of the biggest companies ~~on~~ *in* the world.

At, on, *and* in *to show time and place*

Showing time

AT $\quad$ *at* a specific time: *at* 7:20, *at* dawn, *at* dinner

ON $\quad$ *on* a specific day or date: *on* Tuesday, *on* June 4

IN $\quad$ *in* a part of a 24-hour period: *in* the afternoon, *in* the daytime [but *at* night]

$\quad$ *in* a year or month: *in* 1999, *in* July

$\quad$ *in* a period of time: finished *in* three hours

Showing place

AT $\quad$ *at* a meeting place or location: *at* home, *at* the club

$\quad$ *at* the edge of something: sitting *at* the desk

$\quad$ *at* the corner of something: turning *at* the intersection

$\quad$ *at* a target: throwing the snowball *at* Lucy

ON $\quad$ *on* a surface: placed *on* the table, hanging *on* the wall

$\quad$ *on* a street: the house *on* Spring Street

$\quad$ *on* an electronic medium: *on* television, *on* the Internet

IN $\quad$ *in* an enclosed space: *in* the garage, *in* an envelope

$\quad$ *in* a geographic location: *in* San Diego, *in* Texas

$\quad$ *in* a print medium: *in* a book, *in* a magazine

EXERCISE 31–1 $\quad$ In the following sentences, replace prepositions that are not used correctly. If a sentence is correct, write "correct" after it. Answers to lettered sentences appear in the back of the book. Example:

$\qquad$ *at*
The play begins ~~on~~ 7:20 p.m.
$\qquad\quad\quad$ ^

a. Whenever we eat at the Centerville Diner, we sit at a small table on the corner of the room.

b. At the beginning of the dotcom wave, students created new businesses in record numbers.

c. In Thursday, Nancy will attend her first Pilates class at the community center.

d. Alex began looking for her lost mitten in another location.

e. We decided to go to a restaurant because there was no fresh food on the refrigerator.

1. I don't feel safe walking on my neighborhood in night.
2. If the train is on time, it will arrive on six o'clock at the morning.
3. In the corner of the room is a large bookcase with a pair of small Russian dolls standing at the top shelf.
4. She licked the stamp, stuck it in the envelope, put the envelope on her pocket, and walked to the nearest mailbox.
5. The mailbox was in the intersection of Laidlaw Avenue and Williams Street.

ON THE WEB > dianahacker.com/rules
Grammar exercises > ESL challenges > E-ex 31–1

31b Use nouns (including *-ing* forms) after prepositions.

In a prepositional phrase, use a noun (not a verb) after the preposition. Sometimes the noun will be a gerund, the *-ing* verb form that functions as a noun (see 64c).

>   *saving*
> Our student government is good at ~~save~~ money.

Distinguish between the preposition *to* and the infinitive marker *to*. If *to* is a preposition, it should be followed by a noun or a gerund.

>   *helping*
> We are dedicated to ~~help~~ the poor.

If *to* is an infinitive marker, it should be followed by the base form of the verb.

>   *help*
> We want to ~~helping~~ the poor.

TIP: To test whether *to* is a preposition or an infinitive marker, insert a word that you know is a noun after the word *to*. If the noun sounds right in that position, *to* is a preposition.

    Zoe is addicted to _____.

In this case, a noun (such as *magazines*) makes sense after *to*, so *to* is a preposition and should be followed by a noun or a gerund: *Zoe is addicted to magazines. Zoe is addicted to reading.*

They are planning to _____.

In this case, a noun (such as *house*) does not make sense after *to*, so *to* is an infinitive marker and must be followed by the base form of the verb: *They are planning to build a new house.*

31c Become familiar with common adjective + preposition combinations.

Some adjectives appear only with certain prepositions. These expressions are idiomatic and may be different from the combinations used in your native language.

▶ Paula is married ~~with~~ *to* Jon.

Check an ESL dictionary for combinations that are not listed in the following chart.

Adjective + preposition combinations

accustomed to	connected to	interested in	proud of
addicted to	covered with	involved in	responsible for
afraid of	dedicated to	involved with	satisfied with
angry with	devoted to	known as	scared of
ashamed of	different from	known for	similar to
aware of	engaged to	made of (*or* made from)	tired of
committed to	excited about		worried about
concerned about	familiar with	married to	
concerned with	full of	opposed to	
	guilty of	preferable to	

31d Become familiar with common verb + preposition combinations.

Many verbs and prepositions appear together in idiomatic phrases. Pay special attention to the combinations that are different from the combinations used in your native language.

► Your success depends ~~of~~ ^{on} your effort.

Check an ESL dictionary for combinations that are not listed in the following chart.

Verb + preposition combinations

agree with	compare with	forget about	speak to (*or* speak with)
apply to	concentrate on	happen to	stare at
approve of	consist of	hope for	succeed at
arrive in	count on	insist on	succeed in
arrive at	decide on	listen to	take advantage of
ask for	depend on	participate in	take care of
believe in	differ from	rely on	think about
belong to	disagree with	reply to	think of
care about	dream about	respond to	wait for
care for	dream of	result in	wait on
compare to	feel like	search for	

Punctuation

32

The comma

The comma was invented to help readers. Without it, sentence parts can collide into one another unexpectedly, causing misreadings.

> **CONFUSING**   If you cook Elmer will do the dishes.

> **CONFUSING**   While we were eating a rattlesnake approached our campsite.

Add commas in the logical places (after *cook* and *eating*), and suddenly all is clear. No longer is Elmer being cooked, the rattlesnake being eaten.

Various rules have evolved to prevent such misreadings and to speed readers along through complex grammatical structures. Those rules are detailed in this section. (Section 33 explains when not to use commas.)

32a Use a comma before a coordinating conjunction joining independent clauses.

When a coordinating conjunction connects two or more independent clauses — word groups that could stand alone as separate sentences — a comma must precede it. There are seven coordinating conjunctions in English: *and, but, or, nor, for, so,* and *yet.*

A comma tells readers that one independent clause has come to a close and that another is about to begin.

▶ Nearly everyone has heard of love at first sight, but I fell in

love at first dance.

EXCEPTION: If the two independent clauses are short and there is no danger of misreading, the comma may be omitted.

The plane took off and we were on our way.

GRAMMAR CHECKERS rarely flag missing or misused commas. They sometimes recognize that a comma belongs before a *which* clause but not before a *that* clause (see 32e). For all other uses of the comma — after introductory word groups, between items in a series, between coordinate adjectives, around appositives, and so on — they are unreliable. When a grammar checker does note a missing comma, its suggested revision is often incorrect and sometimes even amusing. One program, for example, suggested a comma after the word *delivery* in the following sentence: *While I was driving a huge delivery truck ran through a red light.*

TIP: As a rule, do *not* use a comma to separate coordinate word groups that are not independent clauses. (See 33a.)

▶ A good money manager controls expenses/ and invests

surplus dollars to meet future needs.

The word group following *and* is not an independent clause; it is the second half of a compound predicate.

32b Use a comma after an introductory clause or phrase.

The most common introductory word groups are clauses and phrases functioning as adverbs. Such word groups usually tell when, where, how, why, or under what conditions the main action of the sentence occurred. (See 64a–64c.)

A comma tells readers that the introductory clause or phrase has come to a close and that the main part of the sentence is about to begin.

▶ When Irwin was ready to iron, his cat tripped on the cord.

Without the comma, readers may have Irwin ironing his cat. The comma signals that *his cat* is the subject of a new clause, not part of the introductory one.

▶ Near a small stream at the bottom of the canyon, the park

rangers discovered an abandoned mine.

The comma tells readers that the introductory prepositional phrase has come to a close.

EXCEPTION: The comma may be omitted after a short adverb clause or phrase if there is no danger of misreading.

In no time we were at 2,800 feet.

Sentences also frequently begin with participial phrases describing the noun or pronoun immediately following them. The comma tells readers that they are about to learn the identity of the person or thing described; therefore, the comma is usually required even when the phrase is short. (See 64c.)

▶ Thinking his motorcade drive through Dallas was routine,

President Kennedy smiled and waved at the crowds.

▶ Buried under layers of younger rocks, the earth's oldest

rocks contain no fossils.

NOTE: Other introductory word groups include transitional expressions and absolute phrases (see 32f).

EXERCISE 32–1 Add or delete commas where necessary in the following sentences. If a sentence is correct, write "correct" after it. Answers to lettered sentences appear in the back of the book. Example:

Because we had been saving molding for a few weeks, we had

enough wood to frame all thirty paintings.

a. Alisa brought the injured bird home, and fashioned a splint out of Popsicle sticks for its wing.
b. Considered a classic of early animation *The Adventures of Prince Achmed* used hand-cut silhouettes against colored backgrounds.
c. If you complete the enclosed evaluation form, and return it within two weeks, you will receive a free breakfast during your next stay.
d. After retiring from the New York City Ballet in 1965, legendary dancer Maria Tallchief went on to found the Chicago City Ballet.
e. Roger had always wanted a handmade violin but he couldn't afford one.

1. While I was driving a huge delivery truck ran through a red light.
2. He pushed the car beyond the tollgate, and poured a bucket of water on the smoking hood.
3. Lit by bright halogen lamps hundreds of origami cranes sparkled like diamonds in sunlight.
4. As the first chord sounded, Aileen knew that her spirits were about to rise.
5. Many musicians of Bach's time played several instruments but few mastered them as early or played with as much expression as Bach.

32c Use a comma between all items in a series.

When three or more items are presented in a series, those items should be separated from one another with commas. Items in a series may be single words, phrases, or clauses.

▶ Bubbles of air, leaves, ferns, bits of wood, and insects are

often found trapped in amber.

Although some writers view the comma between the last two items as optional, most experts advise using the comma because its omission can result in ambiguity or misreading.

▶ Uncle David willed me all of his property, houses, and

warehouses.

Did Uncle David will his property *and* houses *and* warehouses — or simply his property, consisting of houses and warehouses? If the former meaning is intended, a comma is necessary to prevent ambiguity.

▶ The activities include a search for lost treasure, dubious

financial dealings, much discussion of ancient heresies, and

midnight orgies.

Without the comma, the activities seem to include discussing orgies, not participating in them. The comma makes it clear that *midnight orgies* is a separate item in the series.

ON THE WEB > dianahacker.com/rules
Language Debates > Commas with items in a series

32d Use a comma between coordinate adjectives not joined with *and*. Do not use a comma between cumulative adjectives.

When two or more adjectives each modify a noun separately, they are coordinate.

> Roberto is a *warm, gentle, affectionate* father.

Adjectives are coordinate if they can be joined with *and* (warm *and* gentle *and* affectionate).

Adjectives that do not modify the noun separately are cumulative.

> *Three large gray* shapes moved slowly toward us.

Beginning with the adjective closest to the noun *shapes,* these modifiers lean on one another, piggyback style, with each modifying a larger word group. *Gray* modifies *shapes, large* modifies *gray shapes,* and *three* modifies *large gray shapes.* Cumulative adjectives cannot be joined with *and* (three *and* large *and* gray shapes).

COORDINATE ADJECTIVES

▶ Patients with severe‸ irreversible brain damage should not be

put on life support systems.

> Adjectives are coordinate if they can be connected with *and*: *severe and irreversible.*

CUMULATIVE ADJECTIVES

▶ Ira ordered a rich⁄ chocolate⁄ layer cake.

> Ira didn't order a cake that was rich and chocolate and layer: He ordered a *layer cake* that was *chocolate,* a *chocolate layer cake* that was *rich.*

EXERCISE 32-2   Add or delete commas where necessary in the following sentences. If a sentence is correct, write "correct" after it. Answers to lettered sentences appear in the back of the book. Example:

> We gathered our essentials, took off for the great outdoors,
>
> and ignored the fact that it was Friday the 13th.

a. The cold impersonal atmosphere of the university was unbearable.
b. An ambulance threaded its way through police cars, fire trucks and irate citizens.
c. The *1812 Overture* is a stirring, magnificent piece of music.
d. After two broken arms, three cracked ribs and one concussion, Ken quit the varsity football team.
e. My cat's pupils had constricted to small black shining slits.

1. We prefer our staff to be orderly, prompt and efficient.
2. For breakfast the children ordered cornflakes, English muffins with peanut butter and cherry Cokes.
3. It was a small, unimportant part, but I was happy to have it.
4. Cyril was clad in a luminous orange rain suit and a brilliant white helmet.
5. Animation master Hironobu Sakaguchi makes computer-generated scenes look realistic, vivid and seductive.

32e   Use commas to set off nonrestrictive elements. Do not use commas to set off restrictive elements.

Word groups describing nouns or pronouns (adjective clauses, adjective phrases, and appositives) are restrictive or nonrestrictive. A *restrictive* element defines or limits the meaning of the word it modifies and is therefore essential to the meaning of the sentence. Because it contains essential information, a restrictive element is not set off with commas.

> **RESTRICTIVE**   For camp the children need clothes *that are washable.*

If you remove a restrictive element from a sentence, the meaning changes significantly, becoming more general than you intended. The writer of the example sentence does not mean that the children need clothes in general. The intended meaning is more limited: the children need *washable clothes.*

A *nonrestrictive* element describes a noun or pronoun whose meaning has already been clearly defined or limited. Because it contains nonessential or parenthetical information, a nonrestrictive element is set off with commas.

> **NONRESTRICTIVE** For camp the children need sturdy shoes, *which are expensive.*

If you remove a nonrestrictive element from a sentence, the meaning does not change dramatically. Some meaning is lost, to be sure, but the defining characteristics of the person or thing described remain the same as before. The children need *sturdy shoes,* and these happen to be expensive.

NOTE: Often it is difficult to tell whether a word group is restrictive or nonrestrictive without seeing it in context and considering the writer's meaning. Both of the following sentences are grammatically correct, but their meaning is slightly different.

> The dessert made with fresh raspberries was delicious.
>
> The dessert, made with fresh raspberries, was delicious.

In the example without commas, the phrase *made with fresh raspberries* tells readers which of two or more desserts the writer is referring to. In the example with commas, the phrase merely adds information about the particular dessert.

Adjective clauses

Adjective clauses are patterned like sentences, containing subjects and verbs, but they function within sentences as modifiers of nouns or pronouns. They always follow the word they modify, usually immediately. Adjective clauses begin with a relative pronoun (*who, whom, whose, which, that*) or with a relative adverb (*where, when*).

Nonrestrictive adjective clauses are set off with commas; restrictive adjective clauses are not.

NONRESTRICTIVE CLAUSE

▶ Ed's house, which is located on thirteen acres, was completely

furnished with bats in the rafters and mice in the kitchen.

The adjective clause *which is located on thirteen acres* does not restrict the meaning of *Ed's house,* so the information is nonessential.

RESTRICTIVE CLAUSE

▶ Ramona's cat⁄ that just had kittens⁄ became defensive around

the other cats in the house.

Because the adjective clause *that just had kittens* identifies the particular cat, the information is essential.

NOTE: Use *that* only with restrictive clauses. Many writers prefer to use *which* only with nonrestrictive clauses, but usage varies.

ON THE WEB > **dianahacker.com/rules**
Language Debates > *that* versus *which*

Phrases functioning as adjectives

Prepositional or verbal phrases functioning as adjectives may be restrictive or nonrestrictive. Nonrestrictive phrases are set off with commas; restrictive phrases are not.

NONRESTRICTIVE PHRASE

▶ The helicopter‸ with its million-candlepower spotlight

illuminating the area‸ circled above.

The *with* phrase is nonessential because its purpose is not to specify which of two or more helicopters is being discussed.

RESTRICTIVE PHRASE

▶ One corner of the attic was filled with newspapers⁄ dating

from the turn of the century.

Dating from the turn of the century restricts the meaning of *newspapers,* so the comma should be omitted.

Appositives

An appositive is a noun or noun phrase that renames a nearby noun. Nonrestrictive appositives are set off with commas; restrictive appositives are not.

NONRESTRICTIVE APPOSITIVE

▶ Darwin's most important book‸ *On the Origin of Species*‸ was

the result of many years of research.

Most important restricts the meaning to one book, so the appositive *On the Origin of Species* is nonrestrictive and should be set off
with commas.

RESTRICTIVE APPOSITIVE

▶ The song⁄ "Vertigo⁄" was blasted out of huge amplifiers at the

concert.

Once they've read *song,* readers still don't know precisely which
song the writer means. The appositive following *song* restricts its
meaning.

EXERCISE 32–3 Add or delete commas where necessary in the following sentences. If a sentence is correct, write "correct" after
it. Answers to lettered sentences appear in the back of the book.
Example:

My youngest sister‸ who plays left wing on the soccer

team‸ now lives at The Sands‸ a beach house near

Los Angeles.

a. Choreographer Alvin Ailey's best-known work *Revelations* is
   more than just a crowd pleaser.
b. Twyla Tharp's contemporary ballet *Push Comes to Shove* was
   made famous by Russian dancer Baryshnikov. [Tharp has written
   more than one contemporary ballet.]
c. The glass sculptor sifting through hot red sand explained her technique to the other glassmakers.
d. A member of an organization, that provides housing for AIDS patients, was also appointed to the commission.
e. Brian Eno who began his career as a rock musician turned to meditative compositions in the late seventies.

1. I had the pleasure of talking to a woman who had just returned
   from India where she had lived for ten years.

2. Patrick's oldest sister Fiona graduated from MIT with a degree in aerospace engineering.
3. The artist painting a portrait of Aung San Suu Kyi, the Burmese civil rights leader, was once a political prisoner himself.
4. *The Polar Express,* the 1986 Caldecott Medal winner, is my nephew's favorite book.
5. The flame crawled up a few blades of grass to reach a low-hanging palmetto branch which quickly ignited.

32f Use commas to set off transitional and parenthetical expressions, absolute phrases, and elements expressing contrast.

Transitional expressions

Transitional expressions serve as bridges between sentences or parts of sentences. They include conjunctive adverbs such as *however, therefore,* and *moreover* and transitional phrases such as *for example, as a matter of fact,* and *in other words.* (For more complete lists, see 34b.)

When a transitional expression appears between independent clauses in a compound sentence, it is preceded by a semicolon and is usually followed by a comma. (See 34b.)

▶ Minh did not understand our language; moreover, he was

unfamiliar with our customs.

When a transitional expression appears at the beginning of a sentence or in the middle of an independent clause, it is usually set off with commas.

▶ As a matter of fact, American football was established by

fans who wanted to play a more organized game of rugby.

▶ Natural foods are not always salt free; celery, for example,

contains more sodium than most people would imagine.

EXCEPTION: If a transitional expression blends smoothly with the rest of the sentence, calling for little or no pause in reading, it does not need to be set off with a comma. Expressions such as *also, at least, certainly, consequently, indeed, of course, moreover, no doubt, perhaps, then,* and *therefore* do not always call for a pause.

> Alice's bicycle is broken; *therefore* you will need to borrow Sue's.

Parenthetical expressions

Expressions that are distinctly parenthetical should be set off with commas. Providing supplemental information, they interrupt the flow of a sentence or appear at the end as afterthoughts.

▶ Evolution, as far as we know, doesn't work this way.

▶ The bass weighed about twelve pounds, give or take a few

ounces.

Absolute phrases

An absolute phrase, which modifies the whole sentence, usually consists of a noun followed by a participle or participial phrase. (See 64e.) Absolute phrases may appear at the beginning or at the end of a sentence. Wherever they appear, they should be set off with commas.

▶ The sun appearing for the first time in a week, we were at

last able to begin the archaeological dig.

▶ Elvis Presley made music industry history in the 1950s, his

records having sold more than ten million copies.

CAUTION: Do not insert a comma between the noun and the participle in an absolute construction.

▶ The next contestant/ being five years old, the emcee

adjusted the height of the microphone.

Contrasted elements

Sharp contrasts beginning with words such as *not, never,* and *unlike* are set off with commas.

▶ The Epicurean philosophers sought mental, not bodily, pleasures.

▶ Unlike Uncle Robert, Aunt Celia loved entering swing dance contests.

32g Use commas to set off nouns of direct address, the words *yes* and *no*, interrogative tags, and mild interjections.

▶ Forgive us, Dr. Atkins, for having rolls with dinner tonight.

▶ Yes, the loan for the renovations will probably be approved by tomorrow.

▶ The film was faithful to the book, wasn't it?

▶ Well, cases like these are difficult to decide.

32h Use commas with expressions such as *he said* to set off direct quotations. (See also 37f.)

▶ Naturalist Arthur Cleveland Bent remarked, "In part the peregrine declined unnoticed because it is not adorable."

▶ "Convictions are more dangerous foes of truth than lies," wrote philosopher Friedrich Nietzsche.

32i Use commas with dates, addresses, titles, and numbers.

Dates

In dates, the year is set off from the rest of the sentence with a pair of commas.

> On December 12, 1890, orders were sent out for the arrest of Sitting Bull.

EXCEPTIONS: Commas are not needed if the date is inverted or if only the month and year are given.

> The recycling plan went into effect on 15 April 2001.

> January 2006 was an extremely cold month.

Addresses

The elements of an address or a place name are separated by commas. A zip code, however, is not preceded by a comma.

> John Lennon was born in Liverpool, England, in 1940.

▶ Please send the package to Greg Tarvin at 708 Spring Street‸

Washington‸ IL 61571.

Titles

If a title follows a name, separate the title from the rest of the sentence with a pair of commas.

▶ Sandra Belinsky‸ MD‸ has been appointed to the board.

Numbers

In numbers more than four digits long, use commas to separate the numbers into groups of three, starting from the right. In numbers four digits long, a comma is optional.

> 3,500 [*or* 3500]   100,000   5,000,000

EXCEPTIONS: Do not use commas in street numbers, zip codes, telephone numbers, or years.

32j Use a comma to prevent confusion.

In certain contexts, a comma is necessary to prevent confusion. If the writer has omitted a word or phrase, for example, a comma may be needed to signal the omission.

▶ To err is human; to forgive, divine.

If two words in a row echo each other, a comma may be needed for ease of reading.

▶ All of the catastrophes that we had feared might happen, happened.

Sometimes a comma is needed to prevent readers from grouping words in ways that do not match the writer's intention.

▶ Patients who can, walk up and down the halls several times a day.

EXERCISE 32–4 Major uses of the comma This exercise covers the major uses of the comma explained in section 32. Add or delete commas where necessary. If a sentence is correct, write "correct" after it. Answers to lettered sentences appear in the back of the book. Example:

Even though Pavel had studied Nigella Lawson's recipes for a week, he underestimated how long it would take to juice two hundred lemons.

a. Cricket, which originated in England is also popular in Australia, South Africa and India.

b. At the sound of the starting pistol the horses surged forward toward the first obstacle, a sharp incline three feet high.
c. After seeing an exhibition of Western art Gerhard Richter escaped from East Berlin in 1961, and smuggled out many of his notebooks.
d. Corrie's new wet suit has an intricate, blue pattern.
e. The cookies will keep for two weeks in sturdy airtight plastic containers.

1. Research on Andean condors has shown that high levels of the chemical pesticide chlorinated hydrocarbon can cause the thinning of eggshells.
2. Founded in 1868 Hampton University was one of the first colleges for African Americans.
3. Aunt Emilia was an impossible demanding guest.
4. The French Mirage, a high-tech fighter, is an astonishing machine to fly.
5. At the bottom of the ship's rusty hold sat several, well-preserved trunks, reminders of a bygone era of sea travel.

EXERCISE 32–5 All uses of the comma   Add or delete commas where necessary in the following sentences. If a sentence is correct, write "correct" after it. Answers to lettered sentences appear in the back of the book. Example:

> "Yes, dear, you can have dessert," my mother said.

a. On January 15, 2004 our office moved to 29 Commonwealth Avenue, Mechanicsville VA 23111.
b. The coach having bawled us out thoroughly for our lackluster performance, we left the locker room with his harsh words ringing in our ears.
c. Ms. Carlson you are a valued customer whose satisfaction is very important to us.
d. Mr. Mundy was born on July 22, 1939 in Arkansas, where his family had lived for four generations.
e. Her board poised at the edge of the half-pipe, Nina waited her turn to drop in.

1. President Lincoln's original intention was to save the Union, not to destroy slavery.
2. For centuries people believed that Greek culture had developed in isolation from the world. Today however scholars are acknowledging the contributions made by Egypt and the Middle East.

3. Putting together a successful fundraiser, Patricia discovered, requires creativity and good timing.
4. Fortunately science is creating many alternatives to research performed on animals.
5. While the machine was printing the oversize paper jammed.

ON THE WEB > **dianahacker.com/rules**
Grammar exercises > Punctuation > E-ex 32–1 to 32–3

33

Unnecessary commas

Many common misuses of the comma result from an incomplete understanding of the major comma rules presented in 32. In particular, writers frequently form misconceptions about rules 32a–32e, either extending the rules inappropriately or misinterpreting them. Such misconceptions can lead to the errors described in 33a–33e; rules 33f–33h list other common misuses of the comma.

33a Do not use a comma between compound elements that are not independent clauses.

Though a comma should be used before a coordinating conjunction joining independent clauses (see 32a), this rule should not be extended to other compound word groups.

▶ Marie Curie discovered radium, and later applied her work

on radioactivity to medicine.

▶ Jake still doesn't realize that his illness is serious, and that

he will have to alter his diet to improve his chances of survival.

In the first example, *and* links two verbs in a compound predicate: *discovered* and *applied*. In the second example, *and* links two subordinate clauses, each beginning with *that*.

33b Do not use a comma after a phrase that begins an inverted sentence.

Though a comma belongs after most introductory phrases (see 32b), it does not belong after phrases that begin an inverted sentence. In an inverted sentence, the subject follows the verb, and a phrase that ordinarily would follow the verb is moved to the beginning (see 63c).

▶ At the bottom of the hill̸ sat the stubborn mule.

33c Do not use a comma before the first or after the last item in a series.

Though commas are required between items in a series (32c), do not place them either before or after the whole series.

▶ Other causes of asthmatic attacks are̸ stress, change in

temperature, and cold air.

▶ Ironically, this job that appears so glamorous, carefree, and

easy̸ carries a high degree of responsibility.

33d Do not use a comma between cumulative adjectives, between an adjective and a noun, or between an adverb and an adjective.

Commas are required between coordinate adjectives (those that can be joined with *and*), but they do not belong between cumulative adjectives (those that cannot be joined with *and*). (For a full discussion, see 32d.)

▶ In the corner of the closet we found an old̸ maroon hatbox

from Sears.

A comma should never be used between an adjective and the noun that follows it.

▶ It was a senseless, dangerous/ mission.

Nor should a comma be used between an adverb and an adjective that follows it.

▶ The Hillside is a good home for severely/ disturbed youths.

33e Do not use commas to set off restrictive or mildly parenthetical elements.

Restrictive elements are modifiers or appositives that restrict the meaning of the nouns they follow. Because they are essential to the meaning of the sentence, they are not set off with commas. (For a full discussion of both restrictive and nonrestrictive elements, see 32e.)

▶ Drivers/ who think they own the road/ can cause accidents.

The modifier *who think they own the road* restricts the meaning of *Drivers* and is therefore essential to the meaning of the sentence. Putting commas around the *who* clause falsely suggests that all drivers think they own the road.

▶ Margaret Mead's book/ *Coming of Age in Samoa/* stirred up considerable controversy when it was published in 1928.

Since Mead wrote more than one book, the appositive contains information essential to the meaning of the sentence.

Although commas should be used with distinctly parenthetical expressions (see 32f), do not use them to set off elements that are only mildly parenthetical.

▶ Charisse believes that the Internet is/ essentially/ a bastion of advertising.

33f Do not use a comma to set off a concluding adverb clause that is essential to the meaning of the sentence.

When adverb clauses introduce a sentence, they are nearly always followed by a comma (see 32b). When they conclude a sentence, however, they are not set off by commas if their content is essential to the meaning of the earlier part of the sentence. Adverb clauses beginning with *after, as soon as, because, before, if, since, unless, until,* and *when* are usually essential.

▶ Don't visit Paris at the height of the tourist season/ unless

you have booked hotel reservations.

Without the *unless* clause, the meaning of the sentence might at first seem broader than the writer intended.

When a concluding adverb clause is nonessential, it should be preceded by a comma. Clauses beginning with *although, even though, though,* and *whereas* are usually nonessential.

▶ The lecture seemed to last only a short time‸ although the

clock said it had gone on for more than an hour.

33g Do not use a comma to separate a verb from its subject or object.

A sentence should flow from subject to verb to object without unnecessary pauses. Commas may appear between these major sentence elements only when a specific rule calls for them.

▶ Zoos large enough to give the animals freedom to roam/ are

becoming more popular.

The comma should not separate the subject, *Zoos,* from the verb, *are becoming.*

▶ Francesca explained to him,/ that she was busy and would

see him later.

The comma should not separate the verb *explained* from its object, the subordinate clause *that she was busy and would see him later*.

33h Avoid other common misuses of the comma.

Do not use a comma in the following situations.

AFTER A COORDINATING CONJUNCTION (*AND, BUT, OR, NOR, FOR, SO, YET*)

▶ Occasionally soap operas are performed live, but,/ more often

they are taped.

AFTER *SUCH AS* OR *LIKE*

▶ Many shade-loving plants, such as,/ begonias, impatiens, and

coleus, can add color to a shady garden.

BEFORE *THAN*

▶ Touring Crete was more thrilling for us,/ than visiting the

Greek islands frequented by rich Europeans.

AFTER *ALTHOUGH*

▶ Although,/ the air was balmy, the water was too cold for

swimming.

BEFORE A PARENTHESIS

▶ At Nextel Sylvia began at the bottom,/ (with only three and a

half walls and a swivel chair), but within three years she had

been promoted to supervisor.

TO SET OFF AN INDIRECT (REPORTED) QUOTATION

▶ Samuel Goldwyn once said⁄ that a verbal contract isn't worth

the paper it's written on.

WITH A QUESTION MARK OR AN EXCLAMATION POINT

▶ "Why don't you try it?⁄" she coaxed. "You can't do any worse

than the rest of us."

EXERCISE 33–1 Delete commas where necessary in the following sentences. If a sentence is correct, write "correct" after it. Answers to lettered sentences appear in the back of the book. Example:

In his Silk Road Project, Yo-Yo Ma has incorporated work by

musicians such as⁄ Kayhan Kahlor and Richard Danielpour.

a. After the morning rains cease, the swimmers emerge from their cottages.
b. Tricia's first artwork was a big, blue, clay dolphin.
c. Some modern musicians, (trumpeter John Hassell is an example) blend several cultural traditions into a unique sound.
d. Myra liked hot, spicy foods such as, chili, jambalaya, and buffalo wings.
e. On the display screen, was a soothing pattern of light and shadow.

1. Mesquite, the hardest of the softwoods, grows primarily in the Southwest.
2. Jolie's parents encouraged independent thinking, but required respect for others' opinions.
3. Miranda told her boss, that she had discovered a new plastic as strong as metal.
4. The streets that three hours later would be bumper to bumper with commuters, were quiet and empty except for a few prowling cats.
5. Some first-year architecture students, expect to design intricate structures immediately.

ON THE WEB > **dianahacker.com/rules**
Grammar exercises > Punctuation > E-ex 33–1

34

The semicolon

The semicolon is used to connect major sentence elements of equal grammatical rank.

> **GRAMMAR CHECKERS** flag some, but not all, misused semicolons (34d). In addition, they can alert you to some run-on sentences (34a). However, they miss more run-on sentences than they identify, and they sometimes flag correct sentences as possible run-ons.

34a Use a semicolon between closely related independent clauses not joined with a coordinating conjunction.

When related independent clauses appear in one sentence, they are ordinarily linked with a comma and a coordinating conjunction (*and, but, or, nor, for, so, yet*). The coordinating conjunction signals the relation between the clauses. If the clauses are closely related and the relation is clear without a conjunction, they may be linked with a semicolon instead.

> Injustice is relatively easy to bear; what stings is justice.
> —H. L. Mencken

A semicolon must be used whenever a coordinating conjunction has been omitted between independent clauses. To use merely a comma creates a kind of run-on sentence known as a *comma splice*. (See 20.)

▶ In 1800, a traveler needed six weeks to get from New York

City to Chicago/; in 1860, the trip by railroad took only

two days.

TIP: Do not overuse the semicolon as a means of revising run-on sentences. For other revision strategies, see 20a, 20c, and 20d.

34b Use a semicolon between independent clauses linked with a transitional expression.

Transitional expressions include conjunctive adverbs and transitional phrases.

CONJUNCTIVE ADVERBS

accordingly	furthermore	moreover	still
also	hence	nevertheless	subsequently
anyway	however	next	then
besides	incidentally	nonetheless	therefore
certainly	indeed	now	thus
consequently	instead	otherwise	
conversely	likewise	similarly	
finally	meanwhile	specifically	

TRANSITIONAL PHRASES

after all	for example	in the first place
as a matter of fact	for instance	on the contrary
as a result	in addition	on the other hand
at any rate	in conclusion	
at the same time	in fact	
even so	in other words	

When a transitional expression appears between independent clauses, it is preceded by a semicolon and usually followed by a comma.

▶ Many corals grow very gradually/; in fact, the creation of a

coral reef can take centuries.

When a transitional expression appears in the middle or at the end of the second independent clause, the semicolon goes *between the clauses*.

▶ Most singers gain fame through hard work and dedication/;

Evita, however, found other means.

Transitional expressions should not be confused with the coordinating conjunctions *and, but, or, nor, for, so,* and *yet,* which are preceded by a comma when they link independent clauses. (See 32a.)

34c Use a semicolon between items in a series containing internal punctuation.

▶ Classic science fiction sagas are *Star Trek,* with Mr. Spock/;

  Battlestar Galactica, with Cylon Raiders/; and *Star Wars,*

  with Han Solo, Luke Skywalker, and Darth Vader.

Without the semicolons, the reader would have to sort out the major groupings, distinguishing between important and less important pauses according to the logic of the sentence. By inserting semicolons at the major breaks, the writer does this work for the reader.

34d Avoid common misuses of the semicolon.

Do not use a semicolon in the following situations.

BETWEEN A SUBORDINATE CLAUSE AND THE REST OF THE SENTENCE

▶ Unless you brush your teeth within ten or fifteen minutes

  after eating/, brushing does almost no good.

BETWEEN AN APPOSITIVE AND THE WORD IT REFERS TO

▶ The scientists were fascinated by the species *Argyroneta*

  aquatica/, a spider that lives underwater.

TO INTRODUCE A LIST

▶ Some of my favorite film stars have home pages on the Web/:

  Uma Thurman, Billy Bob Thornton, and Halle Berry.

BETWEEN INDEPENDENT CLAUSES JOINED BY *AND, BUT, OR, NOR, FOR, SO,* OR *YET*

▶ Five of the applicants had worked with spreadsheets**;** but

only one was familiar with database management.

EXCEPTIONS: If at least one of the independent clauses contains internal punctuation, you may use a semicolon even though the clauses are joined with a coordinating conjunction.

> As a vehicle [the model T] was hard-working, commonplace, and heroic; and it often seemed to transmit those qualities to the person who rode in it. — E. B. White

Although a comma would also be correct in this sentence, the semicolon is more effective, for it indicates the relative weights of the pauses.

Occasionally, a semicolon may be used to emphasize a sharp contrast or a firm distinction between clauses joined with a coordinating conjunction.

> We hate some persons because we do not know them; and we will not know them because we hate them.
> — Charles Caleb Colton

EXERCISE 34–1 Add commas or semicolons where needed in the following well-known quotations. If a sentence is correct, write "correct" after it. Answers to lettered sentences appear in the back of the book. Example:

> If an animal does something**,** we call it instinct**;** if we do the
>
> same thing**,** we call it intelligence.   — Will Cuppy

a. Do not ask me to be kind just ask me to act as though I were.
   —Jules Renard
b. When men talk about defense they always claim to be protecting women and children but they never ask the women and children what they think.   — Pat Schroeder
c. When I get a little money I buy books if any is left I buy food and clothes.   — Desiderius Erasmus
d. America is a country that doesn't know where it is going but is determined to set a speed record getting there.
   — Lawrence J. Peter
e. Wit has truth in it wisecracking is simply calisthenics with words.
   — Dorothy Parker

1. Standing in the middle of the road is very dangerous you get knocked down by the traffic from both sides.
   —Margaret Thatcher
2. I do not believe in an afterlife, although I am bringing a change of underwear.
   —Woody Allen
3. Once the children were in the house the air became more vivid and more heated every object in the house grew more alive.
   — Mary Gordon
4. We don't know what we want but we are ready to bite someone to get it.
   — Will Rogers
5. I've been rich and I've been poor rich is better.
   — Sophie Tucker

EXERCISE 34–2 Edit the following sentences to correct errors in the use of the comma and the semicolon. If a sentence is correct, write "correct" after it. Answers to lettered sentences appear in the back of the book. Example:

Love is blind; envy has its eyes wide open.
_∧

a. Strong black coffee will not sober you up, the truth is that time is the only way to get alcohol out of your system.
b. It is not surprising that our society is increasingly violent, after all, television desensitizes us to brutality at a very early age.
c. There is often a fine line between right and wrong; good and bad; truth and deception.
d. At Weight Watchers, we believe that being fat is not hereditary; it is a choice.
e. Severe, unremitting pain is a ravaging force; especially when the patient tries to hide it from others.

1. Another delicious dish is the chef's special; a roasted duck rubbed with spices and stuffed with wild rice.
2. Martin Luther King Jr. had not intended to be a preacher, initially, he had planned to become a lawyer.
3. We all assumed that the thief had been Jean's boyfriend; even though we had seen him only from the back.
4. The Victorians avoided the subject of sex but were obsessed with death, our contemporaries are obsessed with sex but avoid thinking about death.
5. Some educators believe that African American history should be taught in separate courses, others prefer to see it integrated into survey courses.

ON THE WEB > **dianahacker.com/rules**
Grammar exercises > Punctuation > E-ex 34–1 and 34–2

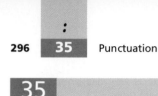

35

The colon

The colon is used primarily to call attention to the words that follow it. In addition, the colon has some conventional uses.

GRAMMAR CHECKERS are fairly good at flagging colons that incorrectly follow a verb (*The office work includes: typing, filing, and answering the phone*). They also point out semicolons used where colons are needed, although they don't suggest revisions.

35a Use a colon after an independent clause to direct attention to a list, an appositive, or a quotation.

A LIST

The daily routine should include at least the following: twenty knee bends, fifty sit-ups, fifteen leg lifts, and five minutes of running in place.

AN APPOSITIVE

My roommate is guilty of two of the seven deadly sins: gluttony and sloth.

A QUOTATION

Consider the words of Benjamin Franklin: "There never was a good war or a bad peace."

For other ways of introducing quotations, see "Introducing quoted material" on pages 306–07.

35b Use a colon between independent clauses if the second summarizes or explains the first.

Faith is like love: It cannot be forced.

NOTE: When an independent clause follows a colon, it may begin with a capital or a lowercase letter (see 45f).

35c Use a colon after the salutation in a formal letter, to indicate hours and minutes, to show proportions, between a title and subtitle, and between city and publisher in bibliographic entries.

Dear Sir or Madam:

5:30 p.m.

The ratio of women to men was 2:1.

The Glory of Hera: Greek Mythology and the Greek Family

Boston: Bedford, 2007

NOTE: In biblical references, a colon is ordinarily used between chapter and verse (Luke 2:14). The Modern Language Association recommends a period instead (Luke 2.14).

35d Avoid common misuses of the colon.

A colon must be preceded by a full independent clause. Therefore, avoid using it in the following situations.

BETWEEN A VERB AND ITS OBJECT OR COMPLEMENT

▶ Some important vitamins found in vegetables are: vitamin A,

thiamine, niacin, and vitamin C.

BETWEEN A PREPOSITION AND ITS OBJECT

▶ The heart's two pumps each consist of: an upper chamber,

or atrium, and a lower chamber, or ventricle.

AFTER *SUCH AS, INCLUDING,* OR *FOR EXAMPLE*

▶ The trees on our campus include many fine Japanese speci-

mens such as: black pines, ginkgos, and weeping cherries.

EXERCISE 35–1 Edit the following sentences to correct errors in the use of the comma, the semicolon, or the colon. If a sentence is correct, write "correct" after it. Answers to lettered sentences appear in the back of the book. Example:

Lifting the cover gently, Luca found the source of the odd

sound⁀: a marble in the gears.

a. We always looked forward to Thanksgiving in Vermont: It was our only chance to see our Grady cousins.

b. If we have come to fight, we are far too few, if we have come to die, we are far too many.

c. The travel package includes: a round-trip ticket to Athens, a cruise through the Cyclades, and all hotel accommodations.

d. The media portray my generation as lazy; although polls show that we work as hard as the twentysomethings before us.

e. Fran Lebowitz has this advice for parents, "Never allow your child to call you by your first name. He hasn't known you long enough."

1. Harry Potter prevails against pain and evil for one reason, his heart is pure.

2. While traveling through France, Rose visited: the Loire Valley, Chartres, the Louvre, and the McDonald's stand at the foot of the Eiffel Tower.

3. There are three types of leave; annual leave, used for vacations, sick leave, used for medical appointments and illness, and personal leave, used for a variety of personal reasons.

4. Carl Sandburg once asked these three questions, "Who paid for my freedom? What was the price? And am I somehow beholden?"

5. Amelie had four goals: to be encouraging, to be effective, to be efficient, and to be elegant.

ON THE WEB > dianahacker.com/rules
Grammar exercises > Punctuation > E-ex 35–1

36

The apostrophe

> **GRAMMAR CHECKERS** flag only some missing or misused apostrophes. They catch missing apostrophes in contractions, such as *don't*. They also flag problems with possessives (*sled dogs feet, a babys eyes*), although they miss as many problems as they identify. Only you can decide when to add an apostrophe and whether to put it before or after the *-s* in possessives.

36a Use an apostrophe to indicate that a noun is possessive.

Possessive nouns usually indicate ownership, as in *Tim's hat* or *the lawyer's desk.* Frequently, however, ownership is only loosely implied: *the tree's roots, a day's work.* If you are not sure whether a noun is possessive, try turning it into an *of* phrase: *the roots of the tree, the work of a day.*

When to add -'s

1. If the noun does not end in *-s,* add *-'s.*

   Roy managed to climb out on the driver's side.

   Thank you for refunding the children's money.

2. If the noun is singular and ends in *-s* or an *s* sound, add *-'s.*

   Lois's sister spent last year in India.

   Her article presents an overview of Marx's teachings.

NOTE: To avoid potentially awkward pronunciation, some writers use only the apostrophe with a singular noun ending in *-s: Sophocles'.*

ON THE WEB > **dianahacker.com/rules**
   Language Debates > -'s for singular nouns ending in -s or an s sound

When to add only an apostrophe

If the noun is plural and ends in *-s,* add only an apostrophe.

   Both diplomats' briefcases were searched by guards.

Joint possession

To show joint possession, use *-'s* or *(-s')* with the last noun only; to show individual possession, make all nouns possessive.

   Have you seen Joyce and Greg's new camper?

   John's and Marie's expectations of marriage couldn't have been more different.

Joyce and Greg jointly own one camper. John and Marie individually have different expectations.

Compound nouns

If a noun is compound, use *-'s* (or *-s'*) with the last element.

My father-in-law's sculpture won first place.

36b Use an apostrophe and *-s* to indicate that an indefinite pronoun is possessive.

Indefinite pronouns refer to no specific person or thing: *everyone, someone, no one, something.* (See 62b.)

Someone's raincoat has been left behind.

36c Use an apostrophe to mark omissions in contractions and numbers.

In contractions the apostrophe takes the place of missing letters.

It's a shame that Frank can't go on the tour.

It's stands for *it is, can't* for *cannot.*
    The apostrophe is also used to mark the omission of the first two digits of a year (*the class of '95*) or years (*the '60s generation*).

36d Do not use an apostrophe to form the plural of numbers, letters, abbreviations, and words mentioned as words.

An apostrophe typically is not used to pluralize numbers, letters, abbreviations, and words mentioned as words. Note the few exceptions and be consistent throughout your paper.

PLURAL NUMBERS   Omit the apostrophe in the plural of all numbers, including decades.

Oksana skated nearly perfect figure 8s.

The 1920s are known as the Jazz Age.

PLURAL LETTERS Italicize the letter and use roman (regular) font style for the *-s* ending. Do not italicize academic grades.

Two large *J*s were painted on the door.

He received two Ds for the first time in his life.

EXCEPTIONS: To avoid misreading, use an apostrophe to form the plural of lowercase letters and the capital letters *A* and *I*: *p*'s, *A*'s.

Beginning readers often confuse *b*'s and *d*'s.

MLA NOTE: The Modern Language Association recommends using an apostrophe for the plural of both capital and lowercase letters: *J*'s, *p*'s.

PLURAL ABBREVIATIONS Do not use an apostrophe to pluralize an abbreviation.

We collected only four IOUs out of forty.

Marco earned two PhDs before his thirtieth birthday.

PLURAL OF WORDS MENTIONED AS WORDS Generally, omit the apostrophe to form the plural of words mentioned as words. If the word is italicized, the *-s* ending appears in roman type.

We've heard enough *maybe*s.

Words mentioned as words may also appear in quotation marks. When you choose this option, use the apostrophe.

We've heard enough "maybe's."

36e Avoid common misuses of the apostrophe.

Do not use an apostrophe in the following situations.

WITH NOUNS THAT ARE PLURAL BUT NOT POSSESSIVE

▶ Some resident's have special parking permits. *residents*

IN THE POSSESSIVE PRONOUNS *ITS, WHOSE, HIS, HERS, OURS, YOURS,* AND *THEIRS*

▶ Each area has it's own conference room. *its*

It's means "it is." The possessive pronoun *its* contains no apostrophe despite the fact that it is possessive.

> *whose*
> This course was taught by a professional florist ~~who's~~
>   ^
>
> technique was Japanese.

Who's means "who is." The possessive pronoun is *whose*.

EXERCISE 36–1 Edit the following sentences to correct errors in the use of the apostrophe. If a sentence is correct, write "correct" after it. Answers to lettered sentences appear in the back of the book. Example:

> We rented an art studio above a barbecue restaurant, Poor
>
> *Richard's*
> ~~Richards~~ Ribs.
>   ^

a. This diet will improve almost anyone's health.
b. The innovative shoe fastener was inspired by the designers son.
c. Each days menu features a different European country's dish.
d. Sue worked overtime to increase her families earnings.
e. Ms. Jacobs is unwilling to listen to students complaints about computer failures and damaged disks.

1. Siddhartha sat by the river and listened to its many voices.
2. Three teenage son's can devour about as much food as four full-grown field hands. The only difference is that they dont do half as much work.
3. We handle contracts with NASA and many other government agency's.
4. Patience and humor are key tools in a travelers survival kit.
5. My sister-in-law's quilts are being shown at the Fendrick Gallery.

ON THE WEB > dianahacker.com/rules
Grammar exercises > Punctuation > E-ex 36–1

37

Quotation marks

 GRAMMAR CHECKERS are no help with quotation marks. They do not recognize direct and indirect quotations, they fail to identify quotation marks used incorrectly inside periods and commas, and they do not point out a missing quotation mark in a pair.

37a Use quotation marks to enclose direct quotations.

Direct quotations of a person's words, whether spoken or written, must be in quotation marks.

> "A foolish consistency is the hobgoblin of little minds," wrote Ralph Waldo Emerson.

NOTE: Do not use quotation marks around indirect quotations. An indirect quotation reports someone's ideas without using that person's exact words.

> Ralph Waldo Emerson believed that consistency for its own sake is the mark of a small mind.

In dialogue, begin a new paragraph to mark a change in speaker.

> "Mom, his name is Willie, not William. A thousand times I've told you, it's *Willie*."
> "Willie is a derivative of William, Lester. Surely his birth certificate doesn't have Willie on it, and I like calling people by their proper names."
> "Yes, it does, ma'am. My mother named me Willie K. Mason."
> — Gloria Naylor

If a single speaker utters more than one paragraph, introduce each paragraph with quotation marks, but do not use closing quotation marks until the end of the speech.

37b Set off long quotations of prose or poetry by indenting.

The guidelines in this section are those of the Modern Language Association (MLA). The American Psychological Association (APA) has slightly different guidelines (see pp. 484–85).

When a quotation of prose runs to more than four typed lines in your paper, set it off by indenting one inch (or ten spaces) from the left margin. Quotation marks are not required because the indented format tells readers that the quotation is taken word-for-word from a source. Long quotations are ordinarily introduced by a sentence ending with a colon.

After making an exhaustive study of the historical record, James Horan evaluates Billy the Kid like this:

> The portrait that emerges of [the Kid] from the thousands of pages of affidavits, reports, trial transcripts, his letters, and his testimony is neither the mythical Robin Hood nor the stereotyped adenoidal moron and pathological killer. Rather Billy appears as a disturbed, lonely young man, honest, loyal to his friends, dedicated to his beliefs, and betrayed by our institutions and the corrupt, ambitious, and compromising politicians in his time. (158)

The number in parentheses is a citation handled according to MLA style. (See 55a.)

NOTE: When you quote two or more paragraphs from the source, indent the first line of each paragraph an additional one-half inch (or five spaces).

When you quote more than three lines of a poem, set the quoted lines off from the text by indenting one inch (or ten spaces) from the left margin. Use no quotation marks unless they appear in the poem itself. (To quote two or three lines of poetry, see 39e.)

> Although many anthologizers "modernize" her punctuation, Emily Dickinson relied heavily on dashes, using them, perhaps, as a musical device. Here, for example, is the original version of the opening stanza from "The Snake":
>
>> A narrow Fellow in the Grass
>> Occasionally rides--
>> You may have met Him--did you not
>> His notice sudden is--

37c Use single quotation marks to enclose a quotation within a quotation.

According to Paul Eliott, Eskimo hunters "chant an ancient magic song to the seal they are after: 'Beast of the sea! Come and place yourself before me in the early morning!' "

37d Use quotation marks around the titles of short works: newspaper and magazine articles, poems, short stories, songs, episodes of television and radio programs, and chapters or subdivisions of books.

Katherine Mansfield's "The Garden Party" provoked a lively discussion in our short-story class last night.

NOTE: Titles of books, plays, Web sites, television and radio programs, films, magazines, and newspapers are put in italics or underlined. (See 42a.)

37e Quotation marks may be used to set off words used as words.

Although words used as words are ordinarily italicized (see 42d), quotation marks are also acceptable. Just be sure to follow consistent practice throughout a paper.

The words "accept" and "except" are frequently confused.

The words *accept* and *except* are frequently confused.

37f Use punctuation with quotation marks according to convention.

This section describes the conventions used by American publishers in placing various marks of punctuation inside or outside quotation marks. It also explains how to punctuate when introducing quoted material.

Periods and commas

Place periods and commas inside quotation marks.

"This is a stick-up," said the well-dressed young couple. "We want all your money."

This rule applies to single quotation marks as well as double quotation marks. (See 37c.) It also applies to all uses of quotation marks: for quoted material, for titles of works, and for words used as words.

EXCEPTION: In the Modern Language Association's style of parenthetical in-text citations (see 55a), the period follows the citation in parentheses.

> James M. McPherson comments, approvingly, that the Whigs "were not averse to extending the blessings of American liberty, even to Mexicans and Indians" (48).

Colons and semicolons

Put colons and semicolons outside quotation marks.

> Harold wrote, "I regret that I am unable to attend the fundraiser for AIDS research"; his letter, however, came with a substantial contribution.

Question marks and exclamation points

Put question marks and exclamation points inside quotation marks unless they apply to the whole sentence.

> Contrary to tradition, bedtime at my house is marked by "Mommy, can I tell you a story now?"

> Have you heard the old proverb "Do not climb the hill until you reach it"?

In the first sentence, the question mark applies only to the quoted question. In the second sentence, the question mark applies to the whole sentence.

NOTE: In MLA style for a quotation that ends with a question mark or an exclamation point, the parenthetical citation and a period should follow the entire quotation: *Rosie Thomas asks, "Is nothing in life ever straight and clear, the way children see it?" (77).*

Introducing quoted material

After a word group introducing a quotation, choose a colon, a comma, or no punctuation at all, whichever is appropriate in context.

FORMAL INTRODUCTION If a quotation has been formally introduced, a colon is appropriate. A formal introduction is a full independent clause, not just an expression such as *he said* or *she remarked.*

Morrow views personal ads in the classifieds as an art form: "The personal ad is like a haiku of self-celebration, a brief solo played on one's own horn."

EXPRESSION SUCH AS *HE SAID* If a quotation is introduced with an expression such as *he said* or *she remarked* — or if it is followed by such an expression — a comma is needed.

Stephan Leacock once said, "I am a great believer in luck, and I find the harder I work the more I have of it."

"You can be a little ungrammatical if you come from the right part of the country," writes Robert Frost.

BLENDED QUOTATION When a quotation is blended into the writer's own sentence, either a comma or no punctuation is appropriate, depending on the way in which the quotation fits into the sentence structure.

The future champion could, as he put it, "float like a butterfly and sting like a bee."

Charles Hudson notes that the prisoners escaped "by squeezing through a tiny window eighteen feet above the floor of their cell."

BEGINNING OF SENTENCE If a quotation appears at the beginning of a sentence, set it off with a comma unless the quotation ends with a question mark or an exclamation point.

"We shot them like dogs," boasted Davy Crockett, who was among Jackson's troops.

"What is it?" I asked, bracing myself.

INTERRUPTED QUOTATION If a quoted sentence is interrupted by explanatory words, use commas to set off the explanatory words.

"A great many people think they are thinking," observed William James, "when they are merely rearranging their prejudices."

If two successive quoted sentences from the same source are interrupted by explanatory words, use a comma before the explanatory words and a period after them.

"I was a flop as a daily reporter," admitted E. B. White. "Every piece had to be a masterpiece — and before you knew it, Tuesday was Wednesday."

37g Avoid common misuses of quotation marks.

Do not use quotation marks to draw attention to familiar slang, to disown trite expressions, or to justify an attempt at humor.

▶ Between Thanksgiving and Super Bowl Sunday, many American wives become ⫻football widows.⫻

Do not use quotation marks around indirect quotations. (See also 37a.)

▶ After leaving the scene of the domestic quarrel, the officer said that ⫻he was due for a coffee break.⫻

Do not use quotation marks around the title of your own essay.

ON THE WEB > dianahacker.com/rules
Grammar exercises > Punctuation > E-ex 37–1

EXERCISE 37–1 Add or delete quotation marks as needed and make any other necessary changes in punctuation in the following sentences. If a sentence is correct, write "correct" after it. Answers to lettered sentences appear in the back of the book. Example:

Gandhi once said, "An eye for an eye only ends up making the whole world blind."

a. As for the advertisement "Sailors have more fun", if you consider chipping paint and swabbing decks fun, then you will have plenty of it.
b. Even after forty minutes of discussion, our class could not agree on an interpretation of Robert Frost's poem "The Road Not Taken."
c. After winning the lottery, Juanita said that "she would give half the money to charity."
d. After the movie Vicki said, "The reviewer called this flick "trash of the first order." I guess you can't believe everything you read."
e. "Cleaning your house while your kids are still growing," quipped Phyllis Diller, "is like shoveling the walk before it stops snowing."

1. "That's the most beautiful seashell I've ever seen!", shouted Alexa.
2. "Get your head in the game, and the rest will come" advised the coach just before the whistle.
3. Gloria Steinem once twisted an old proverb like this, "A woman without a man is like a fish without a bicycle."
4. "Even when freshly washed and relieved of all obvious confections," says Fran Lebowitz, "children tend to be sticky."
5. Have you heard the Cowboy Junkies' cover of Hank Williams's "I'm So Lonesome I Could Cry?"

38

End punctuation

> **GRAMMAR CHECKERS** occasionally flag sentences beginning with words like *Why* or *Are* and suggest that a question mark may be needed. On the whole, however, grammar checkers are of little help with end punctuation. Most notably, they neglect to tell you when your sentence is missing end punctuation.

38a The period

Use a period to end all sentences except direct questions or genuine exclamations. Also use periods in abbreviations according to convention.

To end sentences

Everyone knows that a period should be used to end most sentences. The only problems that arise concern the choice between a period and a question mark or between a period and an exclamation point.

If a sentence reports a question instead of asking it directly, it should end with a period, not a question mark.

▶ Joelle asked whether the picnic would be canceled?.
                                                 ^

If a sentence is not a genuine exclamation, it should end with a period, not an exclamation point.

▶ After years of working her way through school, Geeta finally

graduated with high honors~~!~~.
　　　　　　　　　　　　　　　　　^

In abbreviations

A period is conventionally used in abbreviations of titles and Latin words or phrases, including the time designations for morning and afternoon.

Mr.	i.e.	a.m. (or AM)
Ms.	e.g.	p.m. (or PM)
Dr.	etc.	

NOTE: If a sentence ends with a period marking an abbreviation, do not add a second period.

A period is not used with US Postal Service abbreviations for states: MD, TX, CA.

Current usage is to omit the period in abbreviations of organization names, academic degrees, and designations for eras.

NATO	UNESCO	UCLA	BS	BC
IRS	AFL-CIO	NIH	PhD	AD
USA	NAACP	SEC	RN	BCE

38b The question mark

A direct question should be followed by a question mark.

What is the horsepower of a 777 engine?

If a polite request is written in the form of a question, it may be followed by a period.

Would you please send me your catalog of lilies.

TIP: Do not use a question mark after an indirect question, one that is reported rather than asked directly. Use a period instead.

▶ He asked me who was teaching the mythology course

this year~~?~~.
　　　　　^

NOTE: Questions in a series may be followed by question marks even when they are not complete sentences.

> We wondered where Calamity had hidden this time. Under the sink? Behind the furnace? On top of the bookcase?

38c The exclamation point

Use an exclamation point after a word group or sentence to express exceptional feeling or to provide special emphasis.

> When Gloria entered the room, I switched on the lights and we all yelled, "Surprise!"

TIP: Do not overuse the exclamation point.

> ▶ Whenever I see Serena lunging forward to put away an overhead
>
> smash, it might as well be me̷. She does it just the way I would!

The first exclamation point should be deleted so that the second one will have more force.

39

Other punctuation marks: the dash, parentheses, brackets, the ellipsis mark, the slash

> GRAMMAR CHECKERS rarely flag problems with the punctuation marks in this section: the dash, parentheses, brackets, the ellipsis mark, and the slash.

39a The dash

When typing, use two hyphens to form a dash (--). Do not put spaces before or after the dash. (If your word processing program has what is known as an "em-dash," you may use it instead, with no space before or after it.) Dashes are used for the following purposes.

To set off parenthetical material that deserves emphasis

Everything that went wrong — from the peeping Tom at her window last night to my head-on collision today — we blamed on our move.

To set off appositives that contain commas

An appositive is a noun or noun phrase that renames a nearby noun. Ordinarily most appositives are set off with commas (32e), but when the appositive itself contains commas, a pair of dashes helps readers see the relative importance of all the pauses.

In my small hometown, basic needs — food, clothing, and shelter — are less costly than in Los Angeles.

To prepare for a list, a restatement, an amplification, or a dramatic shift in tone or thought

Along the wall are the bulk liquids — sesame seed oil, honey, safflower oil, and that half-liquid "peanuts only" peanut butter.

Consider the amount of sugar in the average person's diet — 104 pounds per year, 90 percent more than that consumed by our ancestors.

Everywhere we looked there were little kids — a box of Cracker Jacks in one hand and mommy or daddy's sleeve in the other.

Kiere took a few steps back, came running full speed, kicked a mighty kick — and missed the ball.

In the first two examples, the writer could also use a colon. (See 35a.) The colon is more formal than the dash and not quite as dramatic.

TIP: Unless there is a specific reason for using the dash, avoid it. Unnecessary dashes create a choppy effect.

▶ Insisting that students use computers as instructional

tools ⫝̸ for information retrieval ⫝̸ makes good sense. Herding

them ⫝̸ sheeplike ⫝̸ into computer technology does not.

39b Parentheses

Use parentheses to enclose supplemental material, minor digressions, and afterthoughts.

> After taking her vital signs (temperature, pulse, and blood pressure), the nurse made Becky as comfortable as possible.

> The weights James was first able to move (not lift, mind you) were measured in ounces.

Use parentheses to enclose letters or numbers labeling items in a series.

> Regulations stipulated that only the following equipment could be used on the survival mission: (1) a knife, (2) thirty feet of parachute line, (3) a book of matches, (4) two ponchos, (5) an *E* tool, and (6) a signal flare.

TIP: Do not overuse parentheses. Rough drafts are likely to contain more afterthoughts than necessary. As writers head into a sentence, they often think of additional details, occasionally working them in as best they can with parentheses. Usually such sentences should be revised so that the additional details no longer seem to be afterthoughts.

▶ Researchers have said that ~~thirteen million (estimates run as~~ *from thirteen to eighteen million*
∧

~~high as eighteen million)~~ Americans have diabetes.

39c Brackets

Use brackets to enclose any words or phrases that you have inserted into an otherwise word-for-word quotation.

> *Audubon* reports that "if there are not enough young to balance deaths, the end of the species [California condor] is inevitable."

The sentence quoted from the *Audubon* article did not contain the words *California condor* (since the context made clear what species was meant), so the writer needed to add the name in brackets.

The Latin word "sic" in brackets indicates that an error in a quoted sentence appears in the original source.

According to the review, Nelly Furtado's performance was brilliant, "exceding [sic] the expectations of even her most loyal fans."

Do not overuse "sic," however, since calling attention to others' mistakes can appear snobbish. The preceding quotation, for example, might have been paraphrased instead: *According to the review, even Nelly Furtado's devoted fans were surprised by the brilliance of her performance.*

39d The ellipsis mark

The ellipsis mark consists of three spaced periods. Use an ellipsis mark to indicate that you have deleted words from an otherwise word-for-word quotation.

> Reuben reports that "when the amount of cholesterol circulating in the blood rises over . . . 300 milligrams per 100, the chances of a heart attack increase dramatically."

If you delete a full sentence or more in the middle of a quoted passage, use a period before the three ellipsis dots.

> "Most of our efforts," writes Dave Erikson, "are directed toward saving the bald eagle's wintering habitat along the Mississippi River. . . . It's important that the wintering birds have a place to roost, where they can get out of the cold wind."

TIP: Ordinarily, do not use the ellipsis mark at the beginning or at the end of a quotation. Readers will understand that the quoted material is taken from a longer passage. If you have cut some words from the end of the final sentence quoted, however, MLA requires an ellipsis mark, as in the first example on page 420.

In quoted poetry, use a full line of ellipsis dots to indicate that you have dropped a line or more from the poem.

> Had we but world enough, and time,
> This coyness, lady, were no crime.
> . . . .
> But at my back I always hear
> Time's winged chariot hurrying near;   — Andrew Marvell

The ellipsis mark may also be used to indicate a hesitation or an interruption in speech or to suggest unfinished thoughts.

> Before falling into a coma, the victim whispered, "It was a man with a tattoo on his . . ."

39e The slash

Use the slash to separate two or three lines of poetry that have been run into your text. Add a space both before and after the slash.

> In the opening lines of "Jordan," George Herbert pokes gentle fun at popular poems of his time: "Who says that fictions only and false hair / Become a verse? Is there in truth no beauty?"

More than three lines of poetry should be handled as an indented quotation. (See 37b.)

The slash may occasionally be used to separate paired terms such as *pass/fail* and *producer/director*. Do not use a space before or after the slash.

> Roger, the producer/director, announced a casting change.

Be sparing, however, in this use of the slash. In particular, avoid the use of *and/or, he/she,* and *his/her*. (See 17f.)

EXERCISE 39–1 Edit the following sentences to correct errors in punctuation, focusing especially on appropriate use of the dash, parentheses, brackets, ellipsis mark, and slash. If a sentence is correct, write "correct" after it. Answers to lettered sentences appear in the back of the book. Example:

Social insects/— bees, for example/— are able to communicate

quite complicated messages to one another.

a. A client has left his/her cell phone in our conference room.
b. The films we made of Kilauea — on our trip to Hawaii Volcanoes National Park — illustrate a typical spatter cone eruption.
c. Samantha selected the pass/fail option for Chemistry 101.
d. Masahiro poked through his backpack — laptop, digital camera, guidebook — to make sure he was ready for a day's study at the Ryoanji Temple garden.

e. Of three engineering fields, chemical, mechanical, and materials, Keegan chose materials engineering for its application to toy manufacturing.

1. The old Valentine verse we used to chant says it all: "Sugar is sweet, / And so are you."
2. In studies in which mothers gazed down at their infants in their cribs but remained facially unresponsive, for example, not smiling, laughing, or showing any change of expression, the infants responded with intense weariness and eventual withdrawal.
3. There are three points of etiquette in poker: 1. always allow someone to cut the cards, 2. don't forget to ante up, and 3. never stack your chips.
4. In *Lifeboat,* Alfred Hitchcock appears [some say without his knowledge] in a newspaper advertisement for weight loss.
5. The writer Chitra Divakaruni explained her work with other Indian American immigrants: "Many women who came to Maitri [a women's support group in San Francisco] needed to know simple things like opening a bank account or getting citizenship. . . . Many women in Maitri spoke English, but their English was functional rather than emotional. They needed someone who understands their problems and speaks their language."

ON THE WEB > **dianahacker.com/rules**
Grammar exercises > Punctuation > E-ex 39–1

Mechanics

40

Abbreviations

> **GRAMMAR CHECKERS** can flag a few inappropriate abbreviations, such as *Xmas* and *e.g.,* but do not assume that a program will catch all problems with abbreviations.

40a Use standard abbreviations for titles immediately before and after proper names.

TITLES BEFORE PROPER NAMES	TITLES AFTER PROPER NAMES
Mr. Rafael Zabala	William Albert Sr.
Ms. Nancy Linehan	Thomas Hines Jr.
Mrs. Edward Horn	Anita Lor, PhD
Dr. Margaret Simmons	Robert Simkowski, MD
the Rev. John Stone	Margaret Chin, LLD
Prof. James Russo	Polly Stein, DDS

Do not abbreviate a title if it is not used with a proper name.

professor
▶ My history ~~prof.~~ is an expert on race relations in South Africa.
    ^

Avoid redundant titles such as *Dr. Amy Day, MD.* Choose one title or the other: *Dr. Amy Day* or *Amy Day, MD.*

40b Use abbreviations only when you are sure your readers will understand them.

Familiar abbreviations, written without periods, are acceptable.

CIA	FBI	MD	NAACP
NBA	NEA	PhD	CD-ROM
YMCA	CBS	USA	ESL

The YMCA has opened a new gym close to my office.

NOTE: When using an unfamiliar abbreviation (such as NASW for National Association of Social Workers) throughout a paper, write the full name followed by the abbreviation in parentheses at the first mention of the name. Then use the abbreviation throughout the rest of the paper.

40c Use *BC, AD, a.m., p.m., No.,* and *$* only with specific dates, times, numbers, and amounts.

The abbreviation *BC* ("before Christ") follows a date, and *AD* (*"anno Domini"*) precedes a date. Acceptable alternatives are *BCE* ("before the common era") and *CE* ("common era"), both of which follow a date.

40 BC (or 40 BCE)	4:00 a.m. (or AM)	No. 12 (or no. 12)
AD 44 (or 44 CE)	6:00 p.m. (or PM)	$150

Avoid using *a.m., p.m., No.,* or *$* when not accompanied by a specific figure.

▶ We set off for the lake early in the a.m.   *morning.*

40d Be sparing in your use of Latin abbreviations.

Latin abbreviations are acceptable in footnotes and bibliographies and in informal writing for comments in parentheses.

cf. (Latin *confer,* "compare")
e.g. (Latin *exempli gratia,* "for example")
et al. (Latin *et alia,* "and others")
etc. (Latin *et cetera,* "and so forth")
i.e. (Latin *id est,* "that is")
N.B. (Latin *nota bene,* "note well")

Harold Simms et al., *The Race for Space*

Alfred Hitchcock directed many classic thrillers (e.g., *Psycho, Rear Window,* and *Vertigo*).

In formal writing, use the appropriate English phrases.

▶ Many obsolete laws remain on the books, e.g., a law in   *for example,*

Vermont forbidding an unmarried man and woman to sit

closer than six inches apart on a park bench.

40e Avoid inappropriate abbreviations.

In formal writing, abbreviations for the following are not commonly accepted: personal names, units of measurement, days of the week, holidays, months, courses of study, divisions of written works, states, and countries (except in complete addresses and except Washington, DC). Do not abbreviate *Company* and *Incorporated* unless their abbreviated forms are part of an official name.

PERSONAL NAME   Charles (not Chas.)

UNITS OF MEASUREMENT   feet (not ft.)

DAYS OF THE WEEK   Monday (not Mon.)

HOLIDAYS   Christmas (not Xmas)

MONTHS   January, February, March (not Jan., Feb., Mar.)

COURSES OF STUDY   political science (not poli. sci.)

DIVISIONS OF WRITTEN WORKS   chapter, page (not ch., p.)

STATES AND COUNTRIES   Massachusetts (not MA or Mass.)

PARTS OF A BUSINESS NAME   Adams Lighting Company (not Adams Lighting Co.); Kim and Brothers (not Kim and Bros.)

▶ The American Red Cross requires that blood donors be at
        years   *pounds,*
  least seventeen ~~yrs.~~ old, weigh at least 110 ~~lbs.,~~ and not have
                                      weeks.
  given blood in the past eight ~~wks.~~

EXERCISE 40–1   Edit the following sentences to correct errors in abbreviations. If a sentence is correct, write "correct" after it. Answers to lettered sentences appear in the back of the book. Example:

          Christmas   *Tuesday.*
     This year ~~Xmas~~ will fall on a ~~Tues.~~

a. Since its inception, the BBC has maintained a consistently high standard of radio and television broadcasting.
b. Some combat soldiers are trained by govt. diplomats to be sensitive to issues of culture, history, and religion.
c. "Mahatma" Gandhi has inspired many modern leaders, including Martin Luther King Jr.

d. How many lb. have you lost since you began running four miles a day?
e. Denzil spent all night studying for his psych. exam.

1. My favorite prof., Dr. Barker, is on sabbatical this semester.
2. When we visited NYU in early September, we were charmed by the lull of summer crickets in Washington Square Park.
3. Some historians think that the New Testament was completed by AD 100.
4. My mother's birthday was on Fri. the 13th this year.
5. Many first-time users of Flash panic before the complex menus — i.e., some develop a blank stare and the tingling of a migraine.

ON THE WEB > **dianahacker.com/rules**
Grammar exercises > Mechanics > E-ex 40–1

41

Numbers

 GRAMMAR CHECKERS can tell you to spell out certain numbers, such as *thirty-three* and numbers that begin a sentence, but they won't help you understand when it is acceptable to use figures.

41a Spell out numbers of one or two words or those that begin a sentence. Use figures for numbers that require more than two words to spell out.

▶ It's been 8̶ years since I visited Peru.
                eight

▶ I counted ~~one hundred seventy-six~~ DVDs on the shelf.
                                176

If a sentence begins with a number, spell out the number or rewrite the sentence.

▶ ~~150~~ children in our program need expensive dental treatment.
   One hundred fifty

Rewriting the sentence will also correct the error and may be less awkward if the number is long: *In our program, 150 children need expensive dental treatment.*

EXCEPTIONS: In technical and some business writing, figures are preferred even when spellings would be brief, but usage varies. When in doubt, consult the style guide of the organization for which you are writing.

When several numbers appear in the same passage, many writers choose consistency rather than strict adherence to the rule.

When one number immediately follows another, spell out one and use figures for the other: *three 100-meter events, 25 four-poster beds.*

41b Generally, figures are acceptable for dates, addresses, percentages, fractions, decimals, scores, statistics and other numerical results, exact amounts of money, divisions of books and plays, pages, identification numbers, and the time.

DATES   July 4, 1776, 56 BC, AD 30

ADDRESSES   77 Latches Lane, 519 West 42nd Street

PERCENTAGES   55 percent (or 55%)

FRACTIONS, DECIMALS   ¹/₂, 0.047

SCORES   7 to 3, 21–18

STATISTICS   average age 37, average weight 180

SURVEYS   4 out of 5

EXACT AMOUNTS OF MONEY $105.37, $106,000

DIVISIONS OF BOOKS   volume 3, chapter 4, page 189

DIVISIONS OF PLAYS   act 3, scene 3 (or act III, scene iii)

IDENTIFICATION NUMBERS   serial number 10988675

TIME OF DAY   4:00 p.m., 1:30 a.m.

▶ Several doctors put up ~~two hundred fifty-five thousand~~ *$255,000*

~~dollars~~ for the construction of a golf course.

NOTE: When not using *a.m.* or *p.m.,* write out the time in words (*two o'clock in the afternoon, twelve noon, seven in the morning*).

EXERCISE 41–1 Edit the following sentences to correct errors in the use of numbers. If a sentence is correct, write "correct" after it. Answers to lettered sentences appear in the back of the book. Example:

> *$3.06*
> By the end of the evening, Ashanti had only ~~three dollars and~~
> ^
> ~~six cents~~ left.

a. The carpenters located 3 maple timbers, 21 sheets of cherry, and 10 oblongs of polished ebony for the theater set.
b. The program's cost is well over one billion dollars.
c. The score was tied at 5–5 when the momentum shifted and carried the Standards to a decisive 12–5 win.
d. 8 students in the class had been labeled "learning disabled."
e. The Vietnam Veterans Memorial in Washington, DC, had fifty-eight thousand one hundred thirty-two names inscribed on it when it was dedicated in 1982.

1. One of my favorite scenes in Shakespeare is the property division scene in act 1 of *King Lear*.
2. The botany lecture will begin at precisely 3:30 p.m.
3. 50 percent of the gamers who play *The Sims* are female.
4. In two thousand and four, Fox TV's *American Idol* earned more advertising dollars than any other reality show.
5. On a normal day, I spend at least 4 to 5 hours surfing the Internet.

ON THE WEB > dianahacker.com/rules
Grammar exercises > Mechanics > E-ex 41–1

42

Italics (underlining)

Italics, a slanting font style used in printed material, is in widespread use in word processing programs. In handwritten material, <u>underlining</u> is used instead. While italics is accepted by most academic style guides, some instructors may prefer underlining in student papers. If that is the case in your course, simply substitute underlining for italics in the examples in this section.

NOTE: Some computer and online applications do not allow for italics or underlining. To indicate words that should be italicized, you can use underscore marks or asterisks before and after the italic words. Punctuation should follow the coding.

> I am planning to write my senior thesis on _Memoirs of a
>
> Geisha_.

In informal situations, such as e-mail, normally italicized words aren't marked at all.

> I stayed up all night to finish reading Memoirs of a Geisha--what a
>
> story!

TIP: In Web documents, underlining indicates a link. When creating a Web document, use italics, not underlining, for the conventions described in this section.

> **GRAMMAR CHECKERS** do not flag problems with italics or underlining.

42a Italicize or underline the titles of works according to convention.

Titles of the following works, including electronic works, should be italicized or underlined.

TITLES OF BOOKS	*The Color Purple, Middlesex, Encarta*
MAGAZINES	*Time, Scientific American, Salon.com*
NEWSPAPERS	the *Baltimore Sun,* the *New York Times on the Web*
PAMPHLETS	*Common Sense, Facts about Marijuana*
LONG POEMS	*The Waste Land, Paradise Lost*
PLAYS	*King Lear, Rent*

FILMS   *Casablanca, American Beauty*

TELEVISION PROGRAMS   *Survivor, 60 Minutes*

RADIO PROGRAMS   *All Things Considered*

MUSICAL COMPOSITIONS   *Porgy and Bess*

CHOREOGRAPHIC WORKS   *Brief Fling*

WORKS OF VISUAL ART   Rodin's *The Thinker*

COMIC STRIPS   *Dilbert*

ELECTRONIC DATABASES   *InfoTrac*

WEB SITES   *ZDNet, Google*

ELECTRONIC GAMES   *Free Cell, Zuma*

The titles of other works, such as short stories, essays, episodes of radio and television programs, songs, and short poems, are enclosed in quotation marks. (See 37d.)

NOTE: Do not use italics or underlining when referring to the Bible; titles of books in the Bible (Genesis, not *Genesis*); titles of historical documents (the Constitution, not the *Constitution*); titles of computer software (WordPerfect, Photoshop); and the title of your own paper.

42b Italicize or underline the names of spacecraft, aircraft, and ships.

Challenger, Spirit of St. Louis, Queen Mary 2

▶ The success of the Soviets' <u>Sputnik</u> galvanized the US

space program.

42c Italicize or underline foreign words used in an English sentence.

▶ Caroline's <u>joie de vivre</u> should be a model for all of us.

EXCEPTION: Do not italicize or underline foreign words that have become a standard part of the English language — "laissez-faire," "fait accompli," "modus operandi," and "per diem," for example.

42d Italicize or underline words mentioned as words, letters mentioned as letters, and numbers mentioned as numbers.

▶ Tim assured us that the howling probably came from

his bloodhound, Hill Billy, but his <u>probably</u> stuck in

our minds.

▶ Sarah called her father by his given name, Johnny, but she

was unable to pronounce the <u>J</u>.

▶ A big <u>3</u> was painted on the door.

NOTE: Quotation marks may be used instead of italics or underlining to set off words mentioned as words. (See 37e.)

42e Avoid excessive italics or underlining for emphasis.

Italicizing or underlining to emphasize words or ideas is distracting and should be used sparingly.

▶ In-line skating is a popular sport that has become ~~almost~~

~~an addiction.~~

EXERCISE 42–1 Edit the following sentences to correct errors in the use of italics. If a sentence is correct, write "correct" after it. Answers to lettered sentences appear in the back of the book. Example:

We had a lively discussion about Gini Alhadeff's memoir

The Sun at Midday.

a. Howard Hughes commissioned the Spruce Goose, a beautifully built but thoroughly impractical wooden aircraft.

b. The old man *screamed* his anger, *shouting* to all of us, "I will not leave my money to you worthless layabouts!"

c. I learned the Latin term *ad infinitum* from an old nursery rhyme about fleas: "Great fleas have little fleas upon their back to bite 'em, / Little fleas have lesser fleas and so on *ad infinitum*."

d. Cinema audiences once gasped at hearing the word *damn* in *Gone with the Wind*.

e. Neve Campbell's lifelong interest in ballet inspired her involvement in the film "The Company," which portrays a season with the Joffrey Ballet.

1. Yasmina spent a year painting white flowers in imitation of Georgia O'Keeffe's Calla Lilies.

2. On the monastery walls are murals depicting scenes from the book of Kings and the book of Proverbs.

3. My per diem allowance was two hundred dollars.

4. Cecily watched in amazement as the tattoo artist made angles and swooping loops into the Gothic letter G.

5. The blend of poetic lyrics and progressive instruments on Seal's "Human Being" makes it one of my favorite CDs.

ON THE WEB > **dianahacker.com/rules**
Grammar exercises > Mechanics > E-ex 42–1

43

Spelling

You learned to spell from repeated experience with words in both reading and writing, but especially writing. Words have a look, a sound, and even a feel to them as the hand moves across the page. As you proofread, you can probably tell if a word doesn't look quite right. In such cases, the solution is obvious: Look up the word in the dictionary.

SPELL CHECKERS are useful alternatives to a dictionary, but only to a point. A spell checker will not tell you how to spell words not listed in its dictionary; nor will it help you catch words commonly confused, such as *accept* and *except,* or some typographical errors, such as *own* for *won.* You will still need to proofread, and for some words you may need to turn to the dictionary.

43a Become familiar with your dictionary.

A good dictionary, whether print or online — such as *The American Heritage Dictionary of the English Language, The Random House College Dictionary, Merriam-Webster's Collegiate Dictionary,* or *Webster's New World Dictionary of the American Language* — is an indispensable writer's aid.

A sample print dictionary entry, taken from *The American Heritage Dictionary,* appears on page 330. Labels show where various kinds of information about a word can be found in that dictionary.

A sample online dictionary entry, taken from *Merriam-Webster Online,* appears on page 331.

Spelling, word division, pronunciation

The main entry (*re•gard* in the sample entries) shows the correct spelling of the word. When there are two correct spellings of a word (as in *collectible, collectable,* for example), both are given, with the preferred spelling usually appearing first.

The main entry also shows how the word is divided into syllables. The dot between *re* and *gard* separates the word's two syllables and indicates where the word should be divided if it can't fit at the end of a line of type (see 44f). When a word is compound, the main entry shows how to write it: as one word (*crossroad*), as a hyphenated word (*cross-stitch*), or as two words (*cross section*).

The word's pronunciation is given just after the main entry. The accents indicate which syllables are stressed; the other marks are explained in the dictionary's pronunciation key. In print dictionaries this key usually appears at the bottom of every page or every other page. Many online entries include an audio link to a person's voice pronouncing the word. And most online dictionaries have an audio pronunciation guide.

Word endings and grammatical labels

When a word takes endings to indicate grammatical functions (called *inflections*), the endings are listed in boldface, as with *-garded, -garding,* and *-gards* in the sample print entry.

Labels for the parts of speech and for other grammatical terms are sometimes abbreviated, as they are in the print entry. The most commonly used abbreviations are these:

n.	noun	adj.	adjective
pl.	plural	adv.	adverb
sing.	singular	pron.	pronoun
v.	verb	prep.	preposition
tr.	transitive verb	conj.	conjunction
intr.	intransitive verb	interj.	interjection

Meanings, word origin, synonyms, and antonyms

Each meaning for the word is given a number. Occasionally a word's use is illustrated in a quoted sentence.

Sometimes a word can be used as more than one part of speech (*regard,* for instance, can be used as either a verb or a noun). In such a case, all the meanings for one part of speech are given before all the meanings for another, as in the sample entries. The entries also give idiomatic uses of the word.

The origin of the word, called its *etymology,* appears in brackets after all the meanings in the print version; in the on-line version, it appears before the meanings.

Synonyms, words similar in meaning to the main entry, are frequently listed. In the sample print entry, the dictionary draws distinctions in meaning among the various synonyms. In the online entry, synonyms appear as hyperlinks. Antonyms, which do not appear in the sample entries, are words having a meaning opposite from that of the main entry.

Usage

Usage labels indicate when, where, or under what conditions a particular meaning for a word is appropriately used. Common labels are *informal* (or *colloquial*), *slang, nonstandard, dialect, obsolete, archaic, poetic,* and *British.* In the print entry, two meanings of *regard* are labeled *obsolete* because they are no longer in use. The online entry has meanings labeled both *archaic* and *obsolete.*

sp

PRINT DICTIONARY ENTRY

Grammatical
label

Pronunciation

Word   Part of   Word endings   Usage label
division   speech label   (inflections)

Spelling —— **re•gard** (rĭ-gärd′) *v.* **-gard•ed, -gard•ing, -gards** —*tr.* **1.** To look at attentively; observe closely. **2.** To look upon or consider in a particular way: *I regard him as a fool.* **3.** To hold in esteem or respect: *She regards*

Meanings —— *her teachers highly.* **4.** To relate or refer to; concern: *This item regards their liability.* **5.** To take into account; consider. **6.** *Obsolete* To take care of. —*intr.* **1.** To look or gaze. **2.** To give heed; pay attention. ❖ *n.* **1.** A look or gaze. **2.** Careful thought or attention; heed: *She gives little regard to her sister's teasing.* **3a.** Respect, affection, or esteem: *He has high regard for your work.* **b. regards** Good wishes expressing such sentiment: *Give the family my best regards.* **4.** A particular point or aspect; respect: *She was lucky in that regard.* **5.** Basis for action; motive. **6.** *Obsolete* Appear-

Idioms —— ance or aspect. —*idioms:* **as regards** Concerning. **in (or with) regard to** With respect to. [Middle English *regarden,* from Old French *regarder* : *re-,* re- + *guarder,* to guard (of Germanic origin; see GUARD).]

Synonyms *regard, esteem, admiration, respect* These nouns refer to a feeling based on perception of and approval for the worth of a person or thing. *Regard* is the most general: *"I once thought you had a kind of regard for her"* (George Borrow). *Esteem* connotes considered appraisal and pos-

Synonyms —— itive regard: *"The near-unanimity of esteem he enjoyed during his lifetime has by no means been sustained since"* (Will Crutchfield). *Admiration* is a feeling of keen approbation: *"Greatness is a spiritual condition worthy to excite love, interest, and admiration"* (Matthew Arnold). *Respect* implies appreciative, often deferential regard resulting from careful assessment: *"I have a great respect for any man who makes his own way in life"* (Win-ston Churchill). See also synonyms at **consider.**

Usage Note *Regard* is traditionally used in the singular in the phrase *in regard* (not *in regards*) *to. Regarding* and *as regards* are also standard in

Usage note —— the sense "with reference to." In the same sense *with respect to* is accept-able, but *respecting* is not. • *Respects* is sometimes considered preferable to *regards* in the sense of "particulars": *In some respects* (not *regards*) *the books are alike.*

Word origin ——
(etymology)

    Dictionaries sometimes include usage notes as well. In the sample print entry, the dictionary offers advice on several uses of *regard* not specifically covered by the meanings. Such advice is based on the opinions of many experts and on actual usage in current magazines, newspapers, and books.

ON THE WEB > **dianahacker.com/rules**
   Links Library > Grammar, style, and punctuation

ONLINE DICTIONARY ENTRY

Merriam-Webster Online Dictionary

Thesaurus

Alternative entries ——————

3 entries found for **regard**.
To select an entry, click on it.

regard[1,noun]   Go
regard[2,verb]
self-regard

Audio
pronunciation link

Spelling and word division ——————

Pronunciation ——————

Part of speech label ——————

Main Entry: ¹**re·gard** ◀)

Etymology
(word origin)

Pronunciation: ri-'gärd
Function: *noun*
Etymology: Middle English, from Middle
French, from Old French, from *regarder*

Usage label ——————

1 *archaic* : APPEARANCE
2 a : ATTENTION, CONSIDERATION <due
regard should be given to all facets of the
question> **b** : a protective interest : CARE
<ought to have more *regard* for his health>
3 : LOOK, GAZE
4 a : the worth or estimation in which
something or someone is held <a man of

Meanings (synonyms
shown as hyperlinks)

small *regard*> **b (1)** : a feeling of respect and
affection : ESTEEM <his hard work won him
the *regard* of his colleagues> **(2)** *plural* :
friendly greetings implying such feeling <give
him my *regards*>
5 : a basis of action or opinion : MOTIVE
6 : an aspect to be taken into consideration :
RESPECT <is a small school, and is fortunate
in this *regard*>
7 *obsolete* : INTENTION

Idioms ——————

- **in regard to** : with respect to :
CONCERNING
- **with regard to** : in regard to

43b Discriminate between words that sound alike but have different meanings.

Words that sound alike or nearly alike but have different meanings and spellings are called *homophones*. The following sets of words are so commonly confused that a good proofreader will double-check their every use.

affect (verb: to exert an influence)
effect (verb: to accomplish; noun: result)

its (possessive pronoun: of or belonging to it)
it's (contraction for *it is*)

loose (adjective: free, not securely attached)
lose (verb: to fail to keep, to be deprived of)

principal (adjective: most important; noun: head of a school)
principle (noun: a general or fundamental truth)

their (possessive pronoun: belonging to them)
they're (contraction for *they are*)
there (adverb: that place or position)

who's (contraction for *who is*)
whose (possessive form of *who*)

your (possessive form of *you*)
you're (contraction of *you are*)

To check for correct use of these and other commonly confused words, consult the Glossary of Usage, which begins on page 565.

43c Become familiar with the major spelling rules.

i *before* e *except after* c

Use *i* before *e* except after *c* or when sounded like *ay,* as in *neighbor* and *weigh.*

I BEFORE E	relieve, believe, sieve, niece, fierce, frieze
E BEFORE I	receive, deceive, sleigh, freight, eight
EXCEPTIONS	seize, either, weird, height, foreign, leisure

Suffixes

FINAL SILENT -E   Generally, drop a final silent *-e* when adding a suffix that begins with a vowel. Keep the final *-e* if the suffix begins with a consonant.

combine, combination	achieve, achievement
desire, desiring	care, careful
prude, prudish	entire, entirety
remove, removable	gentle, gentleness

Words such as *changeable, judgment, argument,* and *truly* are exceptions.

FINAL -Y When adding *-s* or *-d* to words ending in *-y,* ordinarily change *-y* to *-ie* when the *-y* is preceded by a consonant but not when it is preceded by a vowel.

comedy, comedies   monkey, monkeys

dry, dried   play, played

With proper names ending in *-y,* however, do not change the *-y* to *-ie* even if it is preceded by a consonant: *the Dougherty family, the Doughertys.*

FINAL CONSONANTS If a final consonant is preceded by a single vowel *and* the consonant ends a one-syllable word or a stressed syllable, double the consonant when adding a suffix beginning with a vowel.

bet, betting   occur, occurrence

commit, committed

ESL Spelling varies slightly among English-speaking countries. This can prove particularly confusing for ESL students, who may have learned British or Canadian English. Following is a list of some common words spelled differently in American and British English. Consult a dictionary for others.

AMERICAN	BRITISH
canceled, traveled	cancelled, travelled
color, humor	colour, humour
judgment	judgement
check	cheque
realize, apologize	realise, apologise
defense	defence
anemia, anesthetic	anaemia, anaesthetic
theater, center	theatre, centre
fetus	foetus
mold, smolder	mould, smoulder
civilization	civilisation
connection, inflection	connexion, inflexion
licorice	liquorice

Plurals

-S OR -ES   Add *-s* to form the plural of most nouns; add *-es* to singular nouns ending in *-s, -sh, -ch,* and *-x.*

table, tables	church, churches
paper, papers	dish, dishes

Ordinarily add *-s* to nouns ending in *-o* when the *-o* is preceded by a vowel. Add *-es* when it is preceded by a consonant.

radio, radios	hero, heroes
video, videos	tomato, tomatoes

OTHER PLURALS   To form the plural of a hyphenated compound word, add *-s* to the chief word even if it does not appear at the end.

mother-in-law, mothers-in-law

English words derived from other languages such as Latin or French sometimes form the plural as they would in their original language.

medium, media	chateau, chateaux
criterion, criteria	

43d Be alert to commonly misspelled words.

absence	arrangement	committed	eligible
academic	ascend	committee	embarrass
accidentally	athlete	competitive	emphasize
accommodate	athletics	completely	entirely
achievement	attendance	conceivable	environment
acknowledge	basically	conscience	especially
acquaintance	beautiful	conscientious	exaggerated
acquire	beginning	conscious	exercise
address	believe	criticism	exhaust
all right	benefited	criticize	existence
amateur	bureau	decision	extraordinary
analyze	business	definitely	extremely
answer	calendar	descendant	familiar
apparently	candidate	desperate	fascinate
appearance	cemetery	dictionary	February
arctic	changeable	different	foreign
argument	column	disastrous	forty
arithmetic	commitment	eighth	fourth

friend	marriage	prejudice	siege
government	mathematics	presence	similar
grammar	mischievous	prevalent	sincerely
guard	necessary	privilege	sophomore
harass	noticeable	proceed	strictly
height	occasion	professor	subtly
humorous	occurred	pronunciation	succeed
incidentally	occurrence	publicly	surprise
incredible	pamphlet	quiet	thorough
independence	parallel	quite	tomorrow
indispensable	particularly	quizzes	tragedy
inevitable	pastime	receive	transferred
intelligence	permanent	recognize	tries
irrelevant	permissible	referred	truly
irresistible	perseverance	restaurant	unnecessarily
knowledge	phenomenon	rhythm	usually
library	physically	roommate	vacuum
license	playwright	sandwich	vengeance
lightning	practically	schedule	villain
loneliness	precede	seize	weird
maintenance	preference	separate	whether
maneuver	preferred	sergeant	writing

EXERCISE 43–1 The following memo has been run through a spell checker. Proofread it carefully, editing the spelling and typographical errors that remain.

November 1, 2006

To: Patricia Wise
cc: Richard Chang
From: Constance Mayhew
Subject: Express Tours annual report

Thank you for agreeing to draft the annual report for Express Tours. Before you begin you're work, let me outline the initial steps.

First, its essential for you to include brief profiles of top management. Early next week, I'll provide profiles for all manages accept Samuel Heath, who's biographical information is being revised. You should edit these profiles carefully, than format them according to the enclosed instructions. We may ask you to include other employee's profiles at some point.

Second, you should arrange to get complete financial information for fiscal year 2006 from our comptroller, Richard Chang. (Helen Boyes, to, can provide the necessary figures.) When you get this

information, precede according tot he plans we discuss in yesterday's meeting. By the way, you will notice from the figures that
the sale of our Charterhouse division did not significantly effect
net profits.

Third, you should submit first draft of the report by December
15. I assume that you won a laser printer, but if you don't, you
can submit a disk and we'll print out a draft here. Of coarse, you
should proofread you writing.

I am quiet pleased that you can take on this project. If I or anyone
else at Express Tours can answers questions, don't hesitate to call.

44

The hyphen

> ✓ **GRAMMAR CHECKERS** can flag some, but not all, missing or mis-
> used hyphens. For example, the programs can often tell you
> that a hyphen is needed in compound numbers, such as *sixty-*
> *four*. They can also tell you how to spell certain compound
> words, such as *breakup* (not *break-up*).

44a Consult the dictionary to determine how to treat a compound word.

A dictionary indicates whether to treat a compound word as
hyphenated (*water-repellent*), as one word (*waterproof*), or as
two words (*water table*). If the compound word is not in the dictionary, treat it as two words.

▶ The prosecutor chose not to cross-examine any witnesses.

▶ Imogene kept her sketches in a small note book.

▶ Alice walked through the looking/glass into a backward

world.

44b Use a hyphen to connect two or more words functioning together as an adjective before a noun.

▶ Mrs. Douglas gave Toshiko a seashell and some newspaper-

wrapped fish to take home to her mother.

▶ Richa Gupta is not yet a well-known candidate.

Newspaper-wrapped and *well-known* are adjectives used before the nouns *fish* and *candidate*.

Generally, do not use a hyphen when such compounds follow the noun.

▶ After our television campaign, Richa Gupta will be well /

known.

Do not use a hyphen to connect *-ly* adverbs to the words they modify.

▶ A slowly/moving truck tied up traffic.

NOTE: In a series, hyphens are suspended.

Do you prefer first-, second-, or third-class tickets?

44c Hyphenate the written form of fractions and of compound numbers from twenty-one to ninety-nine.

▶ One-fourth of my income goes to pay my child care expenses.

44d Use a hyphen with the prefixes *all-, ex-* (meaning "former"), and *self-* and with the suffix *-elect*.

▶ The charity is funneling more money into self-help projects.

▶ Anne King is our club's president-elect.

44e Use a hyphen in certain words to avoid ambiguity or to separate awkward double or triple letters.

Without the hyphen there would be no way to distinguish between words such as *recreation* and *re-creation*.

Bicycling in the city is my favorite form of recreation.

The film was praised for its astonishing re-creation of nineteenth-century London.

Hyphens are sometimes used to separate awkward double or triple letters in compound words (*anti-intellectual, cross-stitch*). Always check a dictionary for the standard form of the word.

44f If a word must be divided at the end of a line, divide it correctly.

1. Divide words between syllables.

▶ When I returned from my semester overseas, I didn't reco- *recog-*
-nize ∧
~~gnize~~ one face on the magazine covers.
∧

2. Never divide one-syllable words.

▶ He didn't have the courage or the ~~stren-~~
strength
~~gth~~ to open the door.
∧

3. Never divide a word so that a single letter stands alone at the end of a line or fewer than three letters begin a line.

▶ She'll bring her brother with her when she comes a-
again.
gain. ~~.~~
∧

▶ As audience to the play *The Mousetrap,* Hamlet is a ~~watch-~~
watcher
~~er~~ watching watchers.
∧

4. When dividing a compound word at the end of a line, either make the break between the words that form the compound or put the whole word on the next line.

▶ My niece Marielena is determined to become a long-dis-
distance
~~tance~~ runner when she grows up.
^

5. To divide long e-mail and Internet addresses, do not use a hyphen. Break an e-mail address after the @ symbol or before a period. Break a URL after a colon, a slash, or a double slash or before a period or other punctuation mark.

I repeatedly e-mailed Janine at janine.r.rose@dunbaracademy .org before I gave up and called her cell phone.

To find a zip code quickly, I always use the United States Postal Service Web site at http://zip4.usps.com/zip4/ welcome.jsp.

NOTE: For breaks in URLs in MLA and APA documentation styles, see 56a and 61a.

EXERCISE 44–1 Edit the following sentences to correct errors in hyphenation. If a sentence is correct, write "correct" after it. Answers to lettered sentences appear in the back of the book. Example:

Zola's first readers were scandalized by his slice-of-life
^ ^

novels.

a. Gold is the seventy-ninth element in the periodic table.
b. The swiftly-moving tugboat pulled alongside the barge and directed it away from the oil spill in the harbor.
c. The Moche were a pre-Columbian people who established a sophisticated culture in ancient Peru.
d. Your dog is well-known in our neighborhood.
e. Road-blocks were set up along all the major highways leading out of the city.

1. We knew we were driving too fast when our tires skidded on the rain slick surface.

2. The Black Death reduced the population of some medieval villages by two thirds.
3. Sewing forty-eight sequined tutus for the ballet recital nearly made Karyn cross-eyed.
4. Olivia had hoped to find a pay as you go plan to finance the construction of her observatory.
5. Gail Sheehy writes that at age twenty five many people assume that the choices they make are irrevocable.

ON THE WEB > **dianahacker.com/rules**
Grammar exercises > Mechanics > E-ex 44–1

45

Capital letters

In addition to the rules in this section, a good dictionary can tell you when to use capital letters.

 GRAMMAR CHECKERS remind you that sentences should begin with capital letters and that some words, such as *Cherokee,* are proper nouns. Many words, however, should be capitalized only in certain contexts, and you must determine when to do so.

45a Capitalize proper nouns and words derived from them; do not capitalize common nouns.

Proper nouns are the names of specific persons, places, and things. All other nouns are common nouns. The following types of words are usually capitalized: names for the deity, religions, religious followers, sacred books; words of family relationship used as names; particular places; nationalities and their languages, races, tribes; educational institutions, departments, degrees, particular courses; government departments, organizations, political parties; historical movements, periods, events, documents; specific electronic sources; and trade names.

PROPER NOUNS	COMMON NOUNS
God (used as a name)	a god
Book of Common Prayer	a book
Uncle Pedro	my uncle
Father (used as a name)	my father
Lake Superior	a picturesque lake
the Capital Center	a center for advanced studies
the South	a southern state
Wrigley Field	a baseball stadium
University of Wisconsin	a good university
Geology 101	geology
Environmental Protection Agency	a federal agency
Phi Kappa Psi	a fraternity
a Democrat	an independent
the Enlightenment	the eighteenth century
the Declaration of Independence	a treaty
the World Wide Web, the Web	a home page
the Internet, the Net	a computer network
Advil	a painkiller

Months, holidays, and days of the week are treated as proper nouns; the seasons and numbers of the days of the month are not.

> Our academic year begins on a Tuesday in early September, right after Labor Day.

> My mother's birthday is in early summer, on the second of June.

EXCEPTION: Capitalize Fourth of July (or July Fourth) when referring to the holiday.

Names of school subjects are capitalized only if they are names of languages. Names of particular courses are capitalized.

> This semester Austin is taking math, geography, geology, French, and English.

> Professor Obembe offers Modern American Fiction 501 to graduate students.

CAUTION: Do not capitalize common nouns to make them seem important: *Our company is currently hiring computer programmers* (not *Company, Computer Programmers*).

45b Capitalize titles of persons when used as part of a proper name but usually not when used alone.

Professor Margaret Barnes; Dr. Sinyee Sein; John Scott Williams Jr.; Anne Tilton, LLD

District Attorney Marshall was reprimanded for badgering the witness.

The district attorney was elected for a two-year term.

Usage varies when the title of an important public figure is used alone: *The president* [or *President*] *vetoed the bill.*

45c Capitalize the first, last, and all major words in titles and subtitles of works such as books, articles, songs, and online documents.

In both titles and subtitles, major words such as nouns, pronouns, verbs, adjectives, and adverbs should be capitalized. Minor words such as articles, prepositions, and coordinating conjunctions are not capitalized unless they are the first or last word of a title or subtitle. Capitalize the second part of a hyphenated term in a title if it is a major word but not if it is a minor word. Capitalize chapter titles and the titles of other major divisions of a work following the same guidelines used for titles of complete works.

Seizing the Enigma: The Race to Break the German U-Boat Codes

"Fire and Ice"

"I Want to Hold Your Hand"

The Canadian Green Page

"Work and Play" in Santayana's *The Nature of Beauty*

To see why some of the titles in the list are italicized and some are put in quotation marks, see 42a and 37d.

45d Capitalize the first word of a sentence.

The first word of a sentence should be capitalized.

When lightning struck the house, the chimney collapsed.

When a sentence appears within parentheses, capitalize its first word unless the parentheses appear within another sentence.

> Early detection of breast cancer significantly increases survival rates. (See table 2.)

> Early detection of breast cancer significantly increases survival rates (see table 2).

45e Capitalize the first word of a quoted sentence but not a quoted phrase.

> In *Time* magazine Robert Hughes writes, "There are only about sixty Watteau paintings on whose authenticity all experts agree."

> Russell Baker has written that in our country, sports are "the opiate of the masses."

If a quoted sentence is interrupted by explanatory words, do not capitalize the first word after the interruption. (See 37f.)

> "If you want to go out," he said, "tell me now."

When quoting poetry, copy the poet's capitalization exactly. Many poets capitalize the first word of every line of poetry; a few contemporary poets dismiss capitalization altogether.

> When I consider everything that grows
> Holds in perfection but a little moment   — Shakespeare

> it was the week   that
> i felt the city's narrow breezes rush about
> me   — Don L. Lee

45f Capitalize the first word after a colon if it begins an independent clause.

> I came to a startling conclusion: The house must be haunted.

NOTE: MLA style uses a lowercase letter to begin an independent clause following a colon; APA style uses a capital letter.

Use lowercase after a colon to introduce a list or an appositive.

> The students were divided into two groups: residents and commuters.

45g Capitalize abbreviations for departments and agencies of government, other organizations, and corporations; capitalize the call letters of radio and television stations.

EPA, FBI, OPEC, IBM, WCRB, KNBC-TV

EXERCISE 45–1 Edit the following sentences to correct errors in capitalization. If a sentence is correct, write "correct" after it. Answers to lettered sentences appear in the back of the book. Example:

> On our trip to the West we visited the grand canyon and the
> $\overset{G}{\quad}$ $\overset{C}{\quad}$
>
> great salt desert.
> $\overset{G}{\quad}$ $\overset{S}{\quad}$ $\overset{D}{\quad}$

a. Assistant dean Shirin Ahmadi recommended offering more world language courses.
b. We went to the Mark Taper Forum to see a production of *Angels in America.*
c. Kalindi has an ambitious semester, studying differential calculus, classical hebrew, brochure design, and greek literature.
d. Lydia's Aunt and Uncle make modular houses as beautiful as modernist works of art.
e. We amused ourselves on the long flight by discussing how Spring in Kyoto stacks up against Summer in London.

1. When the Ducati will not start, I try a few tricks with the ignition key: Jiggling it to the left, pulling it out a quarter of an inch, and gently pulling down on it.
2. When you slowly bake a clove of garlic, the most amazing thing happens: It loses its bitter tang and becomes sweet and buttery.
3. After World War II, aunt Helena left Poland to study in Italy.
4. When we drove through the south last summer, we were amazed to see kudzu growing wild along the road.
5. Following in his sister's footsteps, Leonid is pursuing a degree in Marketing Research.

ON THE WEB > **dianahacker.com/rules**
    Grammar exercises > Mechanics > E-ex 45–1

Academic Writing

46

Writing about texts

The word *texts* can refer to a variety of works: essays, periodical articles, government reports, books, and even visuals such as advertisements and photographs. Most assignments that ask you to respond to a text call for a summary or an analysis or both.

A summary is neutral in tone and demonstrates that you have understood the author's key ideas. Assignments calling for an analysis of a text vary widely, but they will usually ask you to look at how the text's parts contribute to its central argument or purpose, often with the aim of judging its evidence or overall effect.

When you write about a written text, you will need to read it several times to digest its full meaning. Two techniques will help you move beyond a superficial first reading: (1) annotating the text with your observations and questions and (2) outlining the text's key points. The same techniques will help you analyze visual texts.

46a Read actively: Annotate the text.

Read actively by jotting down your questions and thoughts in the margins of the text or visual or in a notebook. When you annotate a text as you read, you are doing something — engaging with the work, not just letting the words slip past you. Use a pencil instead of a highlighter; with a pencil you can underline key concepts, mark points, or circle elements that intrigue you. If you change your mind, you can erase your early annotations and replace them with new ones. (See the chart on p. 347 for advice about active reading.)

On pages 348 and 349 are an article from a consumer-oriented newsletter and a magazine advertisement, both annotated by students. The students, Emilia Sanchez and Albert Lee, were assigned to write a summary and an analysis. Each began by annotating the text.

Guidelines for active reading

Familiarize yourself with the basic features and structure of a text.

- What kind of text are you reading? An essay? An editorial? A scholarly article? An advertisement? A photograph?
- What is the author's purpose? To inform? To persuade? To call to action?
- Who is the audience? How does the author attempt to appeal to the audience?
- What is the author's thesis? What question does the text attempt to answer?
- What evidence does the author provide to support the thesis?

Note details that surprise, puzzle, or intrigue you.

- Has the author revealed a fact or made a point that runs counter to what you had assumed was true? What exactly is surprising?
- Has the author made a generalization you disagree with? Can you think of evidence that would challenge the generalization?
- Are there any contradictions or inconsistencies in the text?
- Are there any words, statements, or phrases in the text that you don't understand? If so, what reference materials do you need to consult?

Read and reread to discover meaning.

- What do you notice on a second or third reading that you didn't notice earlier?
- Does the text raise questions that it does not resolve?
- If you could address the author directly, what questions would you pose? Where do you agree and disagree with the author? Why?

Apply critical thinking strategies to visual texts.

- What first strikes you about the image? What elements do you notice immediately?
- Who or what is the main subject of the image?
- What colors and textures dominate?
- What is in the background? In the foreground?
- What role, if any, do words play in the visual text?

ANNOTATED ARTICLE

Big Box Stores Are Bad for Main Street

BETSY TAYLOR

Opening strategy — the problem is not x, it's y.

There is plenty of reason to be concerned about the proliferation of Wal-Marts and other so-called "big box" stores. The question, however, is not whether or not these types of stores create jobs (although several studies claim they produce a net job loss in local communities) or whether they ultimately save consumers money. The real concern about having a 25-acre slab of concrete with a 100,000 square foot box of stuff land on a town is whether it's good for a community's soul.

Sentimental — what is a community's soul?

Lumps all big boxes together.

Assumes all small businesses are attentive.

The worst thing about "big boxes" is that they have a tendency to produce Ross Perot's famous "big sucking sound" — sucking the life out of cities and small towns across the country. On the other hand, small businesses are great for a community. They offer more personal service; they won't threaten to pack up and leave town if they don't get tax breaks, free roads and other blandishments; and small-business owners are much more responsive to a customer's needs. (Ever try to complain about bad service or poor quality products to the president of Home Depot?)

Logic problem? Why couldn't customer complain to store manager?

True?

Yet, if big boxes are so bad, why are they so successful? One glaring reason is that we've become a nation of hyper-consumers, and the big-box boys know this. Downtown shopping districts comprised of small businesses take some of the efficiency out of overconsumption. There's all that hassle of having to travel from store to store, and having to pull out your credit card so many times. Occasionally, we even find ourselves chatting with the shopkeeper, wandering into a coffee shop to visit with a friend or otherwise wasting precious time that could be spent on acquiring more stuff.

Nostalgia for a time that is long gone or never was.

Community vs. economy. What about prices?

But let's face it — bustling, thriving city centers are fun. They breathe life into a community. They allow cities and towns to stand out from each other. They provide an atmosphere for people to interact with each other that just cannot be found at Target, or Wal-Mart or Home Depot.

Ends with emotional appeal.

Is it anti-American to be against having a retail giant set up shop in one's community? Some people would say so. On the other hand, if you board up Main Street, what's left of America?

ANNOTATED ADVERTISEMENT

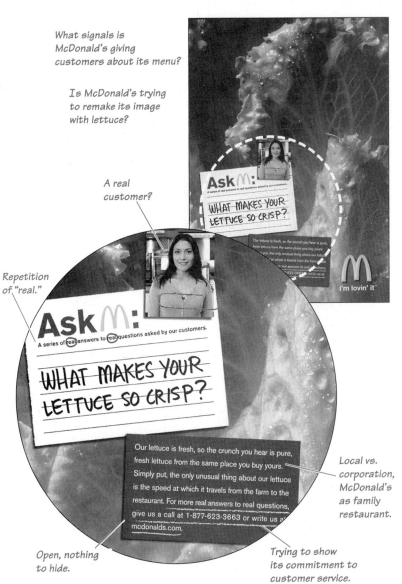

What signals is McDonald's giving customers about its menu?

Is McDonald's trying to remake its image with lettuce?

A real customer?

Repetition of "real."

Ask M: A series of real answers to real questions asked by our customers.

WHAT MAKES YOUR LETTUCE SO CRISP?

Our lettuce is fresh, so the crunch you hear is pure, fresh lettuce from the same place you buy yours. Simply put, the only unusual thing about our lettuce is the speed at which it travels from the farm to the restaurant. For more real answers to real questions, give us a call at 1-877-623-3663 or write us at mcdonalds.com.

Local vs. corporation, McDonald's as family restaurant.

Open, nothing to hide.

Trying to show its commitment to customer service.

i'm lovin' it

46b Try sketching a brief outline of the text.

After reading, rereading, and annotating a text, attempt to outline it. Seeing how the author has constructed a text can help you understand it. As you sketch an outline, pay special attention to the text's thesis (central idea) and its topic sentences. The thesis of a written text usually appears in the introduction, often in the first or second paragraph. Topic sentences can be found at the beginnings of most body paragraphs, where they announce a shift to a new topic. (See 2a and 4a.)

In your outline, put the author's thesis and key points in your own words. Here, for example, is the outline that Emilia Sanchez developed as she prepared to write her summary and analysis of the text printed on page 348. Notice that the outline does not simply trace the author's ideas paragraph by paragraph; instead, it sums up the article's central points.

OUTLINE OF "BIG BOX STORES ARE BAD FOR MAIN STREET"

Thesis: Whether or not they take jobs away from a community or offer low prices to consumers, we should be worried about "big-box" stores like Wal-Mart, Target, and Home Depot because they harm communities by taking the life out of downtown shopping districts.

I. Small businesses are better for cities and towns than big-box stores are.
   A. Small businesses offer personal service and big-box stores do not.
   B. Small businesses don't make demands on community resources as big-box stores do.
   C. Small businesses respond to customer concerns and big-box stores do not.

II. Big-box stores are successful because they cater to consumption at the expense of benefits to the community.
   A. Buying everything in one place is convenient.
   B. Shopping at small businesses may be inefficient, but it provides opportunities for socializing.
   C. Downtown shopping districts give each city or town a special identity.

Conclusion: While some people say that it's anti-American to oppose big-box stores, actually these stores threaten the communities that make up America by encouraging buying at the expense of the traditional interactions of Main Street.

A visual, of course, doesn't state an explicit thesis or an explicit line of reasoning. Instead, you must infer the meaning beneath the image's surface and interpret its central point and supporting ideas from the elements of its design. One way to outline a visual text is to try to define its purpose and sketch a list of its key elements. Here, for example, are the key features that Albert Lee identified for the advertisement printed on page 349.

Purpose: To persuade readers that McDonald's is concerned about its customers' health.

Key features:

- A close-up of a fresh, green lettuce leaf makes up the entire background.
- Near the center there's a comment card with a handwritten question from a "real" McDonald's customer: "What makes your lettuce so crisp?"
- A photograph of a smiling woman is clipped to the card.
- Beneath the comment card is the company's response, which emphasizes the farm-fresh quality and purity of its vegetables and urges customers to ask other candid questions.
- At the bottom of the ad is the McDonald's slogan "I'm lovin' it."

ON THE WEB > dianahacker.com/rules
Model papers > MLA analysis papers > Albert Lee

46c Summarize to demonstrate your understanding.

Your goal in summarizing a text is to state the work's main ideas and key points simply, briefly, and accurately. If you have sketched a brief outline of the text (see 46b), refer to it as you draft your summary.

To summarize a written text, first find the author's central idea — the thesis. Then divide the whole piece into a few major and perhaps minor ideas. Since a summary must be fairly short, you must make judgments about what is most important. To summarize a visual text, begin with information about who created the visual, who the intended audience is, and when and where the visual appeared. Briefly explain the visual's main point or purpose and point to its key features.

Following is Emilia Sanchez's summary of the article that is printed on page 348.

Guidelines for writing a summary

- In the first sentence, mention the title of the text, the name of the author, and the author's thesis or the visual's central point.

- Maintain a neutral tone; be objective.

- Use the third-person point of view and the present tense: *Taylor argues.* . . .

- Keep your focus on the text. Don't state the author's ideas as if they were your own.

- Put all or most of your summary in your own words; if you borrow a phrase or a sentence from the text, put it in quotation marks and give the page number in parentheses.

- Limit yourself to presenting the text's key points.

- Be concise; make every word count.

In her essay "Big Box Stores Are Bad for Main Street," Betsy Taylor argues that chain stores harm communities by taking the life out of downtown shopping districts. Explaining that a community's "soul" is more important than low prices or consumer convenience, she argues that small businesses are better than stores like Wal-Mart, Target, and Home Depot because they emphasize personal interactions and don't place demands on a community's resources. Taylor asserts that big-box stores are successful because "we've become a nation of hyper-consumers," although the convenience of shopping in these stores comes at the expense of benefits to the community. She concludes by suggesting that it's not "anti-American" to oppose big-box stores because the damage they inflict on downtown shopping districts extends to America itself. — Emilia Sanchez, student

46d Analyze to demonstrate your critical thinking.

When you analyze, you separate the whole to study the parts. Whereas a summary most often answers the question of *what* a text says, an analysis looks at *how* a text makes its point.

Typically, an analysis takes the form of an essay that makes its own argument about a text. Include an introduction that texts

briefly summarizes the text, a thesis that states your own judgment about the text, and body paragraphs that support your thesis with evidence. If you are analyzing an image, examine it as a whole and then reflect on how the individual elements contribute to its overall meaning. If you have written a summary of the text, you may find it useful to refer to the main points of the summary as you write your analysis.

Beginning on the next page is Emilia Sanchez's analysis of the article by Betsy Taylor (see p. 348).

Guidelines for analyzing a text

Written texts. Instructors who ask you to analyze a written nonfiction text often expect you to address some of the following questions.

■ What is the author's thesis or central idea? Who is the audience?

■ What questions does the author address (implicitly or explicitly)?

■ How does the author structure the text? What are the key parts and how do they relate to one another and to the thesis?

■ What strategies has the author used to generate interest in the argument and to persuade readers of its merit?

■ What evidence does the author use to support the thesis? How persuasive is the evidence?

■ Does the author anticipate objections and counter opposing views?

■ Does the author fall prey to any faulty reasoning?

Visual texts. If you are analyzing a visual text, the following additional questions will help you evaluate an image's purpose and meaning.

■ What surprises, perplexes, or intrigues you about the image?

■ What clues suggest the visual text's intended audience? How does the image appeal to its audience?

■ If the text is an advertisement, what product is it selling? Does it attempt to sell an idea or a message as well?

■ If the visual text includes words, how do the words contribute to the meaning of the image?

■ How do design elements — colors, shapes, perspective, background, foreground — shape the visual text's meaning or serve its purpose?

Sanchez 1

Emilia Sanchez

Professor Goodwin

English 10

23 October 2006

Rethinking Big-Box Stores

Opening summarizes the article's purpose and thesis.

In her essay "Big Box Stores Are Bad for Main Street," Betsy Taylor focuses not on the economic effects of large chain stores but on the effects these stores have on the "soul" of America. She argues that stores like Home Depot, Target, and Wal-Mart are bad for America because they draw people out of downtown shopping districts and cause them to focus exclusively on consumption. In contrast, she believes that small businesses are good for America because they provide personal attention, foster community interaction, and make each city unique. But Taylor's argument is ultimately unconvincing because it is based on nostalgia-- on idealized images of a quaint Main Street--rather than on the roles that businesses play in consumers'

Thesis expresses Sanchez's judgment of Taylor's article.

lives and communities. By ignoring the more complex, economically driven relationships between large chain stores and their communities, Taylor incorrectly assumes that simply getting rid of big-box stores would have a positive effect on America's communities.

Taylor's use of colorful language reveals that she has a nostalgic view of American society and does not understand economic realities. In her first paragraph,

Sanchez 2

Taylor refers to a big-box store as a "25-acre slab of concrete with a 100,000 square foot box of stuff" that "lands on a town," evoking images of a monolithic monster crushing the American way of life (1011). But her assessment oversimplifies a complex issue. Taylor does not consider that many downtown business districts failed long before chain stores moved in, when factories and mills closed and workers lost their jobs. In cities with struggling economies, big-box stores can actually provide much-needed jobs. Similarly, while Taylor blames big-box stores for harming local economies by asking for tax breaks, free roads, and other perks, she doesn't acknowledge that these stores also enter into economic partnerships with the surrounding communities by offering financial benefits to schools and hospitals.

Taylor's assumption that shopping in small businesses is always better for the customer also seems driven by nostalgia for an old-fashioned Main Street rather than by the facts. While she may be right that many small businesses offer personal service and are responsive to customer complaints, she does not consider that many customers appreciate the service at big-box stores. Just as customer service is better at some small businesses than at others, it is impossible to generalize about service at all big-box stores. For example, customers depend on the lenient return

Signal phrase introduces quotations from the source; Sanchez uses an MLA in-text citation.

Sanchez begins to identify and challenge Taylor's assumptions.

Clear topic sentence announces a shift to a new topic.

Sanchez refutes Taylor's claim.

Sanchez 3

policies and the wide variety of products at stores like Target and Home Depot.

Taylor blames big-box stores for encouraging American "hyper-consumerism," but she oversimplifies by equating big-box stores with bad values and small businesses with good values. Like her other points, this claim ignores the economic and social realities of American society today. Big-box stores do not force Americans to buy more. By offering lower prices in a convenient setting, however, they allow consumers to save time and purchase goods they might not be able to afford from small businesses. The existence of more small businesses would not change what most Americans can afford, nor would it reduce their desire to buy affordable merchandise.

Sanchez treats the author fairly.

Taylor may be right that some big-box stores have a negative impact on communities and that small businesses offer certain advantages. But she ignores the economic conditions that support big-box stores as well as the fact that Main Street was in decline before the big-box store arrived. Getting rid of big-box stores will not bring back a simpler America populated by thriving, unique Main Streets; in reality, Main Street will not survive if consumers cannot afford to shop there.

Conclusion returns to the thesis and shows the wider significance of Sanchez's analysis.

Sanchez 4

Work Cited

Taylor, Betsy. "Big Box Stores Are Bad for Main
Street." *CQ Researcher* 9.44 (1999): 1011. Print.

Work cited page
is in MLA style.

46e Understand the types of texts analyzed in different disciplines.

In your college writing, you may be asked to analyze a variety
of texts in different fields of study. Each field has its own questions, ideas about acceptable evidence, and language conventions. But all disciplines share certain expectations for good
writing, and the guidelines for summarizing and analyzing texts
(see pp. 352 and 353) can be adapted for use in all disciplines.
The following chart shows the types of texts you might be
asked to analyze in different disciplines.

Types of texts analyzed in various disciplines

Humanities: Literature, art, film, music, philosophy

- Passages of a fiction or nonfiction work or lines of a poem
- An image or a work of art
- Passages of a musical composition
- Critical essays that analyze original works such as books, poems, films, music, or works of art

Humanities: History

- Firsthand sources such as photographs, letters, maps, and government documents
- Scholarly books and articles

Social sciences: Psychology, sociology, political science, anthropology

- Data from original experiments
- Results of field research such as interviews, observations, or surveys
- Reports that interpret or analyze data or that place data in context

Sciences: Biology, chemistry, physics

- Data from original experiments
- Scholarly articles that report findings from experiments

47

Constructing reasonable arguments

In writing an argument, you take a stand on a debatable issue. The question being debated might be a matter of public policy:

> Should religious groups be allowed to meet on public school property?

What is the least dangerous way to dispose of nuclear waste?

Should a state enact laws rationing medical care?

On such questions, reasonable people may disagree.

Reasonable men and women also disagree about many scholarly issues. Psychologists debate the role of genes and environment in determining behavior; historians interpret the causes of the Civil War quite differently; biologists challenge one another's predictions about the effects of global warming.

When you construct a *reasonable* argument, your goal is not simply to win or to have the last word. Your aim is to explain your understanding of the truth about a subject or to propose the best solution available for solving a problem — without being needlessly combative. In constructing your argument, you join a conversation with other writers and readers. Your aim is to convince readers to reconsider their opinions by offering new reasons to question an old viewpoint.

ACADEMIC ENGLISH Some cultures value writers who argue with force; other cultures value writers who argue subtly or indirectly. Academic audiences in the United States will expect your writing to be assertive and confident — neither aggressive nor passive. Create an assertive tone by acknowledging different opinions and supporting your view with specific evidence.

TOO AGGRESSIVE	Of course prayer should be discouraged in public schools. Only foolish people think that organized prayer is good for everyone.
TOO PASSIVE	I might be wrong, but I think that organized prayer should be discouraged in public schools.
ASSERTIVE TONE	Organized prayer should be discouraged in public schools because it violates the religious freedom guaranteed by the First Amendment.

If you are uncertain about the tone of your work, ask for help at your school's writing center.

47a Examine your issue's social and intellectual contexts.

Arguments appear in social and intellectual contexts. Public policy debates obviously arise in social contexts. Grounded in specific times and places, such debates are conducted among groups with competing values and interests. For example, the debate over nuclear power plants has been renewed in the United States in light of skyrocketing energy costs and terrorism concerns — with environmentalists, nuclear industry officials, and consumers all weighing in on the argument. Most public policy debates also have intellectual dimensions that address scientific or theoretical questions. In the case of the nuclear power issue, physicists, biologists, and economists all contribute their expertise.

Scholarly debates clearly play themselves out in intellectual contexts, but they have a social dimension too. Scholars and researchers rarely work in a vacuum: They respond to the contributions of other specialists in the field, often building on others' views and refining them, but at times challenging them.

Because many of your readers will be aware of the social and intellectual contexts in which your issue is grounded, you will be at a serious disadvantage if you are not informed. That's why it is a good idea to conduct some research before preparing your argument; consulting even a few sources can help. For example, the student whose paper appears on pages 367–71 became more knowledgeable about his issue — the ethics of performance-enhancing procedures in sports — after consulting a handful of brief sources.

47b View your audience as a panel of jurors.

Do not assume that your audience already agrees with you; instead, envision skeptical readers who, like a panel of jurors, will make up their minds after listening to all sides of the argument. If you are arguing a public policy issue, aim your paper at readers who represent a variety of opinions. In the case of the debate over nuclear power, for example, imagine a jury representative of those who have a stake in the matter: environmentalists, nuclear industry officials, and consumers.

At times, you can deliberately narrow your audience. If you are working within a word limit, for example, you might not have the space in which to address the concerns of all parties to the nuclear energy debate. Or you might be primarily interested in reaching one segment of a general audience, such as consumers. In such instances, you can still view your audience as a panel of jurors; the jury will simply be a less diverse group.

In the case of scholarly debates, you will be addressing readers who share your interest in a discipline such as literature or psychology. Such readers belong to a group with an agreed-upon way of investigating and talking about issues. Though they generally agree about procedures, scholars in an academic discipline often disagree about particular issues. Once you see how they disagree about your issue, you should be able to imagine a jury that reflects the variety of opinions they hold.

47c In your introduction, establish credibility and state your position.

When you are constructing an argument, make sure your introduction contains a thesis sentence that states your position on the issue you have chosen to debate (see 2a). In the sentences leading up to the thesis, establish your credibility with readers by showing that you are knowledgeable and fair-minded. If possible, build common ground with readers who may not be in initial agreement with your views and show them why they need to consider your thesis.

In the following introduction, student Kevin Smith presents himself as someone worth listening to. His opening sentence shows that he is familiar with the legal issues surrounding school prayer. His next sentence reveals him to be fair-minded, as he presents the views of both sides. Even Smith's thesis builds common ground: "Prayer is too important to be trusted to our public schools." Because Smith introduces both sides of the debate, readers are likely to approach his essay with an open mind.

> Although the Supreme Court has ruled against prayer in public schools on First Amendment grounds, many people still feel that prayer should be allowed. Such people value prayer as a practice central to their faith and believe that prayer is a way for

schools to reinforce moral principles. They also compellingly point out a paradox in the First Amendment itself: at what point does the separation of church and state restrict the freedom of those who wish to practice their religion? What proponents of school prayer fail to realize, however, is that the Supreme Court's decision, although it was made on legal grounds, makes sense on religious grounds as well. Prayer is too important to be trusted to our public schools.   — Kevin Smith, student

TIP: A good way to test a thesis while drafting and revising is to imagine a counterargument to your argument (see 47f). If you can't think of an opposing point of view, rethink your thesis or ask a classmate to respond to your argument.

47d Back up your thesis with persuasive lines of argument.

Arguments of any complexity contain lines of argument that, when taken together, might reasonably persuade readers that the thesis has merit. The following, for example, are the main lines of argument used by Jamal Hammond, whose thesis was that athletes' use of biotechnology constitutes an unfair advantage in sports (see pp. 367–71).

> Thesis: Athletes who use any type of biotechnology give themselves an unfair advantage and disrupt the sense of fair play, and they should be banned from competition.
>
> - Athletic achievement nowadays increasingly results from biological and high-tech intervention rather than strictly from hard work.
> - There is a difference between the use of state-of-the-art equipment and drugs and the modification of the body itself.
> - If the rules that guarantee an even playing field are violated, competitors and spectators alike are deprived of a sound basis of comparison on which to judge athletic effort and accomplishment.
> - If we let athletes alter their bodies through biotechnology, we might as well dispense with the human element altogether.

If you sum up your main lines of argument, as Hammond did, you will have a rough outline of your essay. The outline will consist of your central claim — the thesis — and any supporting claims that back it up. In your paper, you will provide evidence for each of these claims.

arg

47e Support your claims with specific evidence.

You will need to support your central claim and any subordinate claims with evidence: facts, statistics, examples and illustrations, expert opinion, and so on. Depending on the issue you have chosen to write about, you may or may not need to do some reading to gather evidence. Some topics, such as whether your college should continue to support its travel study program, can be developed through personal experience and research tools such as questionnaires and interviews. Most debatable topics, however, require that you consult some written sources.

If any of your evidence is based on reading, you must document your sources. Documentation gives credit to the authors and shows readers how to locate a source if they want to assess its credibility or explore the issue further (see 55 and 60).

Using facts and statistics

A fact is something that is known with certainty because it has been objectively verified: The capital of Wyoming is Cheyenne. Carbon has an atomic weight of 12. John F. Kennedy was assassinated on November 22, 1963. Statistics are collections of numerical facts: Alcohol abuse is a factor in nearly 40 percent of traffic fatalities. More than four in ten businesses in the United States are owned by women. As of 2006, about 22 percent of Americans own a high-definition TV.

Most arguments are supported at least to some extent by facts and statistics. For example, in the following passage the writer uses statistics to show that college students are carrying unreasonably high credit card debt.

> A 2001 study by Nellie Mae revealed that while the average credit card debt per college undergraduate is $2,327, more than 20% of undergraduates who have at least one credit card maintain a much higher debt level, from $3,000 to $7,000 (Barrett).

Writers often use statistics in selective ways to bolster their own views. If you suspect that a writer's handling of statistics is not quite fair, read authors with opposing views, who may give you a fuller understanding of the numbers.

Using examples and illustrations

Examples and illustrations (extended examples, often in story form) rarely prove a point by themselves, but when used in combination with other forms of evidence they flesh out an argument and bring it to life. Because they often have an emotional dimension, they can reach readers in ways that statistics cannot.

In a paper arguing that any athletes who use gene therapy should be banned from competition, Jamal Hammond gives a thought-provoking example of how running with genetically modified limbs is no different from riding a motorcycle in a footrace.

Citing expert opinion

Although they are no substitute for careful reasoning of your own, the views of an expert can contribute to the force of your argument. For example, to help him make the case that biotechnology could degrade the meaning of sports, Jamal Hammond quotes the remarks of an expert:

> Thomas Murray, chair of the ethics advisory panel for the World Anti-Doping Agency, says he hopes, not too optimistically, for an "alternative future . . . where we still find meaning in great performances as an alchemy of two factors, natural talents . . . and virtues" (qtd. in Jenkins D11).

When you rely on expert opinion, make sure that your source is an expert in the field you are writing about. In some cases, you may need to provide credentials showing why your source is worth listening to. When including expert testimony in your paper, you can summarize or paraphrase the expert's opinion or you can quote the expert's exact words. You will of course need to document the source, as Hammond did in the example just given (see 55 and 60).

47f Anticipate objections; counter opposing arguments.

Readers who already agree with you need no convincing, but indifferent or skeptical readers may resist your arguments. To be willing to give up a position that seems reasonable, a reader has to see that there is an even more reasonable one. In addition to presenting your own case, therefore, you should review the opposing arguments and attempt to counter them.

Anticipating and countering objections

To anticipate a possible objection, consider the following questions:

- Could a reasonable person draw a different conclusion from your facts or examples?
- Might a reader question any of your assumptions?
- Could a reader offer an alternative explanation of this issue?
- Is there any evidence that might undermine your position?

The following questions may help you respond to a potential objection:

- Can you concede the point to the opposition but challenge the point's importance or usefulness?
- Can you explain why readers should consider a new perspective or question a piece of evidence?
- Should you qualify your position in light of contradictory evidence?
- Can you suggest a different interpretation of the evidence?

When you write, use phrasing to signal to readers that you're about to present an objection. Often the signal phrase can go in the lead sentence of a paragraph:

Critics of this view argue that. . . .

Some readers might point out that. . . .

There might appear to be compelling challenges to. . . .

But isn't it possible that . . . ?

It might seem at first that drawing attention to an opposing point of view or contradictory piece of evidence would weaken your argument. But by anticipating and countering objections to your argument, you show yourself as a reasonable and well-informed writer. You also establish your purpose, demonstrate the significance of the issue you are debating, and ultimately strengthen your argument.

There is no best place in an essay to deal with opposing views. Often it is useful to summarize the opposing position early in your essay. After stating your thesis but before developing your own arguments, you might have a paragraph that takes up the most important counterargument. Or you can anticipate objections paragraph by paragraph as you develop your case. Wherever you decide to deal with opposing arguments, do your best to explain the arguments of others accurately and fairly (see 48c).

47g Build common ground.

As you counter opposing arguments, try to build common ground with readers who do not initially agree with your views. If you can show that you share their concerns, your readers will be more likely to acknowledge the validity of your argument. For example, to persuade people opposed to shooting deer, a state wildlife commission would have to show that it too cares about preserving deer and does not want them to die needlessly. Having established these values in common, the commission might be able to persuade critics that a carefully controlled hunting season is good for the deer population because it prevents starvation caused by overpopulation.

People believe that intelligence and decency support their side of an argument. To change sides, they must continue to feel intelligent and decent. Otherwise they will persist in their opposition.

47h Sample argument paper

In the following paper, student Jamal Hammond argues that athletes who enhance their performance through biotechnology should be banned from athletic competition. Notice that he is careful to present opposing views fairly before providing his counterarguments.

In writing the paper, Hammond consulted three newspaper articles, two in print and one online. When he quotes or uses information from a source, he cites the source with an MLA (Modern Language Association) in-text citation. Citations in the paper refer readers to the list of works cited at the end of the paper. (See 55.)

ON THE WEB > **dianahacker.com/rules**
   Model papers > MLA argument papers: Hammond; Lund; Sanghvi
             > MLA papers: Orlov; Daly; Levi

Hammond 1

Jamal Hammond

Professor Paschal

English 102

19 March 2007

Performance Enhancement through Biotechnology

Has No Place in Sports

The debate over athletes' use of performance-
enhancing substances is getting more complicated as
biotechnologies such as gene therapy become a reality.
The availability of these new methods of boosting
performance will force us to decide what we value most
in sports--displays of physical excellence developed
through hard work or victory at all costs. For centuries,
spectators and athletes have cherished the tradition of
fairness in sports. While sports competition is, of
course, largely about winning, it is also about the
means by which a player or team wins. Athletes who
use any type of biotechnology give themselves an
unfair advantage and disrupt the sense of fair play,
and they should be banned from competition.

Researchers are experimenting with techniques
that could manipulate an athlete's genetic code to
build stronger muscles or increase endurance. Searching
for cures for diseases like Parkinson's and muscular
dystrophy, scientists at the University of Pennsylvania
have created "Schwarzenegger mice," rodents that grew
larger-than-normal muscles after receiving injections
with a gene that stimulates growth protein. The

Opening sentences provide background for Hammond's thesis.

Thesis states the main point.

Hammond establishes his credibility by summarizing medical research.

Hammond 2

researchers also found that a combination of gene

manipulation and exercise led to a 35% increase in the

Source is cited in MLA style.

strength of rats' leg muscles (Lamb 13).

Such therapies are breakthroughs for humans

suffering from muscular diseases; for healthy athletes,

they could mean new world records in sports involving

speed and endurance--but at what cost to the integrity

Hammond uses specific evidence to support his thesis.

of athletic competition? The International Olympic

Committee's World Anti-Doping Agency has become so

alarmed about the possible effects of new gene tech-

nology on athletic competition that it has banned the

use of gene therapies and urged researchers to devise

a test for detecting genetic modification (Lamb 13).

Opposing views are presented fairly.

Some bioethicists argue that this next wave of

performance enhancement is an acceptable and unavoidable

feature of competition. As Dr. Andy Miah, who supports the

regulated use of gene therapies in sports, claims, "The idea

of the naturally perfect athlete is romantic nonsense. . . .

An athlete achieves what he or she achieves through all sorts

of means--technology, sponsorship, support and so on" (qtd.

"Qtd. in" is used for an indirect source: words quoted in another source.

in Rudebeck). Miah, in fact, sees athletes' imminent turn to

genetic modification as "merely a continuation of the way

sport works; it allows us to create more extraordinary

performances" (Rudebeck). Miah's approval of

"extraordinary performances" as the goal of competition

reflects our culture's tendency to demand and reward new

heights of athletic achievement. The problem is that

Hammond 3

achievement nowadays increasingly results from biological and high-tech intervention rather than strictly from hard work.

Better equipment, such as aerodynamic bicycles and fiberglass poles for pole vaulting, have made it possible for athletes to record achievements unthinkable a generation ago. But athletes themselves must put forth the physical effort of training and practice--they must still build their skills--even in the murky area of legal and illegal drug use (Jenkins D11). There is a difference between the use of state-of-the-art equipment and drugs and the modification of the body itself. Athletes who use medical technology to alter their bodies can bypass the hard work of training by taking on the powers of a machine. If they set new records this way, we lose the opportunity to witness sports as a spectacle of human effort and are left marveling at scientific advances, which have little relation to the athletic tradition of fair play.

Such a tradition has long defined athletic competition. Sports rely on equal conditions to ensure fair play, from regulations that demand similar equipment to referees who evenhandedly apply the rules to all participants. If the rules that guarantee an even playing field are violated, competitors and spectators alike are deprived of a sound basis of comparison on which to judge athletic effort and accomplishment. When major league baseball rules call for solid-wood bats,

Hammond counters opposing arguments.

Hammond develops the thesis.

Transition moves from the writer's main argument to specific examples.

Hammond 4

the player who uses a corked bat enhances his hitting statistics at the expense of players who use regulation equipment. When Ben Johnson tested positive for steroids after setting a world record in the 100-meter dash in the 1988 Olympics, his "achievement" devalued the intense training that his competitors had undergone to prepare for the event--and the International Olympic Committee responded by stripping Johnson of his medal and his world record. Likewise, athletes who use gene therapy to alter their bodies and enhance their performance will create an uneven playing field.

If we let athletes alter their bodies through biotechnology, we might as well dispense with the human element altogether. Instead of watching the 100-meter dash to see who the fastest runner in the world is, we might just as well watch the sprinters mount motorcycles and race across the finish line. The absurdity of such an example, however, points to the damage that we will do to sports if we allow these therapies. Thomas Murray, chair of the ethics advisory panel for the World Anti-Doping Agency, says he hopes, not too optimistically, for an "alternative future . . . where we still find meaning in great performances as an alchemy of two factors, natural talents . . . and virtues" (qtd. in Jenkins D11).

Unless we are willing to organize separate sporting events and leagues--an Olympics, say, for athletes who have opted for a boost from the test tube and another for athletes who have chosen to keep their bodies natural--we should ask from our athletes that they dazzle us less with extraordinary performance and more with the fruits of their hard work.

A vivid example helps the writer make his point.

Conclusion echoes the thesis without dully repeating it.

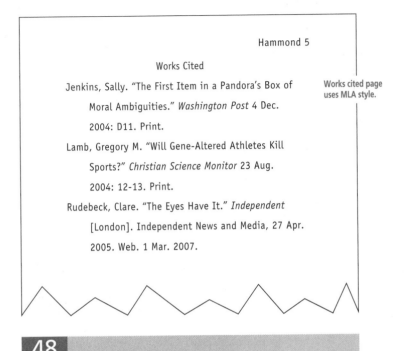

Hammond 5

Works Cited

Jenkins, Sally. "The First Item in a Pandora's Box of Moral Ambiguities." *Washington Post* 4 Dec. 2004: D11. Print.

Lamb, Gregory M. "Will Gene-Altered Athletes Kill Sports?" *Christian Science Monitor* 23 Aug. 2004: 12-13. Print.

Rudebeck, Clare. "The Eyes Have It." *Independent* [London]. Independent News and Media, 27 Apr. 2005. Web. 1 Mar. 2007.

Works cited page uses MLA style.

48

Evaluating arguments

In your reading and in your own writing, evaluate all arguments for logic and fairness. Many arguments can stand up to critical scrutiny. Often, however, a line of argument that at first seems reasonable turns out to be fallacious, unfair, or both.

ON THE WEB > dianahacker.com/rules
Links Library > Academic writing

48a Distinguish between reasonable and fallacious argumentative tactics.

A number of unreasonable argumentative tactics are known as *logical fallacies.* Most of the fallacies—such as hasty generalizations and false analogies—are misguided or dishonest uses of legitimate argumentative strategies. The examples in this section suggest when such strategies are reasonable and when they are not.

Generalizing (inductive reasoning)

Writers and thinkers generalize all the time. We look at a sample of data and conclude that data we have not observed will most likely conform to what we have seen. From a spoonful of soup, we conclude just how salty the whole bowl will be. After numerous bad experiences with an airline, we decide to book future flights with a competitor.

When we draw a conclusion from an array of facts, we are engaged in inductive reasoning. Such reasoning deals in probability, not certainty. For a conclusion to be highly probable, it must be based on evidence that is sufficient, representative, and relevant. (See the chart on p. 373.)

The fallacy known as *hasty generalization* is a conclusion based on insufficient or unrepresentative evidence.

HASTY GENERALIZATION

In a single year, scores on standardized tests in California's public schools rose by ten points. Therefore, more children than ever are succeeding in America's public school systems.

Data from one state do not justify a conclusion about the whole United States.

A *stereotype* is a hasty generalization about a group. Here are a few examples.

STEREOTYPES

Women are bad bosses.

Politicians are corrupt.

Asian students are exceptionally intelligent.

Stereotyping is common because of our human tendency to perceive selectively. We tend to see what we want to see; that is, we notice evidence confirming our already formed opinions and fail to notice evidence to the contrary. For example, if you have concluded that politicians are corrupt, your stereotype will be confirmed by news reports of legislators being indicted — even though every day the media describe conscientious officials serving the public honestly and well.

ACADEMIC ENGLISH Many hasty generalizations contain words like *all, ever, always,* and *never,* when qualifiers such as *most, many, usually,* and *seldom* would be more accurate.

Testing inductive reasoning

Though inductive reasoning leads to probable and not absolute truth, you can assess a conclusion's likely probability by asking three questions. This chart shows how to apply those questions to a sample conclusion based on a survey.

CONCLUSION   The majority of students on our campus would subscribe to wireless Internet access if it were available.

EVIDENCE   In a recent survey, 923 of 1,515 students questioned say they would subscribe to wireless Internet access.

1. Is the evidence sufficient?
   That depends. On a small campus (say, 3,000 students), the pool of students surveyed would be sufficient for market research, but on a large campus (say, 30,000), 1,515 students are only 5 percent of the population. If that 5 percent were known to be truly representative of the other 95 percent, however, even such a small sample would be sufficient (see question 2).
2. Is the evidence representative?
   The evidence is representative if those responding to the survey reflect the characteristics of the entire student population: age, sex, level of technical expertise, amount of disposable income, and so on. If most of those surveyed are majoring in technical fields, for example, the researchers would be wise to question the survey's conclusion.
3. Is the evidence relevant?
   Yes. The results of the survey are directly linked to the conclusion. A question about the number of hours spent online, by contrast, would not be relevant, because it would not be about *subscribing to wireless Internet access*.

Drawing analogies

An analogy points out a similarity between two things that are otherwise different. Analogies can be an effective means of arguing a point. Our system of judicial decision making, or case law, which relies heavily on previous decisions, makes extensive use of reasoning by analogy. One lawyer may point out, for example, that specific facts or circumstances resemble those from a previous case and will thus argue for a similar result or decision. In response, the opposing lawyer may maintain that such facts or circumstances bear only a superficial resemblance to those in the previous case and that in legally relevant respects they are quite different and thus require a different result or decision.

It is not always easy to draw the line between a reasonable and an unreasonable analogy. At times, however, an analogy is clearly off base, in which case it is called a *false analogy*.

FALSE ANALOGY

If we can put humans on the moon, we should be able to find a cure for the common cold.

The writer has falsely assumed that because two things are alike in one respect, they must be alike in others. Putting human beings on the moon and finding a cure for the common cold are both scientific challenges, but the problems confronting medical researchers are quite different from those solved by space scientists.

Tracing causes and effects

Demonstrating a connection between causes and effects is rarely a simple matter. For example, to explain why a chemistry course has a high failure rate, you would begin by listing possible causes: inadequate preparation of students, poor teaching, large class size, lack of qualified tutors, and so on. Next you would investigate each possible cause. To see whether inadequate preparation contributes to the high failure rate, for instance, you might compare the math and science backgrounds of successful and failing students. To see whether large class size is a contributing factor, you might run a pilot program of small classes and compare grades in the small classes with those in the larger ones. Only after investigating the possible causes would you be able to weigh the relative impact of each cause and suggest appropriate remedies.

Because cause-and-effect reasoning is so complex, it is not surprising that writers frequently oversimplify it. In particular, writers sometimes assume that because one event follows another, the first is the cause of the second. This common fallacy is known as *post hoc,* from the Latin *post hoc, ergo propter hoc,* meaning "after this, therefore because of this."

POST HOC FALLACY

Since Governor Cho took office, unemployment of minorities in the state has decreased by 7 percent. Governor Cho should be applauded for reducing unemployment among minorities.

The writer must show that Governor Cho's policies are responsible for the decrease in unemployment; it is not enough to show that the decrease followed the governor's taking office.

Weighing options

Especially when reasoning about problems and solutions, writers must weigh options. To be fair, a writer should mention the full range of options, showing why one is superior to the others or might work well in combination with others.

It is unfair to suggest that there are only two alternatives when in fact there are more. Writers who set up a false choice between their preferred option and one that is clearly unsatisfactory are guilty of the *either . . . or* fallacy.

EITHER . . . OR FALLACY

Our current war against drugs has not worked. Either we should legalize drugs or we should turn the drug war over to our armed forces and let them fight it.

Clearly there are other options, such as increased funding for drug prevention and treatment.

Making assumptions

An assumption is a claim that is taken to be true — without the need of proof. Most arguments are based to some extent on assumptions, since writers rarely have the time and space to prove all of the conceivable claims on which their argument is based. For example, someone arguing about the best means of limiting population growth in developing countries might well assume that the goal of limiting population growth is worthwhile. For most audiences, there would be no need to articulate this assumption or to defend it.

There is a danger, however, in failing to spell out and prove a claim that is clearly controversial. Consider the following short argument, in which a key claim is missing.

ARGUMENT WITH MISSING CLAIM

Violent crime is increasing.

Therefore, we should vigorously enforce the death penalty.

The writer seems to be assuming that the death penalty deters violent criminals — and that most audiences will agree. Neither is a safe assumption.

When a missing claim is an assertion that few would agree with, we say that a writer is guilty of a *non sequitur* (Latin for "does not follow").

NON SEQUITUR

Leah loves good food; therefore, she will be an excellent chef.

Few people would agree with the missing claim — that lovers of good food always make excellent chefs.

Deducing conclusions (deductive reasoning)

When we deduce a conclusion, we — like Sherlock Holmes — put things together. We establish that a general principle is true, that a specific case is an example of that principle, and that therefore a particular conclusion about that case is a certainty. In real life, such absolute reasoning rarely happens. Approximations of it, however, sometimes occur.

Deductive reasoning can often be structured in a three-step argument called a *syllogism.* The three steps are the major premise, the minor premise, and the conclusion.

1. Anything that increases radiation in the environment is dangerous to public health. (Major premise)
2. Nuclear reactors increase radiation in the environment. (Minor premise)
3. Therefore, nuclear reactors are dangerous to public health. (Conclusion)

The major premise is a generalization. The minor premise is a specific case. The conclusion follows from applying the generalization to the specific case.

Deductive arguments break down if one of the premises is not true or if the conclusion does not logically follow from the premises. In the following short argument, the major premise is very likely untrue.

UNTRUE PREMISE

The police do not give speeding tickets to people driving less than five miles per hour over the limit. Sam is driving fifty-nine miles per hour in a fifty-five-mile-per-hour zone. Therefore, the police will not give Sam a speeding ticket.

The conclusion is true only if the premises are true. If the police sometimes give tickets for less than five-mile-per-hour violations, Sam cannot safely conclude that he will avoid a ticket.

In the following argument, both premises might be true, but the conclusion does not follow logically from them.

CONCLUSION DOES NOT FOLLOW

> All members of our club ran in this year's Boston Marathon. Jay ran in this year's Boston Marathon. Therefore, Jay is a member of our club.

The fact that Jay ran the marathon is no guarantee that he is a member of the club. Presumably, many runners are nonmembers.

Assuming that both premises are true, the following argument holds up.

CONCLUSION FOLLOWS

> All members of our club ran in this year's Boston Marathon. Jay is a member of our club. Therefore, Jay ran in this year's Boston Marathon.

48b Distinguish between legitimate and unfair emotional appeals.

There is nothing wrong with appealing to readers' emotions. After all, many issues worth arguing about have an emotional as well as a logical dimension. Even the Greek logician Aristotle lists *pathos* (emotion) as a legitimate argumentative tactic. For example, in an essay criticizing big-box stores, writer Betsy Taylor has a good reason for tugging at readers' emotions: Her subject is the decline of city and town life. In her conclusion, Taylor appeals to readers' emotions by invoking their national pride.

LEGITIMATE EMOTIONAL APPEAL

> Is it anti-American to be against having a retail giant set up shop in one's community? Some people would say so. On the other hand, if you board up Main Street, what's left of America?

As we all know, however, emotional appeals are frequently misused. Many of the arguments we see in the media, for instance, strive to win our sympathy rather than our intelligent agreement. A TV commercial suggesting that you will be thin and sexy if you drink a certain diet beverage is making a pitch to emotions, as is a political speech that recommends electing a candidate because he is a devoted husband and father who serves as a volunteer firefighter.

The following passage illustrates several types of unfair emotional appeals.

UNFAIR EMOTIONAL APPEALS

This progressive proposal to build a ski resort in the state park has been carefully researched by Western Trust, the largest bank in the state; furthermore, it is favored by a majority of the local merchants. The only opposition comes from narrow-minded, do-gooder environmentalists who care more about trees than they do about people; one of their leaders was actually arrested for disturbing the peace several years ago.

Words with strong positive or negative connotations, such as *progressive* and *do-gooder,* are examples of *biased language.* Attacking the persons who hold a belief (environmentalists) rather than refuting their argument is called *ad hominem*, a Latin term meaning "to the man." Associating a prestigious name (Western Trust) with the writer's side is called *transfer.* Claiming that an idea should be accepted because a large number of people are in favor (the majority of merchants) is called the *bandwagon appeal.* Bringing in irrelevant issues (the arrest) is a *red herring,* named after a trick used in fox hunts to mislead the dogs by dragging a smelly fish across the trail.

48c Judge how fairly a writer handles opposing views.

The way in which a writer deals with opposing views is telling. Some writers address the arguments of the opposition fairly, conceding points when necessary and countering others, all in a civil spirit. Other writers will do almost anything to win an argument: either ignoring opposing views altogether or misrepresenting such views and attacking their proponents.

In your own writing, you build credibility by addressing opposing arguments fairly. (See also 47f.) In your reading, you can assess the credibility of your sources by looking at how they deal with views not in agreement with their own.

Describing the views of others

Writers and politicians often deliberately misrepresent the views of others. One way they do this is by setting up a "straw man," a character so weak that he is easily knocked down. The *straw man* fallacy consists of an oversimplification or outright distortion of opposing views. For example, in a California debate over attempts to control the mountain lion population, pro-lion groups characterized their opponents as trophy hunters bent on shooting harmless lions and sticking them on the walls of their dens. In truth, such hunters were only one faction of those who saw a need to control the lion population.

In response to the District of Columbia's request for voting representation, some politicians have set up a straw man, as shown in the following example.

STRAW MAN FALLACY

Washington, DC, residents are lobbying for statehood. Giving a city such as the District of Columbia the status of a state would be unfair.

The straw man wants statehood. In fact, most District citizens are lobbying for voting representation in any form, not necessarily through statehood.

Quoting opposing views

Writers often quote the words of writers who hold opposing views. In general, this is a good idea, for it assures some level of fairness and accuracy. At times, though, both the fairness and accuracy are an illusion.

A source may be misrepresented when it is quoted out of context. All quotations are to some extent taken out of context, but a fair writer will explain the context to readers. To select a provocative sentence from a source and to ignore the more moderate sentences surrounding it is both unfair and misleading. Sometimes a writer deliberately distorts a source through the device of ellipsis dots. Ellipsis dots tell readers that words have been omitted from the original source. When those words are crucial to an author's meaning, omitting them is obviously unfair. (See also 39d.)

ORIGINAL SOURCE

Johnson's *History of the American West* is riddled with inaccuracies and astonishing in its blatantly racist description of the Indian wars.   — B. R., reviewer

MISLEADING QUOTATION

According to B. R., Johnson's *History of the American West* is "astonishing in its . . . description of the Indian wars."

EXERCISE 48–1   Explain what is illogical in the following brief arguments. It may be helpful to identify the logical fallacy or fallacies by name. Answers to lettered sentences appear in the back of the book.

a. My roommate, who is an engineering major, is taking a course called Structures of Tall Buildings. All engineers have to know how to design tall buildings.

b. If you're old enough to vote, you're old enough to drink. Therefore, the drinking age should be lowered to eighteen.

c. Cable stations that rely on nauseating reality shows, annoying infomercials for useless products, idiotic talk shows, and second-rate movies should have their licenses pulled.

d. Most young people can't afford to buy a house in Silicon Valley because they spend too much money on new clothes and computer games.

e. If you're not part of the solution, you're part of the problem.

1. Whenever I wash my car, it rains. I have discovered a way to end all droughts — get all the people to wash their cars.

2. Either learn how to build a Web site or you won't be able to get a decent job after college.

3. College professors tend to be sarcastic. Three of my five professors this semester make sarcastic remarks.

4. Although Ms. Bell's book on Joe DiMaggio was well researched, I doubt that an Australian historian can contribute much to our knowledge of an American baseball player.

5. Slacker co-workers and crazy, big-mouthed clients make our spineless managers impose ridiculous workloads on us hardworking, conscientious employees.

6. If professional sports teams didn't pay athletes such high salaries, we wouldn't have so many kids breaking their legs at hockey and basketball camps.

7. Ninety percent of the students oppose a tuition increase; therefore, the board of trustees should not pass the proposed increase.

8. If more people would take a long, close look at businesses like Microsoft and Amazon, they could reorganize their family lives to run successfully.

9. A mandatory ten-cent deposit on bottles and cans will eliminate litter because everyone I know will return the containers for the money rather than throw them away.

10. Researching what voters think during an election campaign is useless when most citizens don't vote anyway.

Research

College research assignments ask you to pose a question worth exploring, to read widely in search of possible answers, to interpret what you read, to draw reasoned conclusions, and to support those conclusions with valid and well-documented evidence.

The process takes time: time for researching and time for drafting, revising, and documenting the paper in the appropriate style (see 55 and 60). Before beginning a research project, set a realistic schedule of deadlines. One student created a calendar to map out her tasks for a research paper assigned on October 3 and due October 31.

SAMPLE CALENDAR FOR A RESEARCH ASSIGNMENT

2	3	4	5	6	7	8
	Receive assignment.	Pose questions worth exploring.	Talk with a librarian; plan a search strategy.		Settle on a topic. Locate sources.	
9	**10**	**11**	**12**	**13**	**14**	**15**
		Read and take notes.		Draft a tentative thesis and an outline.	Draft the paper.	
16	**17**	**18**	**19**	**20**	**21**	**22**
	Draft the paper.		Visit the writing center to get help with ideas for revision.	Do further research if necessary.		
23	**24**	**25**	**26**	**27**	**28**	**29**
Revise the paper.					Prepare a list of works cited.	
30	**31**					
Proofread the final draft.	**Final draft due.**					

49

Conducting research

Throughout this section, you will encounter examples related to three sample research papers:

- A paper on the dangers of Internet surveillance in the workplace, written by a student in an English composition class (see pp. 467–75). The student, Anna Orlov, uses the MLA (Modern Language Association) style of documentation.

- A paper on the limitations of medications to treat childhood obesity, written by a student in a psychology class (see pp. 515–28). The student, Luisa Mirano, uses the APA (American Psychological Association) style of documentation.

- A paper on the extent to which Civil War general Nathan Bedford Forrest can be held responsible for the Fort Pillow massacre, written by a student in a history class. The student, Ned Bishop, uses the *Chicago Manual of Style* documentation system. Bishop's paper and guidelines for *Chicago*-style documentation appear on the *Rules for Writers* Web site <dianahacker.com/rules>.

49a Pose possible questions worth exploring.

Working within the guidelines of your assignment, pose a few questions that seem worth researching. Here, for example, are some preliminary questions jotted down by students enrolled in a variety of classes in different disciplines.

- Should the FCC broaden its definition of indecent programming to include violence?

- Which geological formations are the safest repositories for nuclear waste?

- What was Marcus Garvey's contribution to the fight for racial equality?

- How can governments and zoos help preserve Asia's endangered snow leopard?

- Why was amateur archaeologist Heinrich Schliemann such a controversial figure in his own time?

As you formulate possible questions, make sure that they are appropriate lines of inquiry for a research paper. Choose questions that are narrow (not too broad), challenging (not too bland), and grounded (not too speculative).

Choosing a narrow question

If your initial question is too broad, given the length of the paper you plan to write, look for ways to restrict your focus. Here, for example, is how two students narrowed their initial questions.

> **TOO BROAD**
>
> What are the hazards of fad diets?
>
> Is the United States seriously addressing the problem of prisoner abuse?
>
> **NARROWER**
>
> What are the hazards of low-carbohydrate diets?
>
> To what extent has the US military addressed the problem of prisoner abuse since the Abu Ghraib discoveries?

Choosing a challenging question

Your research paper will be more interesting to both you and your audience if you base it on an intellectually challenging line of inquiry. Avoid bland questions that fail to provoke thought or engage readers in a debate.

> **TOO BLAND**
>
> What is obsessive-compulsive disorder?
>
> How does DNA testing work?
>
> **CHALLENGING**
>
> What treatments for obsessive-compulsive disorder show the most promise?
>
> How reliable is DNA testing?

You may well need to address a bland question in the course of answering a more challenging one. For example, if you were writing about promising treatments for obsessive-compulsive disorder, you would no doubt answer the question "What is obsessive-compulsive disorder?" at some point in your paper. It would be a mistake, however, to use the bland question as the focus for the whole paper.

Choosing a grounded question

Finally, you will want to make sure that your research question is grounded, not too speculative. Although speculative questions — such as those that address philosophical, ethical, or religious issues — are worth asking and may receive some attention in a research paper, they are inappropriate central questions. The central argument of a research paper should be grounded in facts; it should not be based entirely on beliefs.

TOO SPECULATIVE

Is it wrong to share music files on the Internet?

Do medical scientists have the right to experiment on animals?

GROUNDED

How has Internet file sharing affected the earning potential of musicians?

How have technical breakthroughs made medical experiments on animals increasingly unnecessary?

ON THE WEB > **dianahacker.com/rules**
Research exercises > Researching > E-ex 49–1

49b Map out a search strategy.

A search strategy is a systematic plan for tracking down sources. To create a search strategy appropriate for your research question, consult a reference librarian and take a look at your library's Web site, which will give you an overview of available resources.

Getting started

Reference librarians are information specialists who can save you time by steering you toward relevant and reliable sources. With the help of an expert, you can make the best use of electronic databases, Web search engines, and other reference tools.

When you ask a reference librarian for help, be prepared to answer a number of questions:

- What is your assignment?
- In which academic discipline are you writing?
- What is your tentative research question?
- How long will the paper be?
- How much time can you spend on the project?

It's a good idea to bring a copy of the assignment with you.

In addition to speaking with a reference librarian, take some time to explore your library's Web site (see the bottom of this page). You will typically find links to the library's catalog and to a variety of databases and electronic sources that you can access from any networked computer. In addition, you may find resources listed by subject, research guides, information about interlibrary loans, and links to Web sites selected by librarians for their quality. What's more, many libraries offer online reference assistance to help you locate information and refine your search strategy.

LIBRARY HOME PAGE

Choosing an appropriate search strategy

No single search strategy works for every topic. For some topics, it may be appropriate to search for information in newspapers, magazines, and Web sites. For others, the best sources might be found in scholarly journals and books and specialized reference works. Still other topics might be enhanced by field research — interviews, surveys, or direct observation.

With the help of a reference librarian, each of the students mentioned on page 383 constructed a search strategy appropriate for his or her research question.

ANNA ORLOV   Anna Orlov's topic, the dangers of Internet surveillance in the workplace, was so current that books were an unlikely source. To find up-to-date information on her topic, Orlov decided to

- search a general database for articles in magazines, newspapers, and journals
- use Web search engines, such as *Google*, to locate relevant sites, online articles, and government publications

LUISA MIRANO   Luisa Mirano's topic, the limitations of medications for childhood obesity, has recently become the subject of psychological studies as well as articles in the popular press (newspapers and magazines aimed at the general public). Thinking that both popular and scholarly works would be appropriate, Mirano decided to

- locate books through the library's online catalog
- check a specialized encyclopedia, *Encyclopedia of Psychology*
- search a general database for popular articles
- search a specialized database, *PsycINFO,* for scholarly articles

NED BISHOP   Ned Bishop's topic, the role played by Nathan Bedford Forrest in the Fort Pillow massacre, is an issue that has been investigated and debated by professional historians. Given the nature of his historical topic, Ned Bishop decided to

- locate books through the library's online catalog
- locate scholarly articles by searching a specialized database, *America: History and Life*
- locate newspaper articles from 1864 by using a print index
- search the Web for other historical primary sources

49c To locate articles, search a database or consult a print index.

Libraries subscribe to a variety of electronic databases (sometimes called *periodical databases*) that give students access to articles and other materials without charge. Because many databases are limited to recent works, you may need to consult a print index as well.

What databases offer

Your library has access to databases that can lead you to articles in periodicals such as newspapers, magazines, and scholarly or technical journals. Some databases cover several subjects; others cover one subject in depth. Though each library is unique, your library might subscribe to some of the following databases and collections of databases.

GENERAL DATABASES

EBSCOhost. A portal to more than one hundred databases that include periodical articles, government documents, pamphlets, and other types of documents.

InfoTrac. A collection of databases, some of which index periodical articles.

LexisNexis. A set of databases that are particularly strong in coverage of news, business, legal, and political topics.

ProQuest. A database of periodical articles.

SUBJECT-SPECIFIC DATABASES

ERIC. An education database.

PubMed. A database offering millions of abstracts of medical research studies.

MLA Bibliography. A database of literary criticism.

PsycINFO. A comprehensive database of psychology research.

Many databases include the full text of at least some articles; others list only citations or citations with short summaries called *abstracts*. In the case of full-text articles, you may have the option to print an article, save it to a disk, or e-mail it to yourself.

Refining keyword searches in databases and search engines

Although command terms and characters vary among electronic databases and Web search engines, some of the most commonly used functions are listed here.

- Use quotation marks around words that are part of a phrase: "Broadway musicals".

- Use AND to connect words that must appear in a document: Ireland AND peace. In some search engines — *Google,* for example — *and* is assumed, so typing it is unnecessary. Other search engines require a plus sign instead: Ireland +peace.

- Use NOT in front of words that must not appear in a document: Titanic NOT movie. Some search engines require a minus sign (hyphen) instead: Titanic -movie.

- Use OR if only one of the terms must appear in a document: "mountain lion" OR cougar.

- Use an asterisk as a substitute for letters that might vary: "marine biolog*" (to find *marine biology* or *marine biologist,* for example).

- Use parentheses to group a search expression and combine it with another: (cigarettes OR tobacco OR smok*) AND lawsuits.

NOTE: Many search engines and databases offer an advanced search option that makes it easy to refine your search.

How to search a database

To find articles on your topic in a database, start with a keyword search. If the first keyword you try results in no matches, experiment with synonyms or ask a librarian for suggestions. For example, if you're searching for sources on a topic related to education, you might also want to try the terms *teaching, learning, pedagogy,* and *curriculum.* If your keyword search results in too many matches, narrow it by using one of the strategies in the chart on this page.

For her paper on Internet surveillance in the workplace, Anna Orlov conducted a keyword search in a general periodical database. She typed in *employee* and *privacy* and *"internet use"* and *surveillance;* her search brought up nineteen possible articles, some of which looked promising.

When to use a print index

If you want to search for articles published before the 1980s, you may need to turn to a print index. For example, Ned Bishop consulted the *New York Times Index* to locate newspaper articles written in April 1864, just after the battle at Fort Pillow. To find older magazine articles, consult the *Readers' Guide to Periodical Literature* or *Poole's Index to Periodical Literature* or ask a librarian for help.

49d To locate books, consult the library's catalog.

The books your library owns are listed in its computer catalog, along with other resources such as videos. You can search the catalog by author, title, or topic keywords.

Don't be surprised if your first search calls up too few or too many results. If you have too few results, try different keywords or search for books on broader topics. If a search gives you too many results, use the strategies in the chart on page 389 or try an advanced search tool to combine concepts and limit your results. If those strategies don't work, ask a librarian for suggestions.

When Luisa Mirano, whose topic was childhood obesity, entered the term *obesity* into the computer catalog, she was faced with an unmanageable number of hits. She narrowed her search by adding two more specific terms to *obesity*: *child** (to include the terms *child*, *children*, and *childhood*) and *treatment*. When she still got too many results, she limited the first two terms to subject searches to find books that had obesity in children as their primary subject (see screen 1). Screen 2 shows the complete record for one of the books she found. The call number, listed beside *Availability*, is the book's address on the library shelf. (When you're retrieving a book from the shelf, scan other books in the area since they are likely to be on the same topic.)

LIBRARIAN'S TIP: The record for a book lists related subject headings. These headings are a good way to locate other books on your subject. For example, the record in screen 2 lists the terms *obesity in children* and *obesity in adolescence* as related subject headings. By clicking on these new terms, Mirano found a few more books on her subject.

LIBRARY CATALOG SCREEN 1: ADVANCED SEARCH

Search:	Enter word or phrase:
All Subject Keywords	obesity
Combine (AND) with:	
All Subject Keywords	child*
Combine (AND) with:	
General Keywords	treatment
	Submit Clear

MNCAT Twin Cities - Advanced Search - Microsoft Internet Explorer

File Edit View Favorites Tools Help

MNCAT Twin Cities – Advanced Search   [Search Tips]

For Boolean OR or NOT searches, enter your search statement in a single box
(e.g. horse? or equine) or use "Command Search."

Search: Enter word or phrase:
All Subject Keywords   obesity
Combine (AND) with:
All Subject Keywords   child*
Combine (AND) with:
General Keywords   treatment

Limit search to:
Year: All Years
Language: All Languages
Format: Books
Location: All Libraries

LIBRARY CATALOG SCREEN 2: COMPLETE RECORD FOR A BOOK

MNCAT Twin Cities - Full View of Record - Microsoft Internet Explorer

File Edit View Favorites Tools Help

MNCAT Twin Cities – Full View of Record

Availability	UM MORRIS Briggs Library RA777 .B59 2001 Circulating
Availability	TC Bio-Medical Library WS130 B668 2001 Regular Loan

Record 2 out of 7

Title   Body image, eating disorders, and obesity in youth : assessment, prevention, and treatment / edited by J. Kevin Thompson and Linda Smolak.
Published   Washington, D.C. : American Psychological Association, c2001.
Description   xiii, 403 p. : ill. ; 27 cm.

Availability   UM MORRIS Briggs Library RA777 .B59 2001 Circulating
Availability   TC Bio-Medical Library WS130 B668 2001 Regular Loan

Contents   Ch. 1. Early experience with food and eating: implications for the development of eating disorders -- Ch. 2. Body image in children -- Ch. 3. Obesity, body image, and eating disorders in ethnically diverse children and adolescents -- Ch. 4. Risk and protective factors in the development of eating disorders -- Ch. 5. Family functioning, body image, and eating disturbances -- Ch. 6. Relationship of sexual abuse to body image and eating problems -- Ch. 7. Assessment of physical status of children and adolescents with eating disorders and obesity -- Ch. 8. Assessment of body image disturbance in children and adolescents -- Ch. 9. Assessment of eating disturbance in children and adolescents with eating disorders and obesity -- Ch. 10. Primary prevention of body image disturbances and disordered eating in childhood and early adolescence -- Ch. 11. Obesity prevention for children and adolescents -- Ch. 12. Treatment of eating disorders in children and adolescents -- Ch. 13. Behavioral treatment of childhood and adolescent obesity: current status, challenges, and future directions -- Ch. 14. Plastic surgery in children and adolescents.

Note   Includes bibliographical references and indexes.
Subject LC   Body image in children.
    Body image in adolescence.
    Obesity in children.
    Eating disorders in children.
    Eating disorders in adolescence.
    Obesity in adolescence.
    Child mental health.
    Adolescent -- Mental health.
Subject Medical   Body image -- adolescent
    Body image -- child
    Eating Disorders -- adolescent
    Eating Disorders -- child
    Obesity -- Adolescence.
    Obesity -- Child.

Contributor   Thompson, J. Kevin.
    Smolak, Linda, 1951-
ISBN   1557987580

Obesity in children.
Eating disorders in children.
Eating disorders in adolescence.
Obesity in adolescence.

49e To locate a wide variety of sources, turn to the Web.

For some (but not all) topics, the Web is an excellent resource. For example, government agencies post information on the Web, and the sites of many organizations are filled with information about the issues they cover. Museums and libraries often post digital versions of primary sources, such as photographs, political speeches, and classic literary texts.

Although the Web can be a rich source of information, some of which can't be found anywhere else, it lacks quality control. Anyone can publish on the Web, so you'll need to evaluate online sources with special care (see p. 403).

This section describes the following Web resources: search engines, directories, digital archives, government and news sites, and discussion forums.

ON THE WEB > dianahacker.com/rules
Additional resources > Links Library > Conducting research

Search engines

Search engines take your search terms and seek matches among millions of Web pages. Some search engines go into more depth than others, but none can search the entire Web.

For information about search engines, visit *Search Engine Showdown* at < http://www.searchengineshowdown.com >. This site classifies search engines, evaluates them, and provides updates on new search features. Following are some popular search engines:

Ask.com <http://search.ask.com>

Google <http://www.google.com>

MSN Search <http://search.msn.com>

Yahoo! <http://www.yahoo.com>

For her paper on Internet surveillance in the workplace, Anna Orlov had difficulty restricting the number of hits. When she typed the words *internet, surveillance, workplace,* and *privacy* into a search engine, she got more than 80,000 matches. To narrow her search, Orlov tried typing in the phrases *"internet*

SEARCH ENGINE SCREEN: RESULTS OF AN ADVANCED SEARCH

Web Results 1 -5 of about 9 over the past 3 months for "Internet surveillance" employee "workplace privacy" site:.org 0.44 seconds)

Tip: Try removing quotes from your search to get more results.

EPIC/PI - Privacy & Human Rights 2000
Now the supervision of **employee**'s performance, behavior and... [89]Information and
Privacy Commissioner/Ontario, **Workplace Privacy**: The Need for a..
www.privacyinternational.org/survey/phr2000/threats.html - 131k Cached - Similar pages

Privacy and Human Rights 2003: Threats to Privacy
Other issues that raise **workplace privacy** concerns are employer requirements that
employees complete medical tests, questionnaires, and polygraph tests..
www.privacyinternational.org/survey/phr2003/threats.htm - 279k Cached - Similar pages
[More results from www.privacyinternational.org]

[PDF] Monitoring **Employee** E-Mail And Internet Usage: Avoiding The..
File Format: PDF/Adobe Acrobat - View as HTML
Internet surveillance by employers in the American workplace. At present, US **employees**
in the private workplace have no constitutional, common law or statu
lsr.nellco.org/cgi/viewcontent.cgi?article=1006&context=suffolk/ip - Similar pages

Previous EPIC Top News
The agencies plan to use RFID to track **employees**' movements and in ID cards... For more
information on **workplace privacy**, see the EPIC **Workplace Privacy**...
www.epic.org/news/2005.html - 163k Cached - Similar pages

surveillance", employee, and "workplace privacy". The result was
422 matches, still too many, so Orlov clicked on Advanced
Search and restricted her search to sites with URLs ending in
.org and to those updated in the last three months. (See the
screen at the top of this page.)

Directories

Unlike search engines, which hunt for Web pages automatically, directories are put together by information specialists
who choose reputable sites and arrange them by topic: education, health, politics, and so on.

Some directories are more selective and therefore more
useful for scholarly research than the directories that typically
accompany a search engine. For example, the directory for the
Internet Scout Project was created for a research audience; it
includes annotations that are both descriptive and evaluative.
The following directories are especially useful for scholarly
research:

Internet Scout Project <http://scout.wisc.edu/Archives>

Librarian's Internet Index <http://lii.org>

Open Directory Project <http://dmoz.org>

WWW Virtual Library <http://vlib.org>

Digital archives

Archives may contain the texts of poems, books, speeches, political cartoons, and historically significant documents such as the Declaration of Independence and the Emancipation Proclamation. The materials in these sites are usually limited to official documents and older works because of copyright laws. The following online archives are impressive collections:

American Memory <http://memory.loc.gov>

Archival Research Catalog <http://archives.gov/research/arc>

Avalon Project <http://yale.edu/lawweb/avalon/avalon.htm>

Electronic Text Center <http://etext.lib.virginia.edu>

Eurodocs <http://eudocs.lib.byu.edu>

Internet History Sourcebooks <http://www.fordham.edu/halsall>

Online Books Page <http://onlinebooks.library.upenn.edu>

Government and news sites

For current topics, both government and news sites can prove useful. Many government agencies at every level provide online information. Government-maintained sites include resources such as legal texts, facts and statistics, government reports, and searchable reference databases. Here are just a few government sites:

Census Bureau <http://www.census.gov>

Fedstats <http://www.fedstats.gov>

FirstGov <http://www.usa.gov>

GPO Access <http://www.gpoaccess.gov>

United Nations <http://www.un.org>

Many news organizations offer up-to-date information on the Web. These online services often allow nonsubscribers to read current stories for free. Some allow users to log on as guests and search archives without cost, but to read actual articles users typically must pay a fee. Check with your library to see if it subscribes to a news archive that you can access at no charge. The following are some free news sites:

Google News <http://news.google.com>

Kidon Media-Link <http://www.kidon.com/media-link>

NewsLink <http://newslink.org>

Discussion forums

The Web offers various ways of communicating with experts and others who have an interest in your topic. You might join an online mailing list, for example, to send and receive e-mail messages relevant to your topic. Or you may wish to search a newsgroup's postings. Newsgroups resemble bulletin boards on which messages are posted and connected through "threads" as others respond. In addition, you might log on to real-time discussion forums. To find mailing lists, newsgroups, and forums, try one of these sites:

CataList <http://www.lsoft.com/catalist.html>

Google Groups <http://groups.google.com>

Tile.Net <http://tile.net/lists>

NOTE: Be aware that many of the people you contact in discussion forums will not be experts on your topic. Although you are more likely to find serious and worthwhile commentary in moderated mailing lists and scholarly discussion forums than in more free-wheeling newsgroups, it is difficult to guarantee the credibility of anyone you meet online.

49f Use other search tools.

In addition to articles, books, and Web sources, you may want to consult references such as encyclopedias and almanacs. Bibliographies (lists of works written on a topic) and citations in scholarly works can lead you to additional sources.

Reference works

The reference section of the library holds both general and specialized encyclopedias, dictionaries, almanacs, atlases, and biographical references, some available in electronic format. Such works often serve as a good overview of a subject and include references to the most significant works on a topic. Check with a reference librarian to see which works are most appropriate for your project.

GENERAL REFERENCE WORKS   General reference works are good places to check facts and get basic information. Here are a few frequently used general references:

> *American National Biography*
>
> *National Geographic Atlas of the World*
>
> *The New Encyclopaedia Britannica*
>
> *The Oxford English Dictionary*
>
> *Statistical Abstract of the United States*
>
> *World Almanac and Book of Facts*

Although general encyclopedias are often a good place to find background about your topic, you should rarely use them in your final paper. Most instructors expect you to rely on more specialized sources.

SPECIALIZED REFERENCE WORKS   Specialized reference works often go into a topic in depth, sometimes in the form of articles written by leading authorities. Many specialized works are available, including these:

> *Contemporary Authors*
>
> *Encyclopedia of Applied Ethics*
>
> *Encyclopedia of Crime and Justice*
>
> *Encyclopedia of Psychology*
>
> *McGraw-Hill Encyclopedia of Science and Technology*

ON THE WEB > **dianahacker.com/rules**
Research and Documentation Online > Finding sources

Bibliographies and scholarly citations

Bibliographies are lists of works written on a particular topic. They include enough information about each work (author's name, title, publication data) so that you can locate the book or article. In some cases, bibliographies are annotated: They contain abstracts giving a brief overview of each work's contents.

In addition to book-length bibliographies, scholarly books and articles list the works the author has cited, usually at the end. These lists are useful shortcuts. For example, most of the scholarly articles Luisa Mirano consulted contained citations to related research studies; through these citations, she quickly located additional relevant sources on her topic, treatments for childhood obesity.

49g Conduct field research, if appropriate.

Writing projects may be enhanced by, and sometimes focused on, your own field research. For a composition class, for example, you might want to interview a local politician about some aspect of a current issue, such as the use of cell phones while driving. For a sociology class, you might decide to conduct a survey regarding campus trends in community service. At work, you might need to learn how food industry executives have responded to reports that their products are contributing to health problems.

50

Evaluating sources

With electronic search tools, you can often locate dozens or even hundreds of potential sources for your topic — far more than you will have time to read. Your challenge will be to determine what kinds of sources you need and to zero in on a reasonable number of quality sources, those truly worthy of your time and attention.

Later, once you have decided on some sources worth consulting, your challenge will be to read them with an open mind and a critical eye.

50a Determine how a source will contribute to your writing.

Before you even begin to research your topic, think about how the sources you encounter could help you make your argument. How you plan to use a source will affect how you will evaluate it. Not every source must directly support your thesis. Sources can have various functions in a paper. They can

- provide background information or context for your topic
- explain terms or concepts that your readers might not understand
- provide evidence for your argument
- lend authority to your argument
- offer counterevidence and alternative interpretations to your argument

For examples of how student writers use sources for a variety of purposes, see 52c and 57c.

50b Select sources worth your time and attention.

Sections 49c and 49d show how to refine your searches in the library's book catalog, in databases, and in search engines. This section explains how to scan through the results for the most promising sources and how to preview them — without actually reading them — to see whether they are likely to live up to your expectations and meet your needs.

Scanning search results

You will need to use somewhat different strategies when scanning search results from a book catalog, a database, and a Web search engine.

BOOK CATALOGS The library's book catalog usually gives you a fairly short list of hits. A book's title and date of publication will often be your first clues as to whether the book is worth consulting. If a title looks interesting, you can click on it for further information: the book's subject matter and its length, for example.

DATABASES   Most databases, such as *ProQuest* and *LexisNexis*, list at least the following information, which can help you decide if a source is relevant, current, scholarly enough (see the chart on p. 401), and a suitable length for your purposes.

Title and brief description (How relevant?)

Date (How current?)

Name of periodical (How scholarly?)

Length (How extensive in coverage?)

At the bottom of this page are just a few of the hits Ned Bishop came up with when he consulted a general database for articles on the Fort Pillow massacre, using the search term *Fort Pillow*.

By scanning the titles, Bishop saw that only one contained the words *Fort Pillow*. This title and the name of the periodical, *Journal of American History*, suggested that the source was scholarly. The 1989 publication date was not a problem, since currency is not necessarily a key issue for historical topics. The article's length (eight pages) is given in parentheses at the end of the citation. While the article may seem short, the topic — a statistical note — is narrow enough to ensure adequate depth of coverage. Bishop decided the article was worth consulting.

Bishop chose not to consult the other sources. The first is a brief article in a popular magazine, the second is a movie review, and the third surveys a topic that is far too broad, "black soldiers in the Civil War."

WEB SEARCH ENGINES   Anyone can publish on the Web, and unreliable sites often masquerade as legitimate sources of information. As you scan through search results, look for the

---

☐ **Black, blue and gray: the other Civil War; African-American soldiers, sailors and spies were the unsung heroes.** *Ebony* Feb 1991 v46 n4 p96(6)
Mark   View text and retrieval choices

☐ **The Civil War.** (movie reviews) Lewis Cole. *The Nation* Dec 3, 1990 v251 n19 p694(5)
Mark   View text and retrieval choices

☐ **The hard fight was getting into the fight at all.** (black soldiers in the Civil War) Jack Fincher. *Smithsonian* Oct 1990 v21 n7 p46(13)
Mark   View text and retrieval choices

☑ **The Fort Pillow massacre: a statistical note.** John Cimprich, Robert C. Mainfort Jr.. *Journal of American History* Dec 1989 v76 n3 p830(8)
Mark   View extended citation and retrieval choices

following clues about the probable relevance, currency, and reliability of a site — but be aware that the clues are by no means foolproof.

Title, keywords, and lead-in text (How relevant?)

A date (How current?)

An indication of the site's sponsor or purpose (How reliable?)

The URL, especially the domain name: .com, .edu, .gov, or .org (How relevant? How reliable?)

At the bottom of this page are a few of the results that Luisa Mirano retrieved after typing the keywords *childhood obesity* into a search engine; she limited her search to works with those words in the title.

Mirano found the first site, sponsored by a research-based organization, promising enough to explore for her paper. The second and fourth sites held less promise, because they seemed to offer popular rather than scholarly information. In addition, the *KidSource* site was populated by advertisements. Mirano rejected the third source not because of its reliability — in fact, research from the National Institutes of Health was what she was hoping to locate — but because a quick skim of its contents revealed that the information was too general for her purposes.

American **Obesity** Association - **Childhood Obesity**
Childhood Obesity. **Obesity** in **children** ... Note: The term "**childhood obesity**" may refer to both **children** and adolescents. In general, we ...
www.**obesity**.org/subs/**childhood**/ - 17k - Jan 8, 2005 - <u>Cached</u> - <u>Similar pages</u>

Childhood Obesity
KS Logo, **Childhood Obesity**. advertisement. Source. ERIC Clearinghouse on Teaching and Teacher Education. Contents. ... Back to the Top Causes of **Childhood Obesity**. ...
www.kidsource.com/kidsource/content2/**obesity**.html - 18k - <u>Cached</u> - <u>Similar pages</u>

Childhood Obesity, June 2002 Word on Health - National Institutes ...
Childhood Obesity on the Rise, an article in the June 2002 edition of The NIH Word on Health - Consumer Information Based on Research from the National ...
www.nih.gov/news/WordonHealth/ jun2002/**childhoodobesity**.htm - 22k -
<u>Cached</u> - <u>Similar pages</u>

MayoClinic.com - **Childhood obesity**: Parenting advice
... **Childhood obesity**: Parenting advice By Mayo Clinic staff. ... Here are some other tips to help your **obese child** — and yourself: Be a positive role model. ...
www.mayoclinic.com/invoke.cfm?id=FL00058 - 42k - Jan 8, 2005 - <u>Cached</u> - <u>Similar pages</u>

Determining if a source is scholarly

For many college assignments, you will be asked to use scholarly sources. These are written by experts for a knowledgeable audience and usually go into more depth than books and articles written for a general audience. (Scholarly sources are sometimes called *refereed* or *peer-reviewed* because the work is evaluated by experts in the field before publication.) To determine if a source is scholarly, you should look for the following:

- Formal language and presentation
- Authors who are academics or scientists, not journalists
- Footnotes or a bibliography documenting the works cited in the source
- Original research and interpretation (rather than a summary of other people's work)
- Quotations from and analysis of primary sources (in humanities disciplines such as literature, history, and philosophy)
- A description of research methods or a review of related research (in the sciences and social sciences)

NOTE: In some databases, searches can be limited to refereed or peer-reviewed journals.

50c Read with an open mind and a critical eye.

As you begin reading the sources you have chosen, keep an open mind. Do not let your personal beliefs prevent you from listening to new ideas and opposing viewpoints. Your research question — not a snap judgment about the question — should guide your reading.

When you read critically, you are not necessarily judging an author's work harshly; you are simply examining its assumptions, assessing its evidence, and weighing its conclusions.

ACADEMIC ENGLISH When you research on the Web, it is easy to ignore views different from your own. Web pages that appeal to you will often link to other pages that support the same viewpoint. If your sources all seem to agree with you — and with one another — try to find sources with opposing views and evaluate them with an open mind.

Distinguishing between primary and secondary sources

As you begin assessing evidence in a source, determine whether you are reading a primary or a secondary source. Primary sources are original documents such as letters, diaries, legislative bills, laboratory studies, field research reports, and eyewitness accounts. Secondary sources are commentaries on primary sources — another source's opinions about or interpretation of a primary source. A primary source for Ned Bishop was Nathan Bedford Forrest's official report on the battle at Fort Pillow. Bishop also consulted a number of secondary sources, some of which relied heavily on primary sources such as letters.

Although a primary source is not necessarily more reliable than a secondary source, it has the advantage of being a firsthand account. Naturally, you can better evaluate what a secondary source says if you have first read any primary sources it discusses.

Being alert for signs of bias

Both in print and online, some sources are more objective than others. If you were exploring the conspiracy theories surrounding John F. Kennedy's assassination, for example, you wouldn't look to a supermarket tabloid, such as the *National Enquirer*, for answers. Even publications that are considered reputable can be editorially biased. For example, *USA Today*, *National Review*, and *Ms.* are all credible sources, but they are also likely to interpret events quite differently from one another. If you are uncertain about a periodical's special interests, consult *Magazines for Libraries*. To check for bias in a book, see *Book Review Digest*. A reference librarian can help you locate these resources.

Like publishers, some authors are more objective than others. If you have reason to believe that a writer is particularly biased, you will want to assess his or her arguments with special care. For a list of questions worth asking, see the chart on page 403.

Assessing the author's argument

In nearly all subjects worth writing about, there is some element of argument, so don't be surprised to encounter experts who disagree. When you find areas of disagreement, you will want to read each source's arguments with special care, testing them with your own critical intelligence. For a list of questions worth asking, see the chart on page 403.

Evaluating all sources

Checking for signs of bias

- Does the author or publisher have political leanings or religious views that could affect objectivity?
- Is the author or publisher associated with a special-interest group, such as Greenpeace or the National Rifle Association, that might see only one side of an issue?
- Are alternative views presented and addressed? How fairly does the author treat opposing views?
- Does the author's language show signs of bias?

Assessing an argument

- What is the author's central claim or thesis?
- How does the author support this claim — with relevant and sufficient evidence or with just a few anecdotes or emotional examples?
- Are statistics consistent with those you encounter in other sources? Have they been used fairly? Does the author explain where the statistics come from? (It is possible to "lie" with statistics by using them selectively or by omitting mathematical details.)
- Are any of the author's assumptions questionable?
- Does the author consider opposing arguments and refute them persuasively? (See 48c.)
- Does the author fall prey to any logical fallacies? (See 48a.)

50d Assess Web sources with special care.

Web sources can be deceptive. Sophisticated-looking sites can be full of dubious information, and the identities of those who created a site are often hidden, along with their motives for having created it. Even hate sites may be cleverly disguised to look legitimate. Sites with reliable information, however, can stand up to careful scrutiny. For a checklist on evaluating Web sources, see the chart on page 404.

In researching her topic on Internet surveillance and workplace privacy, Anna Orlov encountered sites that raised her suspicions. In particular, some sites were authored by surveillance software companies, which have an obvious interest in focusing on the benefits of such software to company management.

res

Evaluating Web sources

Authorship

- Does the Web site or document have an author? You may need to do some clicking and scrolling to find the author's name. If you have landed directly on an internal page of a site, for example, you may need to navigate to the home page or find an "about this site" link.

- If there is an author, can you tell whether he or she is knowledgeable and credible? When the author's qualifications aren't listed on the site itself, look for links to the author's home page, which may provide evidence of his or her interests and expertise.

Sponsorship

- Who, if anyone, sponsors the site? The sponsor of a site is often named and described on the home page.

- What does the URL tell you? The URL ending often specifies the type of group hosting the site: commercial (.com), educational (.edu), nonprofit (.org), governmental (.gov), military (.mil), or network (.net). URLs may also indicate a country of origin: .uk (United Kingdom) or .jp (Japan), for instance.

Purpose and audience

- Why was the site created: To argue a position? To sell a product? To inform readers?

- Who is the site's intended audience?

Currency

- How current is the site? Check for the date of publication or the latest update, often located at the bottom of the home page.

- How current are the site's links? If many of the links no longer work, the site may be too dated and unreliable.

TIP: If the authorship and the sponsorship of a site are both unclear, think twice about using the site for your research.

To discover a site's sponsor, you may have to truncate the URL. To find the sponsor of a Web article on responsible neighborhood development, you might need to shorten the full URL to its base URL.

FULL URL   <http://www.bankofamerica.com/environment/dex.cfm ?template=env_reports_speeches&context=smartgrowth>

BASE URL   <http://www.bankofamerica.com>

SPONSOR   Bank of America

51

Managing information; avoiding plagiarism

An effective researcher is a good record keeper. Whether you decide to keep records on paper or on your computer — or both — your challenge as a researcher will be to find systematic ways of managing information. More specifically, you will need methods for maintaining a working bibliography (see 51a), keeping track of source materials (see 51b), and taking notes without plagiarizing (stealing from) your sources (see 51c).

51a Maintain a working bibliography.

Keep a record of any sources you decide to consult. You will need this record, called a *working bibliography*, when you compile the list of sources that will appear at the end of your paper. (The format of this list depends on the documentation style you are using. For MLA style, see 55b; for APA style, see 60b). Your working bibliography will probably contain more sources than you will actually include in your list of works cited.

Most researchers print or save bibliographic information from the library's computer catalog, its periodical databases, and the Web. The information you need to collect is given in the chart on page 407. If you download a visual, you must gather the same information as for a print source.

For Web sources, some bibliographic information may not be available, but spend time looking for it before assuming that it doesn't exist. When information isn't available on the home page, you may have to drill into the site, following links to interior pages. Look especially for the author's name, the date of publication (or latest update), and the name of any sponsoring organization. Do not omit such information unless it is genuinely unavailable.

Once you have created a working bibliography, you can annotate it. Writing several brief sentences summarizing key points of a source will help you to identify the source's role in your paper. Also, clarifying the source's ideas at this stage will help you avoid plagiarizing them later.

ON THE WEB > dianahacker.com/rules
> Model papers > MLA annotated bibliography: Orlov
> APA annotated bibliography: Haddad

51b Keep track of source materials.

The best way to keep track of source materials is to photocopy them or print them out. Many database subscription services will allow you to e-mail citations or full copies of articles to yourself. Some researchers choose to save these and online sources on a computer or disk.

Working with photocopies, printouts, and electronic files — as opposed to relying on memory or hastily written notes — has several benefits. You save time spent in the library. You can highlight key passages, perhaps even color-coding them to reflect topics in your outline. You can annotate the source in the margins and get a head start on note taking. Finally, you reduce the chances of unintentional plagiarism, since you will be able to compare your use of a source in your paper with the actual source, not just with your notes (see 51c).

NOTE: It's especially important to keep print or electronic copies of Web sources, which may change or even become inaccessible. Make sure that your copy includes the site's URL and your date of access, information needed for your list of works cited.

51c As you take notes, avoid unintentional plagiarism.

When you take notes and jot down ideas, be very careful not to borrow language from your sources. Even if you half-copy the author's sentences — either by mixing the author's phrases with your own without using quotation marks or by plugging your synonyms into the author's sentence structure — you are committing plagiarism, a serious academic offense. (For examples of this kind of plagiarism, see 53 and 58.)

To prevent unintentional borrowing, resist the temptation to look at the source as you take notes — except when you are quoting. Keep the source close by so you can check for accuracy, but don't try to put ideas in your own words with the

Information for a working bibliography

For a book

- All authors; any editors or translators
- Title and subtitle
- Edition (if not the first)
- Publication information: city, publisher, and date

For a periodical article

- All authors of the article
- Title and subtitle of the article
- Title of the magazine, journal, or newspaper
- Date; volume, issue, and page numbers, if available

For a periodical article retrieved from a database (in addition to preceding information)

- Name of the database and an item number, if available
- Name of the subscription service
- URL of the subscription service (for an online database)
- Digital object identifier (DOI), if there is one
- Date you retrieved the source

NOTE: Use particular care when printing or saving articles in PDF files. These may not include some of the elements you need to cite the electronic source properly.

For a Web source (including visuals)

- All authors, editors, or creators of the source
- Editor or compiler of the Web site, if there is one
- Title and subtitle of the source and title of the longer work, if applicable
- Title of the site, if available
- Publication information for the source, if available
- Page or paragraph numbers, if any
- Date of online publication (or latest update), if available
- Sponsor of the site
- Date you accessed the source
- The site's URL

NOTE: For the exact bibliographic format to use in the final paper, see 55b and 60b.

source's sentences in front of you. When you need to quote the exact words of a source, make sure you copy the words precisely and put quotation marks around them. (For strategies for avoiding Internet plagiarism, see p. 410.)

ACADEMIC ENGLISH Even when you are in the early stages of note taking, it is important to keep in mind that, in the United States, written texts are considered to be an author's property. (This "property" isn't a physical object, so it is often referred to as *intellectual property*.) The author (or publisher) owns the language as well as any original ideas contained in the writing, whether the source is published in print or electronic form. When you use another author's property in your own writing, you are required to follow certain conventions or risk committing the ethical and legal offense known as *plagiarism*.

There are three kinds of note taking: summarizing, paraphrasing, and quoting. Be sure to include exact page references for all three types of notes, since you will need the page numbers later if you use the information in your paper.

Summarizing without plagiarizing

A summary condenses information, perhaps reducing a chapter to a short paragraph or a paragraph to a single sentence. A summary should be written in your own words; if you use phrases from the source, put them in quotation marks.

ORIGINAL SOURCE

In some respects, the increasing frequency of mountain lion encounters in California has as much to do with a growing *human* population as it does with rising mountain lion numbers. The scenic solitude of the western ranges is prime cougar habitat, and it is falling swiftly to the developer's spade. Meanwhile, with their ideal habitat already at its carrying capacity, mountain lions are forcing younger cats into less suitable terrain, including residential areas. Add that cougars have generally grown bolder under a lengthy ban on their being hunted, and an unsettling scenario begins to emerge.

— Ray Rychnovsky, "Clawing into Controversy," p. 40

SUMMARY

Source: Rychnovsky, "Clawing into Controversy" (40)

Encounters between mountain lions and humans are on the rise in California because increasing numbers of lions are competing for a shrinking habitat. As the lions' wild habitat shrinks, older lions force younger lions into residential areas. These lions have lost some of their fear of humans because of a ban on hunting.

Paraphrasing without plagiarizing

Like a summary, a paraphrase is written in your own words; but whereas a summary reports significant information in fewer words than the source, a paraphrase retells the information in roughly the same number of words. If you retain occasional choice phrases from the source, use quotation marks so you will know later which phrases are not your own.

Note that in the following paraphrase of the original source (see p. 408), the language is significantly different from that in the original.

PARAPHRASE

Source: Rychnovsky, "Clawing into Controversy" (40)

Californians are encountering mountain lions more frequently because increasing numbers of humans and a rising population of lions are competing for the same territory. Humans have moved into mountainous regions once dominated by the lions, and the wild habitat that is left cannot sustain the current lion population. Therefore, the older lions are forcing younger lions into residential areas. And because of a ban on hunting, these younger lions have become bolder — less fearful of encounters with humans.

Using quotation marks to avoid plagiarizing

A quotation consists of the exact words from a source. In your notes, put all quoted material in quotation marks; do not assume that you will remember later which words, phrases, and passages you have quoted and which are your own. When you quote, be sure to copy the words of your source exactly, including punctuation and capitalization.

QUOTATION

Source: Rychnovsky, "Clawing into Controversy" (40)

Rychnovsky explains that as humans expand residential areas into mountain ranges, the cougar's natural habitat "is falling swiftly to the developer's spade."

Avoiding Internet plagiarism

Understand what plagiarism, is. When you use another author's intellectual property — language, visuals, or ideas — in your own writing without giving proper credit, you commit a kind of academic theft called *plagiarism*.

Treat Web sources in the same way you treat print sources. Any language that you find on the Internet must be carefully cited, even if the material is in the public domain or is publicly accessible on free sites. When you use material from Web sites authored by federal, state, or municipal governments (.gov sites) and by nonprofit organizations (.org sites), you must acknowledge that material, too, as intellectual property owned by those agencies.

Keep track of which words come from sources and which are your own. To prevent unintentional plagiarism when you copy passages from Web sources to an electronic file, put quotation marks around any text that you have inserted into your own work. In addition, during note taking and drafting, you might use a different color font or your word processor's highlighting feature to indicate text taken from sources — so that source material stands out unmistakably as someone else's words.

Avoid Web sites that bill themselves as "research services" and sell essays. When you use Web search engines to research a topic, you will often see links to sites that appear to offer legitimate writing support but that actually sell term papers. Of course, submitting a paper that you have purchased is cheating, but even using material from such a paper is considered plagiarism.

Writing MLA Papers

Most English instructors and some humanities instructors will ask you to document your sources with the Modern Language Association (MLA) system of citations described in 55. When writing an MLA paper that is based on sources, you face three main challenges: (1) supporting a thesis, (2) citing your sources and avoiding plagiarism, and (3) integrating quotations and other source material.

Examples in this section are drawn from research a student conducted on online monitoring of employees' computer use. Anna Orlov's research paper, which argues that electronic surveillance in the workplace threatens employees' privacy and autonomy, appears on pages 467–75.

52

Supporting a thesis

Most research assignments ask you to form a thesis, or main idea, and to support that thesis with well-organized evidence.

52a Form a tentative thesis.

Once you have read a variety of sources and considered all sides of your issue, you are ready to form a tentative thesis: a one-sentence (or occasionally a two-sentence) statement of your central idea (see 2a). In a research paper, your thesis will answer the central research question you posed earlier (see 49a). Here, for example, are Anna Orlov's research question and her tentative thesis statement.

ORLOV'S RESEARCH QUESTION

Should employers monitor their employees' online activities in the workplace?

ORLOV'S TENTATIVE THESIS

Employers should not monitor their employees' online activities because electronic surveillance can compromise workers' privacy.

After you have written a rough draft and perhaps done more reading, you may decide to revise your tentative thesis, as Orlov did.

ORLOV'S REVISED THESIS

Although companies often have legitimate concerns that lead them to monitor employees' Internet usage--from expensive security breaches to reduced productivity--the benefits of electronic surveillance are outweighed by its costs to employees' privacy and autonomy.

The thesis usually appears at the end of the introductory paragraph. To read Anna Orlov's thesis in the context of her introduction, see page 467.

ON THE WEB > dianahacker.com/rules
Research exercises > MLA > E-ex 52–1

52b Organize your evidence.

The body of your paper will consist of evidence in support of your thesis. Instead of getting tangled up in a complex, formal outline, sketch an informal plan that organizes your ideas in bold strokes. Anna Orlov, for example, used this simple plan to outline the structure of her argument:

- Electronic surveillance allows employers to monitor workers more efficiently than older types of surveillance.
- Some experts have argued that companies have important financial and legal reasons to monitor employees' Internet usage.
- But monitoring employees' Internet usage may lower worker productivity when the threat to privacy creates distrust.
- Current laws do little to protect employees' privacy rights, so employees and employers have to negotiate the potential risks and benefits of electronic surveillance.

After you have written a rough draft, a more formal outline can be a useful way to shape the complexities of your argument. See 1d for an example.

52c Use sources to inform and support your argument.

Used thoughtfully, the source materials you have gathered will make your argument more complex and convincing for readers. Sources can play several different roles as you develop your points.

Providing background information or context

You can use facts and statistics to support generalizations or to establish the importance of your topic, as student writer Anna Orlov does in her introduction.

> As the Internet has become an integral tool of businesses, company policies on Internet usage have become as common as policies regarding vacation days or sexual harassment. A 2005 study by the American Management Association and ePolicy Institute found that 76% of companies monitor employees' use of the Web, and the number of companies that block employees' access to certain Web sites has increased 27% since 2001 (1).

Explaining terms or concepts

If readers are unlikely to be familiar with a word or an idea important to your topic, you must explain it for them. Quoting or paraphrasing a source can help you define terms and concepts in accessible language.

> One popular monitoring method is keystroke logging, which is done by means of an undetectable program on employees' computers. . . . As Lane explains, these programs record every key entered into the computer in hidden directories that can later be accessed or uploaded by supervisors; at their most sophisticated, the programs can even scan for keywords tailored to individual companies (128-29).

Supporting your claims

As you draft your argument, make sure to back up your assertions with facts, examples, and other evidence from your research (see also 47e). Orlov, for example, uses an anecdote from one of her sources to support her claim that limiting computer access causes resentment among a company's staff.

> Monitoring online activities can have the unintended effect of
> making employees resentful. . . . Kesan warns that "prohibiting
> personal use can seem extremely arbitrary and can seriously harm
> morale. . . . Imagine a concerned parent who is prohibited from
> checking on a sick child by a draconian company policy" (315-16).
> As this analysis indicates, employees can become disgruntled when
> Internet usage policies are enforced to their full extent.

Lending authority to your argument

Expert opinion can give weight to your argument (see also 47e). But don't rely on experts to make your argument for you. Construct your argument in your own words and, when appropriate, cite the judgment of an authority in the field for support.

> Additionally, many experts disagree with employers' assumption
> that online monitoring can increase productivity. Employment law
> attorney Joseph Schmitt argues that, particularly for employees who
> are paid a salary rather than by the hour, "a company shouldn't care
> whether employees spend one or 10 hours on the Internet as long as
> they are getting their jobs done--and provided that they are not
> accessing inappropriate sites" (qtd. in Verespej).

Anticipating and countering objections

Do not ignore sources that seem contrary to your position or that offer arguments different from your own. Instead, use them to give voice to opposing points of view before you counter them (see 47f). Anna Orlov, for example, cites conflicting evidence to acknowledge that readers may disagree with her position that online monitoring is bad for businesses.

> On the one hand, computers and Internet access give employees
> powerful tools to carry out their jobs; on the other hand, the same
> technology offers constant temptations to avoid work. As a 2005
> study by Salary.com and America Online indicates, the Internet

ranked as the top choice among employees for ways of wasting time on the job; it beat talking with co-workers--the second most popular method--by a margin of nearly two to one (Frauenheim).

53

Citing sources; avoiding plagiarism

Your research paper is a collaboration between you and your sources. To be fair and ethical, you must acknowledge your debt to the writers of those sources. If you don't, you commit plagiarism, a serious academic offense.

Three different acts are considered plagiarism: (1) failing to cite quotations and borrowed ideas, (2) failing to enclose borrowed language in quotation marks, and (3) failing to put summaries and paraphrases in your own words.

53a Cite quotations and borrowed ideas.

You must of course cite all direct quotations. You must also cite any ideas borrowed from a source: summaries and paraphrases; statistics and other specific facts; and visuals such as cartoons, graphs, and diagrams.

The only exception is common knowledge — information your readers could easily find in any number of general sources. For example, it is well known that Martin Luther King Jr. won the Nobel Peace Prize in 1964 and that Emily Dickinson published only a handful of her many poems during her lifetime.

As a rule, when you have seen information repeatedly in your reading, you don't need to cite it. However, when information has appeared in only one or two sources or when it is controversial, you should cite the source. If a topic is new to you and you are not sure what is considered common knowledge or what is controversial, ask someone with expertise. When in doubt, cite the source.

The Modern Language Association recommends a system of in-text citations. Here, briefly, is how the MLA citation system usually works:

1. The source is introduced by a signal phrase that names its author.
2. The material being cited is followed by a page number in parentheses.
3. At the end of the paper, a list of works cited (arranged alphabetically according to authors' last names) gives complete publication information about the source.

IN-TEXT CITATION

Legal scholar Jay Kesan points out that the law holds employers liable for employees' actions such as violations of copyright laws, the distribution of offensive or graphic sexual material, and illegal disclosure of confidential information (312).

ENTRY IN THE LIST OF WORKS CITED

Kesan, Jay P. "Cyber-Working or Cyber-Shirking? A First Principles Examination of Electronic Privacy in the Workplace." *Florida Law Review* 54.2 (2002): 289-332. Print.

Handling an MLA citation is not always this simple. For a detailed discussion of possible variations, see 55.

53b Enclose borrowed language in quotation marks.

To indicate that you are using a source's exact phrases or sentences, you must enclose them in quotation marks unless they have been set off from the text by indenting (see pp. 420–21). To omit the quotation marks is to claim — falsely — that the language is your own. Such an omission is plagiarism even if you have cited the source.

ORIGINAL SOURCE

Without adequate discipline, the World Wide Web can be a tremendous time sink; no other medium comes close to matching the Internet's depth of materials, interactivity, and sheer distractive potential.

— Frederick Lane, *The Naked Employee*, p. 142

PLAGIARISM

Frederick Lane points out that if people do not have adequate discipline, the World Wide Web can be a tremendous time sink; no other medium comes close to matching the Internet's depth of materials, interactivity, and sheer distractive potential (142).

BORROWED LANGUAGE IN QUOTATION MARKS

Frederick Lane points out that for those not exercising self-control, "the World Wide Web can be a tremendous time sink; no other medium comes close to matching the Internet's depth of materials, interactivity, and sheer distractive potential" (142).

53c Put summaries and paraphrases in your own words.

A summary condenses information from a source; a paraphrase repeats the information in about the same number of words as in the source. When you summarize or paraphrase, it is not enough to name the source; you must restate the source's meaning using your own language. (See also 51c.) You commit plagiarism if you half-copy the author's sentences — either by mixing the author's phrases with your own without using quotation marks or by plugging your synonyms into the author's sentence structure.

The first paraphrase of the following source is plagiarized — even though the source is cited — because too much of its language is borrowed from the original. The underlined strings of words have been copied word-for-word (without quotation marks). In addition, the writer has closely echoed the sentence structure of the source, merely substituting some synonyms (*restricted* for *limited, modern era* for *computer age, monitoring* for *surveillance,* and *inexpensive* for *cheap*).

ORIGINAL SOURCE

In earlier times, surveillance was limited to the information that a supervisor could observe and record firsthand and to primitive counting devices. In the computer age surveillance can be instantaneous, unblinking, cheap, and, maybe most importantly, easy.
— Carl Botan and Mihaela Vorvoreanu, "What Do Employees Think about Electronic Surveillance at Work?" p. 126

PLAGIARISM: UNACCEPTABLE BORROWING

Scholars Carl Botan and Mihaela Vorvoreanu argue that in earlier times monitoring of employees was restricted to the information that a supervisor could observe and record firsthand.

In the modern era, monitoring <u>can be instantaneous</u>, inexpensive, and, <u>most importantly, easy</u> (126).

To avoid plagiarizing an author's language, resist the temptation to look at the source while you are summarizing or paraphrasing. Close the book, write from memory, and then open the book to check for accuracy. This technique prevents you from being captivated by the words on the page.

ACCEPTABLE PARAPHRASE

Scholars Carl Botan and Mihaela Vorvoreanu claim that the nature of workplace surveillance has changed over time. Before the arrival of computers, managers could collect only small amounts of information about their employees based on what they saw or heard. However, because computers are now standard workplace technology, employers can monitor employees efficiently (126).

ON THE WEB > **dianahacker.com/rules**
Research exercises > MLA > E-ex 53–1 to 53–6

54

Integrating sources

Quotations, summaries, paraphrases, and facts will help you make your argument, but they cannot speak for you. You can use several strategies to integrate information from research sources into your paper while maintaining your own voice.

54a Limit your use of quotations.

Using quotations appropriately

Although it is tempting to insert many quotations in your paper and to use your own words only for connecting passages, do not quote excessively. It is almost impossible to integrate numerous long quotations smoothly into your own text.

Except for the following legitimate uses of quotations, use your own words to summarize and paraphrase your sources and to explain your own ideas.

WHEN TO USE QUOTATIONS

- When language is especially vivid or expressive
- When exact wording is needed for technical accuracy
- When it is important to let the debaters of an issue explain their positions in their own words
- When the words of an important authority lend weight to an argument
- When language of a source is the topic of your discussion (as in an analysis or interpretation)

It is not always necessary to quote full sentences from a source. To reduce your reliance on the words of others, you can often integrate language from a source into your own sentence structure. (For the use of signal phrases in integrating quotations, see 54b.)

> Kizza and Ssanyu observe that technology in the workplace has been accompanied by "an array of problems that needed quick answers" such as electronic monitoring to prevent security breaches (4).

Using the ellipsis mark and brackets

Two useful marks of punctuation, the ellipsis mark and brackets, allow you to keep quoted material to a minimum and to integrate it smoothly into your text.

THE ELLIPSIS MARK To condense a quoted passage, you can use the ellipsis mark (three periods, with spaces between) to indicate that you have omitted words. What remains must be grammatically complete.

> Lane acknowledges the legitimate reasons that many companies have for monitoring their employees' online activities, particularly management's concern about preventing "the theft of information that can be downloaded to a . . . disk, e-mailed to oneself . . . , or even posted to a Web page for the entire world to see" (12).

The writer has omitted from the source the words *floppy or Zip* before *disk* and *or a confederate* after *oneself.*

On the rare occasions when you want to omit one or more full sentences, use a period before the three ellipsis dots.

> Charles Lewis, director of the Center for Public Integrity, points
> out that "by 1987, employers were administering nearly 2,000,000
> polygraph tests a year to job applicants and employees. . . .
> Millions of workers were required to produce urine samples under
> observation for drug testing . . ." (22).

Ordinarily, do not use an ellipsis mark at the beginning or at the end of a quotation. Your readers will understand that the quoted material is taken from a longer passage, so such marks are not necessary. The only exception occurs when words have been dropped at the end of the final quoted sentence. In such cases, put three ellipsis dots before the closing quotation mark and parenthetical reference, as in the previous example.

Do not use an ellipsis mark to distort the meaning of your source.

BRACKETS Brackets allow you to insert your own words into quoted material. You can insert words in brackets to explain a confusing reference or to keep a sentence grammatical in your context.

> Legal scholar Jay Kesan notes that "a decade ago, losses [from
> employees' computer crimes] were already mounting to five billion
> dollars annually" (311).

To indicate an error such as a misspelling in a quotation, insert [sic] after the error.

> Johnson argues that "while online monitoring is often imagined as
> harmles [sic], the practice may well threaten employees' rights to
> privacy" (14).

Setting off long quotations

When you quote more than four typed lines of prose or more than three lines of poetry, set off the quotation by indenting it one inch (or ten spaces) from the left margin.

Long quotations should be introduced by an informative sentence, usually followed by a colon. Quotation marks are unnecessary because the indented format tells readers that the words are taken word-for-word from the source.

> Botan and Vorvoreanu examine the role of gender in company practices of electronic surveillance:
>
>> There has never been accurate documentation of the extent of gender differences in surveillance, but by the middle 1990s, estimates of the proportion of surveilled employees that were women ranged from 75% to 85%. . . . Ironically, this gender imbalance in workplace surveillance may be evening out today because advances in surveillance technology are making surveillance of traditionally male dominated fields, such as long-distance truck driving, cheap, easy, and frequently unobtrusive. (127)

Notice that at the end of an indented quotation the parenthetical citation goes outside the final mark of punctuation. (When a quotation is run into your text, the opposite is true. See the sample citations on p. 420.)

54b Use signal phrases to integrate sources.

Whenever you include a paraphrase, summary, or direct quotation of another writer in your paper, prepare your readers for it with an introduction called a *signal phrase*. A signal phrase names the author of the source and often provides some context for the source material.

When you write a signal phrase, choose a verb that is appropriate for the way you are using the source (see 52c). Are you providing background, explaining a concept, supporting a claim, lending authority, or refuting a belief? See the chart on page 422 for a list of verbs commonly used in signal phrases. Note that MLA style calls for present-tense verbs (*argues*) to introduce source material unless a date specifies the time of writing.

Using signal phrases in MLA papers

To avoid monotony, try to vary both the language and the placement of your signal phrases.

Model signal phrases

In the words of researchers Greenfield and Davis, ". . ."

As legal scholar Jay Kesan has noted, ". . ."

The ePolicy Institute, an organization that advises companies about reducing risks from technology, reported that ". . ."

". . . ," writes Daniel Tynan, ". . ."

". . . ," claims attorney Schmitt.

Kizza and Ssanyu offer a persuasive counterargument: ". . ."

Verbs in signal phrases

acknowledges	comments	endorses	reasons
adds	compares	grants	refutes
admits	confirms	illustrates	rejects
agrees	contends	implies	reports
argues	declares	insists	responds
asserts	denies	notes	suggests
believes	disputes	observes	thinks
claims	emphasizes	points out	writes

Marking boundaries

Readers need to move from your words to the words of a source without feeling a jolt. Avoid dropping quotations into the text without warning. Instead, provide clear signal phrases, including at least the author's name, to indicate the boundary between your words and the source's words.

DROPPED QUOTATION

Some experts have argued that a range of legitimate concerns justifies employer monitoring of employee Internet usage. "Employees could accidentally (or deliberately) spill confidential corporate information . . . or allow worms to spread throughout a corporate network" (Tynan).

QUOTATION WITH SIGNAL PHRASE

Some experts have argued that a range of legitimate concerns
justifies employer monitoring of employee Internet usage. As
PC World columnist Daniel Tynan explains, companies that don't
monitor network traffic can be penalized for their ignorance:
"Employees could accidentally (or deliberately) spill confidential
information . . . or allow worms to spread throughout a corporate
network."

NOTE: Because this quotation is from an unpaginated Web
source, no page number appears in parentheses after the quotation. See item 4 on page 429.

Establishing authority

Good research writing uses evidence from reliable sources. The
first time you mention a source, briefly include the author's
title, credentials, or experience — anything that would help
your readers recognize the source's authority.

SOURCE WITH NO CREDENTIALS

Jay Kesan points out that the law holds employers liable for
employees' actions such as violations of copyright laws, the
distribution of offensive or graphic sexual material, and illegal
disclosure of confidential information (312).

SOURCE WITH CREDENTIALS

Legal scholar Jay Kesan points out that the law holds employers
liable for employees' actions such as violations of copyright laws,
the distribution of offensive or graphic sexual material, and illegal
disclosure of confidential information (312).

When you establish your source's authority, as with the phrase
Legal scholar in the previous example, you also signal to readers your own credibility as a responsible researcher, one who
has located trustworthy sources.

Introducing summaries and paraphrases

Introduce most summaries and paraphrases with a signal phrase that names the author and places the material in the context of your argument. Readers will then understand that everything between the signal phrase and the parenthetical citation summarizes or paraphrases the cited source.

Without the signal phrase (underlined) in the following example, readers might think that only the quotation at the end is being cited, when in fact the whole paragraph is based on the source.

> <u>Frederick Lane believes that</u> the personal computer has posed new challenges for employers worried about workplace productivity. Whereas early desktop computers were primitive enough to prevent employees from using them to waste time, the machines have become so sophisticated that they now make non-work-related computer activities easy and inviting. Many employees enjoy adjusting and readjusting features of their computers, from the desktop wallpaper to software they can quickly download. Many workers spend considerable company time playing games on their computers. But perhaps most problematic from the employer's point of view, Lane asserts, is giving employees access to the Internet, "roughly the equivalent of installing a gazillion-channel television set for each employee" (15-16).

There are times when a summary or paraphrase does not require a signal phrase. When the context makes clear where the cited material begins, you may omit the signal phrase and include the author's last name in parentheses.

Putting direct quotations in context

Because a source cannot reveal its meaning or function by itself, you must make the connection between a source and your own ideas. A signal phrase can show readers how a quotation supports or challenges a point you are making.

> Efforts by the music industry to stop Internet file sharing have been unsuccessful and, worse, divisive. Industry analysts share this view. *Salon*'s Scott Rosenberg, for example, writes that the

only thing the music industry's "legal strategy has accomplished is to radicalize the community of online music fans and accelerate the process of technological change" (2).

Readers should not have to guess why a quotation appears in your paper. If you use another writer's words, you must explain how they contribute to your point. It's a good idea to embed a quotation — especially a long one — between sentences of your own. In addition to introducing it with a signal phrase, follow it with interpretive comments that link the quotation to your paper's argument.

QUOTATION WITH INSUFFICIENT CONTEXT

The difference, Lane argues, between these old methods of data gathering and electronic surveillance involves quantity:

> Technology makes it possible for employers to gather enormous amounts of data about employees, often far beyond what is necessary to satisfy safety or productivity concerns. And the trends that drive technology--faster, smaller, cheaper--make it possible for larger and larger numbers of employers to gather ever-greater amounts of personal data. (3-4)

QUOTATION WITH EFFECTIVE CONTEXT

The difference, Lane argues, between these old methods of data gathering and electronic surveillance involves quantity:

> Technology makes it possible for employers to gather enormous amounts of data about employees, often far beyond what is necessary to satisfy safety or productivity concerns. And the trends that drive technology--faster, smaller, cheaper--make it possible for larger and larger numbers of employers to gather ever-greater amounts of personal data. (3-4)

In an age when employers can collect data whenever employees use their computers--when they send e-mail, surf the Web, or even arrive at or depart from their workstations--the challenge for both employers and employees is to determine how much is too much.

Integrating statistics and other facts

When you are citing a statistic or another specific fact, a signal phrase is often not necessary. In most cases, readers will understand that the citation refers to the statistic or fact (not the whole paragraph).

> According to a 2002 survey, 60% of responding companies reported disciplining employees who had used the Internet in ways the companies deemed inappropriate; 30% had fired their employees for those transgressions (Greenfield and Davis 347).

There is nothing wrong, however, with using a signal phrase to introduce a statistic or another fact.

ON THE WEB > **dianahacker.com/rules**
Research exercises > MLA > E-ex 54–1 to 54–4

55

Documenting sources

In English and in some humanities classes, you will be asked to use the MLA (Modern Language Association) system for documenting sources, which is set forth in the *MLA Handbook for Writers of Research Papers,* 7th ed. (New York: MLA, 2009). MLA recommends in-text citations that refer readers to a list of works cited.

An in-text citation names the author of the source, often in a signal phrase, and gives the page number in parentheses. At the end of the paper, a list of works cited provides publication information about the source; the list is alphabetized by authors' last names (or by titles for works without authors). There is a direct connection between the in-text citation and the alphabetical listing. In the following example, that link is highlighted in orange.

IN-TEXT CITATION

Jay Kesan notes that even though many companies now routinely monitor employees through electronic means, "there may exist less intrusive safeguards for employers" (293).

ENTRY IN THE LIST OF WORKS CITED

> Kesan, Jay P. "Cyber-Working or Cyber-Shirking? A First Principles
> Examination of Electronic Privacy in the Workplace."
> *Florida Law Review* 54.2 (2002): 289-332. Print.

For a list of works cited that includes this entry, see page 474.

NOTE: If your instructor requires underlining for the titles of long works and for the names of publications, substitute underlining for italics in all the models in this section.

55a MLA in-text citations

MLA in-text citations are made with a combination of signal phrases and parenthetical references. A signal phrase introduces information taken from a source (a quotation, summary, paraphrase, or fact); usually the signal phrase includes the author's name. The parenthetical reference, which comes after the cited material, normally includes at least a page number. In the models in this section, the elements of the in-text citation are highlighted in orange.

Directory to MLA in-text citation models

BASIC RULES FOR PRINT AND ELECTRONIC SOURCES

1. Author named in a signal phrase, 428
2. Author named in parentheses, 429
3. Author unknown, 429
4. Page number unknown, 429
5. One-page source, 430

VARIATIONS ON THE BASIC RULES

6. Two or more titles by the same author, 430
7. Two or three authors, 431
8. Four or more authors, 431
9. Corporate author, 431
10. Authors with the same last name, 432

11. Indirect source (source quoted in another source), 432
12. Encyclopedia or dictionary, 432
13. Multivolume work, 432
14. Two or more works, 433
15. An entire work, 433
16. Work in an anthology, 433
17. Historical and legal documents, 433

LITERARY WORKS AND SACRED TEXTS

18. Literary works without parts or line numbers, 434
19. Verse plays and poems, 434
20. Novels with numbered divisions, 435
21. Sacred texts, 435

IN-TEXT CITATION

> Kwon points out that the Fourth Amendment does not give
> employees any protections from employers' "unreasonable
> searches and seizures" (6).

Readers can look up the author's last name in the alphabetized list of works cited, where they will learn the work's title and other publication information. If readers decide to consult the source, the page number will take them straight to the passage that has been cited.

Basic rules for print and electronic sources

The MLA system of in-text citations, which depends heavily on authors' names and page numbers, was created in the early 1980s with print sources in mind. Because some of today's electronic sources have unclear authorship and lack page numbers, they present a special challenge. Nevertheless, the basic rules are the same for both print and electronic sources.

The models in this section (items 1–5) show how the MLA system usually works and explain what to do if your source has no author or page numbers.

■ **1. AUTHOR NAMED IN A SIGNAL PHRASE** Ordinarily, introduce the material being cited with a signal phrase that includes the author's name. In addition to preparing readers for the source, the signal phrase allows you to keep the parenthetical citation brief.

> Frederick Lane reports that employers do not necessarily have to
> use software to monitor how their employees use the Web:
> employers can "use a hidden video camera pointed at an
> employee's monitor" and even position a camera "so that a
> number of monitors [can] be viewed at the same time" (147).

The signal phrase — *Frederick Lane reports that* — names the author; the parenthetical citation gives the page number of the book in which the quoted words may be found.

Notice that the period follows the parenthetical citation. When a quotation ends with a question mark or an exclamation point, leave the end punctuation inside the quotation mark and add a period after the parentheses: ". . . ?" (8). (See also the note on p. 306.)

■ **2. AUTHOR NAMED IN PARENTHESES** If a signal phrase does not name the author, put the author's last name in parentheses along with the page number.

> Companies can monitor employees' every keystroke without legal
>
> penalty, but they may have to combat low morale as a result
>
> (Lane 129).

Use no punctuation between the name and the page number.

■ **3. AUTHOR UNKNOWN** Either use the complete title in a signal phrase or use a short form of the title in parentheses. Titles of books are italicized; titles of articles are put in quotation marks.

> A popular keystroke logging program operates invisibly on workers'
>
> computers yet provides supervisors with details of the workers'
>
> online activities ("Automatically").

TIP: Before assuming that a Web source has no author, do some detective work. Often the author's name is available but is not easy to find. For example, it may appear at the end of the source, in tiny print. Or it may appear on another page of the site, such as the home page.

NOTE: If a source has no author and is sponsored by a corporate entity, such as an organization or a government agency, name the corporate entity as the author (see item 9 on p. 431).

■ **4. PAGE NUMBER UNKNOWN** You may omit the page number if a work lacks page numbers, as is the case with many Web sources. Although printouts from Web sites usually show page numbers, printers don't always provide the same page breaks; for this reason, MLA recommends treating such sources as unpaginated.

> As a 2005 study by *Salary.com* and *America Online* indicates, the
>
> Internet ranked as the top choice among employees for ways of
>
> wasting time on the job; it beat talking with co-workers--the second
>
> most popular method--by a margin of nearly two to one (Frauenheim).

When the pages of a Web source are stable (as in PDF files), however, supply a page number in your in-text citation.

NOTE: If a Web source numbers its paragraphs or screens, give the abbreviation "par." or "pars." or the word "screen" or "screens" in the parentheses: (Smith, par. 4).

■ **5. ONE-PAGE SOURCE** If the source is one page long, MLA allows (but does not require) you to omit the page number. Many instructors will want you to supply the page number because without it readers may not know where your citation ends or, worse, may not realize that you have provided a citation at all.

> *No page number in citation*
>
> Anush Yegyazarian reports that in 2000 the National Labor Relations Board's Office of the General Counsel helped win restitution for two workers who had been dismissed because their employers were displeased by the employees' e-mails about work-related issues. The case points to the ongoing struggle to define what constitutes protected speech in the workplace.

> *Page number in citation*
>
> Anush Yegyazarian reports that in 2000 the National Labor Relations Board's Office of the General Counsel helped win restitution for two workers who had been dismissed because their employers were displeased by the employees' e-mails about work-related issues (62). The case points to the ongoing struggle to define what constitutes protected speech in the workplace.

Variations on the basic rules

This section describes the MLA guidelines for handling a variety of situations not covered by the basic rules just given. These rules on in-text citations are the same for both print sources and electronic sources.

■ **6. TWO OR MORE WORKS BY THE SAME AUTHOR** If your list of works cited includes two or more works by the same author, mention the title of the work in the signal phrase or include a short version of the title in the parentheses.

> The American Management Association and ePolicy Institute have tracked employers' practices in monitoring employees' e-mail use. The groups' 2003 survey found that one-third of companies had a

policy of keeping and reviewing employees' e-mail messages
("2003 E-mail" 2); in 2005, more than 55% of companies engaged
in e-mail monitoring ("2005 Electronic" 1).

Titles of articles and other short works are placed in quotation
marks, as in the example just given. Titles of books are italicized.

In the rare case when both the author's name and a short
title must be given in parentheses, separate them with a comma.

A 2004 survey found that 20% of employers responding had
employees' e-mail "subpoenaed in the course of a lawsuit or
regulatory investigation," up 7% from the previous year
(Amer. Management Assn. and ePolicy Inst., "2004 Workplace" 1).

■ **7. TWO OR THREE AUTHORS** Name the authors in a signal
phrase, as in the following example, or include their last names
in the parenthetical reference: (Kizza and Ssanyu 2).

Kizza and Ssanyu note that "employee monitoring is a dependable,
capable, and very affordable process of electronically or otherwise
recording all employee activities at work" and elsewhere (2).

When three authors are named in the parentheses, separate the
names with commas: (Alton, Davies, and Rice 56).

■ **8. FOUR OR MORE AUTHORS** Name all of the authors or include only the first author's name followed by "et al." (Latin for
"and others"). Make sure that your citation matches the entry in
the list of works cited (see item 2 on pp. 436 and 438).

The study was extended for two years, and only after results were
reviewed by an independent panel did the researchers publish their
findings (Blaine et al. 35).

■ **9. CORPORATE AUTHOR** When the author is a corporation,
an organization, or a government agency, name the corporate
author either in the signal phrase or in the parentheses.

According to a 2001 survey of human resources managers by the
American Management Association, more than three-quarters of the
responding companies reported disciplining employees for "misuse
or personal use of office telecommunications equipment" (2).

In the list of works cited, the American Management Association is treated as the author and alphabetized under *A*.

When a government agency is treated as the author, it will be alphabetized in the list of works cited under the name of the government, such as "United States" (see item 3 on p. 438). For this reason, you must name the government in your in-text citation.

> The United States Department of Transportation provides
>
> nationwide statistics on traffic fatalities.

■ **10. AUTHORS WITH THE SAME LAST NAME** If your list of works cited includes works by two or more authors with the same last name, include the author's first name in the signal phrase or first initial in the parentheses.

> Estimates of the frequency with which employers monitor
>
> employees' use of the Internet each day vary widely (A. Jones 15).

■ **11. INDIRECT SOURCE (SOURCE QUOTED IN ANOTHER SOURCE)** When a writer's or a speaker's quoted words appear in a source written by someone else, begin the parenthetical citation with the abbreviation "qtd. in."

> Researchers Botan and McCreadie point out that "workers are objects
>
> of information collection without participating in the process of
>
> exchanging the information . . ." (qtd. in Kizza and Ssanyu 14).

■ **12. ENCYCLOPEDIA OR DICTIONARY** Unless an encyclopedia or a dictionary has an author, it will be alphabetized in the list of works cited under the word or entry that you consulted — not under the title of the reference work itself (see item 13 on p. 442). Either in your text or in your parenthetical reference, mention the word or the entry. No page number is required, since readers can easily look up the word or entry.

> The word *crocodile* has a surprisingly complex etymology ("Crocodile").

■ **13. MULTIVOLUME WORK** If your paper cites more than one volume of a multivolume work, indicate in the parentheses the volume you are referring to, followed by a colon and the page number.

> In his studies of gifted children, Terman describes a pattern of
>
> accelerated language acquisition (2: 279).

If your paper cites only one volume of a multivolume work, you will include the volume number in the list of works cited and will not need to include it in the parentheses. (See the second example in item 12 on p. 440.)

■ **14. TWO OR MORE WORKS** To cite more than one source in the parentheses, give the citations in alphabetical order and separate them with a semicolon.

> The effects of sleep deprivation have been well documented
>
> (Cahill 42; Leduc 114; Vasquez 73).

Multiple citations can be distracting, however, so you should not overuse the technique. If you want to alert readers to several sources that discuss a particular topic, consider using an information note instead (see 55c).

■ **15. AN ENTIRE WORK** Use the author's name in a signal phrase or a parenthetical reference. There is of course no need to use a page number.

> Lane explores the evolution of surveillance in the workplace.

■ **16. WORK IN AN ANTHOLOGY** Put the name of the author of the work (not the editor of the anthology) in the signal phrase or the parentheses.

> In "A Jury of Her Peers," Mrs. Hale describes both a style of
>
> quilting and a murder weapon when she utters the last words of
>
> the story: "We call it--knot it, Mr. Henderson" (Glaspell 210).

In the list of works cited, the work is alphabetized under Glaspell, not under the name of the editor of the anthology.

> Glaspell, Susan. "A Jury of Her Peers." *Literature and Its Writers: A Compact*
>
> *Introduction to Fiction, Poetry, and Drama.* Ed. Ann Charters and
>
> Samuel Charters. 3rd ed. Boston: Bedford, 2004. 194-210. Print.

■ **17. HISTORICAL AND LEGAL DOCUMENTS** For well-known historical documents, such as the United States Constitution, provide a parenthetical citation using common abbreviations: (US Const., art. 1, sec. 2). For other historical documents, cite as you would any other work, by the first element in the works cited entry. For legislative acts (laws) and court cases, your in-text citation should name the act or case either in a signal phrase or in parentheses. In the text of a paper, names of acts are not italicized, but names of cases are. (See item 55 on p. 459.)

> The Jones Act of 1917 granted US citizenship to Puerto Ricans.

> In 1857, Chief Justice Roger B. Taney declared in the case of *Dred Scott v. Sandford* that blacks, whether enslaved or free, could not be citizens of the United States.

Literary works and sacred texts

Literary works and sacred texts are usually available in a variety of editions. Your list of works cited will specify which edition you are using, and your in-text citation will usually consist of a page number from the edition you consulted (see item 18).

When possible you should give enough information — such as book parts, play divisions, or line numbers — so that readers can locate the cited passage in any edition of the work (see items 19–21).

■ **18. LITERARY WORKS WITHOUT PARTS OR LINE NUMBERS** Many literary works, such as most short stories and many novels and plays, do not have parts or line numbers that you can refer to. In such cases, simply cite the page number.

> At the end of Kate Chopin's "The Story of an Hour," Mrs. Mallard drops dead upon learning that her husband is alive. In the final irony of the story, doctors report that she has died of a "joy that kills" (25).

■ **19. VERSE PLAYS AND POEMS** For verse plays, MLA recommends giving act, scene, and line numbers that can be located in any edition of the work. Use arabic numerals, and separate the numbers with periods.

> In Shakespeare's *King Lear*, Gloucester, blinded for suspected treason, learns a profound lesson from his tragic experience: "A man may see how this world goes / with no eyes" (4.2.148-49).

For a poem, cite the part, stanza, and line numbers, if it has them, separated by periods.

> The Green Knight claims to approach King Arthur's court "because the praise of you, prince, is puffed so high, / And your manor and your men are considered so magnificent" (1.12.258-59).

For poems that are not divided into numbered parts or stanzas, use line numbers. For a first reference, use the word "lines": (lines 5-8). Thereafter use just the numbers: (12-13).

■ **20. NOVELS WITH NUMBERED DIVISIONS** Give the page number, followed by a semicolon and the book, part, or chapter in which the passage may be found. Use abbreviations such as "pt." and "ch."

> One of Kingsolver's narrators, teenager Rachel, pushes her vocabulary beyond its limits. For example, Rachel complains that being forced to live in the Congo with her missionary family is "a sheer tapestry of justice" because her chances of finding a boyfriend are "dull and void" (117; bk. 2, ch. 10).

■ **21. SACRED TEXTS** When citing a sacred text such as the Bible or the Qur'an, name the edition in your works cited entry (see item 14 on p. 442). In your parenthetical citation, give the book, chapter, and verse (or their equivalent), separated by periods. Common abbreviations for books of the Bible are acceptable.

> Consider the words of Solomon: "If your enemy is hungry, give him bread to eat; and if he is thirsty, give him water to drink" (*Oxford Annotated Bible*, Prov. 25.21).

ON THE WEB > dianahacker.com/rules
Research exercises > MLA > E-ex 55–1 and 55–2

55b MLA list of works cited

An alphabetized list of works cited, which appears at the end of your research paper, gives publication information for each of the sources you have cited in the paper. (For information about preparing the list, see p. 465; for a sample list of works cited, see pp. 474–75.)

Unless your instructor asks for them, omit sources not actually cited in the paper, even if you read them.

NOTE: MLA requires the medium of publication in all works cited entries, usually at the end of the entry (neither italicized nor in quotation marks): "Print," "Web," "Television," "Film," "Lecture," and so on. (See specific items throughout this section.)

General guidelines for listing authors

Alphabetize entries in the list of works cited by authors' last names (or by title if a work has no author). The author's name is important because citations in the text refer to it and readers will look for it at the beginning of an entry in the list.

NAME CITED IN TEXT

According to Nancy Flynn, . . .

BEGINNING OF WORKS CITED ENTRY

Flynn, Nancy.

Items 1–5 show how to begin an entry for a work with a single author, multiple authors, a corporate author, an unknown author, and multiple works by the same author. What comes after this first element of your citation will depend on the kind of source you are citing. (See items 6–63.)

NOTE: For a book, an entry in the works cited list will sometimes begin with an editor (see item 9 on p. 439).

■ **1. SINGLE AUTHOR** For a work with one author, begin with the author's last name, followed by a comma; then give the author's first name, followed by a period.

Tannen, Deborah.

■ **2. MULTIPLE AUTHORS** For works with two or three authors, name the authors in the order in which they are listed in the source. Reverse the name of only the first author.

Walker, Janice R., and Todd Taylor.

Wilmut, Ian, Keith Campbell, and Colin Tudge.

For a work with four or more authors, either name all of the authors or name the first author followed by "et al." (Latin for "and others"). See the examples at the top of page 438.

Directory to MLA works cited models

ON THE WEB > **dianahacker.com/rules**
Research exercises > MLA > E-ex 55–3

Sloan, Frank A., Emily M. Stout, Kathryn Whetten-Goldstein, and Lan Liang.

Sloan, Frank A., et al.

■ **3. CORPORATE AUTHOR** When the author of a print document or Web site is a corporation, a government agency, or some other organization, begin your entry with the name of the group.

First Union.

United States. Bureau of the Census.

American Management Association.

NOTE: Your in-text citation should also treat the organization as the author (see item 9 on p. 431).

■ **4. UNKNOWN AUTHOR** When the author of a work is unknown, begin with the work's title. Titles of articles and other short works, such as brief documents from Web sites, are put in quotation marks. Titles of books and other long works, such as entire Web sites, are italicized.

Article or other short work
"Media Giants."

Book, entire Web site, or other long work
Atlas of the World.

Before concluding that the author of a Web source is unknown, check carefully (see the tip on p. 429). Also remember that an organization may be the author (see item 3 at the top of this page).

■ **5. TWO OR MORE WORKS BY THE SAME AUTHOR** If your list of works cited includes two or more works by the same author, first alphabetize the works by title (ignoring the article *A*, *An*, or *The* at the beginning of a title). Use the author's name for the first entry only; for subsequent entries, use three hyphens followed by a period. The three hyphens must stand for exactly the same name or names as in the first entry.

Knopp, Lisa. *Field of Vision*. Iowa City: U of Iowa P, 1996. Print.

---. *The Nature of Home: A Lexicon and Essays*. Lincoln: U of Nebraska
    P, 2002. Print.

Books

Items 6–19 apply to print books. For online books, see item 29. For an annotated example, see page 441.

■ **6. BASIC FORMAT FOR A BOOK** For most books, arrange the information into four units, each followed by a period: the author's name; the title and subtitle, italicized; the place of publication, the publisher, and the date; and the medium.

Tan, Amy. *Saving Fish from Drowning*. New York: Putnam, 2005. Print.

Take the information about the book from its title page and copyright page. Use a short form of the publisher's name; omit terms such as *Press, Inc.*, and *Co.* except when naming university presses (Harvard UP, for example). If the copyright page lists more than one date, use the most recent one.

■ **7. AUTHOR WITH AN EDITOR** Begin with the author and title, followed by the name of the editor. In this case the abbreviation "Ed." means "Edited by," so it is the same for one or multiple editors.

Plath, Sylvia. *The Unabridged Journals of Sylvia Plath*. Ed. Karen V. Kukil.

New York: Anchor-Doubleday, 2000. Print.

■ **8. AUTHOR WITH A TRANSLATOR** Begin with the name of the author. After the title, write "Trans." (for "Translated by") and the name of the translator.

Allende, Isabel. *Zorro*. Trans. Margaret Sayers Peden. London: Fourth

Estate, 2005. Print.

■ **9. EDITOR** An entry for a work with an editor is similar to that for a work with an author except that the name is followed by a comma and the abbreviation "ed." for "editor" (or "eds." for "editors").

Craig, Patricia, ed. *The Oxford Book of Travel Stories*. Oxford: Oxford UP,

1996. Print.

■ **10. WORK IN AN ANTHOLOGY** Begin with (1) the name of the author of the selection, not with the name of the editor of the anthology. Then give (2) the title of the selection; (3) the title of

the anthology; (4) the name of the editor (preceded by "Ed." for "Edited by"); (5) publication information; (6) the pages on which the selection appears; and (7) the medium.

```
   ┌─── 1 ───┐ ┌─────── 2 ───────┐┌──────── 3 ────────┐
Desai, Anita. "Scholar and Gypsy." The Oxford Book of Travel Stories.

      ┌──────── 4 ────────┐ ┌──────── 5 ────────┐ ┌─ 6 ─┐ ┌─ 7 ─┐
      Ed. Patricia Craig. Oxford: Oxford UP, 1996. 251-73. Print.
```

If you use two or more selections from the same anthology, provide an entry for the entire anthology (see item 9) and give a shortened entry for each selection. Begin with the author and title of the selection; follow with the editor(s) of the anthology and the page number(s) on which the selection appears. Use the medium of publication only in the entry for the complete anthology. Alphabetize the entries in the list of works cited by authors' last names.

Desai, Anita. "Scholar and Gypsy." Craig 251-73.

Malouf, David. "The Kyogle Line." Craig 390-96.

■ **11. EDITION OTHER THAN THE FIRST** If you are citing an edition other than the first, include the number of the edition after the title (or after the names of any translators or editors that appear after the title): 2nd ed., 3rd ed., and so on.

Auletta, Ken. *The Underclass*. 2nd ed. Woodstock: Overlook, 2000. Print.

■ **12. MULTIVOLUME WORK** Include the total number of volumes before the city and publisher, using the abbreviation "vols." If the volumes were published over several years, give the inclusive dates of publication. The abbreviation "Ed." means "Edited by," so it is the same for one or more editors.

Stark, Freya. *Letters*. Ed. Lucy Moorehead. 8 vols. Salisbury: Compton,

1974–82. Print.

If your paper cites only one of the volumes, give the volume number before the city and publisher and give the date of publication for that volume. After the date, give the total number of volumes.

Stark, Freya. *Letters*. Ed. Lucy Moorehead. Vol. 5. Salisbury: Compton,

1978. Print. 8 vols.

Citation at a glance: Book (MLA)

To cite a print book in MLA style, include the following elements:

1 Author
2 Title and subtitle
3 City of publication
4 Publisher
5 Date of publication
6 Medium

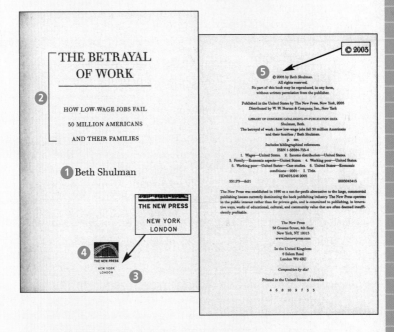

WORKS CITED ENTRY FOR A BOOK

┌──1──┐ ┌────────────2────────────┐
Shulman, Beth. *The Betrayal of Work: How Low-Wage Jobs Fail 30*

┌──3──┐ ┌─4─┐ ┌─5─┐ ┌─6─┐
Million Americans and Their Families. New York: New, 2003. Print.

For more on citing books in MLA style, see pages 439–43.

■ **13. ENCYCLOPEDIA OR DICTIONARY ENTRY** When an encyclopedia or a dictionary is well known, simply list the author of the entry (if there is one), the title of the entry, the title of the reference work, the edition number (if any), the date of the edition, and the medium.

Posner, Rebecca. "Romance Languages." *The Encyclopaedia Britannica: Macropaedia*. 15th ed. 1987. Print.

"Sonata." *The American Heritage Dictionary of the English Language*. 4th ed. 2000. Print.

Volume and page numbers are not necessary because the entries in the source are arranged alphabetically and therefore are easy to locate.

If a reference work is not well known, provide full publication information as well.

■ **14. SACRED TEXT** Give the title of the edition of the sacred text (taken from the title page), italicized; the editor's or translator's name (if any); publication information; and the medium. Add the name of the version, if there is one.

The Oxford Annotated Bible with the Apocrypha. Ed. Herbert G. May and Bruce M. Metzger. New York: Oxford UP, 1965. Print. Rev. Standard Vers.

The Qur'an: Translation. Trans. Abdullah Yusuf Ali. Elmhurst: Tahrike, 2000. Print.

■ **15. FOREWORD, INTRODUCTION, PREFACE, OR AFTERWORD** Give the author of the book part; the name of the part; the book title; the author of the book, preceded by the word "By"; the editor of the book, if any; publication information; page numbers for the book part; and the medium.

Morris, Jan. Introduction. *Letters from the Field, 1925-1975*. By Margaret Mead. New York: Perennial-Harper, 2001. xix-xxiii. Print.

If the book part being cited has a title, include it in quotation marks immediately after the author's name.

Ozick, Cynthia. "Portrait of the Essay as a Warm Body." Introduction. *The Best American Essays 1998*. Ed. Ozick. Boston: Houghton, 1998. xv-xxi. Print.

■ **16. BOOK WITH A TITLE IN ITS TITLE** If the book title contains a title normally italicized, neither italicize the internal title nor place it in quotation marks.

Woodson, Jon. *A Study of Joseph Heller's* Catch-22: Going Around Twice.

New York: Lang, 2001. Print.

If the title within the title is normally put in quotation marks, retain the quotation marks and italicize the entire title.

Hawkins, Hunt, and Brian W. Shaffer, eds. *Approaches to Teaching Conrad's*

Heart of Darkness *and "The Secret Sharer."* New York: MLA, 2002. Print.

■ **17. BOOK IN A SERIES** At the end of the entry, cite the series name as it appears on the title page, followed by the series number, if any.

Malena, Anne. *The Dynamics of Identity in Francophone Caribbean Narrative.*

New York: Lang, 1998. Print. Francophone Cultures and Lits. Ser. 24.

■ **18. REPUBLISHED BOOK** After the title of the book, cite the original publication date, followed by the current publication information. If the republished book contains new material, such as an introduction or afterword, include information about the new material after the original date.

Hughes, Langston. *Black Misery.* 1969. Afterword Robert O'Meally. New

York: Oxford UP, 2000. Print.

■ **19. PUBLISHER'S IMPRINT** If a book was published by an imprint (a division) of a publishing company, link the name of the imprint and the name of the publisher with a hyphen, putting the imprint first.

Truan, Barry. *Acoustic Communication.* Westport: Ablex-Greenwood, 2000.

Print.

Articles in periodicals

This section shows how to prepare works cited entries for articles in magazines, scholarly journals, and newspapers. (See p. 445 for an annotated example.) In addition to consulting the models in this section, you will at times need to turn to other models as well:

- More than one author: see item 2
- Corporate author: see item 3
- Unknown author: see item 4
- Online article: see items 32 and 33
- Article from a database service: see item 31

Put titles of articles in quotation marks; italicize the titles of magazines, journals, and newspapers. For dates requiring a month, abbreviate all months except May, June, and July. Add the medium at the end of the entry.

For articles appearing on consecutive pages, provide the range of pages (see items 21 and 22). When an article does not appear on consecutive pages, give the number of the first page followed by a plus sign: 32+ .

■ **20. ARTICLE IN A MAGAZINE** If the magazine is issued monthly, give just the month and year.

Fay, J. Michael. "Land of the Surfing Hippos." *National Geographic* Aug.

2004: 100+. Print.

If the magazine is issued weekly, give the exact date.

Lord, Lewis. "There's Something about Mary Todd." *US News and*

World Report 19 Feb. 2001: 53. Print.

■ **21. ARTICLE IN A JOURNAL PAGINATED BY VOLUME** Give both volume and issue numbers for all journals, even those with pagination that continues through all issues of the volume. Separate the volume and issue numbers with a period.

Ryan, Katy. "Revolutionary Suicide in Toni Morrison's Fiction." *African*

American Review 34.3 (2000): 389-412. Print.

■ **22. ARTICLE IN A JOURNAL PAGINATED BY ISSUE** Give both volume and issue numbers, separated with a period.

Wood, Michael. "Broken Dates: Fiction and the Century." *Kenyon Review*

22.3 (2000): 50-64. Print.

Citation at a glance: Article in a periodical (MLA)

To cite an article in a print periodical in MLA style, include the following elements:

1 Author
2 Title and subtitle of article
3 Name of periodical
4 Volume and issue number (for scholarly journal)
5 Date or year of publication
6 Page numbers
7 Medium

WORKS CITED ENTRY FOR AN ARTICLE IN A PRINT PERIODICAL

```
┌──1──┐ ┌──────2──────┐ ┌──────3──────┐
McGrath, Anne. "A Loss of Foreign Talent." US News and World Report

  ┌──5──┐ ┌6┐ ┌7┐
  22 Nov. 2004: 76. Print.
```

For more on citing periodical articles in MLA style, see pages 443–46.

■ **23. ARTICLE IN A DAILY NEWSPAPER** Include the section letter if it is part of the page number in the newspaper.

Brummitt, Chris. "Indonesia's Food Needs Expected to Soar." *Boston*

    Globe 1 Feb. 2005: A7. Print.

If the section is marked with a number rather than a letter, handle the entry as follows:

Wilford, John Noble. "In a Golden Age of Discovery, Faraway Worlds

    Beckon." *New York Times* 9 Feb. 1997, late ed., sec. 1: 1+. Print.

When an edition of the newspaper is specified on the masthead, name the edition (eastern ed., late ed., natl. ed., and so on), as in the example just given.

If the city of publication is not obvious, include it in brackets after the name of the newspaper: *Courier-Journal* [Louisville].

■ **24. EDITORIAL IN A NEWSPAPER** Cite an editorial as you would an article with an unknown author, adding the word "Editorial" after the title.

"All Wet." Editorial. *Boston Globe* 12 Feb. 2001: A14. Print.

■ **25. LETTER TO THE EDITOR** Name the writer, followed by the word "Letter" and the publication information for the periodical in which the letter appears.

Shrewsbury, Toni. Letter. *Atlanta Journal-Constitution* 17 Feb. 2001: A13.

    Print.

■ **26. BOOK OR FILM REVIEW** Name the reviewer and the title of the review, if any, followed by the words "Rev. of" and the title and author or director of the work reviewed. Add the publication information for the periodical in which the review appears.

Gleick, Elizabeth. "The Burdens of Genius." Rev. of *The Last Samurai*,

    by Helen DeWitt. *Time* 4 Dec. 2000: 171. Print.

Lane, Anthony. "Dream On." Rev. of *The Science of Sleep* and *Renaissance*,

    dir. Michel Gondry. *New Yorker* 25 Sept. 2006: 155-57. Print.

Online sources

This section shows how to prepare works cited entries for a variety of online sources, including Web sites, online books, articles in online databases and periodicals, blogs, e-mail, and Web postings.

MLA guidelines assume that readers can locate most online sources by entering the author, title, or other identifying information in a search engine or a database. Consequently, MLA does not require a Web address (URL) in citations for online sources. Some instructors may require a URL; for an example, see the note at the end of item 27.

MLA style calls for a sponsor or publisher for most online sources. If a source has no sponsor or publisher, use the abbreviation "N.p." (for "No publisher") in the sponsor position. If there is no date of publication or update, use "n.d." (for "no date") after the sponsor. For an article in an online scholarly journal or an article from a database, give page numbers if they are available; if they are not, use the abbreviation "n. pag." (See item 32.)

■ **27. ENTIRE WEB SITE** Begin with the name of the author, editor, or corporate author (if known) and the title of the site, italicized. Then give the sponsor and the date of publication or last update. End with the medium and your date of access.

With author or editor

Peterson, Susan Lynn. *The Life of Martin Luther*. Susan Lynn Peterson, 2005. Web. 24 Jan. 2009.

Halsall, Paul, ed. *Internet Modern History Sourcebook*. Fordham U, 22 Sept. 2001. Web. 19 Jan. 2009.

With corporate (group) author

United States. Environmental Protection Agency. *Drinking Water Standards*. EPA, 28 Nov. 2006. Web. 24 Jan. 2007.

Author unknown

Margaret Sanger Papers Project. History Dept., New York U, 18 Oct. 2000. Web. 6 Jan. 2009.

If a site has no title, substitute a description, such as "Home page," for the title. Do not italicize the words or put them in quotation marks.

Yoon, Mina. Home page. Oak Ridge Natl. Laboratory, 28 Dec. 2006.

    Web. 12 Jan. 2009.

NOTE: If your instructor requires a URL for Web sources, include the URL, enclosed in angle brackets, at the end of the entry. If you must divide a URL at the end of a line in a works cited entry, break it after a slash. Do not insert a hyphen.

Peterson, Susan Lynn. *The Life of Martin Luther.* Susan Lynn Peterson,

    2005. Web. 24 Jan. 2009. <http://www.susanlynnpeterson.com/

    index_files/luther.htm>.

28. SHORT WORK FROM A WEB SITE Short works include articles, poems, and other documents that are not book length or that appear as internal pages on a Web site. Include the following elements: author's name; title of the short work, in quotation marks; title of the site, italicized; sponsor of the site; date of publication or last update; medium; and your access date.

For an annotated example, see pages 450–51.

With author

Shiva, Vandana. "Bioethics: A Third World Issue." *NativeWeb.*

    NativeWeb, n.d. Web. 22 Jan. 2009.

Author unknown

"Living Old." *Frontline.* PBS Online, 21 Nov. 2006. Web. 19 Jan. 2009.

29. ONLINE BOOK Cite a book or a book-length work, such as a play or a long poem, as you would a short work from a Web site (see item 28), but italicize the title of the work.

Milton, John. *Paradise Lost: Book I. Poetryfoundation.org.* Poetry

    Foundation, 2008. Web. 14 Dec. 2008.

Give the print publication information for the work, if available (see items 6–19), followed by the title of the Web site, the medium, and your date of access.

Jacobs, Harriet A. *Incidents in the Life of a Slave Girl: Written by*
       Herself. Ed. L. Maria Child. Boston, 1861. *Documenting the*
       American South. Web. 3 Feb. 2009.

■ **30. PART OF AN ONLINE BOOK**   Place the title of the book part
before the book's title. If the part is a chapter or a short work
such as a poem or an essay, put its title in quotation marks. If
the part is an introduction or another division of the book, do
not use quotation marks. (See also item 15 on p. 442.) Following the publication information, give the page numbers for the
part (or use "N. pag." if the work is not paginated). End with the
Web site on which you found the work, the medium, and your
date of access.

Adams, Henry. "Diplomacy." *The Education of Henry Adams*. By Adams.
       Boston: Houghton, 1918. N. pag. *Bartleby.com: Great Books Online*.
       Web. 8 Jan. 2009.

■ **31. WORK FROM A DATABASE**   For sources retrieved from a
library's subscription database, first list the publication information for the source (see items 20–26). Then give the name of
the database, italicized; the medium; and your date of access.
An annotated example appears on pages 454–55.

Johnson, Kirk. "The Mountain Lions of Michigan." *Endangered Species Update*
       19.2 (2002): 27-31. *Expanded Academic Index*. Web. 26 Nov. 2008.

Barrera, Rebeca María. "A Case for Bilingual Education." *Scholastic Parent and*
       Child Nov.-Dec. 2004: 72-73. *Academic Search Premier*. Web.
       1 Feb. 2009.

Williams, Jeffrey J. "Why Today's Publishing World Is Reprising the
       Past." *Chronicle of Higher Education* 13 June 2008: 8+. *LexisNexis*
       Academic. Web. 29 Sept. 2008.

When you access a work through a personal subscription
service such as *America Online*, give the same information as
for a library subscription database.

■ **32. ARTICLE IN AN ONLINE JOURNAL**   When citing an article in
an online journal, give publication information as for a print

Citation at a glance: Short work from a Web site (MLA)

To cite a short work from a Web site in MLA style, include the following elements:

1 Author
2 Title of short work
3 Title of Web site
4 Sponsor of Web site
5 Update date ("n.d." if there is no date)
6 Medium
7 Date of access

ON-SCREEN VIEW OF SHORT WORK

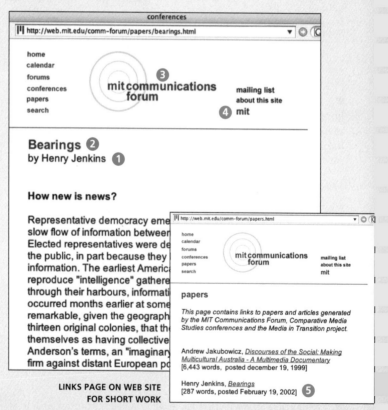

LINKS PAGE ON WEB SITE FOR SHORT WORK

BROWSER PRINTOUT OF SHORT WORK

conferences   http://web.mit.edu/comm-forum/papers/bearings.html

home
calendar
forums
conferences   **mit communications**   mailing list
papers   **forum**   about this site
search   mit

Bearings
by Henry Jenkins

How new is news?

Representative democracy emerged in the context of a relatively slow flow of information between the capital and the periphery. Elected representatives were delegated to make decisions for the public, in part because they had quicker access to reliable information. The earliest American newspapers were content to reproduce "intelligence" gathered from ships as they passed through their harbours, information about events that might have occurred months earlier at some other port of call. It is remarkable, given the geographic distance separating the thirteen original colonies, that they were able to think of themselves as having collective interests, as forming, in Benedict Anderson's terms, an "imaginary community" that could stand firm against distant European powers. The complex balance between federal and state authority established in the U.S. Constitution might be understood as a negotiation between the ideal of local control and the recognition of the slow flow of information across those huge geographic distances. The introduction of the telegraph dramatically accelerated the flow of news, and it has been followed throughout the twentieth century by a succession of faster technologies that allow minute by minute, real time reporting of distance events.

In turn, these technologies have established public expectations about timely delivery of the news. The result of this urgency to give us the news as quickly as possible has been a complex layering of the television newscast – sometimes splitting the screen to report on simultaneous events worldwide (such as the simultaneous impeachment vote and American attacks on Baghdad), sometimes introducing multiple windows and layers of textual information (as with the "crawls" introduced by the cable news networks in response to the complex geopolitics of the post-September 11 world). The impact of this accelerated and intensified news flow has been, many warn, a loss of editorial judgement, the circulation of more misinformation. The speed of the networked computer increases expectations for an even faster news flow, with the public often turning to on-line sources with the anticipation that they will be able to offer in-depth information (a product of what Janet Murray calls our encyclopedic expectations for new media) as rapidly as television news can provide the headlines. This speeded-up dispersion of important information has led some to speculate that the Internet might make participatory democracy practical for the first time in the modern era. But others have argued that new media may undermine the serious and thoughtful deliberation upon which democracy depends.

Who owns the news?

Writers such as Robert McChesney have spoken of the danger of media concentration; today, five major corporations control the bulk of the world's media. Deregulation has enabled these organizations to become significant players across a whole range of media channels. News has increasingly become one commodity among many within multinational media industries, packaged and sold alongside entertainment, evaluated according to costs and audience share, rather than traditional journalistic standards. Some have claimed that digital media have lowered the barriers to

1 of 4   6/16/05 4:56 PM

(7)

6/16/05 4:56 PM

WORKS CITED ENTRY FOR A SHORT WORK FROM A WEB SITE

┌──── **1** ────┐ ┌──── **2** ───┐ ┌──────── **3** ────────┐ ┌**4**┐
Jenkins, Henry. "Bearings." *MIT Communications Forum*. MIT,

          ┌──── **5** ────┐ ┌**6**┐ ┌───── **7** ─────┐
          19 Feb. 2002. Web. 16 June 2005.

For more on citing sources from Web sites in MLA style, see
pages 447–49.

journal (see items 21 and 22), using "n. pag." if the source does not have page numbers. Then give the medium and your date of access.

Belau, Linda. "Trauma and the Material Signifier." *Postmodern Culture*

11.2 (2001): n. pag. Web. 20 Feb. 2009.

33. ARTICLE IN AN ONLINE MAGAZINE OR NEWSPAPER Give the author; the title of the article (in quotation marks); the title of the magazine or newspaper (italicized); the sponsor or publisher of the site (use "N.p." if there is none); the date of publication; the medium; and your date of access.

Online magazine

Paulson, Steve. "Buddha on the Brain." *Salon.com*. Salon Media Group,

27 Nov. 2006. Web. 18 Jan. 2009.

Online newspaper

Rubin, Joel. "Report Faults Charter School." *Los Angeles Times*. Los Angeles

Times, 22 Jan. 2005. Web. 24 Jan. 2009.

34. ENTIRE WEBLOG (BLOG) Cite a blog as you would an entire Web site (see item 27). Give the author's name; the title of the blog, italicized; the sponsor or publisher of the blog (use "N.p." if there is none); and the date of the most recent update. Then give the medium and your date of access.

Mayer, Caroline. *The Checkout*. Washington Post, 28 Feb. 2006. Web.

19 Jan. 2007.

35. ENTRY IN A WEBLOG (BLOG) Cite an entry or a comment (a response to an entry) in a blog as you would a short work from a Web site (see item 28). If the entry or comment has no title, use the label "Weblog entry" or "Weblog comment." Follow with the title of the blog, italicized, and the remaining information as for an entire blog in item 34.

Mayer, Caroline. "Some Surprising Findings about Identity Theft." *The*

Checkout. Washington Post, 28 Feb. 2006. Web. 19 Jan. 2007.

Burdick, Dennis. Weblog comment. *The Checkout*. Washington Post, 28

Feb. 2006. Web. 19 Jan. 2007.

■ **36. CD-ROM** Treat a CD-ROM as you would any other source, but add the medium ("CD-ROM"). For a book on CD-ROM, add the medium after the publication information.

"Pimpernel." *The American Heritage Dictionary of the English Language.*

4th ed. Boston: Houghton, 2000. CD-ROM.

■ **37. E-MAIL** To cite an e-mail, begin with the writer's name and the subject line. Then write "Message to" followed by the name of the recipient. End with the date of the message and the medium.

Lowe, Walter. "Review questions." Message to the author. 15 Mar.

2009. E-mail.

■ **38. POSTING TO AN ONLINE DISCUSSION LIST** When possible, cite archived versions of postings. If you cannot locate an archived version, keep a copy of the posting for your records. Begin with the author's name, followed by the title or subject line, in quotation marks (use the label "Online posting" if the posting has no title); the title of the Web site on which the discussion list is found, italicized; the sponsor or publisher of the site (use "N.p." if there is none); the date of publication; the medium; and your date of access.

Fainton, Peter. "Re: Backlash against New Labour." *Media Lens Message*

Board. Media Lens, 7 May 2008. Web. 2 June 2008.

Multimedia sources (including online versions)

Multimedia sources include visuals (such as works of art), audio works (such as sound recordings), audiovisuals (such as films), podcasts, and live events. Give the medium for all multimedia sources, usually at the end of the citation and not italicized or in quotation marks (for instance, "Print," "Web," "Radio," "Television," "CD," "Audiocassette," "Film," "Videocassette," "DVD," "Performance," "Lecture," "PDF file," "*Microsoft Word* file," "JPEG file").

■ **39. WORK OF ART** Cite the artist's name; the title of the artwork, italicized; the date of composition; the medium of composition (for instance, "Lithograph on paper," "Photograph," "Charcoal on paper"); and the institution and the city in which

Citation at a glance: Article from a database (MLA)

To cite an article from a database in MLA style, include the following elements:

1 Author
2 Title of article
3 Name of periodical, volume and issue numbers
4 Date of publication
5 Inclusive pages
6 Name of database
7 Medium
8 Date of access

EBSCO HOST | Research Databases

Basic Search | Advanced Search | Choose Databases

New Search | View Folder | Preferences | Help

Return to LINK(

Sign In to My EBSCOhost

Keyword | Publications | Subject Terms | Indexes | Cited References

Images

4 of 4 ▶ Result List | Refine Search 🖨 Print ✉ E-mail 💾 Save 📁 Add to folder   📁 Folder is empty.

Formats: 📄 Citation 📄 PDF Full Text (87K) Cited References (9)

Title: IT'S THE *INFORMATION* AGE, SO WHERE'S THE *INFORMATION*? **2**

Authors: Jenson, Jill D.[1] **1**

Source: College Teaching; Summer2004, Vol. 52 Issue 3, p107, 6p

Document Type: Article **4** **3** **5**

Subject Terms: *COLLEGE teachers
*COMPUTER literacy
*DATABASES
*LIBRARIES
*RESEARCH
*STUDENTS
*INTERNET in education

Author-Supplied Keywords: technology
Internet
information literacy
electronic research

NAICS/Industry Codes: 51412 Libraries and Archives
5417 Scientific Research and Development Services

Abstract: Although most college faculty are aware of the problems that students encounter when conducting research using the Internet, fewer recognize why their students lack success when using the electronic databases and indexes to which the institution's library subscribes. In this article, I point to teachers' assumptions about their students' "computer *literacy*," as well as to the students' lack of hands-on experience in an actual library, as potential sources of the problem. I provide practical, detailed suggestions, which are useful across disciplines, for overcoming these obstacles. [ABSTRACT FROM AUTHOR]

Author Affiliations: [1]Assistant Professor, Department of Composition, University of Minnesota Duluth

ISSN: 8756-7555

Accession Number: 13477508

Persistent link to this record: http://search.epnet.com/login.aspx?direct=true&db=aph&an=13477508

Database: Academic Search Premier **6**

View Links: SFX

Formats: 📄 Citation 📄 PDF Full Text (87K)

© 2005 EBSCO Publishing. Privacy Policy - Terms of Use

WORKS CITED ENTRY FOR AN ARTICLE FROM A DATABASE

```
     ┌──1──┐  ┌─────────────2─────────────┐
Jenson, Jill D. "It's the Information Age, so Where's the Information?"

     ┌─────3─────┐ ┌─4─┐ ┌─5─┐ ┌───────6───────┐
     College Teaching 52.3 (2004): 107-12. Academic Search Premier.

     ┌7┐ ┌──8──┐
     Web. 2 Feb. 2009.
```

For more on citing articles from a database in MLA style, see page 449.

the artwork is located. For artworks found online, omit the medium of composition and include the title of the Web site, the medium, and your date of access.

Constable, John. *Dedham Vale*. 1802. Oil on canvas. Victoria and Albert
    Museum, London.

van Gogh, Vincent. *The Starry Night*. 1889. Museum of Mod. Art, New
    York. *MoMA: The Museum of Modern Art*. Web. 14 Jan. 2009.

■ **40. CARTOON** Begin with the cartoonist's name; the title of the cartoon (if it has one) in quotation marks; the word "Cartoon" or "Comic strip"; publication information; and the medium. To cite an online cartoon, instead of publication information give the title of the Web site; the sponsor or publisher; the medium; and your date of access

Sutton, Ward. "Why Wait 'til November?" Cartoon. *Village Voice* 7-13
    July 2004: 6. Print.

■ **41. ADVERTISEMENT** Name the product or company being advertised, followed by the word "Advertisement." Give publication information for the source in which the advertisement appears.

Truth by Calvin Klein. Advertisement. *Vogue* Dec. 2000: 95-98. Print.

■ **42. MAP OR CHART** Cite a map or a chart as you would a book or a short work within a longer work. Use the word "Map" or "Chart" following the title. Add the medium and, for an online source, the sponsor or publisher and the date of access.

Joseph, Lori, and Bob Laird. "Driving While Phoning Is Dangerous."

   Chart. *USA Today* 16 Feb. 2001: 1A. Print.

Serbia. Map. *Syrena Maps*. Syrena, 2 Feb. 2001. Web. 17 Mar. 2009.

■ **43. MUSICAL SCORE** For both print and online versions, begin with the composer's name; the title of the work, italicized; and the date of composition. For a print source, give the place of publication; the name of the publisher and date of publication; and the medium. For an online source, give the title of the Web site; the publisher or sponsor of the site; the date of Web publication; the medium; and your date of access.

Handel, G. F. *Messiah: An Oratorio*. N.d. *CCARH Publications: Scores and*

   Parts. Center for Computer Assisted Research in the Humanities,

   2003. Web. 5 Jan. 2009.

■ **44. SOUND RECORDING** Begin with the name of the person you want to emphasize: the composer, conductor ("Cond."), or performer ("Perf."). For a long work, give the title, italicized; the names of pertinent artists (such as performers, readers, or musicians); and the orchestra and conductor, if relevant. End with the manufacturer, the date, and the medium.

Bizet, Georges. *Carmen*. Perf. Jennifer Laramore, Thomas Moser, Angela

   Gheorghiu, and Samuel Ramey. Bavarian State Orch. and Chorus.

   Cond. Giuseppe Sinopoli. Warner, 1996. CD.

For a song, put the title in quotation marks. If you include the name of the album or CD, italicize it.

Blige, Mary J. "Be without You." *The Breakthrough*. Geffen, 2005. CD.

■ **45. FILM OR VIDEO** Begin with the title, italicized. Cite the director ("Dir.") and the lead actors or narrator ("Perf." or

"Narr."); the distributor; the year of the film's release; and the medium ("Videocassette," "DVD," "Film").

Finding Neverland. Dir. Marc Forster. Perf. Johnny Depp, Kate Winslet,

Julie Christie, Radha Mitchell, and Dustin Hoffman. Miramax,

2004. DVD.

The Hours. Dir. Stephen Daldry. Perf. Meryl Streep, Julianne Moore, and

Nicole Kidman. Paramount, 2002. DVD.

■ **46. SPECIAL FEATURE ON A DVD** Begin with the title of the feature, in quotation marks, and the names of any important contributors. Add the title of the DVD and other relevant information about the DVD, as in item 45. End with the number of the disc on which the feature appears.

"Sweeney's London." Prod. Eric Young. *Sweeney Todd: The Demon*

Barber of Fleet Street. Dir. Tim Burton. DreamWorks, 2007. DVD.

Disc 2.

■ **47. RADIO OR TELEVISION PROGRAM** Begin with the title of the radio segment or television episode (if there is one) in quotation marks, followed by the title of the program, italicized. Next give relevant information about the program's writer ("By"), director ("Dir."), performers ("Perf."), or host ("Host"). Then name the network, the local station (if any) and location, the date of broadcast, and the medium ("Television," "Radio"). For a program you accessed online, after the information about the program give the network, the title of the Web site, the medium ("Web"), and your date of access.

"New Orleans." *American Experience*. Narr. Jeffrey Wright. PBS. WGBH,

Boston, 12 Feb. 2007. Television.

"Elif Shafak: Writing under a Watchful Eye." *Fresh Air*. Host Terry Gross.

Natl. Public Radio, 6 Feb. 2007. *NPR.org*. Web. 22 Feb. 2009.

■ **48. RADIO OR TELEVISION INTERVIEW** Begin with the name of the person who was interviewed, followed by the word "Interview" and the interviewer's name. End with the information about the program as in item 47.

McGovern, George. Interview by Charlie Rose. *Charlie Rose*. PBS. WNET,

New York, 1 Feb. 2001. Television.

■ **49. PODCAST** A podcast can refer to digital audio content — downloadable lectures, interviews, or essays — or to the method of delivery. Treat a podcast as you would a short work from a Web site (see item 28), giving the medium of delivery (such as "Web," "MP3 file," "MPEG-4 video file") before your date of access.

Patterson, Chris. "Will School Consolidation Improve Education?" Host

Michael Quinn Sullivan. *Texas PolicyCast*. Texas Public Policy

Foundation, 13 Apr. 2006. MP3 file. 10 Jan. 2009.

■ **50. ONLINE VIDEO CLIP** Cite a video clip as you would a short work from a Web site (see item 28).

Murphy, Beth. "Tips for a Good Profile Piece." *Project: Report*. YouTube,

7 Sept. 2008. Web. 19 Sept. 2008.

■ **51. LIVE PERFORMANCE** For a live performance of a play, a ballet, an opera, or a concert, begin with the title of the work performed. Then name the author or composer of the work (preceded by the word "By"); relevant information such as the director ("Dir."), the choreographer ("Chor."), the conductor ("Cond."), or performers ("Perf."); the theater, ballet, or opera company; the theater and its city; the date of the performance; and the label "Performance."

Art . By Yasmina Reza. Dir. Matthew Warchus. Perf. Philip Franks, Leigh

Lawson, and Simon Shephard. Whitehall Theatre, London. 3 Dec.

2001. Performance.

Cello Concerto no. 2. By Eric Tanguy. Cond. Seiji Ozawa. Perf. Mstislav

Rostropovich. Boston Symphony Orch. Symphony Hall, Boston. 5

Apr. 2002. Performance.

■ **52. LECTURE OR PUBLIC ADDRESS** Cite the speaker's name, followed by the title of the lecture (if any), in quotation marks;

the organization sponsoring the lecture; the location; the date; and a label such as "Lecture" or "Address."

> Wellbery, David E. "On a Sentence of Franz Kafka." Franke Inst. for the
>
> Humanities. Gleacher Center, Chicago. 1 Feb. 2006. Lecture.

■ **53. PERSONAL INTERVIEW**   To cite an interview that you conducted, begin with the name of the person interviewed. Then write "Personal interview" or "Telephone interview," followed by the date of the interview.

> Akufo, Dautey. Personal interview. 11 Aug. 2007.

Other sources (including online versions)

This section includes a variety of sources not covered elsewhere. For sources obtained on the Web, consult the appropriate model in this section and give required information for an online source (see items 27–38); end the citation with the medium and your date of access.

■ **54. GOVERNMENT PUBLICATION**   Treat the government agency as the author, giving the name of the government followed by the name of the department and the agency, if any. For print sources, add the medium at the end of the entry. For online sources, follow the model for an entire Web site (item 27) or a short work from a Web site (item 28).

> United States. Dept. of Labor. *America's Dynamic Workforce*. Washington:
>
> US Dept. of Labor, 2004. Print.

> United States. Dept. of Transportation. Natl. Highway Traffic Safety
>
> Administration. *An Investigation of the Safety Implications of Wireless*
>
> *Communications in Vehicles*. Natl. Highway Traffic Safety
>
> Administration, Nov. 1999. Web. 20 May 2006.

■ **55. HISTORICAL AND LEGAL SOURCES**   For a well-known historical document, such as the United States Constitution, provide the document title, neither italicized nor in quotation marks, the document date, and publication information. For less familiar documents, begin with the author, if the work has one, and continue with the title, date, and publication information.

Jefferson, Thomas. First Inaugural Address. 1801. *The American Reader*.

Ed. Diane Ravitch. New York: Harper, 1990. 42-44. Print.

For a legislative act (law), give the name of the act, neither italicized nor in quotation marks, followed by the Public Law number, the Statutes at Large information, the date, and the medium.

Electronic Freedom of Information Act Amendments of 1996. Pub. L.

104-231. 110 Stat. 3048. 2 Oct. 1996. Print.

For a court case, name the first plaintiff and the first defendant. Then give the law report number, the court, the year, and publication information. In a works cited entry, do not italicize the name of the case. (For an in-text citation, see item 17 on p. 433.)

Utah v. Evans. 536 US 452. Supreme Court of the US. 2002. *Supreme*

Court Collection. Legal Information Inst., Cornell U Law School,

n.d. Web. 30 Apr. 2008.

■ **56. PAMPHLET**   Cite a pamphlet as you would a book.

Commonwealth of Massachusetts. Dept. of Jury Commissioner. *A Few Facts*

about Jury Duty. Boston: Commonwealth of Massachusetts, 2004.

Print.

■ **57. DISSERTATION**   Begin with the author's name, followed by the dissertation title in quotation marks, the abbreviation "Diss.," the name of the institution, the year the dissertation was accepted, and the medium.

Jackson, Shelley. "Writing Whiteness: Contemporary Southern Literature

in Black and White." Diss. U of Maryland, 2000. Print.

For dissertations that have been published in book form, italicize the title and add publication information and the medium after the dissertation year.

Damberg, Cheryl L. *Healthcare Reform: Distributional Consequences of an*

Employer Mandate for Workers in Small Firms. Diss. Rand Graduate

School, 1995. Santa Monica: Rand, 1996. Print.

■ **58. ABSTRACT OF A DISSERTATION**   Cite an abstract as you would an unpublished dissertation. After the dissertation date, give the abbreviation *DA* or *DAI* (for *Dissertation Abstracts* or *Dissertation Abstracts International*), followed by the volume and issue numbers, the year of publication, the page numbers, and the medium.

Chen, Shu-Ling. "Mothers and Daughters in Morrison, Tan, Marshall,

and Kincaid." Diss. U of Washington, 2000. *DAI* 61.6 (2000): 2289.

Print.

■ **59. PUBLISHED PROCEEDINGS OF A CONFERENCE**   Cite published conference proceedings as you would a book, adding information about the conference after the title.

Kartiganer, Donald M., and Ann J. Abadie, eds. *Faulkner at 100:*

Retrospect and Prospect. Proc. of Faulkner and Yoknapatawpha Conf.,

27 July-1 Aug. 1997, U of Mississippi. Jackson: UP of Mississippi,

2000. Print.

■ **60. PUBLISHED INTERVIEW**   Name the person interviewed, followed by the title of the interview (if there is one). If the interview does not have a title, include the word "Interview" followed by a period after the interviewee's name. Give publication information for the work in which the interview was published.

Armstrong, Lance. "Lance in France." *Sports Illustrated* 28 June 2004: 46+.

Print.

If the name of the interviewer is relevant, include it after the name of the interviewee.

Prince. Interview by Bilge Ebiri. *Yahoo! Internet Life* 7.6 (2001):

82-85. Print.

■ **61. PERSONAL LETTER**   To cite a letter that you have received, begin with the writer's name and add the phrase "Letter to the author," followed by the date. Add the medium ("MS" for "manuscript," or a handwritten letter; "TS" for "typescript," or a typed letter).

Primak, Shoshana. Letter to the author. 6 May 2007. TS.

■ **62. PUBLISHED LETTER** Begin with the writer of the letter, the words "Letter to" and the recipient, and the date of the letter (use "N.d." if the letter is undated). Then add the title of the collection and proceed as for a work in an anthology (see item 10).

Wharton, Edith. Letter to Henry James. 28 Feb. 1915. *Henry James and*
Edith Wharton: Letters, 1900-1915. Ed. Lyall H. Powers. New York:
Scribner's, 1990. 323-26. Print.

■ **63. ENTRY IN A WIKI** A wiki is an online reference that is openly edited by its users. Treat an entry in a wiki as you would a short work from a Web site (see item 28 on p. 448). Because wiki content is, by definition, collectively edited and can be updated frequently, do not include an author. Give the title of the entry; the name of the wiki, italicized; the sponsor or publisher of the wiki (use "N.p." if there is none); the date of the last update; the medium; and your date of access.

"Hip Hop Music." *Wikipedia*. Wikimedia Foundation, 26 Sept. 2008.
Web. 18 Mar. 2009.

"Negation in Languages." *UniLang.org*. UniLang, 25 Oct. 2004. Web. 9 June
2009.

ON THE WEB > **dianahacker.com/rules**
Research exercises > MLA > E-ex 55–4 to 55–6

55c MLA information notes (optional)

Researchers who use the MLA system of parenthetical documentation (see 55a) may also use information notes for one of two purposes:

1. to provide additional material that might interrupt the flow of the paper yet is important enough to include
2. to refer to several sources or to provide comments on sources

Information notes may be either footnotes or endnotes. Footnotes appear at the foot of the page; endnotes appear on a separate page at the end of the paper, just before the list of works

cited. For either style, the notes are numbered consecutively throughout the paper. The text of the paper contains a raised arabic numeral that corresponds to the number of the note.

TEXT

In the past several years, employees have filed a number of lawsuits against employers because of online monitoring practices.[1]

NOTE

[1] For a discussion of federal law applicable to electronic surveillance in the workplace, see Kesan 293.

56

MLA manuscript format; sample paper

56a MLA manuscript format

The following guidelines are consistent with advice given in the *MLA Handbook for Writers of Research Papers,* 7th ed. (New York: MLA, 2009). For a sample MLA paper, see 56b.

Formatting the paper

Papers written in MLA style should be formatted as follows.

MATERIALS Use good-quality 8½″ × 11″ white paper. Secure the pages with a paper clip. Unless your instructor suggests otherwise, do not staple or bind the pages.

TITLE AND IDENTIFICATION MLA does not require a title page. On the first page of your paper, place your name, your instructor's name, the course title, and the date on separate lines against the left margin. Then center your title. (See p. 467 for a sample first page.)

If your instructor requires a title page, ask for guidelines on formatting it. A format similar to the one on page 515 may be acceptable.

PAGINATION   Put the page number preceded by your last name in the upper right corner of each page, one-half inch below the top edge. Use arabic numerals (1, 2, 3, and so on).

MARGINS, LINE SPACING, AND PARAGRAPH INDENTS   Leave margins of one inch on all sides of the page. Left-align the text.

Double-space throughout the paper. Do not add extra space above or below the title of the paper or between paragraphs.

Indent the first line of each paragraph one-half inch (or five spaces) from the left margin.

LONG QUOTATIONS   When a quotation is longer than four typed lines of prose or three lines of verse, set it off from the text by indenting the entire quotation one inch (or ten spaces) from the left margin. Double-space the indented quotation, and do not add extra space above or below it.

Quotation marks are not needed when a quotation has been set off from the text by indenting. See page 468 for an example.

WEB ADDRESSES   When a Web address (URL) mentioned in the text of your paper must be divided at the end of a line, do not insert a hyphen (a hyphen could appear to be part of the address). For MLA rules on dividing Web addresses in your list of works cited, see page 465.

HEADINGS   MLA neither encourages nor discourages the use of headings and currently provides no guidelines for their use. If you would like to insert headings in a long essay or research paper, check first with your instructor.

VISUALS   MLA classifies visuals as tables and figures (figures include graphs, charts, maps, photographs, and drawings). Label each table with an arabic numeral (Table 1, Table 2, and so on) and provide a clear caption that identifies the subject. The label and caption should appear on separate lines above the table, flush left. Below the table, give its source in a note like this one:

Source: David N. Greenfield and Richard A. Davis; "Lost in Cyberspace: The Web @ Work"; *CyberPsychology and Behavior* 5.4 (2002): 349; print.

For each figure, place the figure number (using the abbreviation "Fig.") and a caption below the figure, flush left. Include source information following the caption.

Visuals should be placed in the text, as close as possible to the sentences that relate to them unless your instructor prefers them in an appendix. See page 471 for an example of a visual in the text of a paper.

Preparing the list of works cited

Begin the list of works cited on a new page at the end of the paper. Center the title Works Cited about one inch from the top of the page. Double-space throughout. See pages 474–75 for a sample list of works cited.

ALPHABETIZING THE LIST   Alphabetize the list by the last names of the authors (or editors); if a work has no author or editor, alphabetize by the first word of the title other than *A, An,* or *The.*

If your list includes two or more works by the same author, use the author's name for the first entry only. For subsequent entries, use three hyphens followed by a period. List the titles in alphabetical order. See item 5 on page 438.

INDENTING   Do not indent the first line of each works cited entry, but indent any additional lines one-half inch (or five spaces). This technique highlights the names of the authors, making it easy for readers to scan the alphabetized list.

WEB ADDRESSES   If you need to include a Web addresss (URL) in a works cited entry, do not insert a hyphen when dividing it at the end of a line. Break the URL only after a slash. Insert angle brackets around the URL. (See the note following item 27 on p. 448.)

If your word processing program automatically turns Web addresses into links (by underlining them and highlighting them in color), turn off this feature.

ON THE WEB > **dianahacker.com/rules**
Additional resources > Formatting help

56b Sample MLA research paper

On the following pages is a research paper on the topic of electronic surveillance in the workplace, written by Anna Orlov, a student in a composition class. Orlov's paper is documented with MLA-style in-text citations and list of works cited. Annotations in the margins of the paper draw your attention to Orlov's use of MLA style and her effective writing.

ON THE WEB > **dianahacker.com/rules**
  Model papers > MLA papers: Orlov; Daly; Levi
                > MLA annotated bibliography: Orlov

Orlov 1

Anna Orlov

Professor Willis

English 101

17 March 2006

Online Monitoring:

A Threat to Employee Privacy in the Wired Workplace

As the Internet has become an integral tool of

businesses, company policies on Internet usage have

become as common as policies regarding vacation days

or sexual harassment. A 2005 study by the American

Management Association and ePolicy Institute found that

76% of companies monitor employees' use of the Web,

and the number of companies that block employees'

access to certain Web sites has increased 27% since

2001 (1). Unlike other company rules, however, Internet

usage policies often include language authorizing

companies to secretly monitor their employees, a practice

that raises questions about rights in the workplace.

Although companies often have legitimate concerns that

lead them to monitor employees' Internet usage—from

expensive security breaches to reduced productivity—the

benefits of electronic surveillance are outweighed by its

costs to employees' privacy and autonomy.

While surveillance of employees is not a new

phenomenon, electronic surveillance allows employers

to monitor workers with unprecedented efficiency. In

Title is centered.

Opening sentences provide background for thesis.

Thesis asserts Orlov's main point.

Orlov 2

Summary and long quotation are introduced with a signal phrase naming the author.

his book *The Naked Employee*, Frederick Lane describes offline ways in which employers have been permitted to intrude on employees' privacy for decades, such as drug testing, background checks, psychological exams, lie detector tests, and in-store video surveillance. The difference, Lane argues, between these old methods of data gathering and electronic surveillance involves quantity:

Long quotation is set off from the text; quotation marks are omitted.

> Technology makes it possible for employers to gather enormous amounts of data about employees, often far beyond what is necessary to satisfy safety or productivity concerns. And the trends that drive technology—faster, smaller, cheaper—make it possible for larger and larger numbers of employers to gather ever-greater amounts of personal data. (3-4)

Page number is given in parentheses after the final period.

In an age when employers can collect data whenever employees use their computers—when they send e-mail, surf the Web, or even arrive at or depart from their workstations—the challenge for both employers and employees is to determine how much is too much.

Clear topic sentences, like this one, are used throughout the paper.

Another key difference between traditional surveillance and electronic surveillance is that employers can monitor workers' computer use secretly. One popular monitoring method is keystroke logging, which is done by means of an undetectable program on employees' computers. The Web site of a vendor for Spector Pro, a

Orlov 3

popular keystroke logging program, explains that the software can be installed to operate in "Stealth" mode so that it "does not show up as an icon, does not appear in the Windows system tray, . . . [and] cannot be uninstalled without the Spector Pro password which YOU specify" ("Automatically"). As Lane explains, these programs record every key entered into the computer in hidden directories that can later be accessed or uploaded by supervisors; the programs can even scan for keywords tailored to individual companies (128-29).

> Source with an unknown author is cited by a shortened title.

   Some experts have argued that a range of legitimate concerns justifies employer monitoring of employee Internet usage. As *PC World* columnist Daniel Tynan points out, companies that don't monitor network traffic can be penalized for their ignorance: "Employees could accidentally (or deliberately) spill confidential information . . . or allow worms to spread throughout a corporate network." The ePolicy Institute, an organization that advises companies about reducing risks from technology, reported that breaches in computer security cost institutions $100 million in 1999 alone (Flynn). Companies also are held legally accountable for many of the transactions conducted on their networks and with their technology. Legal scholar Jay Kesan points out that the law holds employers liable for employees' actions such as

> Orlov anticipates objections and provides sources for opposing views.

Orlov 4

violations of copyright laws, the distribution of
offensive or graphic sexual material, and illegal
disclosure of confidential information (312).

Transition helps readers move from one paragraph to the next.

These kinds of concerns should give employers,
in certain instances, the right to monitor employee
behavior. But employers rushing to adopt surveillance
programs might not be adequately weighing the
effect such programs can have on employee morale.
Employers must consider the possibility that employees
will perceive surveillance as a breach of trust that
can make them feel like disobedient children, not
responsible adults who wish to perform their jobs
professionally and autonomously.

Orlov treats both sides fairly; she provides a transition to her own argument.

Yet determining how much autonomy workers
should be given is complicated by the ambiguous
nature of productivity in the wired workplace. On the one
hand, computers and Internet access give employees
powerful tools to carry out their jobs; on the other
hand, the same technology offers constant temptations
to avoid work. As a 2005 study by *Salary.com* and
America Online indicates, the Internet ranked as the top
choice among employees for ways of wasting time on the
job; it beat talking with co-workers—the second most
popular method—by a margin of nearly two to one
(Frauenheim). Chris Gonsalves, an editor for *eWeek.com*,
argues that the technology has changed the terms between
employers and employees: "While bosses can easily detect

Orlov 5

Fig. 1. This "Dilbert" comic strip suggests that personal Internet usage is widespread in the workplace (Adams 106).

Illustration has figure number and source information.

and interrupt water-cooler chatter," he writes, "the employee who is shopping at Lands' End or IMing with fellow fantasy baseball managers may actually appear to be working." The gap between behaviors that are observable to managers and the employee's actual activities when sitting behind a computer has created additional motivations for employers to invest in surveillance programs. "Dilbert," a popular cartoon that spoofs office culture, aptly captures how rampant recreational Internet use has become in the workplace (see fig. 1).

No page number is available for this Web source.

But monitoring online activities can have the unintended effect of making employees resentful. As many workers would be quick to point out, Web surfing and other personal uses of the Internet can provide needed outlets in the stressful work environment; many scholars have argued that limiting and policing these outlets can exacerbate tensions between employees and managers. Kesan warns that "prohibiting personal use can seem extremely arbitrary and can seriously harm morale. . . . Imagine a concerned parent

Orlov counters opposing views and provides support for her argument.

Orlov uses a brief signal phrase to move from her argument to the words of a source.

Orlov 6

who is prohibited from checking on a sick child by a draconian company policy" (315-16). As this analysis indicates, employees can become disgruntled when Internet usage policies are enforced to their full extent.

Additionally, many experts disagree with employers' assumption that online monitoring can increase productivity. Employment law attorney Joseph Schmitt argues that, particularly for employees who are paid a salary rather than by the hour, "a company shouldn't care whether employees spend one or 10 hours on the Internet as long as they are getting their jobs done—and provided that they are not accessing inappropriate sites" (qtd. in Verespej). Other experts even argue that time spent on personal Internet browsing can actually be productive for companies. According to Bill Coleman, an executive at *Salary.com*, "Personal Internet use and casual office conversations often turn into new business ideas or suggestions for gaining operating efficiencies" (qtd. in Frauenheim). Employers, in other words, may benefit from showing more faith in their employees' ability to exercise their autonomy.

Employees' right to privacy and autonomy in the workplace, however, remains a murky area of the law. Although evaluating where to draw the line between employee rights and employer powers is often a duty that falls to the judicial system, the courts have shown little willingness to intrude on employers' exercise of control over their computer networks. Federal law provides few guidelines

Orlov cites an indirect source: words quoted in another source.

Orlov 7

related to online monitoring of employees, and only
Connecticut and Delaware require companies to disclose
this type of surveillance to employees (Tam et al.). "It is
unlikely that we will see a legally guaranteed zone of
privacy in the American workplace," predicts Kesan (293).
This reality leaves employees and employers to sort the
potential risks and benefits of technology in contract
agreements and terms of employment. With continuing
advances in technology, protecting both employers and
employees will require greater awareness of these programs,
better disclosure to employees, and a more public discussion
about what types of protections are necessary to guard
individual freedoms in the wired workplace.

Orlov sums up
her argument and
suggests a course
of action.

Orlov 8

Heading is centered.

Works Cited

Adams, Scott. *Dilbert and the Way of the Weasel*. New York: Harper, 2002. Print.

American Management Association and ePolicy Institute. "2005 Electronic Monitoring and Surveillance Survey." *American Management Association*. Amer. Management Assn., 2005. Web. 15 Feb. 2006.

"Automatically Record Everything They Do Online! Spector Pro 5.0 FAQ's." Netbus.org. *Netbus.Org*, n.d. Web. 17 Feb. 2006.

Flynn, Nancy. "Internet Policies." *ePolicy Institute*. ePolicy Inst., n.d. Web. 15 Feb. 2006.

Frauenheim, Ed. "Stop Reading This Headline and Get Back to Work." *CNET News.com*. CNET Networks, 11 July 2005. Web. 17 Feb. 2006.

Gonsalves, Chris. "Wasting Away on the Web." *eWeek.com*. Ziff Davis Enterprise Holdings, 8 Aug. 2005. Web. 16 Feb. 2006.

Kesan, Jay P. "Cyber-Working or Cyber-Shirking? A First Principles Examination of Electronic Privacy in the Workplace." *Florida Law Review* 54.2 (2002): 289-332. Print.

Lane, Frederick S., III. *The Naked Employee: How Technology Is Compromising Workplace Privacy*. New York: Amer. Management Assn., 2003. Print.

List is alphabetized by authors' last names (or by title when a work has no author).

Abbreviation "n.d." indicates that the online source has no update date.

First line of each entry is at the left margin; extra lines are indented 1/2" (or five spaces).

Double-spacing is used throughout.

Orlov 9

Tam, Pui-Wing, et al. "Snooping E-Mail by Software Is
     Now a Workplace Norm." *Wall Street Journal*
     9 Mar. 2005: B1+. Print.

Tynan, Daniel. "Your Boss Is Watching." *PC World*. PC
     World Communications, 6 Oct. 2004. Web.
     17 Sept. 2006.

Verespej, Michael A. "Inappropriate Internet Surfing."
     Industry Week. Penton Media, 7 Feb. 2000. Web.
     16 Feb. 2006.

A work with four authors is listed by the first author's name and the abbreviation "et al." (for "and others").

Writing APA Papers

Most writing assignments in the social sciences are either reports of original research or reviews of the literature written about a research topic. Often an original research report contains a "review of the literature" section that places the writer's project in the context of previous research.

Most social science instructors will ask you to document your sources with the American Psychological Association (APA) system of in-text citations and references described in 60. You face three main challenges when writing a social science paper that draws on sources: (1) supporting a thesis, (2) citing your sources and avoiding plagiarism, and (3) integrating quotations and other source material.

Examples in this section are drawn from research a student conducted for a review of the literature on treatments for childhood obesity. Luisa Mirano's paper appears on pages 515–28.

57

Supporting a thesis

Most assignments ask you to form a thesis, or main idea, and to support that thesis with well-organized evidence. In a paper reviewing the literature on a topic, this thesis analyzes the often competing conclusions drawn by a variety of researchers.

57a Form a thesis.

A thesis, which usually appears at the end of the introduction, is a one-sentence (or occasionally a two-sentence) statement of your central idea. You will be reading articles and other sources that address a central research question. Your thesis will express a reasonable answer to that question, given the current state of research in the field. Here, for example, is a research question posed by Luisa Mirano, a student in a psychology class, followed by a thesis that answers the question.

RESEARCH QUESTION

Is medication the right treatment for the escalating problem of childhood obesity?

POSSIBLE THESIS

Understanding the limitations of medical treatments for children highlights the complexity of the childhood obesity problem in the United States and underscores the need for physicians, advocacy groups, and policymakers to search for other solutions.

ON THE WEB > **dianahacker.com/rules**
Research exercises > APA > E-ex 57–1

57b Organize your evidence.

The American Psychological Association encourages the use of headings to help readers follow the organization of a paper. For an original research report, the major headings often follow a standard model: Method, Results, Discussion. The introduction is not given a heading; it consists of the material between the title of the paper and the first heading.

For a literature review, headings will vary. The student who wrote about treatments for childhood obesity used four questions to focus her research; the questions then became headings in her paper (see pp. 515–28).

57c Use sources to inform and support your argument.

Used thoughtfully, the source materials you have gathered will make your argument more complex and convincing for readers. Sources can play several different roles as you develop your points.

Providing background information or context

You can use facts and statistics to support generalizations or to establish the importance of your topic, as student writer Luisa Mirano does in her introduction.

In March 2004, U.S. Surgeon General Richard Carmona called
attention to a health problem in the United States that, until
recently, has been overlooked: childhood obesity. Carmona said
that the "astounding" 15% child obesity rate constitutes an
"epidemic." Since the early 1980s, that rate has "doubled in
children and tripled in adolescents." Now more than 9 million
children are classified as obese (paras. 3, 6).

Explaining terms or concepts

If readers are unlikely to be familiar with a word or an idea important to your topic, you must explain it for them. Quoting or
paraphrasing a source can help you define terms and concepts
in accessible language. Luisa Mirano uses a footnote in her
paper to define the familiar word *obesity* in the technical sense
used by researchers.

Obesity is measured in terms of body-mass index (BMI):
weight in kilograms divided by square of height in meters. An
adult with a BMI 30 or higher is considered obese. A child or an
adolescent with a BMI in the 95th percentile for his or her age
and gender is considered obese.

Supporting your claims

As you draft your argument, make sure to back up your assertions with facts, examples, and other evidence from your research (see also 47e). Luisa Mirano, for example, uses one
source's findings to support her central idea that the medical
treatment of childhood obesity has limitations.

As journalist Greg Critser (2003) noted in his book *Fat Land,* use
of weight-loss drugs is unlikely to have an effect without the
proper "support system"--one that includes doctors, facilities,
time, and money (p. 3).

g authority to your argument

inion can give weight to your argument (see also 47e).
ely on experts to make your argument for you. Con-

struct your argument in your own words and, when appropriate, cite the judgment of an authority in the field for support.

> Both medical experts and policymakers recognize that solutions might come not only from a laboratory but also from policy, education, and advocacy. Indeed, a handbook designed to educate doctors on obesity recommended a notably nonmedical course of action, calling for "major changes in some aspects of western culture" (Hoppin & Taveras, 2004, Conclusion section, para. 1).

Anticipating and countering alternative interpretations

Do not ignore sources that seem contrary to your position or that offer interpretations different from your own. Instead, use them to give voice to opposing points of view before you counter them (see 47f). Mirano uses a source to show readers that there is substance to her opponents' position that medication is the preferable approach to treating childhood obesity.

> As researchers Yanovski and Yanovski (2002) have explained, obesity was once considered "either a moral failing or evidence of underlying psychopathology" (p. 592). But this view has shifted: Many medical professionals now consider obesity a biomedical rather than a moral condition, influenced by both genetic and environmental factors. Yanovski and Yanovski have further noted that the development of weight-loss medications in the early 1990s showed that "obesity should be treated in the same manner as any other chronic disease . . . through the long-term use of medication" (p. 592).

58

Citing sources; avoiding plagiarism

Your research paper is a collaboration between you and your sources. To be fair and ethical, you must acknowledge your debt to the writers of those sources. If you don't, you commit plagiarism, a serious academic offense.

Three different acts are considered plagiarism: (1) failing to cite quotations and borrowed ideas, (2) failing to enclose borrowed language in quotation marks, and (3) failing to put summaries and paraphrases in your own words.

58a Cite quotations and borrowed ideas.

You must of course cite all direct quotations. You must also cite any ideas borrowed from a source: summaries and paraphrases; statistics and other specific facts; and visuals such as cartoons, graphs, and diagrams.

The only exception is common knowledge — information that your readers may know or could easily locate in any number of reference sources. For example, the current population of the United States is common knowledge among sociologists and economists, and psychologists are familiar with Freud's theory of the unconscious. As a rule, when you have seen certain information repeatedly in your reading, you don't need to cite it. However, when information has appeared in only a few sources, when it is highly specific (as with statistics), or when it is controversial, you should cite the source.

The American Psychological Association recommends an author-date system of citations. Here, very briefly, is how the author-date system usually works. See 60 for a detailed discussion of variations.

1. The source is introduced by a signal phrase that includes the last names of the authors followed by the date of publication in parentheses.

2. The material being cited is followed by a page number in parentheses.

3. At the end of the paper, an alphabetized list of references gives complete publication information about the source.

N-TEXT CITATION

researchers Yanovski and Yanovski (2002) have explained,

ity was once considered "either a moral failing or evidence of

ving psychopathology" (p. 592).

ENTRY IN THE LIST OF REFERENCES

Yanovski, S. Z., & Yanovski, J. A. (2002). Drug therapy: Obesity.
The New England Journal of Medicine, 346(8), 591-602.

58b Enclose borrowed language in quotation marks.

To indicate that you are using a source's exact phrases or sentences, you must enclose them in quotation marks. To omit the quotation marks is to claim — falsely — that the language is your own. Such an omission is plagiarism even if you have cited the source.

ORIGINAL SOURCE

In an effort to seek the causes of this disturbing trend, experts have pointed to a range of important potential contributors to the rise in childhood obesity that are unrelated to media: a reduction in physical education classes and after-school athletic programs, an increase in the availability of sodas and snacks in public schools, the growth in the number of fast-food outlets across the country, the trend toward "super-sizing" food portions in restaurants, and the increasing number of highly processed high-calorie and high-fat grocery products.

—Henry J. Kaiser Family Foundation,
"The Role of Media in Childhood Obesity" (2004), p. 1

PLAGIARISM

According to the Henry J. Kaiser Family Foundation (2004), experts have pointed to a range of important potential contributors to the rise in childhood obesity that are unrelated to media (p. 1).

BORROWED LANGUAGE IN QUOTATION MARKS

According to the Henry J. Kaiser Family Foundation (2004), "experts have pointed to a range of important potential contributors to the rise in childhood obesity that are unrelated to media" (p. 1).

NOTE: When quoted sentences are set off from the text by indenting, quotation marks are not needed (see pp. 484–85).

58c Put summaries and paraphrases in your own words.

Summaries and paraphrases are written in your own words. A summary condenses information; a paraphrase reports information in about the same number of words as in the source. When you summarize or paraphrase, you must restate the source's meaning using your own language. You commit plagiarism if you half-copy the author's sentences — either by mixing the author's well-chosen phrases with your own without using quotation marks or by plugging your own synonyms into the author's sentence structure. The following paraphrases are plagiarized — even though the source is cited — because their language is too close to that of the source.

ORIGINAL SOURCE

In an effort to seek the causes of this disturbing trend, experts have pointed to a range of important potential contributors to the rise in childhood obesity that are unrelated to media.
— Henry J. Kaiser Family Foundation,
"The Role of Media in Childhood Obesity" (2004), p. 1

UNACCEPTABLE BORROWING OF PHRASES

According to the Henry J. Kaiser Family Foundation (2004), experts have indicated a range of significant potential contributors to the rise in childhood obesity that are not linked to media (p. 1).

UNACCEPTABLE BORROWING OF STRUCTURE

According to the Henry J. Kaiser Family Foundation (2004), experts have identified a variety of significant factors causing a rise in childhood obesity, factors that are not linked to media (p. 1).

To avoid plagiarizing an author's language, set the source aside, write from memory, and consult the source later to check for accuracy. This strategy prevents you from being captivated by the words on the page.

ACCEPTABLE PARAPHRASE

A report by the Henry J. Kaiser Family Foundation (2004) described sources other than media for the childhood obesity crisis.

ON THE WEB > dianahacker.com/rules
Research exercises > APA > E-ex 58–1 to 58–5

59

Integrating sources

Quotations, summaries, paraphrases, and facts will support your argument, but they cannot speak for you. You can use several strategies to integrate information from research sources into your paper while maintaining your own voice.

59a Limit your use of quotations.

Using quotations appropriately

Although it is tempting to insert many quotations in your paper and to use your own words only for connecting passages, do not quote excessively. It is almost impossible to integrate numerous long quotations smoothly into your own text.

It is not always necessary to quote full sentences from a source. At times you may wish to borrow only a phrase or to weave part of a source's sentence into your own sentence structure. (For the use of signal phrases in integrating quotations, see 59b.)

> As researchers continue to face a number of unknowns about obesity, it may be helpful to envision treating the disorder, as Yanovski and Yanovski (2002) suggested, "in the same manner as any other chronic disease" (p. 592).

Using the ellipsis mark and brackets

USING THE ELLIPSIS MARK   To condense a quoted passage, you can use the ellipsis mark (three periods, with spaces between) to indicate that you have omitted words. What remains must be grammatically complete.

> Roman (2003) reported that "social factors are nearly as
> significant as individual metabolism in the formation of . . .
> dietary habits of adolescents" (p. 345).

The writer has omitted the words *both healthy and unhealthy* from the source.

When you want to omit a full sentence or more, use a period before the three ellipsis dots.

> According to Sothern and Gordon (2003), "Environmental factors
> may contribute as much as 80% to the causes of childhood
> obesity. . . . Research suggests that obese children demonstrate
> decreased levels of physical activity and increased psychosocial
> problems" (p. 104).

Ordinarily, do not use an ellipsis mark at the beginning or at the end of a quotation. Readers will understand that the quoted material is taken from a longer passage. The only exception occurs when you think that the author's meaning might be misinterpreted without the ellipsis mark.

USING BRACKETS Brackets allow you to insert your own words into quoted material to explain a confusing reference or to keep a sentence grammatical in your context.

> The cost of treating obesity currently totals $117 billion per year--
> a price, according to the surgeon general, "second only to the
> cost of [treating] tobacco use" (Carmona, 2004, para. 9).

To indicate an error in a quotation, insert [*sic*] right after the error. Notice that the term *sic* is italicized and appears in brackets.

Setting off long quotations

When you quote forty or more words, set off the quotation by indenting it one-half inch (or five spaces) from the left margin. Use the normal right margin and do not single-space.

Long quotations should be introduced by an informative sentence, usually followed by a colon. Quotation marks are unnecessary because the indented format tells readers that the words are taken word-for-word from the source.

Yanovski and Yanovski (2002) have described earlier treatments of obesity that focused on behavior modification:

> With the advent of behavioral treatments for obesity in the 1960s, hope arose that modification of maladaptive eating and exercise habits would lead to sustained weight loss, and that time-limited programs would produce permanent changes in weight. Medications for the treatment of obesity were proposed as short-term adjuncts for patients, who would presumably then acquire the skills necessary to continue to lose weight, reach "ideal body weight," and maintain a reduced weight indefinitely. (p. 592)

Notice that at the end of an indented quotation the parenthetical citation goes outside the final mark of punctuation. (When a quotation is run into your text, the opposite is true. See the sample citations on p. 484.)

59b Use signal phrases to integrate sources.

The information you gather from sources cannot speak for itself. Whenever you include a paraphrase, summary, or direct quotation of another writer in your paper, prepare your readers for it with an introduction called a *signal phrase.* A signal phrase usually names the author of the source and gives the publication year in parentheses.

When the signal phrase includes a verb, choose one that is appropriate for the way you are using the source (see 57c). Are you arguing a point, making an observation, reporting a fact, drawing a conclusion, or refuting an argument? By choosing an appropriate verb, you can make your source's role clear. See the chart on page 486 for a list of verbs commonly used in signal phrases.

The American Psychological Association requires using past tense or present perfect tense in phrases that introduce quotations and other source material: *Davis (2005) noted that* or *Davis (2005) has noted that,* not *Davis (2005) notes that.* Use the present tense only for discussing the results of an experiment (*the results show*) or knowledge that has clearly been established (*researchers agree*).

Using signal phrases in APA papers

To avoid monotony, try to vary the language and placement of your signal phrases.

Model signal phrases

In the words of Carmona (2004), ". . ."

As Yanovski and Yanovski (2002) have noted, ". . ."

Hoppin and Taveras (2004), medical researchers, pointed out that ". . ."

". . .," claimed Critser (2003).

". . .," wrote Duenwald (2004), ". . ."

Researchers McDuffie et al. (2003) have offered a compelling argument for this view: ". . ."

Hilts (2002) answered these objections with the following analysis: ". . ."

Verbs in signal phrases

admitted	contended	reasoned
agreed	declared	refuted
argued	denied	rejected
asserted	emphasized	reported
believed	insisted	responded
claimed	noted	suggested
compared	observed	thought
confirmed	pointed out	wrote

It is generally acceptable in the social sciences to call authors by their last name only, even on a first mention. If your paper refers to two authors with same last name, use initials as well.

Marking boundaries

Readers need to move from your words to the words of a source without feeling a jolt. Avoid dropping direct quotations into your text without warning. Instead, provide clear signal phrases, including at least the author's name and the date of publication. A signal phrase indicates the boundary between your words and the source's words and can also tell readers why a source is trustworthy.

DROPPED QUOTATION

Obesity was once considered in a very different light. "For many years, obesity was approached as if it were either a moral failing or evidence of underlying psychopathology" (Yanovski & Yanovski, 2002, p. 592).

QUOTATION WITH SIGNAL PHRASE

As researchers Yanovski and Yanovski (2002) have explained, obesity was once considered "either a moral failing or evidence of underlying psychopathology" (p. 592).

Introducing summaries and paraphrases

As with quotations, you should introduce most summaries and paraphrases with a signal phrase that mentions the author and the year and places the material in context. Readers will then understand where the summary or paraphrase begins.

Without the signal phrase (underlined) in the following example, readers might think that only the last sentence is being cited, when in fact the whole paragraph is based on the source.

<u>Carmona (2004) advised a Senate subcommittee that</u> the problem of childhood obesity is dire and that the skyrocketing statistics--which put the child obesity rate at 15%--are cause for alarm. More than 9 million children, double the number in the early 1980s, are classified as obese. Carmona warned that obesity can cause myriad physical problems that only worsen as children grow older (para. 6).

There are times, however, when a summary or a paraphrase does not require a signal phrase naming the author. When the context makes clear where the cited material begins, omit the signal phrase and include the author's name in the parentheses. Unless the work is short, also include the page number in the parentheses: (Saltzman, 2004, p. D8).

Putting source material in context

Readers need to understand how your source is relevant to your paper's thesis. It's therefore a good idea to embed your quotation — especially a long one — between sentences of your own, introducing it with a signal phrase and following it with interpretive comments that link the source material to your paper's thesis.

QUOTATION WITH INSUFFICIENT CONTEXT

> A report by the Henry J. Kaiser Family Foundation (2004) outlined trends that may have contributed to the childhood obesity crisis, including food advertising for children as well as
>> a reduction in physical education classes . . . , an increase in the availability of sodas and snacks in public schools, the growth in the number of fast-food outlets . . . , and the increasing number of highly processed high-calorie and high-fat grocery products. (p. 1)

QUOTATION WITH EFFECTIVE CONTEXT

> A report by the Henry J. Kaiser Family Foundation (2004) outlined trends that may have contributed to the childhood obesity crisis, including food advertising for children as well as
>> a reduction in physical education classes . . . , an increase in the availability of sodas and snacks in public schools, the growth in the number of fast-food outlets . . . , and the increasing number of highly processed high-calorie and high-fat grocery products. (p. 1)

> Addressing each of these areas requires more than a doctor armed with a prescription pad; it requires a broad mobilization not just of doctors and concerned parents but of educators, food industry executives, advertisers, and media representatives.

Integrating statistics and other facts

When you are citing a statistic or another specific fact, a signal phrase is often not necessary. In most cases, readers will understand that the citation refers to the statistic or fact (not the whole paragraph).

> In purely financial terms, the drugs cost more than $3 a day on
> average (Duenwald, 2004, paras. 33, 36).

There is nothing wrong, however, with using a signal phrase.

ON THE WEB > dianahacker.com/rules
Research exercises > APA > E-ex 59–1 to 59–4

60

Documenting sources

In most social science classes, you will be asked to use the APA system for documenting sources, which is set forth in the *Publication Manual of the American Psychological Association,* 5th ed. (Washington: APA, 2001) and the *APA Style Guide to Electronic References* (2007). APA recommends in-text citations that refer readers to a list of references.

An in-text citation gives the author of the source (often in a signal phrase), the year of publication, and at times a page number in parentheses. At the end of the paper, a list of references provides publication information about the source (see pp. 527–28). The direct link between the in-text citation and the entry in the reference list is highlighted in the following example.

IN-TEXT CITATION

> Yanovski and Yanovski (2002) reported that "the current state of
> the treatment for obesity is similar to the state of the treatment
> of hypertension several decades ago" (p. 600).

ENTRY IN THE LIST OF REFERENCES

> Yanovski, S. Z., & Yanovski, J. A. (2002). Drug therapy: Obesity.
> *The New England Journal of Medicine, 346*(8), 591-602.

For a reference list that includes this entry, see page 528.

60a APA in-text citations

The APA's in-text citations provide at least the author's last name and the year of publication. For direct quotations and some paraphrases, a page number is given as well.

NOTE: APA style requires the use of the past tense or the present perfect tense in signal phrases introducing cited material: *Smith (2005) reported, Smith (2005) has argued.*

■ 1. BASIC FORMAT FOR A QUOTATION Ordinarily, introduce the quotation with a signal phrase that includes the author's last name followed by the year of publication in parentheses. Put the page number (preceded by "p.") in parentheses after the quotation.

> Critser (2003) noted that despite growing numbers of overweight Americans, many health care providers still "remain either in ignorance or outright denial about the health danger to the poor and the young" (p. 5).

If the author is not named in the signal phrase, place the author's name, the year, and the page number in parentheses after the quotation: (Critser, 2003, p. 5).

NOTE: APA style requires the year of publication in an in-text citation. Do not include a month, even if the entry in the reference list includes the month and year.

■ 2. BASIC FORMAT FOR A SUMMARY OR A PARAPHRASE Include the author's last name and the year either in a signal phrase introducing the material or in parentheses following it. A page number or another locator is not required for a summary or a paraphrase, but include one if it would help readers find the passage in a long work.

> According to Carmona (2004), the cost of treating obesity is
> exceeded only by the cost of treating illnesses from tobacco use
> (para. 9).

> The cost of treating obesity is exceeded only by the cost of
> treating illnesses from tobacco use (Carmona, 2004, para. 9).

■ **3. A WORK WITH TWO AUTHORS**   Name both authors in the signal phrase or parentheses each time you cite the work. In the parentheses, use "&" between the authors' names; in the signal phrase, use "and."

> According to Sothern and Gordon (2003), "Environmental factors
> may contribute as much as 80% to the causes of childhood
> obesity" (p. 104).

> Obese children often engage in limited physical activity (Sothern
> & Gordon, 2003, p. 104).

■ **4. A WORK WITH THREE TO FIVE AUTHORS**   Identify all authors in the signal phrase or parentheses the first time you cite the source.

> In 2003, Berkowitz, Wadden, Tershakovec, and Cronquist concluded,
> "Sibutramine . . . must be carefully monitored in adolescents, as
> in adults, to control increases in [blood pressure] and pulse rate"
> (p. 1811).

In subsequent citations, use the first author's name followed by "et al." in either the signal phrase or the parentheses.

> As Berkowitz et al. (2003) advised, "Until more extensive safety and
> efficacy data are available, . . . weight-loss medications should be
> used only on an experimental basis for adolescents" (p. 1811).

■ **5. A WORK WITH SIX OR MORE AUTHORS**   Use the first author's name followed by "et al." in the signal phrase or the parentheses.

> McDuffie et al. (2002) tested 20 adolescents, aged 12-16, over a
> three-month period and found that orlistat, combined with
> behavioral therapy, produced an average weight loss of 4.4 kg,
> or 9.7 pounds (p. 646).

■ **6. UNKNOWN AUTHOR**   If the author is unknown, mention the work's title in the signal phrase or give the first word or two of the title in the parenthetical citation. Titles of articles and chapters are put in quotation marks; titles of books and reports are italicized.

> Children struggling to control their weight must also struggle with
> the pressures of television advertising that, on the one hand,
> encourages the consumption of junk food and, on the other,
> celebrates thin celebrities ("Television," 2002).

NOTE: In the rare case when "Anonymous" is specified as the author, treat it as if it were a real name: (Anonymous, 2001). In the list of references, also use the name Anonymous as author.

■ **7. ORGANIZATION AS AUTHOR**   If the author is a government agency or another organization, name the organization in the signal phrase or in the parenthetical citation the first time you cite the source.

> Obesity puts children at risk for a number of medical
> complications, including type 2 diabetes, hypertension, sleep
> apnea, and orthopedic problems (Henry J. Kaiser Family
> Foundation, 2004, p. 1).

If the organization has a familiar abbreviation, you may include it in brackets the first time you cite the source and use the abbreviation alone in later citations.

FIRST CITATION   (National Institute of Mental Health [NIMH], 2001)

LATER CITATIONS   (NIMH, 2001)

■ **8. TWO OR MORE WORKS IN THE SAME PARENTHESES**   When your parenthetical citation names two or more works, put them in the same order that they appear in the reference list, separated by semicolons.

Researchers have indicated that studies of pharmacological treatments for childhood obesity are inconclusive (Berkowitz et al., 2003; McDuffie et al., 2003).

■ **9. AUTHORS WITH THE SAME LAST NAME** To avoid confusion, use initials with the last names if your reference list includes two or more authors with the same last name.

Research by E. Smith (1989) revealed that . . .

■ **10. PERSONAL COMMUNICATION** Interviews, memos, letters, e-mail, and similar unpublished person-to-person communications should be cited as follows:

One of Atkinson's colleagues, who has studied the effect of the media on children's eating habits, has contended that advertisers for snack foods will need to design ads responsibly for their younger viewers (F. Johnson, personal communication, October 20, 2004).

Do not include personal communications in your reference list.

■ **11. AN ELECTRONIC DOCUMENT** When possible, cite an electronic document as you would any other document (using the author-date style).

Atkinson (2001) found that children who spent at least four hours a day watching TV were less likely to engage in adequate physical activity during the week.

Electronic sources may lack authors' names or dates. In addition, they may lack page numbers. Here are APA's guidelines for handling sources without authors' names, dates, or page numbers.

Unknown author

If no author is named, mention the title of the document in a signal phrase or give the first word or two of the title in parentheses (see also item 6). (If an organization serves as the author, see item 7.)

The body's basal metabolic rate, or BMR, is a measure of its at-rest energy requirement ("Exercise," 2003).

Unknown date

When the date is unknown, APA recommends using the abbreviation "n.d." (for "no date").

> Attempts to establish a definitive link between television
> programming and children's eating habits have been
> problematic (Magnus, n.d.).

No page numbers

APA ordinarily requires page numbers for quotations, and it recommends them for summaries or paraphrases from long sources. When an electronic source lacks stable numbered pages, your citation should include — if possible — information that will help readers locate the particular passage being cited.

When an electronic document has numbered paragraphs, use the paragraph number preceded by the symbol ¶ or by the abbreviation "para.": (Hall, 2001, ¶ 5) *or* (Hall, 2001, para. 5). If neither a page nor a paragraph number is given and the document contains headings, cite the appropriate heading and indicate which paragraph under that heading you are referring to.

> Hoppin and Taveras (2004) pointed out that several other
> medications were classified by the Drug Enforcement
> Administration as having the "potential for abuse"
> (Weight-Loss Drugs section, para. 6).

NOTE: Electronic files in portable document format (PDF) often have stable page numbers. For such sources, give the page number in the parenthetical citation.

■ **12. INDIRECT SOURCE** If you use a source that was cited in another source (a secondary source), name the original source in your signal phrase. List the secondary source in your reference list and include it in your parenthetical citation, preceded by the words "as cited in." In the following example, Critser is the secondary source.

> Former surgeon general Dr. David Satcher described "a nation of
> young people seriously at risk of starting out obese and dooming
> themselves to the difficult task of overcoming a tough illness"
> (as cited in Critser, 2003, p. 4).

■ **13. TWO OR MORE WORKS BY THE SAME AUTHOR IN THE SAME YEAR** When your list of references includes more than one work by the same author in the same year, use lowercase letters ("a," "b," and so on) with the year to order the entries in the reference list. (See item 6 on p. 497.) Use those same letters with the year in the in-text citation.

> Research by Durgin (2003b) has yielded new findings about the
> role of counseling in treating childhood obesity.

ON THE WEB > **dianahacker.com/rules**
Research exercises > APA > E-ex 60–1 to 60–3

60b APA references

In APA style, the alphabetical list of works cited, which appears at the end of the paper, is titled "References." This section contains models illustrating APA style for entries in the list of references. Observe all details: capitalization, punctuation, use of italics, and so on. For advice on preparing the reference list, see pages 513–14. For a sample reference list, see pages 527–28.

ON THE WEB > **dianahacker.com/rules**
Research exercises > APA > E-ex 60–4

ON THE WEB > **dianahacker.com/rules**
Research and Documentation Online > Social sciences:
Documenting sources (APA)

General guidelines for listing authors

Alphabetize entries in the list of references by authors' last names; if a work has no author, alphabetize it by its title. The first element of each entry is important because citations in the text of the paper refer to it and readers will be looking for it in the alphabetized list. The date of publication appears immediately after the first element of the citation.

NAME AND DATE CITED IN TEXT

Duncan (2006) has reported that . . .

BEGINNING OF ENTRY IN THE LIST OF REFERENCES

Duncan, B. (2006).

Items 1–4 show how to begin an entry for a work with a single author, multiple authors, an organization as author, and an unknown author. Items 5 and 6 show how to begin an entry when your list includes two or more works by the same author or two or more works by the same author in the same year. What comes after the first element of your citation will depend on the kind of source you are citing (see items 7–34).

■ **1. SINGLE AUTHOR** Begin the entry with the author's last name, followed by a comma and the author's initial(s). Then give the date in parentheses.

Perez, E. (2006).

■ **2. MULTIPLE AUTHORS** List up to six authors by last names followed by initials. Use an ampersand (&) between the names of two authors or, if there are more than two authors, before the name of the last author.

DuNann, D. W., & Koger, S. M. (2004).

Sloan, F. A., Stout, E. M., Whetten-Goldstein, K., & Liang, L. (2000).

If there are more than six authors, list the first six and "et al." (meaning "and others") to indicate that there are others.

■ **3. ORGANIZATION AS AUTHOR** When the author is an organization, begin with the name of the organization.

American Psychiatric Association. (2005).

NOTE: If the organization is also the publisher, see item 31 on page 510.

■ **4. UNKNOWN AUTHOR** Begin the entry with the work's title. Titles of books are italicized; titles of articles are neither italicized nor put in quotation marks. (For rules on capitalization of titles, see pp. 513–14.)

Oxford essential world atlas. (2001).

Omega-3 fatty acids. (2004, November 23).

■ **5. TWO OR MORE WORKS BY THE SAME AUTHOR** Use the author's name for all entries. List the entries by year, the earliest first.

Directory to APA references (bibliographic entries)

Schlechty, P. C. (1997).

Schlechty, P. C. (2001).

■ **6. TWO OR MORE WORKS BY THE SAME AUTHOR IN THE SAME YEAR**
List the works alphabetically by title. In the parentheses, following the year add "a," "b," and so on. Use these same letters when giving the year in the in-text citation. (See also p. 513.)

Durgin, P. A. (2003a). At-risk behaviors in children.

Durgin, P. A. (2003b). Treating obesity with psychotherapy.

Articles in periodicals

This section shows how to prepare an entry for an article in a periodical such as a scholarly journal, a magazine, or a newspaper. In addition to consulting the models in this section, you may need to refer to items 1–6 (general guidelines for listing authors). For an annotated example of an article in a periodical, see page 499.

NOTE: For articles on consecutive pages, provide the range of pages at the end of the citation (see item 7 for an example). When an article does not appear on consecutive pages, give all page numbers: A1, A17.

■ 7. ARTICLE IN A JOURNAL PAGINATED BY VOLUME Many professional journals continue page numbers throughout the year instead of beginning each issue with page 1; at the end of the year, the issues are collected in a volume. After the italicized title of the journal, give the volume number (also italicized), followed by the page numbers.

Morawski, J. (2000). Social psychology a century ago. *American*

Psychologist, 55, 427-431.

■ 8. ARTICLE IN A JOURNAL PAGINATED BY ISSUE When each issue of a journal begins with page 1, include the issue number in parentheses after the volume number. Italicize the volume number but not the issue number.

Smith, S. (2003). Government and nonprofits in the modern age.

Society, 40(4), 36-45.

■ 9. ARTICLE IN A MAGAZINE In addition to the year of publication, list the month and, for weekly magazines, the day. If there is a volume number, include it (italicized) after the title.

Raloff, J. (2001, May 12). Lead therapy won't help most kids. *Science*

News, 159, 292.

■ 10. ARTICLE IN A NEWSPAPER Begin with the name of the author, followed by the exact date of publication. (If the author is unknown, see also item 4.) Page numbers are introduced with "p." (or "pp.").

Lohr, S. (2004, December 3). Health care technology is a promise

unfinanced. *The New York Times,* p. C5.

Citation at a glance: Article in a periodical (APA)

To cite an article in a periodical in APA style, include the following elements:

1 Author
2 Date of publication
3 Title of article
4 Name of periodical

5 Volume and issue numbers
6 Page numbers

REFERENCE LIST ENTRY FOR AN ARTICLE IN A PERIODICAL

Hoxby, C. M. (2002). The power of peers. *Education Next, 2*(2), 57-63.

For more on citing periodicals in APA style, see pages 497–500.

■ **11. LETTER TO THE EDITOR** Letters to the editor appear in journals, magazines, and newspapers. Follow the appropriate model and insert the words "Letter to the editor" in brackets before the name of the periodical.

Wright, M. J. (2006, December). Diminutive danger [Letter to the

editor]. *Scientific American, 295*(6), 18.

■ **12. REVIEW** Reviews of books and other media appear in a variety of periodicals. Follow the appropriate model for the periodical. For a review of a book, give the title of the review (if there is one), followed in brackets by the words "Review of the book" and the title of the book.

Gleick, E. (2000, December 14). The burdens of genius [Review of the

book *The Last Samurai*]. *Time, 156,* 171.

For a film review, write "Review of the motion picture," and for a TV review, write "Review of the television program." Treat other media in a similar way.

Books

In addition to consulting the items in this section, you may need to refer to items 1–6 (general guidelines for listing authors). For an annotated example, see page 501.

■ **13. BASIC FORMAT FOR A BOOK** Begin with the author's name, followed by the date and the book's title. End with the place of publication and the name of the publisher. Take the information about the book from its title page and copyright page. If more than one place of publication is given, use only the first; if more than one date is given, use the most recent one.

Highmore, B. (2001). *Everyday life and cultural theory.* New York:

Routledge.

■ **14. BOOK WITH AN EDITOR** For a book with an editor but no author, begin with the name of the editor (or editors) followed by the abbreviation "Ed." (or "Eds.") in parentheses.

Bronfen, E., & Kavka, M. (Eds.). (2001). *Feminist consequences: Theory*

for a new century. New York: Columbia University Press.

Citation at a glance: Book (APA)

To cite a book in APA style, include the following elements:

1 Author
2 Date of publication
3 Title and subtitle
4 City of publication
5 Publisher

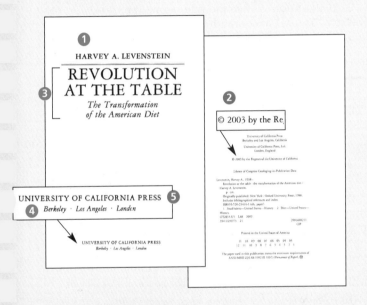

REFERENCE LIST ENTRY FOR A BOOK

Levenstein, H. A. (2003). *Revolution at the table: The transformation of the American diet.* Berkeley: University of California Press.

For more on citing books in APA style, see pages 500–02.

For a book with an author and an editor, begin with the author's name. Give the editor's name in parentheses after the title of the book, followed by the abbreviation "Ed." (or "Eds.").

Plath, S. (2000). *The unabridged journals* (K. V. Kukil, Ed.). New York: Anchor.

15. TRANSLATION   After the title, name the translator, followed by "Trans.," in parentheses. Add the original date of publication at the end of the entry.

Steinberg, M. D. (2003). *Voices of revolution, 1917* (M. Schwartz, Trans.). New Haven, CT: Yale University Press. (Original work published 2001)

16. EDITION OTHER THAN THE FIRST   Include the number of the edition in parentheses after the title.

Helfer, M. E., Keme, R. S., & Drugman, R. D. (1997). *The battered child* (5th ed.). Chicago: University of Chicago Press.

17. ARTICLE OR CHAPTER IN AN EDITED BOOK   Begin with the author, year, and title of the article or chapter. Then write "In" and the editor's name, followed by "Ed." in parentheses; the book title; the page numbers of the article or chapter in parentheses; and the book publication information.

Luban, D. (2000). The ethics of wrongful obedience. In D. L. Rhode (Ed.), *Ethics in practice: Lawyers' roles, responsibilities, and regulation* (pp. 94-120). New York: Oxford University Press.

18. MULTIVOLUME WORK   Give the number of volumes after the title.

Luo, J. (Ed.). (2005). *China today: An encyclopedia of life in the People's Republic* (Vols. 1-2). Westport, CT: Greenwood Press.

Electronic sources

This section shows how to prepare reference list entries for a variety of electronic sources, including articles in online periodicals and databases, Web documents, Weblogs, podcasts, wikis, and e-mail.

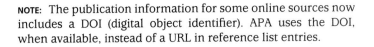

NOTE: The publication information for some online sources now includes a DOI (digital object identifier). APA uses the DOI, when available, instead of a URL in reference list entries.

■ **19. ARTICLE FROM AN ONLINE PERIODICAL** When citing online articles, include publication information as in items 7–12. If the article has a DOI (digital object identifier), include that number. Give the volume and issue numbers for all journals.

Whitmeyer, J. M. (2000). Power through appointment. *Social Science Research, 29*(4), 535-555. doi:10.1006/ssre.2000.0680

If there is no DOI, include the URL for the article or for the journal's home page (if the article is available only by subscription or the URL is very long).

Ashe, D. D., & McCutcheon, L. E. (2001). Shyness, loneliness, and attitude toward celebrities. *Current Research in Social Psychology, 6*(9), 124–133. Retrieved from http://www.uiowa.edu /~grpproc/crisp/crisp.6.9.htm

NOTE: When you have retrieved an article from a newspaper's searchable Web site, give the URL for the site, not for the exact source.

Vogel, N. (2007, January 19). Turning to greener wheels. *Los Angeles Times.* Retrieved from http://www.latimes.com

■ **20. ARTICLE FROM A DATABASE** To cite an article from a library's subscription database, include the publication information for the source (see items 7–12). If the article has a DOI (digital object identifier), give that number at the end and do not include the database name. If there is no DOI, include the name of the database and the document number assigned by the database, if any. (For an annotated example, see p. 504.)

Holliday, R. E., & Hayes, B. K. (2000). Dissociating automatic and intentional processes in children's eyewitness memory. *Journal of Experimental Child Psychology, 75*(1), 1-42. doi:10.1006/jecp.1999.2521

Citation at a glance: Article from a database (APA)

To cite an article from a database in APA style, include the following elements:

1 Author
2 Date of publication
3 Title of article
4 Name of periodical
5 Volume and issue numbers
6 Page numbers
7 DOI (digital object identifier)
8 Name of database (if there is no DOI)
9 Document number (if there is no DOI)

ON-SCREEN VIEW OF DATABASE RECORD

ProQuest® ⑧   Help

| Basic | Advanced | Topics | Publications | 🗎 My Research 0 marked items |

Interface language: English

Databases selected: Criminal Justice Periodicals   What's new

Document View « Back to Results   Document 1 of 1   Publisher Information

Print Email   ⬜ Mark Document   ⧉ Abstract , 🗎 Full Text , 🗎 Page Image - PDF

SOCIAL JUSTICE

③
Crime and justice in American Indian Communities
① *Lisa M Poupart*. **Social Justice**. San Francisco: 2002.Vol.29, Iss. 1/2; pg. 144, 16 pgs
» Jump to full text   ④   ②   ⑤   ⑥
» Translate document into: Select language
» More Like This - Find similar documents

Subjects:	Native Americans, Crime, History, Social conditions & trends, Criminology, Culture, Genocide, Indigenous people, Justice, Law groups, Politics, Race relations, Social services, United States, US
Author(s):	Lisa M Poupart
Document types:	Feature
Publication title:	Social Justice. San Francisco: 2002. Vol. 29, Iss. 1/2; pg. 144, 16 pgs
Source type:	Periodical
ISSN/ISBN:	10431578
ProQuest document ID:	208056261 ⑨
Text Word Count	6624
Document URL:	http://proquest.umi.com/pqdweb?did=208056261&sid=1&Fmt=3&clientId=66

Abstract (Document Summary)

Poupart examines the ways in which the historical domination and oppression of American Indians by Western nations created and continue to perpetuate crime and injustice in American Indian communities. American Indian communities today struggle to cope with devastating social ills that were practically nonexistent in traditional tribal communities before

Looking up proquest.umi.com...

REFERENCE LIST ENTRY FOR AN ARTICLE FROM A DATABASE

```
  ┌───1───┐  ┌─2─┐  ┌──────────────3──────────────┐
```
Poupart, L. M. (2002). Crime and justice in American Indian communities.

```
     ┌───4───┐ ┌─5─┐ ┌─6─┐                    ┌──8──┐
```
   Social Justice, 29(1/2), 144-159. Retrieved from ProQuest

```
        ┌───9───┐
```
   database (208056261).

For more on citing articles from a database in APA style, see item 20.

Howard, K. R. (2007). Childhood overweight: Parental perceptions

   and readiness for change. *The Journal of School Nursing,*

   23(2), 73-79. Retrieved from PsycINFO database

   (2007-05057-003).

21. DOCUMENT FROM A WEB SITE APA refers to non-peer-reviewed work, such as corporate reports, consumer brochures, fact sheets, press releases, hearings, and newsletter articles, as "gray literature." List as many of the following elements as are available: author's name, publication date (or "n.d." if there is no date), title (in italics), and URL. Give your date of access only if the source itself has no date or if its content is likely to change.

Cain, A., & Burris, M. (1999, April). *Investigation of the use of mobile*

   phones while driving. Retrieved from http://www.cutr.eng.usf.edu

   /its/mobile_phone_text.htm

Archer, D. (n.d.). *Exploring nonverbal communication.* Retrieved January

   10, 2007, from http://nonverbal.ucsc.edu

If a source has no author, begin with the title and follow it with the date in parentheses.

NOTE: If you retrieved the source from the Web site of an organization such as a university program, name the organization in your retrieval statement.

Cosmides, L., & Tooby, J. (1997). *Evolutionary psychology: A primer.*
Retrieved from the University of California, Santa Barbara, Center
for Evolutionary Psychology Web site: http://www.psych.ucsb
.edu/research/cep/primer.html

▪ **22. CHAPTER OR SECTION IN A WEB DOCUMENT** Begin with publication information as for a chapter from a book (see item 17), but do not include the city or publisher. End with either the name of the database and the document number or the URL for the chapter or section. (For an annotated example, see p. 508.)

Stephenson, R. H. (2007). Super-sized kids: Obesity, children, moral
panic, and the media. In J. A. Bryant (Ed.), *The children's
television community* (pp. 277-291). Retrieved from PsycINFO
database (2006-21782-008).

▪ **23. WEBLOG (BLOG) POST** Give the writer's name, the date of the post, and the title or subject of the post. Follow with the words "Message posted to" and the URL.

Kellermann, M. (2007, May 23). Disclosing clinical trials. Message
posted to http://www.iq.harvard.edu/blog/sss/archives/2007/05

▪ **24. PODCAST** Begin with the writer or producer of the podcast; the date the podcast was produced or posted; the title; and any other identifying information in brackets. Then give as much of the following information as is available: the series title, in italics; the title of the Web site on which you found the podcast; or the name of the organization on whose Web site you found the podcast. End with a retrieval statement and the URL.

National Academies (Producer). (2007, June 6). Progress in preventing
childhood obesity: How do we measure up? *The sounds of science
podcast.* Podcast retrieved from http://media.nap.edu/podcasts

Chesney, M. (2007, September 13). Gender differences in the use of
complementary and alternative medicine [No. 12827]. Podcast
retrieved from the University of California Television Web site:
http://www.uctv.tv/ondemand/

■ **25. ENTRY IN A WIKI** Begin with the title of the entry and the date of posting, if there is one (use "n.d." for "no date" if there is not). Then add your retrieval date, the name of the wiki, and the URL for the home page of the wiki or the specific entry. Unlike most other entries for electronic sources, the entry for a wiki includes the date of retrieval because the content of a wiki is often not stable. If an author or an editor is identified, include that name at the beginning of the entry.

Ethnomethodology. (n.d.). Retrieved August 22, 2007, from the STS

Wiki: http://en.stswiki.org/index.php/Ethnomethodology

■ **26. E-MAIL** E-mail messages, letters, and other personal communications are not included in the list of references.

■ **27. ONLINE POSTING** If an online posting is not archived, cite it as a personal communication in the text of your paper and do not include it in the list of references. If the posting is archived, give as much information as is available.

McKinney, J. (2006, December 19). Adult education-healthcare

partnerships [Msg 504]. Message posted to the HealthLiteracy

electronic mailing list, archived at http://www.nifl.gov/pipermail

/healthliteracy/2006/000524.html

■ **28. COMPUTER PROGRAM** Add the words "Computer software" in brackets after the title of the program.

Kaufmann, W. J., III, & Comins, N. F. (2003). Discovering the universe

(Version 6.0) [Computer software]. New York: Freeman.

Other sources

■ **29. DISSERTATION ABSTRACT**

Yoshida, Y. (2001). Essays in urban transportation (Doctoral

dissertation, Boston College, 2001). *Dissertation Abstracts*

International, 62, 7741A.

■ **30. GOVERNMENT DOCUMENT**

U.S. Census Bureau. (2006). *Statistical abstract of the United States.*

Washington, DC: U.S. Government Printing Office.

Citation at a glance: Section in a Web document (APA)

To cite a section in a Web document in APA style, include the following elements:

1 Author
2 Date of publication or most recent update
3 Title of document on Web site
4 Title of Web site or section of site
5 URL of document

BROWSER PRINTOUT OF WEB SITE

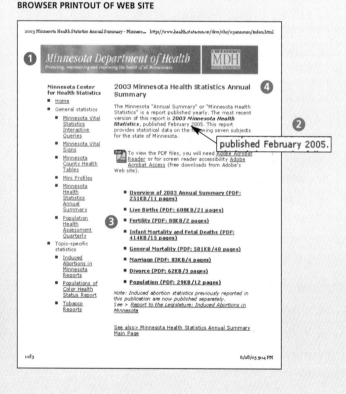

ON-SCREEN VIEW OF DOCUMENT

Fertility Table 1
Total Reported Pregnancies by Outcome and Rate
Minnesota Residents, 1980 - 2003

http://www.health.state.mn.us/divs/chs/03annsum/fertility.pdf

Year	Total Reported Pregnancies	Live Births	Induced Abortions	Fetal Deaths	Female Population Ages 15-44	Pregnancy Rate**
1980	84					
1981	84,934	68,652	15,821	461	967,087	87.8
1982	84,500	68,512	15,559	429	977,905	86.4
1983	80,530	65,559	14,514	457	981,287	82.1
1984	82,736	66,715	15,556	465	985,608	83.9
1985	83,853	67,412	16,002	439	994,249	84.3
1986	81,882	65,766	15,716	400	997,501	82.1
1987	81,318	65,168	15,746	404	1,004,801	80.9
1988	83,335	66,745	16,124	466	1,020,209	81.7
1989	83,426	67,490	15,506	430	1,024,576	81.4
1990	83,714	67,985	15,280	449	1,025,919	81.6

REFERENCE LIST ENTRY FOR A SECTION IN A WEB DOCUMENT

————————1———————— ⌐—2—⌐ ⌐—3—⌐ ⌐————4————

Minnesota Department of Health. (2005). Fertility. In *2003 Minnesota*

⌐————————————————————⌐ ⌐————5————

health statistics annual summary. Retrieved from http://www.health

————————————————————————

.state.mn.us/divs/chs/03annsum/fertility.pdf

For more on citing documents from Web sites in APA style, see
pages 502–07.

■ **31. REPORT FROM A PRIVATE ORGANIZATION** If the publisher and the author are the same, use the word "Author" as the publisher. If a person is named as the author, begin with that person and give the organization as publisher at the end.

American Psychiatric Association. (2000). *Practice guidelines for the*
  treatment of patients with eating disorders (2nd ed.). Washington,
  DC: Author.

■ **32. CONFERENCE PROCEEDINGS**

Stahl, G. (Ed.). (2002). *Proceedings of CSCL '02: Computer support for*
  collaborative learning. Hillsdale, NJ: Erlbaum.

■ **33. MOTION PICTURE** To cite a motion picture (film, video, or DVD), list the director and the year of the picture's release. Give the title, followed by "Motion picture" in brackets, the country where it was made, and the name of the studio. If the motion picture is difficult to find, include instead the name and address of its distributor.

Gaghan, S. (Director). (2005). *Syriana* [Motion picture]. United States:
  Warner Brothers Pictures.

Spurlock, M. (Director). (2004). *Super size me* [Motion picture].
  (Available from IDP Films, 1133 Broadway, Suite 926, New York,
  NY 10010)

■ **34. TELEVISION PROGRAM** To cite a television program, list the producer and the date it was aired. Give the title, followed by "Television broadcast" in brackets, the city, and the television network or service.

Pratt, C. (Executive Producer). (2006, February 19). *Face the nation*
  [Television broadcast]. Washington, DC: CBS News.

For a television series, use the year in which the series was produced, and follow the title with "Television series" in brackets. For an episode in a series, list the writer and director and the year. After the episode title, put "Television series episode" in brackets. Follow with information about the series.

Janows, J. (Executive Producer). (2000). *Culture shock* [Television
  series]. Boston: WGBH.

Loeterman, B. (Writer), & Gale, B. (Director). (2000). Real justice [Television series episode]. In M. Sullivan (Executive Producer), *Frontline*. Boston: WGBH.

ON THE WEB > **dianahacker.com/rules**
Research exercises > APA > E-ex APA 60–5 and 60–6

61

APA manuscript format; sample paper

61a APA manuscript format

The American Psychological Association makes a number of recommendations for formatting a paper and preparing a list of references. The following guidelines are consistent with advice given in the *Publication Manual of the American Psychological Association,* 5th ed. (Washington: APA, 2001) and the *APA Style Guide to Electronic References* (2007).

Formatting the paper

APA guidelines for formatting a paper are endorsed by many instructors in the social sciences.

MATERIALS AND TYPEFACE   Use good-quality 8½″ × 11″ white paper. Avoid a typeface that is unusual or hard to read.

TITLE PAGE   The APA manual does not provide guidelines for preparing the title page of a college paper, but most instructors will want you to include one. See page 515 for an example.

PAGE NUMBERS AND RUNNING HEAD   The title page is numbered as page i; the abstract page, if there is one, is numbered as page ii. Use arabic numerals, beginning with 1, for the rest of the paper. In the upper right-hand corner of each page, type a short version of your title, followed by five spaces and the page number. Number all pages, including the title page.

MARGINS, LINE SPACING, AND PARAGRAPH INDENTS   Use margins of one inch on all sides of the page. Left-align the text.

Double-space throughout the paper, but single-space footnotes. Indent the first line of each paragraph one-half inch (or five spaces).

LONG QUOTATIONS AND FOOTNOTES   When a quotation is longer than forty words, set it off from the text by indenting it one-half inch (or five spaces) from the left margin. Double-space the quotation. Quotation marks are not needed when a quotation has been set off from the text. See page 525 for an example.

Place each footnote, if any, at the bottom of the page on which the text reference occurs. Double-space between the last line of text on the page and the footnote. Indent the first line of the footnote one-half inch (or five spaces). Begin the note with the superscript arabic numeral that corresponds to the number in the text. See page 517 for an example.

ABSTRACT   If your instructor requires one, include an abstract immediately after the title page. Center the word Abstract one inch from the top of the page; double-space the abstract as you do the body of your paper.

An abstract is a 100-to-120-word paragraph that provides readers with a quick overview of your essay. It should express your main idea and your key points; it might also briefly suggest any implications or applications of the research you discuss in the paper. See page 516 for an example.

HEADINGS   Although headings are not always necessary, their use is encouraged in the social sciences. For most undergraduate papers, one level of heading will usually be sufficient.

In APA style, major headings are centered. Capitalize the first word of the heading, along with all words except articles, short prepositions, and coordinating conjunctions.

VISUALS   APA classifies visuals as tables and figures (figures include graphs, charts, drawings, and photographs). Keep visuals as simple as possible. Label each table with an arabic numeral (Table 1, Table 2, and so on) and provide a clear title. The label and title should appear on separate lines above the table, flush left and single-spaced. Below the table, give its source in a note. If any data in the table require an explanatory footnote, use a superscript lowercase letter in the body of the table and in a footnote following the source note. Single-space source notes and footnotes and do not indent the first line of each note. See page 521 for an example.

For each figure, place a label and a caption below the figure, flush left and single-spaced. The label and caption need not appear on separate lines.

In the text of your paper, discuss the most significant features of each visual. Place the visual as close as possible to the sentences that relate to it unless your instructor prefers it in an appendix.

Preparing the list of references

Begin your list of references on a new page at the end of the paper. Center the title References one inch from the top of the page. Double-space throughout. For a sample reference list, see pages 527–28.

INDENTING ENTRIES   APA recommends using a hanging indent: Type the first line of an entry flush left and indent any additional lines one-half inch (or five spaces), as shown on pages 527–28.

ALPHABETIZING THE LIST   Alphabetize the reference list by the last names of the authors (or editors); when a work has no author or editor, alphabetize by the first word of the title other than *A, An,* or *The.*

If your list includes two or more works by the same author, arrange the entries by year, the earliest first. If your list includes two or more works by the same author in the same year, arrange them alphabetically by title. Add the letters "a," "b," and so on within the parentheses after the year. Use only the year for articles in journals: (2002a). Use the full date for articles in magazines and newspapers in the reference list: (2005a, July 7). Use only the year in the in-text citation.

AUTHORS' NAMES   Invert all authors' names and use initials instead of first names. With two or more authors, use an ampersand (&) before the last author's name. Separate the names with commas. Include names for the first six authors; if there are additional authors, end the list with "et al." (Latin for "and others").

TITLES OF BOOKS AND ARTICLES   Italicize the titles and subtitles of books. Do not use quotation marks around the titles of articles. Capitalize only the first word of the title and subtitle (and all proper nouns) of books and articles. Capitalize names of periodicals as you would capitalize them normally (see 45c).

ABBREVIATIONS FOR PAGE NUMBERS Abbreviations for "page" and "pages" ("p." and "pp.") are used before page numbers of newspaper articles and articles in edited books (see item 10 on p. 498 and item 17 on p. 502) but not before page numbers of articles appearing in magazines and scholarly journals (see items 7–9 on p. 498).

BREAKING A URL When a URL must be divided, break it after a double slash or before any other mark of punctuation. Do not insert a hyphen. Do not add a period after a URL or a DOI.

For information about the exact format of each entry in your list, consult the models on pages 496–511.

61b Sample APA research paper

On the following pages is a research paper on the effectiveness of treatments for childhood obesity, written by Luisa Mirano, a student in a psychology class. Mirano's assignment was to write a review of the literature paper documented with APA-style citations and references.

ON THE WEB > **dianahacker.com/rules**
   Model papers > APA papers: Mirano; Shaw
                  > APA annotated bibliography: Haddad

Obesity in Children   i   Short title and page number for student papers. Lowercase roman numerals are used on title page and abstract page, arabic numerals on all text pages.

Can Medication Cure Obesity in Children?   Full title

A Review of the Literature

Luisa Mirano

Psychology 107, Section B

Professor Kang

October 31, 2004

Writer's name, and section number of course, instructor's name, and date (all centered).

Marginal annotations indicate APA-style formatting and effective writing.

Obesity in Children   ii

Abstract appears on a separate page.

Abstract

In recent years, policymakers and medical experts have expressed alarm about the growing problem of childhood obesity in the United States. While most agree that the issue deserves attention, consensus dissolves around how to respond to the problem. This literature review examines one approach to treating childhood obesity: medication. The paper compares the effectiveness for adolescents of the only two drugs approved by the Food and Drug Administration (FDA) for long-term treatment of obesity, sibutramine and orlistat. This examination of pharmacological treatments for obesity points out the limitations of medication and suggests the need for a comprehensive solution that combines medical, social, behavioral, and political approaches to this complex problem.

Can Medication Cure Obesity in Children?

A Review of the Literature

In March 2004, U.S. Surgeon General Richard
Carmona called attention to a health problem in the
United States that, until recently, has been overlooked: childhood obesity. Carmona said that the
"astounding" 15% child obesity rate constitutes an
"epidemic." Since the early 1980s, that rate has
"doubled in children and tripled in adolescents." Now
more than 9 million children are classified as obese
(paras. 3, 6).[1] While the traditional response to a
medical epidemic is to hunt for a vaccine or a cure-all
pill, childhood obesity has proven more elusive. The
lack of success of recent initiatives suggests that
medication might not be the answer for the escalating
problem. This literature review considers whether the
use of medication is a promising approach for solving
the childhood obesity problem by responding to the
following questions:

1. What are the implications of childhood
   obesity?

---

[1]Obesity is measured in terms of body-mass
index (BMI): weight in kilograms divided by square of
height in meters. An adult with a BMI 30 or higher is
considered obese. A child or an adolescent with a BMI
in the 95th percentile for his or her age and gender
is considered obese.

Full title, centered.

The writer uses a
footnote to define
an essential term
that would be
cumbersome to
define within the
text.

Obesity in Children   2

The writer sets up her organization by posing four questions.

2. Is medication effective at treating childhood obesity?

3. Is medication safe for children?

4. Is medication the best solution?

The writer states her thesis.

Understanding the limitations of medical treatments for children highlights the complexity of the childhood obesity problem in the United States and underscores the need for physicians, advocacy groups, and policymakers to search for other solutions.

Headings, centered, help readers follow the organization.

What Are the Implications of Childhood Obesity?

Obesity can be a devastating problem from both an individual and a societal perspective. Obesity puts children at risk for a number of medical complications, including type 2 diabetes, hypertension, sleep apnea, and orthopedic problems (Henry J. Kaiser Family Foundation, 2004, p. 1). Researchers Hoppin and Taveras (2004) have noted that obesity is often associated with psychological issues such as depression, anxiety, and binge eating (Table 4).

In a signal phrase, the word "and" links the names of two authors; the date is given in parentheses.

Because the author (Carmona) is not named in the signal phrase, his name and the date appear in parentheses, along with the paragraph number of the electronic source.

Obesity also poses serious problems for a society struggling to cope with rising health care costs. The cost of treating obesity currently totals $117 billion per year--a price, according to the surgeon general, "second only to the cost of [treating] tobacco use" (Carmona, 2004, para. 9). And as the number of children who suffer from obesity grows, long-term costs will only increase.

Obesity in Children   3

Is Medication Effective at Treating Childhood Obesity?

The widening scope of the obesity problem has prompted medical professionals to rethink old conceptions of the disorder and its causes. As researchers Yanovski and Yanovski (2002) have explained, obesity was once considered "either a moral failing or evidence of underlying psychopathology" (p. 592). But this view has shifted: Many medical professionals now consider obesity a biomedical rather than a moral condition, influenced by both genetic and environmental factors. Yanovski and Yanovski have further noted that the development of weight-loss medications in the early 1990s showed that "obesity should be treated in the same manner as any other chronic disease . . . through the long-term use of medication" (p. 592).

> Ellipsis mark indicates omitted words.

The search for the right long-term medication has been complicated. Many of the drugs authorized by the Food and Drug Administration (FDA) in the early 1990s proved to be a disappointment. Two of the medications--fenfluramine and dexfenfluramine--were withdrawn from the market because of severe side effects (Yanovski & Yanovski, 2002, p. 592), and several others were classified by the Drug Enforcement Administration as having the "potential for abuse" (Hoppin & Taveras, 2004, Weight-Loss Drugs section, para. 6). Currently only two medications have been approved by the FDA for long-term treatment of obesity:

> An ampersand links the names of two authors in parentheses.

Obesity in Children   4

sibutramine (marketed as Meridia) and orlistat
(marketed as Xenical). This section compares studies
on the effectiveness of each.

Sibutramine suppresses appetite by blocking the
reuptake of the neurotransmitters serotonin and
norepinephrine in the brain (Yanovski & Yanovski,
2002, p. 594). Though the drug won FDA approval in
1998, experiments to test its effectiveness for younger
patients came considerably later. In 2003, University
of Pennsylvania researchers Berkowitz, Wadden,
Tershakovec, and Cronquist released the first
double-blind placebo study testing the effect of
sibutramine on adolescents, aged 13-17, over a
12-month period. Their findings are summarized in
Table 1.

After 6 months, the group receiving medication had
lost 4.6 kg (about 10 pounds) more than the control
group. But during the second half of the study, when
both groups received sibutramine, the results were more
ambiguous. In months 6-12, the group that continued to
take sibutramine gained an average of 0.8 kg, or roughly
2 pounds; the control group, which switched from
placebo to sibutramine, lost 1.3 kg, or roughly 3 pounds
(p. 1808). Both groups received behavioral therapy
covering diet, exercise, and mental health.

These results paint a murky picture of the
effectiveness of the medication: While initial data seemed

The writer draws
attention to an
important article.

Table 1

Effectiveness of Sibutramine and Orlistat in Adolescents

> The writer uses a table to summarize the findings presented in two sources.

Medication	Subjects	Treatment[a]	Side effects	Average weight loss/gain
Sibutra-mine	Control	0-6 mos.: placebo 6-12 mos.: sibutra-mine	Mos. 6-12: increased blood pressure; increased pulse rate	After 6 mos.: loss of 3.2 kg (7 lb) After 12 mos.: loss of 4.5 kg (9.9 lb)
	Medicated	0-12 mos.: sibutra-mine	Increased blood pressure; increased pulse rate	After 6 mos.: loss of 7.8 kg (17.2 lb) After 12 mos.: loss of 7.0 kg (15.4 lb)
Orlistat	Control	0-12 mos.: placebo	None	Gain of 0.67 kg (1.5 lb)
	Medicated	0-12 mos.: orlistat	Oily spotting; flatulence; abdominal discomfort	Loss of 1.3 kg (2.9 lb)

Note. The data on sibutramine are adapted from "Behavior Therapy and Sibutramine for the Treatment of Adolescent Obesity," by R. I. Berkowitz, T. A. Wadden, A. M. Tershakovec, & J. L. Cronquist, 2003, *Journal of the American Medical Association, 289,* pp. 1807-1809. The data on orlistat are adapted from *Xenical (Orlistat) Capsules: Complete Product Information,* by Roche Laboratories, December 2003, retrieved from http://www.rocheusa.com/products/xenical/pi.pdf
[a]The medication and/or placebo were combined with behavioral therapy in all groups over all time periods.

> A note gives the source of the data.
>
> A content note explains data common to all subjects.

Obesity in Children 6

promising, the results after one year raised questions
about whether medication-induced weight loss could
be sustained over time. As Berkowitz et al. (2003)
advised, "Until more extensive safety and efficacy data
are available, . . . weight-loss medications should be
used only on an experimental basis for adolescents"
(p. 1811).

When this article was first cited, all four authors were named. In subsequent citations of a work with three to five authors, "et al." is used after the first author's name.

A study testing the effectiveness of orlistat in adolescents showed similarly ambiguous results. The FDA
approved orlistat in 1999 but did not authorize it for
adolescents until December 2003. Roche Laboratories
(2003), maker of orlistat, released results of a one-year
study testing the drug on 539 obese adolescents, aged
12-16. The drug, which promotes weight loss by blocking
fat absorption in the large intestine, showed some
effectiveness in adolescents: an average loss of 1.3 kg,
or roughly 3 pounds, for subjects taking orlistat for one
year, as opposed to an average gain of 0.67 kg, or 1.5
pounds, for the control group (pp. 8-9). See Table 1.

Short-term studies of orlistat have shown slightly
more dramatic results. Researchers at the National
Institute of Child Health and Human Development tested
20 adolescents, aged 12-16, over a three-month period
and found that orlistat, combined with behavioral
therapy, produced an average weight loss of 4.4 kg, or
9.7 pounds (McDuffie et al., 2002, p. 646). The study
was not controlled against a placebo group; therefore,

For a source with six or more authors, the first author's surname followed by "et al." is used for the first and subsequent references.

the relative effectiveness of orlistat in this case remains unclear.

Is Medication Safe for Children?

While modest weight loss has been documented for both medications, each carries risks of certain side effects. Sibutramine has been observed to increase blood pressure and pulse rate. In 2002, a consumer group claimed that the medication was related to the deaths of 19 people and filed a petition with the Department of Health and Human Services to ban the medication (Hilts, 2002). The sibutramine study by Berkowitz et al. (2003) noted elevated blood pressure as a side effect, and dosages had to be reduced or the medication discontinued in 19 of the 43 subjects in the first six months (p. 1809).

The main side effects associated with orlistat were abdominal discomfort, oily spotting, fecal incontinence, and nausea (Roche Laboratories, 2003, p. 13). More serious for long-term health is the concern that orlistat, being a fat-blocker, would affect absorption of fat-soluble vitamins, such as vitamin D. However, the study found that this side effect can be minimized or eliminated if patients take vitamin supplements two hours before or after administration of orlistat (p. 10). With close monitoring of patients taking the medication, many of the risks can be reduced.

Obesity in Children 8

Is Medication the Best Solution?

The data on the safety and efficacy of pharmacological treatments of childhood obesity raise the question of whether medication is the best solution for the problem. The treatments have clear costs for individual patients, including unpleasant side effects, little information about long-term use, and uncertainty that they will yield significant weight loss.

In purely financial terms, the drugs cost more than $3 a day on average (Duenwald, 2004, paras. 33, 36). In each of the clinical trials, use of medication was accompanied by an expensive regime of behavioral therapies, including counseling, nutritional education, fitness advising, and monitoring. As journalist Greg Critser (2003) noted in his book *Fat Land,* use of weight-loss drugs is unlikely to have an effect without the proper "support system"--one that includes doctors, facilities, time, and money (p. 3). For some, this level of care is prohibitively expensive.

A third complication is that the studies focused on adolescents aged 12-16, but obesity can begin at a much younger age. Little data exist to establish the safety or efficacy of medication for treating very young children.

The writer develops the paper's thesis.

While the scientific data on the concrete effects of these medications in children remain somewhat unclear, medication is not the only avenue for addressing the crisis. Both medical experts and policymakers recognize that solutions might come not only from a laboratory but also from policy, education, and advocacy. Indeed, a handbook designed to educate doctors on obesity recommended a notably nonmedical course of action, calling for "major changes in some aspects of western culture" (Hoppin & Taveras, 2004, Conclusion section, para. 1). Cultural change may not be the typical realm of medical professionals, but the handbook urged doctors to be proactive and "focus [their] energy on public policies and interventions" (Conclusion section, para. 1).

Brackets indicate a word not in the original source.

The solutions proposed by a number of advocacy groups underscore this interest in political and cultural change. A report by the Henry J. Kaiser Family Foundation (2004) outlined trends that may have contributed to the childhood obesity crisis, including food advertising for children as well as

> a reduction in physical education classes and after-school athletic programs, an increase in the availability of sodas and snacks in public schools, the growth in the number of fast-food outlets . . . , and the increasing number of highly processed high-calorie and high-fat grocery products. (p. 1)

A quotation longer than 40 words is set off from the text without quotation marks.

Addressing each of these areas requires more than a doctor armed with a prescription pad; it requires a

The writer interprets the evidence; she doesn't just report it.

Obesity in Children   10

broad mobilization not just of doctors and concerned

parents but of educators, food industry executives,

advertisers, and media representatives.

The tone of the con-
clusion is objective.   The barrage of possible approaches to combating

childhood obesity--from scientific research to political

lobbying--indicates both the severity and the

complexity of the problem. While none of the

medications currently available is a miracle drug

for curing the nation's 9 million obese children,

research has illuminated some of the underlying

factors that affect obesity and has shown the need

for a comprehensive approach to the problem that

includes behavioral, medical, social, and political

change.

Obesity in Children   11

References

Berkowitz, R. I., Wadden, T. A., Tershakovec, A. M., & Cronquist, J. L. (2003). Behavior therapy and sibutramine for the treatment of adolescent obesity. *Journal of the American Medical Association, 289,* 1805-1812.

Carmona, R. H. (2004, March 2). *The growing epidemic of childhood obesity.* Testimony before the Subcommittee on Competition, Foreign Commerce, and Infrastructure of the U.S. Senate Committee on Commerce, Science, and Transportation. Retrieved from http://www.hhs.gov /asl/testify/t040302.html

Critser, G. (2003). *Fat land: How Americans became the fattest people in the world.* Boston: Houghton Mifflin.

Duenwald, M. (2004, January 6). Slim pickings: Looking beyond ephedra. *The New York Times,* p. F1. Retrieved from LexisNexis.

Henry J. Kaiser Family Foundation. (2004, February). *The role of media in childhood obesity.* Retrieved from http://www.kff.org/entmedia/7030.cfm

Hilts, P. J. (2002, March 20). Petition asks for removal of diet drug from market. *The New York Times,* p. A26. Retrieved from LexisNexis.

List of references begins on a new page. Heading is centered.

List is alphabetized by authors' last names. All authors' names are inverted.

The first line of an entry is at the left margin; subsequent lines indent ½" (or five spaces).

Double-spacing is used throughout.

Hoppin, A. G., & Taveras, E. M. (2004, June 25). Assessment and management of childhood and adolescent obesity. *Clinical Update.* Retrieved from http://www.medscape.com/viewarticle /481633

McDuffie, J. R., Calis, K. A., Uwaifo, G. I., Sebring, N. G., Fallon, E. M., Hubbard, V. S., et al. (2003). Three-month tolerability of orlistat in adolescents with obesity-related comorbid conditions. *Obesity Research, 10,* 642-650.

Roche Laboratories. (2003, December). *Xenical (orlistat) capsules: Complete product information.* Retrieved from http://www.rocheusa.com/products/xenical/pi.pdf

Yanovski, S. Z., & Yanovski, J. A. (2002). Drug therapy: Obesity. *The New England Journal of Medicine, 346,* 591-602.

Basics

62

Parts of speech

Traditional grammar recognizes eight parts of speech: noun, pronoun, verb, adjective, adverb, preposition, conjunction, and interjection. Many words can function as more than one part of speech. For example, depending on its use in a sentence, the word *paint* can be a noun (*The paint is wet*) or a verb (*Please paint the ceiling next*).

A quick-reference chart of the parts of speech appears on pages 540–42.

62a Nouns

As most schoolchildren can attest, a noun is the name of a person, place, thing, or concept.

> N   N   N
> The *cat* in *gloves* catches no *mice.*

> N   N   N
> *Action* is the *antidote* to *despair.*

Nouns sometimes function as adjectives modifying other nouns. Because of their dual roles, nouns used in this manner may be called *noun/adjectives.*

> N/ADJ   N/ADJ
> You can't make a *silk* purse out of a *sow's* ear.

Nouns are classified for a variety of purposes. When capitalization is the issue, we speak of *proper* versus *common nouns* (see 45a). If the problem is one of word choice, we may speak of *concrete* versus *abstract nouns* (see 18b). The distinction between *count nouns* and *noncount nouns* is useful primarily for nonnative speakers of English (see 29b). The term *collective noun* refers to a set of nouns that may cause problems with subject-verb or pronoun-antecedent agreement (see 21f and 22b).

EXERCISE 62–1 Underline the nouns (and noun/adjectives) in the following sentences. Answers to lettered sentences appear in the back of the book. Example:

Idle <u>hands</u> are the <u>devil's</u> <u>workshop</u>.

a. The sun will set without your assistance.   — Hebrew proverb
b. Pride is at the bottom of all great mistakes.   — John Ruskin
c. Success breeds confidence.   — Beryl Markham
d. The ultimate censorship is the flick of the dial.   — Tom Smothers
e. Our national flower is the concrete cloverleaf.   — Lewis Mumford

1. Truthfulness so often goes with ruthlessness.   — Dodie Smith
2. Luck is a matter of preparation meeting opportunity.
                                                  — Oprah Winfrey
3. Problems are only opportunities in work clothes.   — Henry Kaiser
4. A woman must have money and a room of her own.
                                                  — Virginia Woolf
5. Language helps form the limits of our reality.   — Dale Spender

ON THE WEB > **dianahacker.com/rules**
    Grammar exercises > Basics > E-ex 62–1

62b Pronouns

A pronoun is a word used in place of a noun. Usually the pronoun substitutes for a specific noun, known as its *antecedent*.

> When the *wheel* squeaks, *it* is greased.

Although most pronouns function as substitutes for nouns, some can function as adjectives modifying nouns (*This* bird always catches the worm).

Because they have the form of a pronoun and the function of an adjective, such pronouns may be called *pronoun/adjectives*.

Pronouns are classified as personal, possessive, intensive and reflexive, relative, interrogative, demonstrative, indefinite, and reciprocal.

PERSONAL PRONOUNS   Personal pronouns refer to specific persons or things. They always function as noun equivalents.

> *Singular:* I, me, you, she, her, he, him, it
>
> *Plural:* we, us, you, they, them

POSSESSIVE PRONOUNS   Possessive pronouns indicate ownership.

> *Singular:* my, mine, your, yours, her, hers, his, its
>
> *Plural:* our, ours, your, yours, their, theirs

Some of these possessive pronouns function as adjectives modifying nouns: *my, your, his, her, its, our, their.*

INTENSIVE AND REFLEXIVE PRONOUNS   Intensive pronouns emphasize a noun or another pronoun (The senator *herself* met us at the door). Reflexive pronouns, which have the same form as intensive pronouns, name a receiver of an action identical with the doer of the action (Paula cut *herself*).

> *Singular:* myself, yourself, himself, herself, itself
>
> *Plural:* ourselves, yourselves, themselves

RELATIVE PRONOUNS   Relative pronouns introduce subordinate clauses functioning as adjectives (The man *who robbed us* was never caught). In addition to introducing the clause, the relative pronoun, in this case *who,* points back to a noun or pronoun that the clause modifies (*man*). (See 64b.)

> who, whom, whose, which, that

Some textbooks also treat *whichever, whoever, whomever, what,* and *whatever* as relative pronouns. These words introduce noun clauses; they do not point back to a noun or pronoun. (See "Noun clauses" in 64b.)

INTERROGATIVE PRONOUNS   Interrogative pronouns introduce questions (*Who* is expected to win the election?).

> who, whom, whose, which, what

DEMONSTRATIVE PRONOUNS   Demonstrative pronouns identify or point to nouns. Frequently they function as adjectives (*This* chair is my favorite), but they may also function as noun equivalents (*This* is my favorite chair).

> this, that, these, those

INDEFINITE PRONOUNS   Indefinite pronouns refer to nonspecific persons or things. Most are always singular (*everyone, each*); some are always plural (*both, many*); a few may be singular or plural (see 21e). Most indefinite pronouns function as noun equivalents (*Something* is burning), but some can also function as adjectives (*All* campers must check in at the lodge).

all	anything	everyone	nobody	several
another	both	everything	none	some
any	each	few	no one	somebody
anybody	either	many	nothing	someone
anyone	everybody	neither	one	something

RECIPROCAL PRONOUNS Reciprocal pronouns refer to individual parts of a plural antecedent (By turns, we helped *each other* through college).

each other, one another

NOTE: Pronouns cause a variety of problems for writers. See pronoun-antecedent agreement (22), pronoun reference (23), distinguishing between pronouns such as *I* and *me* (24), and distinguishing between *who* and *whom* (25).

EXERCISE 62–2 Underline the pronouns (and pronoun/adjectives) in the following sentences. Answers to lettered sentences appear in the back of the book. Example:

Always beware of persons <u>who</u> are praised by <u>everyone</u>.

a. He has every attribute of a dog except loyalty.   — Thomas Gore
b. A fall does not hurt those who fly low.   — Chinese proverb
c. I have written some poetry that I myself don't understand.
    — Carl Sandburg
d. I am firm. You are obstinate. He is a pig-headed fool.
    — Katherine Whitehorn
e. If you haven't anything nice to say about anyone, come and sit by me.   — Alice Roosevelt Longworth

1. Men are taught to apologize for their weaknesses, women for their strengths.   — Lois Wyse
2. Nothing is interesting if you are not interested.
    — Helen MacInness
3. We will never have friends if we expect to find them without fault.
    — Thomas Fuller
4. The gods help those who help themselves.   — Aesop
5. I awoke one morning and found myself famous.   — Lord Byron

ON THE WEB > dianahacker.com/rules
Grammar exercises > Basics > E-ex 62–2

62c Verbs

The verb of a sentence usually expresses action (*jump, think*) or being (*is, become*). It is composed of a main verb possibly preceded by one or more helping verbs.

> MV
> The best fish *swim* near the bottom.

> HV   MV
> A marriage *is* not *built* in a day.

Notice that words can intervene between the helping and the main verb (is *not* built).

Helping verbs

There are twenty-three helping verbs in English: forms of *have, do,* and *be,* which may also function as main verbs; and nine modals, which function only as helping verbs. The forms of *have, do,* and *be* change form to indicate tense; the nine modals do not.

FORMS OF *HAVE, DO,* AND *BE*

have, has, had

do, does, did

be, am, is, are, was, were, being, been

MODALS

can, could, may, might, must, shall, should, will, would

The phrase *ought to* is often classified as a modal as well.

Main verbs

The main verb of a sentence is always the kind of word that would change form if put into these test sentences:

BASE FORM	Usually I (*walk, ride*).
PAST TENSE	Yesterday I (*walked, rode*).
PAST PARTICIPLE	I have (*walked, ridden*) many times before.
PRESENT PARTICIPLE	I am (*walking, riding*) right now.
***-S* FORM**	Usually he/she/it (*walks, rides*).

If a word doesn't change form when slipped into these test sentences, you can be certain that it is not a main verb. For example, the noun *revolution,* though it may seem to suggest an action, can never function as a main verb. Just try to make it behave like one (*Today I revolution... Yesterday I revolutioned...*) and you'll see why.

When both the past-tense and the past-participle forms of a verb end in *-ed,* the verb is regular (*walked, walked*). Otherwise, the verb is irregular (*rode, ridden*). (See 27a.)

The verb *be* is highly irregular, having eight forms instead of the usual five: the base form *be*; the present-tense forms *am, is,* and *are*; the past-tense forms *was* and *were*; the present participle *being*; and the past participle *been.*

Helping verbs combine with the various forms of main verbs to create tenses. For a survey of tenses, see 28a.

NOTE: Some verbs are followed by words that look like prepositions but are so closely associated with the verb that they are a part of its meaning. These words are known as *particles.* Common verb-particle combinations include *bring up, call off, drop off, give in, look up, run into,* and *take off.*

> A lot of parents *pack up* their troubles and *send* them *off* to camp.
> — Raymond Duncan

NOTE: Verbs can be challenging for writers. See active verbs (8), subject-verb agreement (21), standard English verb forms (27), verb tense and mood (27), and ESL challenges with verbs (28).

EXERCISE 62-3 Underline the verbs in the following sentences, including helping verbs and particles. If a verb is part of a contraction (such as *is* in *isn't* or *would* in *I'd*), underline only the letters that represent the verb. Answers to lettered sentences appear in the back of the book. Example:

A full cup <u>must</u> <u>be</u> <u>carried</u> steadily.

a. I can pardon everyone's mistakes except my own.   — Cato
b. There are no atheists on turbulent airplanes.   — Erica Jong
c. One arrow does not bring down two birds.   — Turkish proverb
d. Keep your talent in the dark, and you'll never be insulted.
     — Elsa Maxwell
e. Throw a lucky man into the sea, and he will emerge with a fish in his mouth.   — Arab proverb

1. Do not scald your tongue in other people's broth.
   — English proverb
2. Wrong must not win by technicalities.   — Aeschylus
3. Love your neighbor, but don't pull down the hedge.
   — Swiss proverb
4. I'd rather have roses on my table than diamonds around my neck.
   — Emma Goldman
5. He is a fine friend. He stabs you in the front.
   — Leonard Louis Levinson

ON THE WEB > dianahacker.com/rules
Grammar exercises > Basics > E-ex 62–3 and 62–4

62d Adjectives

An adjective is a word used to modify, or describe, a noun or pronoun. An adjective usually answers one of these questions: Which one? What kind of? How many?

> ADJ
> the *lame* elephant [Which elephant?]

> ADJ   ADJ
> *valuable old* stamps [What kind of stamps?]

> ADJ
> *sixteen* candles [How many candles?]

Adjectives usually precede the words they modify. However, they may also follow linking verbs, in which case they describe the subject. (See B2-b.)

> ADJ
> Good medicine always tastes *bitter.*

Articles, sometimes classified as adjectives, are used to mark nouns. There are only three: the definite article *the* and the indefinite articles *a* and *an.*

> ART   ART
> *A* country can be judged by *the* quality of its proverbs.

Some possessive, demonstrative, and indefinite pronouns can function as adjectives: *their, its, this* (see 62b).

NOTE: Writers sometimes misuse adjectives (see 26b). Speakers of English as a second language may encounter problems with the articles *a, an,* and *the* and occasionally have trouble placing adjectives correctly (see 29 and 30h).

62e Adverbs

An adverb is a word used to modify, or qualify, a verb (or verbal), an adjective, or another adverb. It usually answers one of these questions: When? Where? How? Why? Under what conditions? To what degree?

> Pull *gently* at a weak rope. [Pull how?]
>
> Read the best books *first*. [Read when?]

Adverbs modifying adjectives or other adverbs usually intensify or limit the intensity of the word they modify.

> ADV   ADV
> Be *extremely* good, and you will be *very* lonesome.

Adverbs modifying adjectives and other adverbs are not movable. We can't say "Be good *extremely*" or "*Extremely* be good."

The negators *not* and *never* are classified as adverbs. A word such as *cannot* contains the helping verb *can* and the adverb *not*. A contraction such as *can't* contains the helping verb *can* and a contracted form of the adverb *not*.

NOTE: Writers sometimes misuse adverbs (see 26a). Multilingual speakers may have trouble placing adverbs correctly (see 30f).

EXERCISE 62–4 Underline the adjectives and circle the adverbs in the following sentences. If a word is a pronoun in form but an adjective in function, treat it as an adjective. Also treat the articles *a, an,* and *the* as adjectives. Answers to lettered sentences appear in the back of the book. Example:

> A wild goose (never) laid a tame egg.

a. General notions are generally wrong.
— Lady Mary Wortley Montagu
b. The American public is wonderfully tolerant.   — Anonymous

c. Wildflowers sometimes grow in an uncultivated field, but they never bloom in an uncultivated mind. — Anonymous

d. I'd rather be strongly wrong than weakly right.
— Tallulah Bankhead

e. Sleep faster. We need the pillows. — Yiddish proverb

1. Success is a public affair; failure is a private funeral.
— Rosalind Russell

2. Their civil discussions were not interesting, and their interesting discussions were not civil. — Lisa Alther

3. Money will buy a pretty good dog, but it will not buy the wag of its tail. — Josh Billings

4. We cannot be too careful in the choice of our enemies.
— Oscar Wilde

5. Feelings are untidy. — Esther Hautzig

ON THE WEB > dianahacker.com/rules
Grammar exercises > Basics > E-ex 62–5 and 62–6

62f Prepositions

A preposition is a word placed before a noun or pronoun to form a phrase modifying another word in the sentence. The prepositional phrase nearly always functions as an adjective or as an adverb.

P   P
The road *to* hell is usually paved *with* good intentions.

To hell functions as an adjective, modifying the noun *road*; *with good intentions* functions as an adverb, modifying the verb *is paved.* (For more about prepositional phrases, see 64a.)

There are a limited number of prepositions in English. The most common ones are included in the following list.

about	before	considering	like	over
above	behind	despite	near	past
across	below	down	next	plus
after	beside	during	of	regarding
against	besides	except	off	respecting
along	between	for	on	round
among	beyond	from	onto	since
around	but	in	opposite	than
as	by	inside	out	through
at	concerning	into	outside	throughout

till	under	until	upon	without
to	underneath	unto	with	
toward	unlike	up	within	

Some prepositions are more than one word long. *Along with, as well as, in addition to,* and *next to* are common examples.

NOTE: Except for certain idiomatic uses (see 18d), prepositions cause few problems for native speakers of English. For multilingual speakers, however, prepositions can cause considerable difficulty (see 31).

62g Conjunctions

Conjunctions join words, phrases, or clauses, and they indicate the relation between the elements joined.

COORDINATING CONJUNCTIONS   A coordinating conjunction is used to connect grammatically equal elements. The coordinating conjunctions are *and, but, or, nor, for, so,* and *yet.*

A good laugh *and* a long sleep are the best cures.

Admire a little ship, *but* put your cargo in a big one.

In the first sentence, *and* connects two noun phrases; in the second, *but* connects two independent clauses.

CORRELATIVE CONJUNCTIONS   Correlative conjunctions come in pairs: *either...or; neither...nor; not only...but also; whether... or; both...and.* Like coordinating conjunctions, they connect grammatically equal elements.

Either Jack Sprat *or* his wife could eat no fat.

SUBORDINATING CONJUNCTIONS   A subordinating conjunction introduces a subordinate clause and indicates the relation of the clause to the rest of the sentence. (See 64b.) The most common subordinating conjunctions are *after, although, as, as if, because, before, even though, if, in order that, once, rather than, since, so that, than, that, though, unless, until, when, where, whether, and while.*

If you want service, serve yourself.

CONJUNCTIVE ADVERBS   A conjunctive adverb may be used with a semicolon to connect independent clauses; it usually serves as a transition between the clauses. The most common conjunctive adverbs are *consequently, finally, furthermore, however, moreover, nevertheless, similarly, then, therefore,* and *thus.* (See p. 542 for a longer list.)

> When we want to murder a tiger, we call it sport; *however,* when the tiger wants to murder us, we call it ferocity.

NOTE: The ability to distinguish between conjunctive adverbs and coordinating conjunctions will help you avoid run-on sentences and make punctuation decisions (see 20, 32a, and 32b). The ability to recognize subordinating conjunctions will help you avoid sentence fragments (see 19).

62h Interjections

An interjection is a word used to express surprise or emotion (*Oh! Hey! Wow!*).

ON THE WEB > dianahacker.com/rules
  Grammar exercises > Basics > E-ex 62–7

Parts of speech

A **NOUN** names a person, place, thing, or concept.

$$\text{N} \qquad\qquad\qquad \text{N} \qquad \text{N}$$
Repetition does not transform a *lie* into *truth*.

A **PRONOUN** substitutes for a noun.

$$\qquad\qquad\qquad \text{PN} \quad \text{PN} \qquad \text{PN}$$
When the gods wish to punish *us, they* heed *our* prayers.
Personal pronouns: I, me, you, he, him, she, her, it, we, us, they, them
Possessive pronouns: my, mine, your, yours, her, hers, his, its, our, ours, their, theirs
Intensive and reflexive pronouns: myself, yourself, himself, herself, itself, ourselves, yourselves, themselves

→

Parts of speech (continued)

Relative pronouns: that, which, who, whom, whose
Interrogative pronouns: who, whom, whose, which, what
Demonstrative pronouns: this, that, these, those
Indefinite pronouns: all, another, any, anybody, anyone, any-thing, both, each, either, everybody, everyone, everything, few, many, neither, nobody, none, no one, nothing, one, several, some, somebody, someone, something
Reciprocal pronouns: each other, one another

A HELPING VERB comes before a main verb.

Modals: can, could, may, might, must, shall, should, will, would (*also* ought to)
Forms of be: be, am, is, are, was, were, being, been
Forms of have: have, has, had
Forms of do: do, does, did
(The forms of *be, have,* and *do* may also function as main verbs.)

A MAIN VERB asserts action, being, or state of being.

	MV		HV	MV

Charity *begins* at home but *should* not *end* there.

A main verb will always change form when put into these positions in sentences:

Usually I _____ .	(*walk, ride*)
Yesterday I _____ .	(*walked, rode*)
I have _____ many times before.	(*walked, ridden*)
I am _____ right now.	(*walking, riding*)
Usually he _____ .	(*walks, rides*)

There are eight forms of the highly irregular verb *be*: *be, am, is, are, was, were, being, been.*

An ADJECTIVE modifies a noun or pronoun, usually answering one of these questions: Which one? What kind of? How many? The articles *a, an,* and *the* are also adjectives.

→

Parts of speech (continued)

    ADJ   ADJ
Useless laws weaken *necessary* ones.

An ADVERB modifies a verb, an adjective, or an adverb, usually answering one of these questions: When? Where? Why? How? Under what conditions? To what degree?

          ADV   ADV
People think *too historically.*

A PREPOSITION indicates the relationship between the noun or pronoun that follows it and another word in the sentence.

         P   P
A journey *of* a thousand miles begins *with* a single step.

Common prepositions: about, above, across, after, against, along, among, around, as, at, before, behind, below, beside, besides, between, beyond, but, by, concerning, considering, despite, down, during, except, for, from, in, inside, into, like, near, next, of, off, on, onto, opposite, out, outside, over, past, plus, regarding, respecting, since, than, through, throughout, till, to, toward, under, underneath, unlike, until, unto, up, upon, with, within, without

A CONJUNCTION connects words or word groups.

Coordinating conjunctions: and, but, or, nor, for, so, yet

Subordinating conjunctions: after, although, as, as if, because, before, even though, if, in order that, once, rather than, since, so that, than, that, though, unless, until, when, where, whether, while

Correlative conjunctions: either . . . or, neither . . . nor, not only . . . but also, both . . . and, whether . . . or

Conjunctive adverbs: accordingly, also, anyway, besides, certainly, consequently, conversely, finally, furthermore, hence, however, incidentally, indeed, instead, likewise, meanwhile, moreover, nevertheless, next, nonetheless, otherwise, similarly, specifically, still, subsequently, then, therefore, thus

An INTERJECTION expresses surprise or emotion (*Oh! Wow! Hey! Hooray!*).

63

Sentence patterns

Most English sentences flow from subject to verb to any objects or complements. The vast majority of sentences conform to one of these five patterns:

subject / verb / subject complement

subject / verb / direct object

subject / verb / indirect object / direct object

subject / verb / direct object / object complement

subject / verb

Adverbial modifiers (single words, phrases, or clauses) may be added to any of these patterns, and they may appear nearly anywhere — at the beginning, the middle, or the end.

Predicate is the grammatical term given to the verb plus its objects, complements, and adverbial modifiers.

For a quick-reference chart of sentence patterns, see page 549.

63a Subjects

The subject of a sentence names who or what the sentence is about. The *complete subject* is usually composed of a *simple subject,* always a noun or pronoun, plus any words or word groups modifying the simple subject.

The complete subject

To find the complete subject, ask Who? or What?, insert the verb, and finish the question. The answer is the complete subject.

┌── COMPLETE SUBJECT ──┐
The purity of a revolution usually lasts about two weeks.

Who or what lasts about two weeks? *The purity of a revolution.*

┌──────── **COMPLETE SUBJECT** ────────┐
Historical books that contain no lies are extremely tedious.

Who or what are extremely tedious? *Historical books that contain no lies.*

COMPLETE SUBJECT
┌────────┐
In every country the sun rises in the morning.

Who or what rises in the morning? *The sun.* Notice that *In every country the sun* is not a sensible answer to the question. *In every country* is a prepositional phrase modifying the verb *rises.* Since sentences frequently open with such modifiers, it is not safe to assume that the subject must always appear first in a sentence.

The simple subject

To find the simple subject, strip away all modifiers in the complete subject. This includes single-word modifiers such as *the* and *historical,* phrases such as *of a revolution,* and subordinate clauses such as *that contain no lies.*

┌ss┐
The purity of a revolution usually lasts about two weeks.

┌ss┐
Historical books that contain no lies are extremely tedious.

┌ss┐
In every country *the sun* rises in the morning.

A sentence may have a compound subject containing two or more simple subjects joined with a coordinating conjunction such as *and, but,* or *or.*

┌ss┐   ┌ss┐
Much industry and little conscience make us rich.

Understood subjects

In imperative sentences, which give advice or issue commands, the subject is understood but not actually present in the sentence. The subject of an imperative sentence is understood to be *you,* as in the following example.

[*You*] Hitch your wagon to a star.

Subject after the verb

Although the subject ordinarily comes before the verb, occasionally it does not. When a sentence begins with *There is* or *There are* (or *There was* or *There were*), the subject follows the verb. The word *There* is an expletive in such constructions, an empty word serving merely to get the sentence started.

⌐——**SS**——⌐
There is *no substitute* for victory.

Occasionally a writer will invert a sentence for effect.

⌐—**SS**—⌐
Happy is *the nation that has no history.*

Happy is an adjective, so it cannot be the subject. Turn this sentence around and its structure becomes obvious: *The nation that has no history is happy.*

In questions, the subject frequently appears in an unusual position, sandwiched between parts of the verb.

⌐**SS**⌐
Do *married men* make the best husbands?

Turn the question into a statement, and the words will appear in their usual order: *Married men do make the best husbands.* (*Do make* is the verb.)

For more about unusual sentence patterns, see 63c.

NOTE: The ability to recognize the subject of a sentence will help you edit for a variety of problems such as sentence fragments (19), subject-verb agreement (21), and choice of pronouns such as *I* and *me* (24). If English is not your native language, see also 30b and 30c.

EXERCISE 63–1 In the following sentences, underline the complete subject and write *SS* above the simple subject(s). If the subject is an understood *you*, insert it in parentheses. Answers to lettered sentences appear in the back of the book. Example:

    SS   SS
<u>Fools and their money</u> are soon parted.

a. Sticks and stones may break my bones, and words can sting like anything.   — Anonymous

b. In war, all delays are dangerous. — John Dryden
c. Speak softly and carry a big stick. — Theodore Roosevelt
d. There is nothing permanent except change. — Heraclitus
e. Most of the disputes in the world arise from words.
— Lord Mansfield

1. The structure of every sentence is a lesson in logic. — J. S. Mill
2. Don't be humble. You're not that great. — Golda Meir
3. In the eyes of its mother, every beetle is a gazelle.
— Moorish proverb
4. The burden of proof lies on the plaintiff. — Legal maxim
5. There are no signposts in the sea. — Vita Sackville-West

ON THE WEB > **dianahacker.com/rules**
Grammar exercises > Basics > E-ex 63–1 and 63–2

63b Verbs, objects, and complements

Section 62c explains how to find the verb of a sentence, which consists of a main verb possibly preceded by one or more helping verbs. A sentence's verb is classified as linking, transitive, or intransitive, depending on the kinds of objects or complements the verb can (or cannot) take.

Linking verbs and subject complements

Linking verbs link the subject to a subject complement, a word or word group that completes the meaning of the subject by renaming or describing it. If the subject complement renames the subject, it is a noun or noun equivalent (sometimes called a *predicate noun*).

$$\overbrace{\text{The handwriting on the wall}}^{\text{S}} \quad \overbrace{\text{may be}}^{\text{V}} \quad \overbrace{\text{a forgery.}}^{\text{SC}}$$

If the subject complement describes the subject, it is an adjective or adjective equivalent (sometimes called a *predicate adjective*).

```
S    V   SC
Love is blind.
```

Whenever they appear as main verbs (rather than helping verbs), the forms of *be — be, am, is, are, was, were, being, been —* usually function as linking verbs. In the preceding examples, for instance, the main verbs are *be* and *is.*

Verbs such as *appear, become, feel, grow, look, make, seem, smell, sound,* and *taste* are sometimes linking, depending on the sense of the sentence.

```
                      S        V   ┌─SC─┐
```
At the touch of love, everyone becomes a poet.

```
         ┌───S───┐        V    SC
```
At first sight, original art often looks ugly.

When you suspect that a verb such as *becomes* or *looks* is linking, check to see if the word or words following it rename or describe the subject. In the preceding examples, *a poet* renames *everyone,* and *ugly* describes *art.*

Transitive verbs and direct objects

A transitive verb takes a direct object, a word or word group that names a receiver of the action.

```
┌──────S──────┐   V   ┌──────────DO──────────┐
```
The little snake studies the ways of the big serpent.

The simple direct object is always a noun or pronoun, in this case *ways.* To find it, simply strip away all modifiers.

Transitive verbs usually appear in the active voice, with the subject doing the action and a direct object receiving the action. Active-voice sentences can be transformed into the passive voice, with the subject receiving the action instead. (See 63c.)

Transitive verbs, indirect objects, and direct objects

The direct object of a transitive verb is sometimes preceded by an indirect object, a noun or pronoun telling to whom or for whom the action of the sentence is done.

```
 S   V   IO ┌─DO─┐     S┌─V─┐ IO ┌─DO─┐
```
You show me a hero, and I will write you a tragedy.

The simple indirect object is always a noun or pronoun. To test for an indirect object, insert the word *to* or *for* before the word or word group in question. If the sentence makes sense, the word or word group is an indirect object.

You show [to] me a hero, and I will write [for] you a tragedy.

An indirect object may be turned into a prepositional phrase using *to* or *for*: *You show a hero to me, and I will write a tragedy for you.*

Only certain transitive verbs take indirect objects. Some examples are *ask, bring, find, get, give, hand, lend, offer, pay, promise, read, send, show, teach, tell, throw,* and *write.*

Transitive verbs, direct objects, and object complements

The direct object of a transitive verb is sometimes followed by an object complement, a word or word group that completes the direct object's meaning by renaming or describing it.

```
      S          V  ┌─DO─┐┌─────────OC─────────┐
People now call a spade an agricultural implement.

      S     V    ┌─────DO─────┐   OC
Love makes all hard hearts gentle.
```

When the object complement renames the direct object, it is a noun or pronoun (such as *implement*). When it describes the direct object, it is an adjective (such as *gentle*).

Intransitive verbs

Intransitive verbs take no objects or complements. Their pattern is subject/verb.

```
      S     V
Money talks.

      S           V
Revolutions never go backward.
```

Nothing receives the actions of talking and going in these sentences, so the verbs are intransitive. Notice that such verbs may or may not be followed by adverbial modifiers. In the second sentence, *backward* is an adverb modifying *go*.

NOTE: The dictionary will tell you whether a verb is transitive or intransitive. Some verbs have both transitive and intransitive functions.

TRANSITIVE Sandra flew her Cessna over the canyon.

INTRANSITIVE A bald eagle flew overhead.

Sentence patterns

Subject / linking verb / subject complement

┌──S──┐ V ┌──SC──┐
Advertising is legalized lying. [*Legalized lying* renames *Advertising*.]

┌──S──┐ V ┌─SC─┐
Great intellects are skeptical. [*Skeptical* describes *Great intellects*.]

Subject / transitive verb / direct object

┌─S─┐ ┌──V──┐┌DO┐
A stumble may prevent a fall.

Subject / transitive verb / indirect object / direct object

S V IO ┌──DO──┐
Fate gives us our relatives.

Subject / transitive verb / direct object / object complement

┌─S─┐┌─V─┐DO OC
Our fears do make us traitors. [*Traitors* renames *us*.]

┌─S─┐ V ┌─DO─┐ OC
The pot calls the kettle black. [*Black* describes *the kettle*.]

Subject / intransitive verb

S V
Time flies.

In the first example, *flew* has a direct object that receives the action: *her Cessna*. In the second example, the verb is followed by an adverb (*overhead*), not by a direct object.

EXERCISE 63–2 Label the subject complements and direct objects in the following sentences, using these labels: *SC, DO*. If a subject complement or direct object consists of more than one word, bracket and label all of it. Example:

┌──────DO──────┐
You can fool most of the people most of the time.

a. Talk is cheap. — English proverb
b. An elephant never forgets an injury. — American proverb
c. A runaway monk never praises his convent. — Italian proverb
d. Religion is the opium of the people. — Karl Marx
e. Good medicine always tastes bitter. — Japanese proverb

1. You can say the nastiest things about yourself without offending anyone. — Phyllis Diller
2. The quarrels of friends are the opportunities of foes. — Aesop
3. Art is the signature of civilization. — Beverly Sills
4. You can tell the ideals of a nation by its advertising. — Norman Douglas
5. You can never be too rich or too thin. — Wallis Warfield Simpson

EXERCISE 63–3   Each of the following sentences has either an indirect object followed by a direct object or a direct object followed by an object complement. Label the objects and complements, using these labels; *IO, DO, OC.* If an object or a complement consists of more than one word, bracket and label all of it. Example:

```
      ┌────── DO ──────┐ ┌─ OC ─┐
```
Every man thinks his own geese swans.

a. Sorrow makes us wise. — Alfred Lord Tennyson
b. Too many people make money their primary pursuit. — Anonymous
c. Make us happy and you make us good. — Robert Browning
d. Ask me no questions, and I will tell you no lies. — Anonymous
e. Show me a good loser, and I will show you a failure. — Paul Newman

1. Give the devil his due. — English proverb
2. God gives every bird its proper food, but all must fly for it. — Dutch proverb
3. A wide screen makes a bad film worse. — Samuel Goldwyn
4. Trees and fields tell me nothing. — Socrates
5. Necessity can make us surprisingly brave. — Latin proverb

ON THE WEB > **dianahacker.com/rules**
   Grammar exercises > Basics > E-ex 63–3 to 63–5

63c Pattern variations

Although most sentences follow one of the five patterns in the chart on page 549, variations of these patterns commonly occur in questions, commands, sentences with delayed subjects, and passive transformations.

Questions and commands

Questions are sometimes patterned in normal word order, with the subject preceding the verb.

> S ⌐ V ⌐
> Who will take the first step?

Just as frequently, however, the pattern of a question is inverted, with the subject appearing between the helping and main verbs or after the verb.

> HV   S   MV
> Will you take the first step?

> V ⌐ S ⌐
> Why is the first step so difficult?

In commands, the subject of the sentence is an understood *you*.

> S   V
> [You] Keep your eyes on the road.

Sentences with delayed subjects

Writers sometimes choose to delay the subject of a sentence to achieve a special effect such as suspense or humor.

> V ⌐ S ⌐
> Behind the phony tinsel of Hollywood lies the real tinsel.

The subject of the sentence is also delayed in sentences opening with the expletive *There* or *It*. When used as expletives, the words *There* and *It* have no strict grammatical function; they serve merely to get the sentence started.

> V ⌐ S ⌐
> There are too many cooks spoiling the broth.

> V ⌐ S ⌐
> It is not good to wake a sleeping lion.

The subject in the second example is an infinitive phrase. (See 64c.)

Passive transformations

Transitive verbs, those that can take direct objects, usually appear in the active voice. In the active voice, the subject does the action and a direct object receives the action.

ACTIVE   The early bird sometimes catches the early worm.

Sentences in the active voice may be transformed into the passive voice, with the subject receiving the action instead.

PASSIVE   The early worm is sometimes caught by the early bird.

What was once the direct object (*the early worm*) has become the subject in the passive-voice transformation, and the original subject appears in a prepositional phrase beginning with *by*. The *by* phrase is frequently omitted in passive-voice constructions.

PASSIVE   The early worm is sometimes caught.

Verbs in the passive voice can be identified by their form alone. The main verb is always a past participle, such as *caught* (see 62c), preceded by a form of *be* (*be, am, is, are, was, were, being, been*): *is caught*. Sometimes adverbs intervene (*is sometimes caught*).

NOTE: Writers sometimes use the passive voice when the active voice would be more appropriate (see 8a).

Subordinate word groups

Subordinate word groups include prepositional phrases, subordinate clauses, verbal phrases, appositives, and absolutes. Not all of these word groups are subordinate in quite the same way. Some are subordinate because they are modifiers; others function as noun equivalents, not as modifiers.

64a Prepositional phrases

A prepositional phrase begins with a preposition such as *at, by, for, from, in, of, on, to,* or *with* (see 62f) and usually ends with a noun or noun equivalent: *on the table, for him, with great fanfare.* The noun or noun equivalent is known as the *object of the preposition.*

Functions of prepositional phrases

Prepositional phrases function either as adjectives modifying nouns or pronouns or as adverbs modifying verbs, adjectives, or other adverbs. When functioning as an adjective, a prepositional phrase nearly always appears immediately following the noun or pronoun it modifies.

Variety is the *spice of life.*

Adjective phrases usually answer one or both of the questions Which one? and What kind of? If we ask Which spice? or What kind of spice? we get a sensible answer: *the spice of life.*

Adverbial prepositional phrases that modify the verb can appear nearly anywhere in a sentence.

Do not *judge* a tree *by its bark.*

Tyranny will *in time lead* to revolution.

To the ant, a few drops of rain *are* a flood.

Adverbial word groups usually answer one of these questions: When? Where? How? Why? Under what conditions? To what degree?

Do not judge a tree *how? By its bark.*

Tyranny will lead to revolution *when? In time.*

A few drops of rain are a flood *under what conditions? To the ant.*

If a prepositional phrase is movable, you can be certain that it is adverbial; adjectival prepositional phrases are wedded to the words they modify. At least some of the time, adverbial modifiers can be moved to other positions in the sentence.

> *By their fruits* you shall know them.

> You shall know them *by their fruits.*

EXERCISE 64–1 Underline the prepositional phrases in the following sentences. Be prepared to explain the function of each phrase. Answers to lettered sentences appear in the back of the book. Example:

> **Communism is fascism <u>with a human face.</u>** *(Adjective phrase modifying <u>fascism</u>)*

a. On their side, the workers had only the Constitution. The other side had bayonets.
— Mother Jones

b. Any mother could perform the job of several air traffic controllers with ease.
— Lisa Alther

c. To my embarrassment, I was born in bed with a lady.
— Wilson Mizner

d. Language is the road map of a culture. — Rita Mae Brown

e. In France, cooking is a serious art form and a national sport.
— Julia Child

1. We know that the road to freedom has always been stalked by death.
— Angela Davis

2. A society of sheep produces a government of wolves.
— Bertrand de Jouvenal

3. Some people feel with their heads and think with their hearts.
— G. C. Lichtenberg

4. By a small sample, we may know the whole piece.
— Cervantes

5. You and I come by road or rail, but economists travel on infrastructure.
— Margaret Thatcher

ON THE WEB > **dianahacker.com/rules**
Grammar exercises > Basics > E-ex 64–1 to 64–3

64b Subordinate clauses

Subordinate clauses are patterned like sentences, having subjects and verbs and sometimes objects or complements. But they function within sentences as adjectives, adverbs, or nouns. They cannot stand alone as complete sentences.

A subordinate clause usually begins with a subordinating conjunction or a relative pronoun. The chart on page 557 classifies these words according to the kinds of clauses (adjective, adverb, or noun) they introduce.

Adjective clauses

Like other word groups functioning as adjectives, adjective clauses modify nouns or pronouns. An adjective clause nearly always appears immediately following the noun or pronoun it modifies.

> The *arrow that has left the bow* never returns.

> Relatives are *persons who live too near and visit too often.*

To test whether a subordinate clause functions as an adjective, ask the adjective questions: Which one? What kind of? The answer should make sense. Which arrow? *The arrow that has left the bow.* What kind of persons? *Persons who live too near and visit too often.*

Most adjective clauses begin with a relative pronoun (*who, whom, whose, which,* or *that*), which marks them as grammatically subordinate. In addition to introducing the clause, the relative pronoun points back to the noun that the clause modifies.

> The *fur that warms a monarch* once warmed a bear.

Relative pronouns are sometimes "understood."

> The things [*that*] *we know best* are the things [*that*] *we haven't been taught.*

Occasionally an adjective clause is introduced by a relative adverb, usually *when, where,* or *why.*

> Home is the *place where you slip in the tub and break your neck.*

The parts of an adjective clause are often arranged as in sentences (subject/verb/object or complement).

>   S   V   **DO**
> We often forgive the people who bore us.

Frequently, however, the object or complement appears first, violating the normal order of subject/verb/object.

> DO   S   V
> We rarely forgive those whom we bore.

To determine the subject of a clause, ask Who? or What? and insert the verb. Don't be surprised if the answer is an echo, as in the first adjective clause above: Who bore us? *Who.* To find any objects or complements, read the subject and the verb and then ask Who? Whom? or What? Again, be prepared for a possible echo, as in the second adjective clause: We bore whom? *Whom.*

NOTE: For punctuation of adjective clauses, see 32e and 33e. If English is not your native language, see 30d for a common problem with adjective clauses.

Adverb clauses

Adverb clauses usually modify verbs, in which case they may appear nearly anywhere in a sentence — at the beginning, at the end, or in the middle. Like other adverbial word groups, they tell when, where, why, under what conditions, or to what degree an action occurred or a situation existed.

> *When the well is dry,* we *know* the worth of water.

> Venice *would be* a fine city *if it were only drained.*

Adverb clauses are sometimes elliptical, with some of their words being understood but not appearing in the sentence.

> *When [it is] painted,* the room will look larger.

Noun clauses

Because they do not function as modifiers, noun clauses are not subordinate in the same sense as are adjective and adverb clauses. They are called subordinate only because they cannot stand alone: They must function within a sentence, always as nouns.

A noun clause functions just like a single-word noun, usually as a subject, subject complement, direct object, or object of a preposition.

>   S
> Whoever gossips to you will gossip of you.

Words that introduce subordinate clauses

Words introducing adverb clauses

Subordinating conjunctions: after, although, as, as if, because, before, even though, if, in order that, rather than, since, so that, than, that, though, unless, until, when, where, whether, while

Words introducing adjective clauses

Relative pronouns: that, which, who, whom, whose
Relative adverbs: when, where, why

Words introducing noun clauses

Relative pronouns: that, which, who, whom, whose
Other pronouns: whoever, whomever, what, whatever, whichever
Other subordinating words: how, if, when, whenever, where, wherever, whether, why

```
            ┌──────── DO ────────┐
```
We never forget that we buried the hatchet.

A noun clause begins with a word that marks it as subordinate (see the list at the top of this page). The subordinating word may or may not play a significant role in the clause. In the preceding example sentences, *Whoever* is the subject of its clause, but *that* does not perform a function in its clause.

As with adjective clauses, the parts of a noun clause may appear out of their normal order (subject/verb/object).

```
         DO   S     V
```
Talent is what you possess.

The parts of a noun clause may also appear in their normal order.

```
         S     V    DO
```
Genius is what possesses you.

EXERCISE 64–2 Underline the subordinate clauses in the following sentences. Be prepared to explain the function of each clause. Answers to lettered sentences appear in the back of the book. Example:

Dig a well **before you are thirsty.** *(Adverb clause modifying* Dig*)*

a. It is hard to fight an enemy who has outposts in your head.
— Sally Kempton

b. A rattlesnake that doesn't bite teaches you nothing.
— Jessamyn West

c. If love is the answer, could you please rephrase the question?
— Lily Tomlin

d. Dreams say what they mean, but they don't say it in daytime language.
— Gail Godwin

e. I generally avoid temptation unless I cannot resist it.
— Mae West

1. What history teaches us is that we have never learned anything from it.
— Georg Wilhelm Hegel

2. When the insects take over the world, we hope that they will remember our picnics with gratitude.
— Anonymous

3. A woman who will tell her age will tell anything.
— Rita Mae Brown

4. If triangles had a god, it would have three sides.
— C. L. de Montesquieu

5. He gave her a look that you could have poured on a waffle.
— Ring Lardner

ON THE WEB > **dianahacker.com/rules**
Grammar exercises > Basics > E-ex 64–4 to 64–6

64c Verbal phrases

A verbal is a verb form that does not function as the verb of a clause. Verbals include infinitives (the word *to* plus the base form of the verb), present participles (the *-ing* form of the verb), and past participles (the verb form usually ending in *-d, -ed, -n, -en,* or *-t*). (See 27a and 62c.)

Verbals can take objects, complements, and modifiers to form verbal phrases. These phrases are classified as participial, gerund, and infinitive.

NOTE: For advice on editing dangling verbal phrases, see 12e.

Participial phrases

Participial phrases always function as adjectives. Their verbals are either present participles, always ending in *-ing,* or past participles, frequently ending in *-d, -ed, -n, -en,* or *-t* (see 27a).

Participial phrases frequently appear immediately following the noun or pronoun they modify.

Truth kept in the dark will never save the world.

Unlike other adjectival word groups, however, which must always follow the noun or pronoun they modify, participial phrases are often movable. They can precede the word they modify.

Being weak, foxes are distinguished by superior tact.

They may also appear at some distance from the word they modify.

History is *something* that never happened, *written by someone who wasn't there.*

Gerund phrases

Gerund phrases are built around present participles (verb forms ending in -*ing*), and they always function as nouns: usually as subjects, subject complements, direct objects, or objects of a preposition.

┌────S────┐
Justifying a fault doubles it.

┌────SC────┐
The secret of education is respecting the pupil.

┌────DO────┐
Kleptomaniacs can't help helping themselves.

┌────OBJ OF PREP────┐
The hen is an egg's way of producing another egg.

Infinitive phrases

Infinitive phrases, usually constructed around *to* plus the base form of the verb (*to call, to drink*), can function as nouns, as adjectives, or as adverbs.

When functioning as a noun, an infinitive phrase may appear in almost any noun slot in a sentence, usually as a subject, subject complement, or direct object.

```
         ┌──────S──────┐
```
To side with truth is noble.

```
              ┌────────DO────────┐
```
Never try to leap a chasm in two jumps.

Infinitive phrases functioning as adjectives usually appear immediately following the noun or pronoun they modify.

```
                    ┌─────────┐
```
We do not have the *right to abandon the poor*.

The infinitive phrase modifies the noun *right*. Which right? *The right to abandon the poor*.

Adverbial infinitive phrases usually qualify the meaning of the verb, telling when, where, how, why, under what conditions, or to what degree an action occurred.

```
              ┌──────────────┐
```
He *cut off* his nose *to spite his face*.

Why did he cut off his nose? *To spite his face*.

NOTE: In some constructions, the infinitive is unmarked; in other words, the *to* does not appear: *No one can make you [to] feel inferior without your consent*. (See 28f.)

EXERCISE 64–3 Underline the verbal phrases in the following sentences. Be prepared to explain the function of each phrase. Answers to lettered sentences appear in the back of the book. Example:

Do you want <u>to be a writer</u>? Then write. (*Infinitive phrase used as direct object of <u>Do want</u>*)

a. Concealing a disease is no way to cure it. — Ethiopian proverb
b. The trouble with being punctual is that nobody is there to appreciate it. — Franklin P. Jones
c. Fate tried to conceal him by naming him Smith. — Oliver Wendell Holmes Jr.
d. Being weak, children quickly learn to beguile us with charm. — Anonymous
e. Wrestling with words gave me my moments of greatest meaning. — Richard Wright

1. The thing generally raised on city land is taxes. — C. D. Warner
2. Do not use a hatchet to remove a fly from your friend's forehead. — Chinese proverb

3. He has the gall of a shoplifter returning an item for a refund.
— W. I. E. Gates

4. Tact is the ability to describe others as they see themselves.
— Mary Pettibone Poole

5. He could never see a belt without hitting below it.
— Harriet Braiker

ON THE WEB > dianahacker.com/rules
Grammar exercises > Basics > E-ex 64–7 to 64–9

64d Appositive phrases

Though strictly speaking they are not subordinate word groups, appositive phrases function somewhat as adjectives do, to describe nouns or pronouns. Instead of modifying nouns or pronouns, however, appositive phrases rename them. In form they are nouns or noun equivalents.

Appositives are said to be "in apposition" to the nouns or pronouns they rename.

Politicians, *acrobats at heart,* can sit on a fence and yet keep both ears to the ground.

Acrobats at heart is in apposition to the noun *politicians.*

64e Absolute phrases

An absolute phrase modifies a whole clause or sentence, not just one word, and it may appear nearly anywhere in the sentence. It consists of a noun or noun equivalent usually followed by a participial phrase.

His words dipped in honey, the senator mesmerized the crowd.

The senator mesmerized the crowd, *his words dipped in honey.*

65

Sentence types

Sentences are classified in two ways: according to their structure (simple, compound, complex, and compound-complex) and according to their purpose (declarative, imperative, interrogative, and exclamatory).

65a Sentence structures

Depending on the number and types of clauses they contain, sentences are classified as simple, compound, complex, or compound-complex.

Clauses come in two varieties: independent and subordinate. An independent clause contains a subject and a predicate, and it either stands alone or could stand alone. A subordinate clause also contains a subject and a predicate, but it functions within a sentence as an adjective, an adverb, or a noun; it cannot stand alone. (See 64b.)

Simple sentences

A simple sentence is one independent clause with no subordinate clauses.

┌────────────INDEPENDENT CLAUSE────────────┐
Without music, life would be a mistake.

This sentence contains a subject (*life*), a verb (*would be*), a complement (*a mistake*), and an adverbial modifier (*Without music*).

A simple sentence may contain compound elements — a compound subject, verb, or object, for example — but it does not contain more than one full sentence pattern. The following sentence is simple because its two verbs (*enters* and *spreads*) share a subject (*Evil*).

┌──────────────── INDEPENDENT CLAUSE ────────────────┐
Evil enters like a needle and spreads like an oak.

Compound sentences

A compound sentence is composed of two or more independent clauses with no subordinate clauses. The independent clauses are usually joined with a comma and a coordinating conjunction (*and, but, or, nor, for, so, yet*) or with a semicolon. (See 14a.)

┌─── INDEPENDENT CLAUSE ─┐   ┌─── INDEPENDENT CLAUSE ──────┐
One arrow is easily broken, but you can't break a bundle of ten.

┌──────── INDEPENDENT CLAUSE ──────┐ ┌─INDEPENDENT ─
We are born brave, trusting, and greedy; most of us have

┌──── CLAUSE────┐
remained greedy.

Complex sentences

A complex sentence is composed of one independent clause with one or more subordinate clauses. (See 64b.)

SUBORDINATE
┌──── CLAUSE ──┐
ADJECTIVE   They that sow in tears shall reap in joy.

SUBORDINATE
┌──── CLAUSE ──────┐
ADVERB   If you scatter thorns, don't go barefoot.

┌──────── SUBORDINATE CLAUSE ────────┐
NOUN   What the scientists have in their briefcases is terrifying.

Compound-complex sentences

A compound-complex sentence contains at least two independent clauses and at least one subordinate clause. The following sentence contains two full sentence patterns that can stand alone.

┌────IND CL ──────┐   ┌──────── IND CL ──────┐
Tell me what you eat, and I will tell you what you are.

And each independent clause contains a subordinate clause, making the sentence both compound and complex.

┌────IND CL──────┐   ┌──────── IND CL──────┐
    ┌── SUB CL──┐   ┌── SUB CL──┐
Tell me what you eat, and I will tell you what you are.

65b Sentence purposes

Writers use declarative sentences to make statements, imperative sentences to issue requests or commands, interrogative sentences to ask questions, and exclamatory sentences to make exclamations.

DECLARATIVE	The echo always has the last word.
IMPERATIVE	Love your neighbor.
INTERROGATIVE	Are second thoughts always wisest?
EXCLAMATORY	I want to wash the flag, not burn it!

EXERCISE 65–1 Identify the following sentences as simple, compound, complex, or compound-complex. Be prepared to identify the subordinate clauses and classify them according to their function: adjective, adverb, or noun. (See 64b.) Answers to lettered sentences appear in the back of the book. Example:

The frog in the well knows nothing of the ocean. *(Simple)*

a. People who sleep like a baby usually don't have one.
— Leo Burke

b. My folks didn't come over on the *Mayflower*; they were there to meet the boat. — Will Rogers

c. The impersonal hand of the government can never replace the helping hand of a neighbor. — Hubert Humphrey

d. If you don't go to other people's funerals, they won't go to yours.
— Clarence Day

e. Tell us your phobias, and we will tell you what you are afraid of.
— Robert Benchley

1. The tragedy of life is that people don't change. — Agatha Christie

2. Those who cannot remember the past are condemned to repeat it.
— George Santayana

3. The best mind-altering drug is truth. — Lily Tomlin

4. Morality cannot be legislated, but behavior can be regulated.
— Martin Luther King Jr.

5. Science commits suicide when it adopts a creed. — T. H. Huxley

ON THE WEB > **dianahacker.com/rules**
    Grammar exercises > Basics > E-ex 65–1

Glossary of Usage

This glossary includes words commonly confused (such as *accept* and *except*), words commonly misused (such as *aggravate*), and words that are nonstandard (such as *hisself*). It also lists colloquialisms and jargon. Colloquialisms are expressions that may be appropriate in informal speech but are inappropriate in formal writing. Jargon is needlessly technical or pretentious language that is inappropriate in most contexts. If an item is not listed here, consult the index. For irregular verbs (such as *sing, sang, sung*), see 27a. For idiomatic use of prepositions, see 18d.

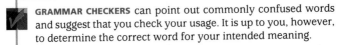

GRAMMAR CHECKERS can point out commonly confused words and suggest that you check your usage. It is up to you, however, to determine the correct word for your intended meaning.

ON THE WEB > **dianahacker.com/rules**
> Language Debates > Absolute concepts such as *unique*
> > *bad* versus *badly*
> > *however* at the beginning of a sentence
> > *lie* versus *lay*
> > *myself*
> > *that* versus *which*
> > *who* versus *which* or *that*
> > *who* versus *whom*
> > *you*

a, an Use *an* before a vowel sound, *a* before a consonant sound: *an apple, a peach.* Problems sometimes arise with words beginning with *h* or *u*. If the *h* is silent, the word begins with a vowel sound, so use *an*: *an hour, an honorable deed.* If the *h* is pronounced, the word begins with a consonant sound, so use *a*: *a hospital, a historian, a hotel.* Words such as *university* and *union* begin with a consonant sound (a *y* sound), so use *a*: *a union.* Words such as *uncle* and *umbrella* begin with a vowel sound, so use *an*: *an underground well.* When an abbreviation or an acronym begins with a vowel sound, use *an*: *an EKG, an MRI, an AIDS prevention program.*

accept, except   *Accept* is a verb meaning "to receive." *Except* is usually a preposition meaning "excluding." *I will accept all the packages except that one. Except* is also a verb meaning "to exclude." *Please except that item from the list.*

adapt, adopt   *Adapt* means "to adjust or become accustomed"; it is usually followed by *to. Adopt* means "to take as one's own." *Our family adopted a Vietnamese orphan, who quickly adapted to his new life.*

adverse, averse   *Adverse* means "unfavorable." *Averse* means "opposed" or "reluctant"; it is usually followed by *to. I am averse to your proposal because it could have an adverse impact on the economy.*

advice, advise   *Advice* is a noun, *advise* a verb. *We advise you to follow John's advice.*

affect, effect   *Affect* is usually a verb meaning "to influence." *Effect* is usually a noun meaning "result." *The drug did not affect the disease, and it had adverse side effects. Effect* can also be a verb meaning "to bring about." *Only the president can effect such a dramatic change.*

aggravate   *Aggravate* means "to make worse or more troublesome." *Overgrazing aggravated the soil erosion.* In formal writing, avoid the colloquial use of *aggravate* meaning "to annoy or irritate." *Her babbling annoyed* (not *aggravated*) *me.*

agree to, agree with   *Agree to* means "to give consent." *Agree with* means "to be in accord" or "to come to an understanding." *He agrees with me about the need for change, but he won't agree to my plan.*

ain't   *Ain't* is nonstandard. Use *am not, are not (aren't),* or *is not (isn't). I am not* (not *ain't*) *going home for spring break.*

all ready, already   *All ready* means "completely prepared." *Already* means "previously." *Susan was all ready for the concert, but her friends had already left.*

all right   *All right* is written as two words. *Alright* is nonstandard.

all together, altogether   *All together* means "everyone gathered." *Altogether* means "entirely." *We were not altogether certain that we could bring the family all together for the reunion.*

allude   To *allude* to something is to make an indirect reference to it. Do not use *allude* to mean "to refer directly." *In his lecture the professor referred* (not *alluded*) *to several pre-Socratic philosophers.*

allusion, illusion   An *allusion* is an indirect reference. An *illusion* is a misconception or false impression. *Did you catch my allusion to Shakespeare? Mirrors give the room an illusion of depth.*

a lot   *A lot* is two words. Do not write *alot. Sam lost a lot of weight.*

among, between   See *between, among.*

amongst   In American English, *among* is preferred.

amoral, immoral   *Amoral* means "neither moral nor immoral"; it also means "not caring about moral judgments." *Immoral* means "morally wrong." *Until recently, most business courses were taught from an amoral perspective. Murder is immoral.*

amount, number Use *amount* with quantities that cannot be counted; use *number* with those that can. *This recipe calls for a large amount of sugar. We have a large number of toads in our garden.*

an See *a, an*.

and etc. *Et cetera* (*etc.*) means "and so forth," so *and etc.* is redundant. See also *etc*.

and/or Avoid the awkward construction *and/or* except in technical or legal documents.

angry at, angry with To write that one is *angry at* another person is nonstandard. Use *angry with* instead.

ante-, anti- The prefix *ante-* means "earlier" or "in front of"; the prefix *anti-* means "against" or "opposed to." *William Lloyd Garrison was a leader of the antislavery movement during the antebellum period.* *Anti-* should be used with a hyphen when it is followed by a capital letter or a word beginning with *i*.

anxious *Anxious* means "worried" or "apprehensive." In formal writing, avoid using *anxious* to mean "eager." *We are eager* (not *anxious*) *to see your new house.*

anybody, anyone *Anybody* and *anyone* are singular. (See 21e and 22a.)

anymore Reserve the adverb *anymore* for negative contexts, where it means "any longer." *Moviegoers are rarely shocked anymore by profanity.* Do not use *anymore* in positive contexts. Use *now* or *nowadays* instead. *Interest rates are so low nowadays* (not *anymore*) *that more people can afford to buy homes.*

anyone See *anybody, anyone*.

anyone, any one *Anyone*, an indefinite pronoun, means "any person at all." *Any one*, the pronoun *one* preceded by the adjective *any*, refers to a particular person or thing in a group. *Anyone from Chicago may choose any one of the games on display.*

anyplace In formal writing, use *anywhere*.

anyways, anywheres *Anyways* and *anywheres* are nonstandard. Use *anyway* and *anywhere*.

as *As* is sometimes used to mean "because." But do not use it if there is any chance of ambiguity. *We canceled the picnic because* (not *as*) *it began raining. As* here could mean "because" or "when."

as, like See *like, as*.

as to *As to* is jargon for *about*. *He inquired about* (not *as to*) *the job.*

averse See *adverse, averse*.

awful The adjective *awful* and the adverb *awfully* are too colloquial for formal writing.

awhile, a while *Awhile* is an adverb; it can modify a verb, but it cannot be the object of a preposition such as *for*. The two-word form *a while* is a noun preceded by an article and therefore can be the object of a preposition. *Stay awhile. Stay for a while.*

back up, backup *Back up* is a verb phrase. *Back up the car carefully. Be sure to back up your hard drive. Backup* is a noun meaning "a duplicate of electronically stored data." *Keep your backup in a safe place. Backup* can also be used as an adjective. *I regularly create backup disks.*

bad, badly *Bad* is an adjective, *badly* an adverb. (See 26a and 26b.) *They felt bad about being early and ruining the surprise. Her arm hurt badly after she slid headfirst into second base.*

being as, being that *Being as* and *being that* are nonstandard expressions. Write *because* instead. *Because* (not *Being as*) *I slept late, I had to skip breakfast.*

beside, besides *Beside* is a preposition meaning "at the side of" or "next to." *Annie Oakley slept with her gun beside her bed. Besides* is a preposition meaning "except" or "in addition to." *No one besides Terrie can have that ice cream. Besides* is also an adverb meaning "in addition." *I'm not hungry; besides, I don't like ice cream.*

between, among Ordinarily, use *among* with three or more entities, *between* with two. *The prize was divided among several contestants. You have a choice between carrots and beans.*

bring, take Use *bring* when an object is being transported toward you, *take* when it is being moved away. *Please bring me a glass of water. Please take these flowers to Mr. Scott.*

burst, bursted; bust, busted *Burst* is an irregular verb meaning "to come open or fly apart suddenly or violently." Its principal parts are *burst, burst, burst.* The past-tense form *bursted* is nonstandard. *Bust* and *busted* are slang for *burst* and, along with *bursted,* should not be used in formal writing.

can, may The distinction between *can* and *may* is fading, but some writers still observe it in formal writing. *Can* is traditionally reserved for ability, *may* for permission. *Can you speak French? May I help you?*

capital, capitol *Capital* refers to a city, *capitol* to a building where lawmakers meet. *Capital* also refers to wealth or resources. *The capitol has undergone extensive renovations. The residents of the state capital protested the development plans.*

censor, censure *Censor* means "to remove or suppress material considered objectionable." *Censure* means "to criticize severely." *The school's policy of censoring books has been censured by the media.*

cite, site *Cite* means "to quote as an authority or example." *Site* is usually a noun meaning "a particular place." *He cited the zoning law in his argument against the proposed site of the gas station.* Locations on the Internet are usually referred to as *sites. The library's Web site improves every week.*

climactic, climatic *Climactic* is derived from *climax,* the point of greatest intensity in a series or progression of events. *Climatic* is derived from *climate* and refers to meteorological conditions. *The climactic period in the dinosaurs' reign was reached just before severe climatic conditions brought on an ice age.*

coarse, course *Coarse* means "crude" or "rough in texture." *The coarse weave of the wall hanging gave it a three-dimensional quality. Course* usually refers to a path, a playing field, or a unit of study; the expression *of course* means "certainly." *I plan to take a course in car repair this summer. Of course, you are welcome to join me.*

compare to, compare with *Compare to* means "to represent as similar." *She compared him to a wild stallion. Compare with* means "to examine similarities and differences." *The study compared the language ability of apes with that of dolphins.*

complement, compliment *Complement* is a verb meaning "to go with or complete" or a noun meaning "something that completes." *Compliment* as a verb means "to flatter"; as a noun it means "flattering remark." *Her skill at rushing the net complements his skill at volleying. Mother's flower arrangements receive many compliments.*

conscience, conscious *Conscience* is a noun meaning "moral principles." *Conscious* is an adjective meaning "aware or alert." *Let your conscience be your guide. Were you conscious of his love for you?*

continual, continuous *Continual* means "repeated regularly and frequently." *She grew weary of the continual telephone calls. Continuous* means "extended or prolonged without interruption." *The broken siren made a continuous wail.*

could care less *Could care less* is a nonstandard expression. Write *couldn't care less* instead. *He couldn't* (not *could*) *care less about his psychology final.*

could of *Could of* is nonstandard for *could have. We could have* (not *could of*) *taken the train.*

council, counsel A *council* is a deliberative body, and a *councilor* is a member of such a body. *Counsel* usually means "advice" and can also mean "lawyer"; *counselor* is one who gives advice or guidance. *The councilors met to draft the council's position paper. The pastor offered wise counsel to the troubled teenager.*

criteria *Criteria* is the plural of *criterion,* which means "a standard or rule or test on which a judgment or decision can be based." *The only criterion for the scholarship is ability.*

data *Data* is a plural noun technically meaning "facts or propositions." But *data* is increasingly being accepted as a singular noun. *The new data suggest* (or *suggests*) *that our theory is correct.* (The singular *datum* is rarely used.)

different from, different than Ordinarily, write *different from. Your sense of style is different from Jim's.* However, *different than* is acceptable to avoid an awkward construction. *Please let me know if your plans are different than* (to avoid *from what*) *they were six weeks ago.*

differ from, differ with *Differ from* means "to be unlike"; *differ with* means "to disagree." *She differed with me about the wording of the agreement. My approach to the problem differed from hers.*

disinterested, uninterested *Disinterested* means "impartial, objective"; *uninterested* means "not interested." *We sought the advice of a* *disinterested counselor to help us solve our problem. He was uninterested in anyone's opinion but his own.*

don't *Don't* is the contraction for *do not. I don't want any. Don't* should not be used as the contraction for *does not,* which is *doesn't. He doesn't* (not *don't*) *want any.*

due to *Due to* is an adjective phrase and should not be used as a preposition meaning "because of." *The trip was canceled because of* (not *due to*) *lack of interest. Due to* is acceptable as a subject complement and usually follows a form of the verb *be. His success was due to hard work.*

each *Each* is singular. (See 21e and 22a.)

effect See *affect, effect.*

e.g. In formal writing, replace the Latin abbreviation *e.g.* with its English equivalent: *for example* or *for instance.*

either *Either* is singular. (See 21e and 22a.) For *either . . . or* constructions, see 21d and 22d.

elicit, illicit *Elicit* is a verb meaning "to bring out" or "to evoke." *Illicit* is an adjective meaning "unlawful." *The reporter was unable to elicit any information from the police about illicit drug traffic.*

emigrate from, immigrate to *Emigrate* means "to leave one country or region to settle in another." *In 1900, my grandfather emigrated from Russia to escape the religious pogroms. Immigrate* means "to enter another country and reside there." *Many Mexicans immigrate to the United States to find work.*

eminent, imminent *Eminent* means "outstanding" or "distinguished." *We met an eminent professor of Greek history. Imminent* means "about to happen." *The announcement is imminent.*

enthused Many people object to the use of *enthused* as an adjective. Use *enthusiastic* instead. *The children were enthusiastic* (not *enthused*) *about going to the circus.*

etc. Avoid ending a list with *etc.* It is more emphatic to end with an example, and in most contexts readers will understand that the list is not exhaustive. When you don't wish to end with an example, *and so on* is more graceful than *etc.*

eventually, ultimately Often used interchangeably, *eventually* is the better choice to mean "at an unspecified time in the future" and *ultimately* is better to mean "the furthest possible extent or greatest extreme." *He knew that eventually he would complete his degree. The existentialists considered suicide the ultimately rational act.*

everybody, everyone *Everybody* and *everyone* are singular. (See 21e and 22a.)

everyone, every one *Everyone* is an indefinite pronoun. *Every one,* the pronoun *one* preceded by the adjective *every,* means "each individual or thing in a particular group." *Every one* is usually followed by *of. Everyone wanted to go. Every one of the missing books was found.*

except See *accept, except.*

expect   Avoid the colloquial use of *expect* meaning "to believe, think, or suppose." *I think* (not *expect*) *it will rain tonight.*

explicit, implicit   *Explicit* means "expressed directly" or "clearly defined"; *implicit* means "implied, unstated." *I gave him explicit instructions not to go swimming. My mother's silence indicated her implicit approval.*

farther, further   *Farther* usually describes distances. *Further* usually suggests quantity or degree. *Chicago is farther from Miami than I thought. You extended the curfew further than you should have.*

fewer, less   *Fewer* refers to items that can be counted; *less* refers to items that cannot be counted. *Fewer people are living in the city. Please put less sugar in my tea.*

finalize   *Finalize* is jargon meaning "to make final or complete." Use ordinary English instead. *The architect prepared final drawings* (not *finalized the drawings*).

firstly   *Firstly* sounds pretentious, and it leads to the ungainly series *firstly, secondly, thirdly,* and so on. Write *first, second, third* instead.

further   See *farther, further.*

get   *Get* has many colloquial uses. In writing, avoid using *get* to mean the following: "to evoke an emotional response" (*That music always gets to me*); "to annoy" (*After a while his sulking got to me*); "to take revenge on" (*I got back at him by leaving the room*); "to become" (*He got sick*); "to start or begin" (*Let's get going*). Avoid using *have got to* in place of *must. I must* (not *have got to*) *finish this paper tonight.*

good, well   *Good* is an adjective, *well* an adverb. (See 26.) *He hasn't felt good about his game since he sprained his wrist last season. She performed well on the uneven parallel bars.*

graduate   Both of the following uses of *graduate* are standard: *My sister was graduated from UCLA last year. My sister graduated from UCLA last year.* It is nonstandard, however, to drop the word *from: My sister graduated UCLA last year.* Though this usage is common in informal English, many readers object to it.

grow   Phrases such as *to grow the economy* and *to grow a business* are jargon. Usually the verb *grow* is intransitive (it does not take a direct object). *Our business has grown very quickly.* When *grow* is used in a transitive sense, with a direct object, it means "to cultivate" or "to allow to grow." *We plan to grow tomatoes this year. John is growing a beard.*

hanged, hung   *Hanged* is the past-tense and past-participle form of the verb *hang* meaning "to execute." *The prisoner was hanged at dawn. Hung* is the past-tense and past-participle form of the verb *hang* meaning "to fasten or suspend." *The stockings were hung by the chimney with care.*

hardly   Avoid expressions such as *can't hardly* and *not hardly,* which are considerable double negatives. *I can* (not *can't*) *hardly describe my elation at getting the job.* (See 26d.)

has got, have got   *Got* is unnecessary and awkward in such constructions. It should be dropped. *We have* (not *have got*) *three days to prepare for the opening.*

he   At one time *he* was commonly used to mean "he or she." Today such usage is inappropriate. (See 17f and 22a.)

he/she, his/her   In formal writing, use *he or she* or *his or her.* For alternatives to these wordy constructions, see 17f and 22a.

hisself   *Hisself* is nonstandard. Use *himself.*

hopefully   *Hopefully* means "in a hopeful manner." *We looked hopefully to the future.* Some usage experts object to the use of *hopefully* as a sentence adverb, apparently on grounds of clarity. To be safe, avoid using *hopefully* in sentences such as the following: *Hopefully, your son will recover soon.* Instead, indicate who is doing the hoping: *I hope that your son will recover soon.*

however   In the past, some writers objected to *however* at the beginning of a sentence, but current experts advise you to place the word according to your meaning and desired emphasis. Any of the following sentences is correct, depending on the intended contrast. *Pam decided, however, to attend Harvard. However, Pam decided to attend Harvard.* (She had been considering other schools.) *Pam, however, decided to attend Harvard.* (Unlike someone else, Pam opted for Harvard.)

hung   See *hanged, hung.*

i.e.   In formal writing, replace the Latin abbreviation *i.e.* with its English equivalent: *that is.*

if, whether   Use *if* to express a condition and *whether* to express alternatives. *If you go on a trip, whether to Nebraska or New Jersey, remember to bring traveler's checks.*

illusion   See *allusion, illusion.*

immigrate   See *emigrate from, immigrate to.*

imminent   See *eminent, imminent.*

immoral   See *amoral, immoral.*

implement   *Implement* is a pretentious way of saying "do," "carry out," or "accomplish." Use ordinary language instead. *We carried out* (not *implemented*) *the director's orders with some reluctance.*

imply, infer   *Imply* means "to suggest or state indirectly"; *infer* means "to draw a conclusion." *John implied that he knew all about computers, but the interviewer inferred that John was inexperienced.*

in, into   *In* indicates location or condition; *into* indicates movement or a change in condition. *They found the lost letters in a box after moving into the house.*

in regards to   *In regards to* confuses two different phrases: *in regard to* and *as regards.* Use one or the other. *In regard to* (or *As regards*) *the contract, ignore the first clause.*

irregardless   *Irregardless* is nonstandard. Use *regardless.*

is when, is where   These mixed constructions are often incorrectly used in definitions. *A run-off election is a second election held to break a tie* (not *is when a second election breaks a tie*). (See 11c.)

its, it's   *Its* is a possessive pronoun; *it's* is a contraction for *it is.* (See 36c and 36e.) *The dog licked its wound whenever its owner walked into the room. It's a perfect day to walk the twenty-mile trail.*

kind(s)   *Kind* is singular and should be treated as such. Don't write *These kind of chairs are rare.* Write instead *This kind of chair is rare. Kinds* is plural and should be used only when you mean more than one kind. *These kinds of chairs are rare.*

kind of, sort of   Avoid using *kind of* or *sort of* to mean "somewhat." *The movie was somewhat* (not *kind of*) *boring.* Do not put *a* after either phrase. *That kind of* (not *kind of a*) *salesclerk annoys me.*

lay, lie   See *lie, lay.*

lead, led   *Lead* is a metallic element; it is a noun. *Led* is the past tense of the verb *lead. He led me to the treasure.*

learn, teach   *Learn* means "to gain knowledge"; *teach* means "to impart knowledge." *I must teach* (not *learn*) *my sister to read.*

leave, let   *Leave* means "to exit." Avoid using it with the nonstandard meaning "to permit." *Let* (not *Leave*) *me help you with the dishes.*

less   See *fewer, less.*

let, leave   See *leave, let.*

liable   *Liable* means "obligated" or "responsible." Do not use it to mean "likely." *You're likely* (not *liable*) *to trip if you don't tie your shoelaces.*

lie, lay   *Lie* is an intransitive verb meaning "to recline or rest on a surface." Its principal parts are *lie, lay, lain. Lay* is a transitive verb meaning "to put or place." Its principal parts are *lay, laid, laid.* (See 27b.)

like, as   *Like* is a preposition, not a subordinating conjunction. It can be followed only by a noun or a noun phrase. *As* is a subordinating conjunction that introduces a subordinate clause. In casual speech you may say *She looks like she hasn't slept* or *You don't know her like I do.* But in formal writing, use *as. She looks as if she hasn't slept. You don't know her as I do.* (See also 62f and 62g.)

loose, lose   *Loose* is an adjective meaning "not securely fastened." *Lose* is a verb meaning "to misplace" or "to not win." *Did you lose your only loose pair of work pants?*

lots, lots of   *Lots* and *lots of* are colloquial substitutes for *many, much,* or *a lot.* Avoid using them in formal writing.

mankind   Avoid *mankind* whenever possible. It offends many readers because it excludes women. Use *humanity, humans, the human race,* or *humankind* instead. (See 17f.)

may   See *can, may.*

maybe, may be   *Maybe* is an adverb meaning "possibly." *May be* is a verb phrase. *Maybe the sun will shine tomorrow. Tomorrow may be a brighter day.*

may of, might of   *May of* and *might of* are nonstandard for *may have* and *might have. We may have* (not *may of*) *had too many cookies.*

media, medium   *Media* is the plural of *medium. Of all the media that cover the Olympics, television is the medium that best captures the spectacle of the events.*

most   *Most* is colloquial when used to mean "almost" and should be avoided. *Almost* (not *Most*) *everyone went to the parade.*

must of   See *may of.*

myself   *Myself* is a reflexive or intensive pronoun. Reflexive: *I cut myself.* Intensive: *I will drive you myself.* Do not use *myself* in place of *I* or *me. He gave the flowers to Melinda and me* (not *myself*). (See also 24.)

neither   *Neither* is singular. (See 21e and 22a.) For *neither . . . nor* constructions, see 21d and 22d.

none   *None* may be singular or plural. (See 21e.)

nowheres   *Nowheres* is nonstandard for *nowhere.*

number   See *amount, number.*

of   Use the verb *have,* not the preposition *of,* after the verbs *could, should, would, may, might,* and *must. They must have* (not *must of*) *left early.*

off of   *Off* is sufficient. Omit *of. The ball rolled off* (not *off of*) *the table.*

OK, O.K., okay   All three spellings are acceptable, but in formal speech and writing avoid these colloquial expressions.

parameters   *Parameter* is a mathematical term that has become jargon for "fixed limit," "boundary," or "guideline." Use ordinary English instead. *The task force worked within certain guidelines* (not *parameters*).

passed, past   *Passed* is the past tense of the verb *pass. Mother passed me another slice of cake. Past* usually means "belonging to a former time" or "beyond a time or place." *Our past president spoke until past midnight. The hotel is just past the next intersection.*

percent, per cent, percentage   *Percent* (also spelled *per cent*) is always used with a specific number. *Percentage* is used with a descriptive term such as *large* or *small,* not with a specific number. *The candidate won 80 percent of the primary vote. Only a small percentage of registered voters turned out for the election.*

phenomena   *Phenomena* is the plural of *phenomenon,* which means "an observable occurrence or fact." *Strange phenomena occur at all hours of the night in that house, but last night's phenomenon was the strangest of all.*

plus   *Plus* should not be used to join independent clauses. *This raincoat is dirty; moreover* (not *plus*), *it has a hole in it.*

precede, proceed   *Precede* means "to come before." *Proceed* means "to go forward." *As we proceeded up the mountain path, we noticed fresh tracks in the mud, evidence that a group of hikers had preceded us.*

principal, principle   *Principal* is a noun meaning "the head of a school or an organization" or "a sum of money." It is also an adjective meaning "most important." *Principle* is a noun meaning "a basic truth or law." *The principal expelled her for three principal reasons. We believe in the principle of equal justice for all.*

Glossary of Usage   575

proceed, precede   See *precede, proceed.*

quote, quotation   *Quote* is a verb; *quotation* is a noun. Avoid using *quote* as a shortened form of *quotation. Her quotations* (not *quotes*) *from Shakespeare intrigued us.*

raise, rise   *Raise* is a transitive verb meaning "to move or cause to move upward." It takes a direct object. *I raised the shades. Rise* is an intransitive verb meaning "to go up." *Heat rises.*

real, really   *Real* is an adjective; *really* is an adverb. *Real* is sometimes used informally as an adverb, but avoid this use in formal writing. *She was really* (not *real*) *angry.* (See 26a.)

reason . . . is because   Use *that* instead of *because. The reason she's cranky is that* (not *because*) *she didn't sleep last night.* (See 11c.)

reason why   The expression *reason why* is redundant. *The reason* (not *The reason why*) *Jones lost the election is clear.*

relation, relationship   *Relation* describes a connection between things. *Relationship* describes a connection between people. *There is a relation between poverty and infant mortality. Our business relationship has cooled over the years.*

respectfully, respectively   *Respectfully* means "showing or marked by respect." *Respectively* means "each in the order given." *He respectfully submitted his opinion to the judge. John, Tom, and Larry were a butcher, a baker, and a lawyer, respectively.*

sensual, sensuous   *Sensual* means "gratifying the physical senses," especially those associated with sexual pleasure. *Sensuous* means "pleasing to the senses," especially those involved in the experience of art, music, and nature. *The sensuous music and balmy air led the dancers to more sensual movements.*

set, sit   *Set* is a transitive verb meaning "to put" or "to place." Its principal parts are *set, set, set. Sit* is an intransitive verb meaning "to be seated." Its principal parts are *sit, sat, sat. She set the dough in a warm corner of the kitchen. The cat sat in the warmest part of the room.*

shall, will   *Shall* was once used as the helping verb with *I* or *we: I shall, we shall, you will, he/she/it will, they will.* Today, however, *will* is generally accepted even when the subject is *I* or *we.* The word *shall* occurs primarily in polite questions (*Shall I find you a pillow?*) and in legalistic sentences suggesting duty or obligation (*The applicant shall file form 1080 by December 31*).

should of   *Should of* is nonstandard for *should have. They should have* (not *should of*) *been home an hour ago.*

since   Do not use *since* to mean "because" if there is any chance of ambiguity. *Because* (not *Since*) *we won the game, we have been celebrating with a pitcher of root beer. Since* here could mean "because" or "from the time that."

sit   See *set, sit.*

site   See *cite, site.*

somebody, someone   *Somebody* and *someone* are singular. (See 21e and 22a.)

something   *Something* is singular. (See 21e.)

sometime, some time, sometimes   *Sometime* is an adverb meaning "at an indefinite or unstated time." *Some time* is the adjective *some* modifying the noun *time* and is spelled as two words to mean "a period of time." *Sometimes* is an adverb meaning "at times, now and then." *I'll see you sometime soon. I haven't lived there for some time. Sometimes I run into him at the library.*

suppose to   Write *supposed to.*

sure and   Write *sure to. We were all taught to be sure to* (not *sure and*) *look both ways before crossing a street.*

take   See *bring, take.*

than, then   *Than* is a conjunction used in comparisons; *then* is an adverb denoting time. *That pizza is more than I can eat. Tom laughed, and then we recognized him.*

that   See *who, which, that.*

that, which   Many writers reserve *that* for restrictive clauses, *which* for nonrestrictive clauses. (See 32e.)

theirselves   *Theirselves* is nonstandard for *themselves. The crash victims pushed the car out of the way themselves* (not *theirselves*).

them   The use of *them* in place of *those* is nonstandard. *Please send those* (not *them*) *flowers to the patient in room 220.*

there, their, they're   *There* is an adverb specifying place; it is also an expletive (placeholder). Adverb: *Sylvia is lying there unconscious.* Expletive: *There are two plums left. Their* is a possessive pronoun. *Fred and Jane finally washed their car. They're* is a contraction of *they are. They're later than usual today.*

they   The use of *they* to indicate possession is nonstandard. Use *their* instead. *Cindy and Sam decided to sell their* (not *they*) *1975 Corvette.*

this kind   See *kind(s).*

to, too, two   *To* is a preposition; *too* is an adverb; *two* is a number. *Too many of your shots slice to the left, but the last two were just right.*

toward, towards   *Toward* and *towards* are generally interchangeable, although *toward* is preferred in American English.

try and   *Try and* is nonstandard for *try to. The teacher asked us all to try to* (not *try and*) *write an original haiku.*

ultimately, eventually   See *eventually, ultimately.*

unique   Avoid expressions such as *most unique, more straight, less perfect, very round.* Either something is unique or it isn't. It is illogical to suggest degrees of uniqueness. (See 26c.)

usage   The noun *usage* should not be substituted for *use* when the meaning is "employment of." *The use* (not *usage*) *of computers dramatically increased the company's profits.*

use to   Write *used to.*

utilize   *Utilize* means "to make use of." It often sounds pretentious; in most cases, *use* is sufficient. *I used* (not *utilized*) *the laser printer.*

wait for, wait on   *Wait for* means "to be in readiness for" or "await." *Wait on* means "to serve." *We're only waiting for* (not *waiting on*) *Ruth to take us to the game.*

ways   *Ways* is colloquial when used to mean "distance." *The city is a long way* (not *ways*) *from here.*

weather, whether   The noun *weather* refers to the state of the atmosphere. *Whether* is a conjunction referring to a choice between alternatives. *We wondered whether the weather would clear.*

well, good   See *good, well.*

where   Do not use *where* in place of *that. I heard that* (not *where*) *the crime rate is increasing.*

which   See *that, which* and *who, which, that.*

while   Avoid using *while* to mean "although" or "whereas" if there is any chance of ambiguity. *Although* (not *While*) *Gloria lost money in the slot machine, Tom won it at roulette.* Here *While* could mean either "although" or "at the same time that."

who, which, that   Do not use *which* to refer to persons. Use *who* instead. *That,* though generally used to refer to things, may be used to refer to a group or class of people. *The player who* (not *that* or *which*) *made the basket at the buzzer was named MVP. The team that scores the most points in this game will win the tournament.*

who, whom   *Who* is used for subjects and subject complements; *whom* is used for objects. (See 25.)

who's, whose   *Who's* is a contraction of *who is; whose* is a possessive pronoun. *Who's ready for more popcorn? Whose coat is this?* (See 36c and 36e.)

will   See *shall, will.*

would of   *Would of* is nonstandard for *would have. She would have* (not *would of*) *had a chance to play if she had arrived on time.*

you   In formal writing, avoid *you* in an indefinite sense meaning "anyone." (See 23d.) *Any spectator* (not *You*) *could tell by the way John caught the ball that his throw would be too late.*

your, you're   *Your* is a possessive pronoun; *you're* is a contraction of *you are. Is that your new bike? You're in the finals.* (See 36c and 36e.)

Answers to Tutorials and Lettered Exercises

TUTORIAL 1, page xix

1. A verb has to agree with its subject. (21)
2. Each pronoun should agree with its antecedent. (22)
3. Avoid sentence fragments. (19)
4. It's important to use apostrophes correctly. (36)
5. Check for *-ed* verb endings that have been dropped. (27d)
6. Discriminate carefully between adjectives and adverbs. (26)
7. If your sentence begins with a long introductory word group, use a comma to separate the word group from the rest of the sentence. (32b)
8. Don't write a run-on sentence; you must connect independent clauses with a comma and a coordinating conjunction or with a semicolon. (20)
9. A writer must be careful not to shift his or her [*not* their] point of view. *Or* Writers must be careful not to shift their point of view. (13a)
10. Watch out for dangling modifiers. (12e)

TUTORIAL 2, page xix

1. The index entry "*each*" mentions that the word is singular, so you might not need to look further to realize that the verb should be *has*, not *have*. The first page reference takes you to section 21, which explains in more detail why *has* is correct. The index entry "*has* vs. *have*" also leads you to section 21.
2. The index entry "*lying* vs. *laying*" takes you to section 27b, where you will learn that lying (meaning "reclining or resting on a surface") is correct.
3. Look up "*only*" and you will be directed to section 12a, which explains that limiting modifiers such as *only* should be placed before the words they modify. The sentence should read *We looked at only two houses before buying the house of our dreams.*
4. Looking up "*you*, inappropriate use of" leads you to section 23d and the Glossary of Usage, which explain that *you* should not be used to mean "anyone in general." You can revise the sentence by using *a person* or *one* instead of *you*, or you can restructure the sentence completely: *In Saudi Arabia, accepting a gift is considered ill mannered.*
5. The index entries "*I* vs. *me*" and "*me* vs. *I*" take you to section 24, which explains why *her sister and me* is correct.

TUTORIAL 3, page xx

1. Section 32c states that, although usage varies, most experts advise using a comma between all items in a series — to prevent possible misreadings or ambiguities. To find this section, Ray Farley would probably use the menu system.
2. Maria Sanchez and Mike Lee would consult section 29, on articles. This section is easy to locate in the menu system.
3. Section 24 explains why *Jane and me* is correct. To find section 24, John Pell could use the menu system if he knew to look under "Problems with pronouns." Otherwise, he could look up "*I* vs. *me*" in the index. Pell could also

look up "*myself*" in the index or he could consult the Glossary of Usage, where a cross-reference would direct him to section 24.
4. Selena Young's employees could turn to sections 21 and 27c for help. Young could use the menu system to find these sections if she knew to look under "Subject-verb agreement" or "Standard English verb forms." If she wasn't sure about the grammatical terminology, she could look up "*-s*, as verb ending" or "Verbs, *-s* form of" in the index.
5. Section 26b explains why "I felt bad about her death" is correct. To find section 26b, Joe Thompson could use the menu system if he knew that *bad* versus *badly* is a choice between an adjective and an adverb. Otherwise he could look up "*bad, badly*" in the index or the Glossary of Usage.

TUTORIAL 4, page xxi

1. Changing attitudes toward alcohol have *affected* the beer industry.
2. It is *human* nature to think wisely and act foolishly.
3. Correct
4. Our goal this year is to *increase* our profits by 9 percent.
5. Most sleds are pulled by no *fewer* than two dogs and no more than ten.

TUTORIAL 5, page xxi

Alim, H. Samy. "360 Degreez of Black Art Comin at You: Sista Sonia Sanchez and the Dimensions of a Black Arts Continuum." *BMa: The Sonia Sanchez Literary Review* 6.1 (2000): 15-33. Print.

Chang, Jeff. *Can't Stop, Won't Stop: A History of the Hip-Hop Generation*. New York: St. Martin's, 2005. Print.

Davis, Kimberly. "The Roots Redefine Hip-Hop's Past." *Ebony* June 2003: 162-64. *Expanded Academic ASAP*. Web. 13 Oct. 2008.

Randall, Kay. "Studying a Hip-Hop Nation." *University of Texas at Austin*. U of Texas at Austin, 9 Oct. 2008. Web. 13 Oct. 2008.

Sugarhill Gang. "Rapper's Delight." *Sugarhill Gang*. DBK Works, 2008. CD.

EXERCISE 8–1, page 83

Possible revisions:

a. The Prussians defeated the Saxons in 1745.
b. Ahmed, the producer, manages the entire operation.
c. The video game programmers awkwardly paddled the sea kayaks.
d. Emphatic and active; no change
e. Protesters were shouting on the courthouse steps.

EXERCISE 9–1, page 87

Possible revisions:

a. Police dogs are used for finding lost children, tracking criminals, and detecting bombs and illegal drugs.

b. Hannah told her rock-climbing partner that she bought a new harness and that she wanted to climb Otter Cliffs.
c. It is more difficult to sustain an exercise program than to start one.
d. During basic training, I was told not only what to do but also what to think.
e. Jan wanted to drive to the wine country or at least to Sausalito.

EXERCISE 10–1, page 92

Possible revisions:

a. A good source of vitamin C is a grapefruit or an orange.
b. The women entering VMI can expect haircuts as short as those of the male cadets.
c. The driver went to investigate, only to find that one of the new tires had blown.
d. The graphic designers are interested in and knowledgeable about producing posters for the balloon race.
e. Reefs are home to more species than any other ecosystem in the sea.

EXERCISE 11–1, page 95

Possible revisions:

a. Using surgical gloves is a precaution now taken by dentists to prevent contact with patients' blood and saliva.
b. A career in medicine, which my brother is pursuing, requires at least ten years of challenging work.
c. The pharaohs had bad teeth because tiny particles of sand found their way into Egyptian bread.
d. Recurring bouts of flu caused the team to forfeit a record number of games.
e. This box contains the key to your future.

EXERCISE 12–1, page 100

Possible revisions:

a. Our English professor asked us to reread the sonnet very carefully, looking for subtleties we had missed on a first reading.
b. The monarch arrived at the gate in a gold carriage pulled by four white horses.
c. Rhonda and Sam talked almost all night about her surgery.
d. A coolhunter is a person who can find the next wave of fashion in the unnoticed corners of modern society.
e. Not all geese fly beyond Narragansett for the winter.

EXERCISE 12–2, page 103

Possible revisions:

a. When I was ten, my parents took me on my first balloon ride.
b. To replace the gear mechanism, you can use the attached form to order the part by mail.
c. As I nestled in the cockpit, the pounding of the engine was muffled only slightly by my helmet.
d. After studying polymer chemistry, Phuong found computer games less complex.
e. When I was a young man, my mother enrolled me in tap dance classes, hoping I would become the next Savion Glover.

EXERCISE 13–3, page 109

Possible revisions:

a. Courtroom lawyers have more than a touch of theater in their blood.
b. The interviewer asked if we had brought our proof of birth and citizenship and our passports.
c. Reconnaissance scouts often have to make fast decisions and use sophisticated equipment to keep their teams from detection.
d. After the animators finish their scenes, the production designer arranges the clips according to the storyboard and makes synchronization notes for the sound editor and the composer.
e. Madame Defarge is a sinister figure in Dickens's *A Tale of Two Cities*. On a symbolic level, she represents fate; like the Greek Fates, she knits the fabric of individual destiny.

EXERCISE 14–1, page 115

Possible revisions:

a. The X-Men comic books and Japanese woodcuts of kabuki dancers, all part of Marlena's research project on popular culture, covered the tabletop and the chairs.
b. Our waitress, costumed in a kimono, had painted her face white and arranged her hair in an upswept lacquered beehive.
c. Students can apply for a spot in the foundation's leadership program, which teaches thinking and communication skills.
d. Shore houses were flooded up to the first floor, beaches were washed away, and Brant's Lighthouse was swallowed by the sea.
e. Laura Thackray, an engineer at Volvo Car Corporation, designed a pregnant crash-test dummy to address women's safety needs.

EXERCISE 14–2, page 117

Possible revisions:

a. These particles, known as "stealth liposomes," can hide in the body for a long time without detection.
b. Irena, a competitive gymnast majoring in biochemistry, intends to apply her athletic experience and her science degree to a career in sports medicine.
c. Because students, textile workers, and labor unions have loudly protested sweatshop abuses, apparel makers have been forced to examine their labor practices.
d. Developed in a European university, IRC (Internet Relay Chat) was created as a way for a group of graduate students to talk about projects from their dorm rooms.
e. The cafeteria's new menu, which has an international flavor, includes everything from enchiladas and pizza to pad thai and sauerbraten.

EXERCISE 14–3, page 118

Possible revisions:

a. Working as an aide for the relief agency, Gina distributed food and medical supplies.
b. Janbir, who spent every Saturday learning tabla drumming, noticed with each hour of practice that his memory for complex patterns was growing stronger.
c. When the rotor hit, it gouged a hole about an eighth of an inch deep in my helmet.

d.   My grandfather, who was born eighty years ago in Puerto Rico, raised his daughters the old-fashioned way.
e.   By reversing the depressive effect of the drug, the Narcan saved the patient's life.

EXERCISE 16–1, page 127

Possible revisions:

a.   Martin Luther King Jr. set a high standard for future leaders.
b.   Arlene has loved cooking since she could first peek over a kitchen tabletop.
c.   Bloom's race for the governorship is futile.
d.   A successful graphic designer must have technical knowledge and an eye for color and balance.
e.   You will deliver mail to employees in every building.

EXERCISE 17–1, page 131

Possible revisions:

a.   In my youth, my family was poor.
b.   This conference will help me serve my clients better.
c.   Have you ever been accused of beating a dead horse?
d.   Government studies show a need for after-school programs.
e.   Passengers should try to complete the customs declaration form before leaving the plane.

EXERCISE 17–2, page 137

Possible revisions:

a.   Dr. Geralyn Farmer is the chief surgeon at University Hospital. Dr. Paul Green is her assistant.
b.   All applicants want to know how much they will make.
c.   Elementary school teachers should understand the concept of nurturing if they intend to be successful.
d.   Students of high-tech architecture pick a favorite when they study such inspirational architects as Renzo Piano and Zaha Hadid.
e.   If we do not stop polluting our environment, we will destroy the Earth.

EXERCISE 18–1, page 141

Possible revisions:

a.   We regret this delay; thank you for your patience.
b.   Ada's plan is to acquire education and experience to prepare herself for a position as property manager.
c.   Tiger Woods, the ultimate competitor, has earned millions of dollars just in endorsements.
d.   Many people take for granted that public libraries have up-to-date networked computer systems.
e.   The effect of Gao Xinjian's novels on Chinese exiles is hard to gauge.

EXERCISE 18–2, page 142

Possible revisions:

a.   Queen Anne was so angry with Sarah Churchill that she refused to see her again.
b.   Correct

c.   The parade moved off the street and onto the beach.
d.   The frightened refugees intend to make the dangerous trek across the mountains.
e.   What type of wedding are you planning?

EXERCISE 18–3, page 145

Possible revisions:

a.   John stormed into the room like a hurricane.
b.   Some people insist that they'll always be available to help, even when they haven't been before.
c.   The Cubs easily beat the Mets, who were in trouble early in the game today at Wrigley Field.
d.   We worked out the problems in our relationship.
e.   My mother accused me of evading her questions when in fact I was just saying the first thing that came to mind.

EXERCISE 19–1, page 155

Possible revisions:

a.   Listening to the CD her sister had sent, Mia was overcome with a mix of emotions: happiness, homesickness, nostalgia.
b.   Cortés and his soldiers were astonished when they looked down from the mountains and saw Tenochtitlán, the magnificent capital of the Aztecs.
c.   Although my spoken Spanish is not very good, I can read the language with ease.
d.   There are several reasons for not eating meat. One reason is that dangerous chemicals are used throughout the various stages of meat production.
e.   To learn how to sculpt beauty from everyday life is my intention in studying art and archaeology.

EXERCISE 20–1, page 163

Possible revisions:

a.   The city had one public swimming pool that stayed packed with children all summer long.
b.   The building is being renovated, so at times we have no heat, water, or electricity.
c.   The view was not what the travel agent had described. Where were the rolling hills, the fields of poppies, and the shimmering rivers?
d.   All those gnarled equations looked like toxic insects; maybe I was going to have to rethink my major.
e.   City officials told FEMA they had good reason to fear a major earthquake: Most [*or* most] of the business district was built on landfill.

EXERCISE 20–2, page 163

Possible revisions:

a.   Wind power for the home is a supplementary source of energy that can be combined with electricity, gas, or solar energy.
b.   Aidan viewed Sofia Coppola's *Lost in Translation* three times, and then he wrote a paper describing the film as the work of a mysterious modern painter.
c.   Correct

d.   "He's not drunk," I said. "He's in a state of diabetic shock."
e.   Are you able to endure boredom, isolation, and potential violence? Then the army may well be the adventure for you.

EXERCISE 21–1, page 174

a. Subject: friendship and support; verb: have; b. Subject: Shelters; verb: offer; c. Subject: source; verb: is; d. Subject: chances; verb: are; e. Subject: card and haiku; verb: were

EXERCISE 21–2, page 174

a.   One of the main reasons for elephant poaching is the profits received from selling the ivory tusks.
b.   Correct
c.   A number of students in the seminar were aware of the importance of joining the discussion.
d.   Batik cloth from Bali, blue and white ceramics from Delft, and a bocce ball from Turin have made Angelie's room the talk of the dorm.
e.   Correct

EXERCISE 22–1, page 180

Possible revisions:

a.   Every presidential candidate must appeal to a wide variety of ethnic and social groups to win the election.
b.   David lent his motorcycle to someone who allowed a friend to use it.
c.   The aerobics teacher motioned for all the students to move their arms in wide, slow circles.
d.   Correct
e.   Applicants should be bilingual if they want to qualify for this position.

EXERCISE 23–1, page 185

Possible revisions:

a.   Some professors say that an engineering student should have hands-on experience with dismantling and reassembling machines.
b.   Because she had decorated her living room with posters from chamber music festivals, her date thought she was interested in classical music. Actually she preferred rock.
c.   In Ethiopia, a person doesn't need much property to be considered well-off.
d.   Marianne told Jenny, "I am worried about your mother's illness." [or ". . . about my mother's illness."]
e.   Though Lewis cried for several minutes after scraping his knee, eventually his crying subsided.

EXERCISE 24–1, page 192

a.   Correct [But the writer could change the end of the sentence: . . . *than he is.*]
b.   Correct [But the writer could change the end of the sentence: . . . *that she was the coach.*]
c.   She appreciated his telling the truth in such a difficult situation.
d.   The director has asked you and me to draft a proposal for a new recycling plan.
e.   Five close friends and I rented a station wagon, packed it with food, and drove two hundred miles to Mardi Gras.

EXERCISE 25–1, page 197

a.   The roundtable featured scholars whom I had never heard of. [*or* . . . scholars I had never heard of.]
b.   Correct
c.   Correct
d.   Daniel donates money to whoever needs it.
e.   So many singers came to the audition that Natalia had trouble deciding whom to select for the choir.

EXERCISE 26–1, page 203

Possible revisions:

a.   Did you do well on last week's chemistry exam?
b.   With the budget deadline approaching, our office has hardly had time to handle routine correspondence.
c.   Correct
d.   The customer complained that he hadn't been treated nicely.
e.   Of all my relatives, Uncle Roberto is the cleverest.

EXERCISE 27–1, page 208

a.   When I get the urge to exercise, I lie down until it passes.
b.   Grandmother had driven our new SUV to the sunrise church service on Savage Mountain, so we were left with the station wagon.
c.   A pile of dirty rags was lying at the bottom of the stairs.
d.   How did the computer know that the gamer had gone from the room with the blue ogre to the hall where the gold was heaped?
e.   Abraham Lincoln took good care of his legal clients; the contracts he drew for the Illinois Central Railroad could never be broken.

EXERCISE 27–2, page 215

a.   The glass sculptures of the Swan Boats were prominent in the brightly lit lobby.
b.   Visitors to the glass museum were not supposed to touch the exhibits.
c.   Our church has all the latest technology, even a closed-circuit television.
d.   Christos didn't know about Marlo's promotion because he never listens. He is always talking.
e.   Correct

EXERCISE 27–3, page 222

Possible revisions:

a.   Correct
b.   Watson and Crick discovered the mechanism that controls inheritance in all life: the workings of the DNA molecule.
c.   When Hitler decided to kill the Jews in 1941, did he know that Himmler and his SS had had mass murder in mind since 1938?
d.   Correct
e.   Correct

EXERCISE 28–1, page 228

a.   In the past, tobacco companies denied any connection between smoking and health problems.
b.   There is nothing in the world that TV has not touched on.

c. I want to register for a summer tutoring session.
d. By the end of the year, the state will have tested 139 birds for avian flu.
e. The benefits of eating fruits and vegetables have been promoted by health care providers.

EXERCISE 28–2, page 231

a. A major league pitcher can throw a baseball over ninety-five miles per hour.
b. The writing center tutors will help you to revise your essay.
c. A reptile must adjust its body temperature to its environment.
d. Correct
e. My uncle, a caricature artist, could sketch a face in less than two minutes.

EXERCISE 28–3, page 239

Possible revisions:

a. The electrician might have discovered the broken circuit if she had gone through the modules one at a time.
b. If Verena wins a scholarship, she will go to graduate school.
c. Whenever there is a fire in our neighborhood, everybody comes out to watch.
d. Sarah will take the paralegal job unless she gets a better offer.
e. If I lived in Budapest with my cousin Szusza, she would teach me Hungarian cooking.

EXERCISE 28–4, page 242

Possible answers:

a. I enjoy riding my motorcycle.
b. The tutor told Samantha to come to the writing center.
c. The team hopes to work hard and win the championship.
d. Ricardo and his brothers miss surfing during the winter.
e. The babysitter let Roger stay up until midnight.

EXERCISE 29–1, page 251

a. Doing volunteer work often brings satisfaction.
b. As I looked out the window of the plane, I could see Cape Cod.
c. Melina likes to drink her coffee with lots of cream.
d. Correct
e. I completed my homework assignment quickly. *Or* I completed the home-work assignment quickly.

EXERCISE 30–1, page 257

a. There are some cartons of ice cream in the freezer.
b. I don't use the subway because I am afraid.
c. The prime minister is the most popular leader in my country.
d. We tried to get in touch with the same manager whom we spoke to earlier.
e. Recently there have been a number of earthquakes in Turkey.

EXERCISE 30–2, page 259

Possible revisions:

a. Although freshwater freezes at 32 degrees Fahrenheit, ocean water freezes at 28 degrees Fahrenheit.
b. Because we switched Internet service providers, our e-mail address has changed.
c. The competitor confidently mounted his skateboard.

d.   My sister performs the *legong,* a Balinese dance, well.
e.   Correct

EXERCISE 30–3, page 262

a.   Listening to everyone's complaints all day was irritating.
b.   The long flight to Singapore was exhausting.
c.   Correct
d.   After a great deal of research, the scientist made a fascinating discovery.
e.   That blackout was one of the most frightening experiences I've ever had.

EXERCISE 30–4, page 263

a.   an attractive young Vietnamese woman
b.   a dedicated Catholic priest
c.   her old blue wool sweater
d.   Joe's delicious Scandinavian bread
e.   many beautiful antique jewelry boxes

EXERCISE 31–1, page 265

a.   Whenever we eat at the Centerville Diner, we sit at a small table in the corner of the room.
b.   Correct
c.   On Thursday, Nancy will attend her first Pilates class at the community center.
d.   Correct
e.   We decided to go to a restaurant because there was no fresh food in the refrigerator.

EXERCISE 32–1, page 272

a.   Alisa brought the injured bird home and fashioned a splint out of Popsicle sticks for its wing.
b.   Considered a classic of early animation, *The Adventures of Prince Achmed* used hand-cut silhouettes against colored backgrounds.
c.   If you complete the enclosed evaluation form and return it within two weeks, you will receive a free breakfast during your next stay.
d.   Correct
e.   Roger had always wanted a handmade violin, but he couldn't afford one.

EXERCISE 32–2, page 275

a.   The cold, impersonal atmosphere of the university was unbearable.
b.   An ambulance threaded its way through police cars, fire trucks, and irate citizens.
c.   Correct
d.   After two broken arms, three cracked ribs, and one concussion, Ken quit the varsity football team.
e.   Correct

EXERCISE 32–3, page 278

a.   Choreographer Alvin Ailey's best-known work, *Revelations,* is more than just a crowd pleaser.
b.   Correct
c.   Correct
d.   A member of an organization that provides housing for AIDS patients was also appointed to the commission.
e.   Brian Eno, who began his career as a rock musician, turned to meditative compositions in the late seventies.

EXERCISE 32–4, page 283

a. Cricket, which originated in England, is also popular in Australia, South Africa, and India.
b. At the sound of the starting pistol, the horses surged forward toward the first obstacle, a sharp incline three feet high.
c. After seeing an exhibition of Western art, Gerhard Richter escaped from East Berlin in 1961 and smuggled out many of his notebooks.
d. Corrie's new wet suit has an intricate blue pattern.
e. Correct

EXERCISE 32–5, page 284

a. On January 15, 2004, our office moved to 29 Commonwealth Avenue, Mechanicsville, VA 23111.
b. Correct
c. Ms. Carlson, you are a valued customer whose satisfaction is very important to us.
d. Mr. Mundy was born on July 22, 1939, in Arkansas, where his family had lived for four generations.
e. Correct

EXERCISE 33–1, page 290

a. Correct
b. Tricia's first artwork was a big blue clay dolphin.
c. Some modern musicians (trumpeter John Hassell is an example) blend several cultural traditions into a unique sound.
d. Myra liked hot, spicy foods such as chili, jambalaya, and buffalo wings.
e. On the display screen was a soothing pattern of light and shadow.

EXERCISE 34–1, page 294

a. Do not ask me to be kind; just ask me to act as though I were.
b. When men talk about defense, they always claim to be protecting women and children, but they never ask the women and children what they think.
c. When I get a little money, I buy books; if any is left, I buy food and clothes.
d. Correct
e. Wit has truth in it; wisecracking is simply calisthenics with words.

EXERCISE 34–2, page 295

a. Strong black coffee will not sober you up; the truth is that time is the only way to get alcohol out of your system.
b. It is not surprising that our society is increasingly violent; after all, television desensitizes us to brutality at a very early age.
c. There is often a fine line between right and wrong, good and bad, truth and deception.
d. Correct
e. Severe, unremitting pain is a ravaging force, especially when the patient tries to hide it from others.

EXERCISE 35–1, page 297

a. Correct [Either *It* or *it* is correct.]
b. If we have come to fight, we are far too few; if we have come to die, we are far too many.
c. The travel package includes a round-trip ticket to Athens, a cruise through the Cyclades, and all hotel accommodations.

d. The media portray my generation as lazy, although polls show that we work as hard as the twentysomethings before us.
e. Fran Lebowitz has this advice for parents: "Never allow your child to call you by your first name. He hasn't known you long enough."

EXERCISE 36–1, page 302

a. Correct
b. The innovative shoe fastener was inspired by the designer's son.
c. Each day's menu features a different European country's dish.
d. Sue worked overtime to increase her family's earnings.
e. Ms. Jacobs is unwilling to listen to students' complaints about computer failures and damaged disks.

EXERCISE 37–1, page 308

a. As for the advertisement "Sailors have more fun," if you consider chipping paint and swabbing decks fun, then you will have plenty of it.
b. Correct
c. After winning the lottery, Juanita said that she would give half the money to charity.
d. After the movie Vicki said, "The reviewer called this flick 'trash of the first order.' I guess you can't believe everything you read."
e. Correct

EXERCISE 39–1, page 315

a. A client has left his or her cell phone in our conference room.
b. The films we made of Kilauea on our trip to Hawaii Volcanoes National Park illustrate a typical spatter cone eruption.
c. Correct
d. Correct
e. Of three engineering fields — chemical, mechanical, and materials — Keegan chose materials engineering for its application to toy manufacturing.

EXERCISE 40–1, page 320

a. Correct
b. Some combat soldiers are trained by government diplomats to be sensitive to issues of culture, history, and religion.
c. Correct
d. How many pounds have you lost since you began running four miles a day?
e. Denzil spent all night studying for his psychology exam.

EXERCISE 41–1, page 323

a. The carpenters located three maple timbers, twenty-one sheets of cherry, and ten oblongs of polished ebony for the theater set.
b. Correct
c. Correct
d. Eight students in the class had been labeled "learning disabled."
e. The Vietnam Veterans Memorial in Washington, DC, had 58,132 names inscribed on it when it was dedicated in 1982.

EXERCISE 42–1, page 326

a. Howard Hughes commissioned the *Spruce Goose*, a beautifully built but thoroughly impractical wooden aircraft.

b. The old man screamed his anger, shouting to all of us, "I will not leave my money to you worthless layabouts!"

c. I learned the Latin term *ad infinitum* from an old nursery rhyme about fleas: "Great fleas have little fleas upon their back to bite 'em, / Little fleas have lesser fleas and so on *ad infinitum*."

d. Correct

e. Neve Campbell's lifelong interest in ballet inspired her involvement in the film *The Company*, which portrays a season with the Joffrey Ballet.

EXERCISE 44–1, page 339

a. Correct

b. The swiftly moving tugboat pulled alongside the barge and directed it away from the oil spill in the harbor.

c. Correct

d. Your dog is well known in our neighborhood.

e. Roadblocks were set up along all the major highways leading out of the city.

EXERCISE 45–1, page 344

a. Assistant Dean Shirin Ahmadi recommended offering more world language courses.

b. Correct

c. Kalindi has an ambitious semester, studying differential calculus, classical Hebrew, brochure design, and Greek literature.

d. Lydia's aunt and uncle make modular houses as beautiful as modernist works of art.

e. We amused ourselves on the long flight by discussing how spring in Kyoto stacks up against summer in London.

EXERCISE 48–1, page 380

a. hasty generalization; b. false analogy; c. biased language; d. faulty cause-and-effect reasoning; e. *either . . . or* fallacy

EXERCISE 62–1, page 530

a. sun, assistance; b. Pride, bottom, mistakes; c. Success, confidence; d. censorship, flick, dial; e. flower, concrete (noun/adjective), cloverleaf

EXERCISE 62–2, page 533

a. He, every (pronoun/adjective); b. those, who; c. I, some (pronoun/adjective), that, I, myself; d. I, You, He; e. you, anything, anyone, me

EXERCISE 62–3, page 535

a. can pardon; b. are; c. does bring down; d. Keep, 'll [will] be insulted; e. Throw, will emerge

EXERCISE 62–4, page 537

a. Adjectives: General, wrong; adverb: generally; b. Adjectives: The (article), American, tolerant; adverb: wonderfully; c. Adjectives: an (article), uncultivated, an (article), uncultivated; adverbs: sometimes, never; d. Adjectives: wrong, right; adverbs: rather, strongly, weakly; e. Adjective: the (article); adverb: faster

EXERCISE 63–1, page 545

a. Complete subjects: Sticks and stones, words; simple subjects: Sticks, stones, words; b. Complete subject: all delays; simple subject: delays; c. Complete subject: (You); d. Complete subject: nothing except change; simple subject: nothing; e. Complete subject: Most of the disputes in the world; simple subject: Most

EXERCISE 63–2, page 549

a. Subject complement: cheap; b. Direct object: an injury; c. Direct object: his convent; d. Subject complement: the opium of the people; e. Subject complement: bitter

EXERCISE 63–3, page 550

a. Direct object: us; object complement: wise; b. Direct object: money; object complement: their primary pursuit; c. Direct objects: us, us; object complements: happy, good; d. Indirect objects: me, you; direct objects: no questions, no lies; e. Indirect objects: me, you; direct objects: a good loser, a failure

EXERCISE 64–1, page 554

a. On their side (adverb phrase modifying *had*); b. of several air traffic controllers (adjective phrase modifying *job*), with ease (adverb phrase modifying *could perform*); c. To my embarrassment (adverb phrase modifying *was born*), in bed (adverb phrase modifying *was born*), with a lady (adverb phrase modifying *was born*); d. of a culture (adjective phrase modifying *map*); e. In France (adverb phrase modifying *is*)

EXERCISE 64–2, page 557

a. who has outposts in your head (adjective clause modifying *enemy*); b. that doesn't bite (adjective clause modifying *rattlesnake*); c. If love is the answer (adverb clause modifying *could rephrase*); d. what they mean (noun clause used as direct object of *say*); e. unless I cannot resist it (adverb clause modifying *avoid*)

EXERCISE 64–3, page 560

a. Concealing a disease (gerund phrase used as subject), to cure it (infinitive phrase modifying *way*); b. being punctual (gerund phrase used as object of the preposition *with*), to appreciate it (infinitive phrase modifying *is*); c. to conceal him (infinitive phrase used as direct object), naming him Smith (gerund phrase used as object of the preposition *by*); d. Being weak (participial phrase modifying *children*), to beguile us with charm (infinitive phrase used as direct object); e. Wrestling with words (gerund phrase used as subject)

EXERCISE 65–1, page 564

a. Complex; who sleep like a baby (adjective clause); b. Compound; c. Simple; d. Complex; If you don't go to other people's funerals (adverb clause); e. Compound-complex; what you are afraid of (noun clause)

(*continued from page iv*)

Screen shot of Center for Women's Business Research Web site, www.womensbusinessresearch .org/national/index.php. Copyright © 2007 by the Center for Women's Business Research. Reprinted with permission.

Columbia University Library. Library Web pages. Copyright © Columbia University Libraries. www.columbia.edu. Reprinted by permission.

Emily Dickinson, excerpt from "A Narrow Fellow in the Grass" from *The Complete Poems of Emily Dickinson*, edited by Thomas H. Johnson (Cambridge, MA: The Belknap Press of Harvard University Press). Copyright © 1952, 1955, 1979, 1983 by the President and Fellows of Harvard College. Reprinted with the permission of The Belknap Press of Harvard University Press and the Trustees of Amherst College.

EBSCO Information Services, various screen shots. Reprinted with the permission of EBSCO Information Services.

Henry J. Kaiser Family Foundation, excerpts from "The Role of Media in Childhood Obesity" (2004). Copyright © 2004 by The Henry J. Kaiser Family Foundation. This information was reprinted with permission from the Henry J. Kaiser Family Foundation.

Carolyn M. Hoxby. "The Power of Peers." Front page of article and the TOC. From *Education Next*, Summer 2002. www.educationnext.org. Reprinted with the permission of *Education Next*.

Jill D. Jenson, excerpt from "It's the Information Age, So Where's the Information?" from *College Teaching* (Summer 2004). Copyright © 2004. Reprinted with the permission of the Helen Dwight Reid Educational Foundation. Published by Heldref Publications, 1319 Eighteenth Street, NW, Washington, DC 20036.

Screen shots of MIT Communications Forum, including excerpt from Henry Jenkins, "Bearings," http://web.mit.edu/comm-forum/papers/bearings.html and related links, http://web.mit.edu/comm-forum/papers. Copyright © 2006 by The Massachusetts Institute of Technology. Reprinted by permission.

McDonald's Corporation, "What makes your lettuce so crisp?" advertisement. Copyright © 2004 by McDonald's Corporation. Reprinted with permission.

Anne McGrath, "A loss of foreign talent" from *U.S. News & World Report* (November 27, 2004). Copyright © 2004 by U.S. News & World Report, LP. Reprinted with permission. This figure includes a photo by Kenneth Dickerman which is reprinted by permission.

Merriam-Webster Online, screen shot of thesaurus entry for "regard" from www.m-w.com. Copyright © 2007 by Merriam-Webster Incorporated. Reprinted with permission.

"The Minnesota Annual Summary" or "Minnesota Health Statistics" report. Copyright © 2005 by the Minnesota Department of Health. www.health.state.mn.us.

L. M. Poupart. Page from "Crime and Justice in American Indian Communities." Copyright © 2002. Reprinted with the permission of *Social Justice*. Screen shot copyright © 2006 by ProQuest Information and Learning. Reprinted by permission.

Roche Laboratories, *Xenical (Orlistat) Capsules: Complete Product Information* (December 2003), www.rocheusa.com/products/xenical/pi.pdf. Reprinted with the permission of Hoffmann-La Roche, Inc.

Beth Shulman. Reprint of title and copyright pages from *The Betrayal of Work* by Beth Shulman. Copyright © 2005 by Beth Shulman. Reprinted with permission of The New Press.

Betsy Taylor, "Big Box Stores Are Bad for Main Street" from *CQ Researcher* (November 1999). Copyright © 1999 by Congressional Quarterly, Inc. Reprinted with permission of the author.

United Nations Department of Public Information, *Africa Recovery* (June 2004), www.un.org/ecosocdev/geninfo/afrec/vol15no1/drugpr1.htm. Reprinted with the permission of the UN Africa Renewal.

University of Minnesota Libraries, screen shots. Reprinted with permission.

University Library, The University of North Carolina at Chapel Hill, screen shot of document menu for Harriet A. Jacobs, *Incidents in the Life of a Slave Girl. Written by Herself*, edited by Lydia Maria Francis Child, http://docsouth.unc.edu/fpn/jacobs/. Screen shot of University of North Carolina at Chapel Hill *Documenting the American South* Web site, including excerpt from Marcella Grendler, Andrew Letter, and Jill Sexton, "Guide to Religious Content in Slave Narrative," http://docsouth.unc.edu/neh/religiouscontent.html. Reprinted with permission.

WGBH Educational Foundation, screen shot of *Newshour Extra* Web page for January 18, 2007, "PlayStation 3 Delay Part of High-Definition Showdown," www.pbs.org/newshour/extra/features/jan-june06/dvds_3-22.htm. Copyright © 2006 by the WGBH Educational Foundation. Reprinted with permission.

WGBH Educational Foundation, screen shot of PBS.org Web page and links for Frontline's "Living Old" program, www.pbs.org/wgbh/pages/frontline/livingold/. Copyright © 1995–2007. WGBH/Boston. Courtesy FRONTLINE/WGBH Educational Foundation.

Index

Rules for Writers describes two commonly used systems of documentation: MLA, used in English and the humanities (see 55), and APA, used in psychology and the social sciences (see 60). Following is a list of style manuals used in a variety of disciplines.

BIOLOGY (See <http://dianahacker.com/resdoc> for more information.)

Council of Science Editors. *Scientific Style and Format: The CSE Manual for Authors, Editors, and Publishers.* 7th ed. Reston: Council of Science Eds., 2006. Print.

BUSINESS

American Management Association. *The AMA Style Guide for Business Writing.* New York: AMACOM, 1996. Print.

CHEMISTRY

Coghill, Anne M., and Lorrin R. Garson, eds. *The ACS Style Guide: Effective Communication of Scientific Information.* 3rd ed. Washington: Amer. Chemical Soc., 2006. Print.

ENGINEERING

Institute of Electrical and Electronics Engineers. *IEEE Standards Style Manual.* IEEE, 2007. Web. 9 Feb. 2009.

ENGLISH AND OTHER HUMANITIES (See 55.)

MLA Handbook for Writers of Research Papers. 7th ed. New York: MLA, 2009. Print.

GEOLOGY

Bates, Robert L., Rex Buchanan, and Marla Adkins-Heljeson, eds. *Geowriting: A Guide to Writing, Editing, and Printing in Earth Science.* 5th ed. Alexandria: Amer. Geological Inst., 1995. Print.

GOVERNMENT DOCUMENTS

Garner, Diane L. *The Complete Guide to Citing Government Information Resources: A Manual for Social Science and Business Research.* 3rd ed. Bethesda: Congressional Information Service, 2002. Print.

United States Government Printing Office. *Style Manual.* Washington: GPO, 2000. Print.

HISTORY

The Chicago Manual of Style. 15th ed. Chicago: U of Chicago P, 2003. Print.

JOURNALISM

Goldstein, Norm, ed. *Associated Press Stylebook and Briefing on Media Law.* Rev. ed. New York: Associated Press, 2005. Print.

LAW

Harvard Law Review et al. *The Bluebook: A Uniform System of Citation.* 18th ed. Cambridge: Harvard Law Rev. Assn., 2005. Print.

LINGUISTICS

Linguistic Society of America. Language *Style Sheet.* LSA, n.d. Web. 9 Feb. 2009.

MATHEMATICS

American Mathematical Society. *Author Resource Center.* AMS, 2009. Web. 9 Feb. 2009.

MEDICINE

Iverson, Cheryl, et al. *American Medical Association Manual of Style: A Guide for Authors and Editors.* 9th ed. Baltimore: Williams, 1998. Print.

MUSIC

Holoman, D. Kern, ed. *Writing about Music: A Style Sheet from the Editors of* 19th-Century Music. Berkeley: U of California P, 1988. Print.

PHYSICS

American Institute of Physics. *Style Manual: Instructions to Authors and Volume Editors for the Preparation of AIP Book Manuscripts.* 5th ed. New York: AIP, 1995. Print.

POLITICAL SCIENCE

American Political Science Association. *Style Manual for Political Science.* Rev. ed. Washington: APSA, 2001. Print.

PSYCHOLOGY AND OTHER SOCIAL SCIENCES (See 60.)

American Psychological Association. *Publication Manual of the American Psychological Association.* 5th ed. Washington: APA, 2001. Print.

SCIENCE AND TECHNICAL WRITING

American National Standards Institute. *American National Standard for the Preparation of Scientific Papers for Written or Oral Presentation.* New York: ANSI, 1979. Print.

Microsoft Corporation. *Microsoft Manual of Style for Technical Publications.* 3rd ed. Redmond: Microsoft, 2004. Print.

Rubens, Philip, ed. *Science and Technical Writing: A Manual of Style.* 2nd ed. New York: Routledge, 2001. Print.

SOCIAL WORK

National Association of Social Workers Press. *NASW Press Author Guidelines.* NASW P, 2009. Web. 9 Feb. 2009.

ESL Menu

Boldface numbers refer to sections of the book.

abbr	faulty abbreviation **40**
ad	misuse of adverb or adjective **26**
add	add needed word **10**
agr	faulty agreement **21, 22**
appr	inappropriate language **17**
art	article (*a, an, the*) **29**
awk	awkward
cap	capital letter **45**
case	error in case **24, 25**
cliché	cliché **18e**
coh	coherence **4d**
coord	faulty coordination **14a**
cs	comma splice **20**
dev	inadequate development **4b**
dm	dangling modifier **12e**
-ed	error in *-ed* ending **27d**
emph	emphasis **14**
ESL	English as a second language **28–31**
exact	inexact language **18**
frag	sentence fragment **19**
fs	fused sentence **20**
gl/us	see Glossary of Usage
hyph	error in use of hyphen **44**
idiom	idioms **18d**
inc	incomplete construction **10**
irreg	error in irregular verb **27a**
ital	italics (underlining) **42**
jarg	jargon **17a**
lc	lowercase letter **45**
mix	mixed construction **11**
mm	misplaced modifier **12a–d**
mood	error in mood **27g**
nonst	nonstandard usage **17d, 27**
num	error in use of numbers **41**

om	omitted word **10, 30b**
p	error in punctuation
$\hat{,}$	comma **32**
no ,	no comma **33**
;	semicolon **34**
:	colon **35**
$\overset{?}{v}$	apostrophe **36**
" "	quotation marks **37**
. ?	period, question mark,
!	exclamation point **38**
— ( )	dash, parentheses,
[ ] . . .	brackets, ellipsis
/	mark, slash **39**
¶	new paragraph **4e**
pass	ineffective passive **8**
pn agr	pronoun agreement **22**
proof	proofreading problem **3b**
ref	error in pronoun reference **23**
run-on	run-on sentence **20**
-s	error in *-s* ending **27c, 21**
sexist	sexist language **17f, 22a**
shift	distracting shift **13**
sl	slang **17d**
sp	misspelled word **43**
sub	faulty subordination **14a**
sv agr	subject-verb agreement **21, 27c**
t	error in verb tense **27f**
trans	transition needed **4d**
usage	see Glossary of Usage
v	voice **8a**
var	lack of variety in sentence structure **14, 15**
vb	verb problem **27, 28**
w	wordy **16**
//	faulty parallelism **9**
∧	insert
x	obvious error
#	insert space
⌣	close up space

Detailed Menu